6/08

Gay
Artists
in
Modern
American
Culture

Gay
Artists
in Modern American Culture

an imagined conspiracy

Michael S. Sherry

THE UNIVERSITY OF NORTH CAROLINA PRESS   Chapel Hill

This book was published with the assistance of the
Anniversary Endowment Fund of the University of
North Carolina Press.

The paper in this book meets the guidelines for
permanence and durability of the Committee on
Production Guidelines for Book Longevity of the
Council on Library Resources.

Library of Congress
Cataloging-in-Publication Data
Sherry, Michael S., 1945–
Gay artists in modern American culture :
an imagined conspiracy / Michael S. Sherry.
p. cm.
Includes bibliographical references and index.
ISBN 978-0-8078-3121-2 (cloth : alk. paper)
1. Homosexuality and art—United States—History—
20th century. 2. Arts, American—20th century.
3. Homosexuality—United States. I. Title.
NX180.H6S54 2007
704'.086640973—dc22 2006039795

A Caravan book. For more information, visit
www.caravanbooks.org.

11 10 09 08 07 5 4 3 2 1

CONTENTS

Acknowledgments *vii*

Introduction: Nixon, Myself, and Others· *1*

1 Discovery *13*

2 Explanation *51*

3 Frenzy *105*

4 Barber at the Met *155*

5 Aftermath *204*

   Notes *239*

   Index *271*

A section of illustrations follows p. 141.

ACKNOWLEDGMENTS

Three research assistants provided essential help in locating and
often shrewdly commenting on primary sources: David K. Johnson,
Miles Becker, and Michael Allen. Allison Quinn provided last-minute
help with sources. Antony Burton did fast and good work obtaining
the images used. Several people read the manuscript, some more than
once—Nadine Hubbs, David K. Johnson, George Chauncey, Marilyn
Young, Lane Fenrich, and Charles Grench (my editor since my first
book three decades ago)—and generously offered corrections, counsel,
conversation, challenges, and encouragement. Others provided
support, comments, and leads in conversations after reading parts
of the manuscript or hearing versions in lectures. Research leaves
underwritten by Northwestern University provided time for work
on this book. Research funds, made possible by former students of
Richard Leopold who endowed a chair in his honor, underwrote many
of the costs involved. Chairs of the Northwestern history department
and colleagues in it provided support in other ways. My partner, James
Beal, and other family members endured many delays in this project
and disruptions caused by it. I thank them for their patience and for
their own insights into this history.

Gay
Artists
in
Modern
American
Culture

Introduction

Nixon, Myself, and Others

In the mid-twentieth century, gay figures created much of modern American culture—the sounds of Aaron Copland's *Appalachian Spring*, the words and moods of Stanley and Blanche in Tennessee Williams's *A Streetcar Named Desire*, the songs and dances of *West Side Story*. If there was a gay moment in American culture, it occurred then as much as now, despite recent attention to television programs like *Queer Eye for the Straight Guy* and queer people from Ellen DeGeneres to Tony Kushner. Uneven across fields, the gay presence was sufficient to disturb many observers, who imagined a vast homintern—a homosexual international conspiracy in the arts parallel to the Comintern, or Communist International, in politics. "Homintern," a word probably invented in jest by gay men but seized upon by their enemies, alternated with terms like "homosexual mafia" to conjure up a queer menace.[1] This book explores the gay presence in the arts, how Americans once understood it, and how we might understand it now.

The arrival of many groups on the stage of cultural production has triggered consternation—witness reactions to Jews and African Americans in the arts early in the twentieth century—but reactions are not uniform across time and groups. They depend on prior perceptions of a group, its cultural role, and the circumstances of its arrival. America's global conflicts—World War II and the Cold War—magnified and defined the contributions of queer artists, this book argues, and shaped a Lavender Scare in the arts.[2] In turn, the disruptions of America's Cold War, culture, and society in the late 1960s fractured the homintern discourse. When anxieties about America's cultural empire peaked, with artists deployed as Cold War weapons alongside astronauts and diplomats, so too did scrutiny of the queer artist. When anxieties subsided, so too did scrutiny.

Three themes—the homintern discourse, authenticity, and cultural empire—run through this story. That discourse expressed anxiety about American cultural empire through a language of authenticity central to American life in the 1950s and 1960s. Anxious observers depicted gay artists as psychologically and creatively inauthentic—at best possessing "a wonderful gift for delightful embroidery," as *Time* quoted writer Somerset Maugham in 1966, but for the most part "failed artists," *Time* claimed.[3] In turn, observers suggested, those artists undermined the nation's cultural prowess. Yet because they made much of the American culture paraded before the world, figures like Williams and Copland could hardly be jettisoned. Hence denunciation of them as queer artists unfolded alongside celebration of them as American artists. Out of national pride, aspirations for cultural empire, and fears of enemy advances, Americans showcased artists as emblems of the nation's freedom and muscular culture. In this context, gay artists were American artists. Often out of the same fears, many Americans denigrated or exaggerated gay creative figures. In this context, they were gay artists, not American ones. That tension between dependence and revulsion structured the homintern discourse and nourished the splenetic and contradictory qualities that make it fascinating.

Despite its subsidence after the 1960s, the tension persists: the labels "gay" and "American" do not yet readily collapse into one, for some gay people as well as for many hostile to them. Likewise, mid-century discourse has shaped recent debates, ones driven by new issues like gays in the military and gay marriage but also embedded in a past. Although silence was often imposed on gay people, many Americans noisily— often meanly—scrutinized homosexuality long before gay liberation in the 1970s. Indeed, this book shows how noisy that scrutiny was. Americans created modern antihomosexuality in part by examining queers and queerness in the arts. They bequeathed to us images of gay people as curiously both silly and sinister, protean and perverse, creative and corrupting, invaluable and insidious: as both outside and inside American life. Gay people contributed to those images, albeit rarely from a position of power. Some prized their "delightful embroidery." Others expressed more serious talents.

Like any study of history, this one is informed by its author's experiences, some noted here to suggest the stakes in this book. When Composers Recordings, Inc. (CRI) released "Gay American Composers" in 1996—one of the first "gay" albums of serious music—its CD jacket asked, "Is there a gay sensibility to American classical music?" Perhaps the "gay sensibility" appeared in the tantalizing album cover featuring a handsome man with his jeans unbuttoned at the waist, who reappears on the back cover with the jeans gone, so far as viewers could see. Was the "gay sensibility" therefore more in the buyer's mind or lust than in the music? CRI answered its own question obliquely, by enjoining the listener to "decide for yourself as you enjoy over 70 minutes of today's most beautiful and soulful classical music—all written by gay American composers." Apparently, the "gay sensibility" was to compose "beautiful and soulful" music, but some of the music was not "beautiful" or "soulful" by most standards, or probably intended to be, and "beautiful" and "soulful" were hardly unique to queer-composed music. Above all, it was not clear whether those qualities were "gay," "American," or somehow both.

Beyond the advertising veneer, liner notes acknowledged complexity. CRI's managing director, pointing to a "landmark double LP of classical music by black composers" released in 1971, stated that "music is an abstract art form and it has no gender." The album's composers (those who had not died of AIDS) offered no single point of view. Robert Helps (1928–2001) denied any "artistic difference" between the compositions of gay and straight composers but added, "Who knows what affects us subliminally?" Lee Hoiby (born 1926) saw "no traces of my sexual preferences in my (or any) music" but set Walt Whitman's words to music and contributed to the 1991 AIDS *Quilt Song Book*, with text by gay poet James Merrill. Lou Harrison (1917–2004) noted that his two main mentors, Henry Cowell and Virgil Thomson, were gay and pointed to Tchaikovsky, "the divine Mr. Handel," the avant-garde's John Cage, and his partner. Although Harrison identified no queer content in music per se, he stressed his inspiration from and collaboration with other artists queer and female, and he restated a dominant late-century idea about gay figures' contributions: "Living and working outside the mainstream is, I believe, a help to those inside the mainstream." Ned Rorem (born 1923), long prolific in music and words, recapitulated apparent paradoxes he had artfully offered for decades: "There is no homosexual music," but "my songs are my soap box" for queer politics, and, besides, "all art is subversive," and perhaps "all music is queer." David Del Tredici (born 1937) flagged his Catholic "sexuality and shame," finding it "a pleasure to speak now in these notes things I once thought unspeakable."[4]

Collectively, these composers summed up recent ideas about how queerness relates to artistic creativity. I do not seek to determine which ideas were valid but rather to place them, and the hostile views that others offered, in history. As CRI's album suggested, the queerness of artists perpetually fluttered between irrelevance and inescapableness, triviality and weightiness, invisibility and omnipresence.

A later moment also alerted me to the issues involved in this book. In June 2002 I heard three pieces performed outdoors by the Grant Park Orchestra in downtown Chicago. Samuel Barber's Violin Concerto

(1939) has become a concert favorite, an American analogue to modern violin concertos like Sibelius's for Finland, Prokofiev's for Russia, and Berg's for central Europe. Detractors deride it as Modernism Lite, easy for audiences obliged to hear something modern. Defenders see it as bridging romanticism and modernism, like eve-of-World-War-II music by Benjamin Britten and Aaron Copland. The big draw for me, because it is rarely performed, was Canadian Colin McPhee's 1936 *Tabuh-Tabuhan, Toccata for Orchestra*, whose Balinese sounds, modernist energy, subtle orchestration, and submerged lyricism anticipate, but, for me, better realize, the hypnotic qualities and cross-cultural aspirations of postmodern music. Last, a warhorse: Tchaikovsky's Symphony No. 4.

Here were three notable gay composers. Program notes mentioned the "homosexuality" only of Tchaikovsky, by retelling — retailing — the familiar tale of his brief, disastrous marriage to Antonina Miliukov, melodrama that Ken Russell luridly filmed (*The Music Lovers*, 1971). It was the standard program-note approach: Tchaikovsky's sexuality is usually suggested only by reference to his marriage, whose failure makes a narrative that both signals his homosexuality and crowds it out. For this concert, the relevance of the tale was the impact it presumably had on his symphony. The "homosexuality" of McPhee and Barber went unremarked, apparently irrelevant to the compositions played, or perhaps less easy to acknowledge than in the case of Tchaikovsky, Russian and long dead.

I glanced at program notes for a previous concert: John Williams's *Music from "Schindler's List,"* Ernest Bloch's *Schelomo, Hebraic Rhapsody for Cello and Orchestra*, and Leonard Bernstein's Symphony No. 3, *"Kaddish."* The names of the composers and compositions marked the pieces as Jewish, and they appeared under the phrase "In Memoriam" (of what was not spelled out). Bernstein's homosexuality was unmentioned, his Jewishness so obvious that it needed no marking. For McPhee, Barber, and Tchaikovsky, queerness lingered in the wings, noted only for Tchaikovsky. The difference was familiar, understandable, and striking, especially given awkward efforts for decades by artists and others to grasp or reject a relationship between Jewishness and queerness in the arts. One program screamed "Jewish!" The other whispered "queer." It's the whispering that I try to decipher here. How had Americans inclined to think about such things come to see the relationship between homosexuality and creativity? What did they whisper about it, and why did they whisper?

It may seem an esoteric matter, but many Americans were inclined to think about it. Richard Nixon, for one. On 13 May 1971, the president, responding to the television sit-com *All in the Family*, whose Meathead character (Archie Bunker's son-in-law) Nixon decided "apparently goes both ways," sputtered about homosexuality to his nearly mute aides:

> You don't glorify it, John [Ehrlichman], any more than you glorify, uh, uh, uh, whores. Now we all know people who have whores and . . . we all have weaknesses and so forth and so on, but God damn it, what do you think that does to kids. . . . Why is it that the Scouts, the, why is it that the Boys Clubs, we were there, we constantly had to clean up the staffs to keep the Goddamned fags out of it. Because, not because of them, they can go out and do anything they damn please, [unintelligible: but?] all those kids? You know, there's a little tendency among them all.

Nixon was on a typical roll, complete with confusions of meaning common in casual conversation but particularly in his rants. Was the "little tendency" among "all those kids" or the grown-up "staffs"? The associations he made among homosexuality, prostitution, and "weaknesses," however, had deep historical roots.

The rant continued: "Well by God can I tell you it [apparently, what he witnessed in the Boys Clubs] outraged me. Most people are outraged for moral reasons, I, it outraged me because I don't want to see this country go that way. . . . you know what happened to the Greeks. Homosexuality destroyed them. Sure, Aristotle was a homo, we all know that, so was Socrates." Ehrlichman interrupted with the insight that Socrates "never had the influence television had." Nixon continued: "Do you know what happened to the Romans? The last six Roman emperors were fags." How Nixon could be "outraged" but not for "moral reasons" was unclear, but as a prude who hated to be regarded as such, Nixon wanted to appear worldly-wise, even to his inner circle. It was more befitting the leader of the world's greatest power to give the fall of empires as the reason for his outrage. His phrasing was again murky: were Aristotle and Socrates exceptions to the peril that homosexuality posed to the Greeks, or the ones who "destroyed" them? Was all creativity dangerous, or only its queer version?

Nixon was still warming up. "You know what happened to the Popes? It's all right that, po-po-Popes were laying the nuns, that's been going on for years, centuries, but, when the popes, when the Catholic Church went to hell, in, I don't know, three or four centuries ago, it was homosexual. And finally it had to be cleaned out." For good measure, Nixon threw in Britain and France and contrasted them to the Soviet Union, the enemy he yearned to copy in order to preserve America's difference from it. "The

Russians. God damn it, they root them [homosexuals] out, they don't let them around at all. I don't know what they do with them." Nor did they allow "dope." Nixon escalated: "You see, homosexuality, dope, uh, immorality in general: These are the enemies of strong societies. That's why the Communists and the left-wingers are pushing it. They're trying to destroy us."[5]

Nixon's hatreds were many, intense, and contradictory, but as Nixon-debunkers often failed to admit, they were rarely far from those of many Americans (he was elected twice). His associations of homosexuality with creativity, corruption, and communism were standard. So too was his confusion: few "Communists" and "left-wingers" were "pushing" homosexuality; indeed, by Nixon's claim, "the Russians" stamped it out. Nixon showed that those associations circulated widely and elicited confusion and consternation. For him, homosexuals seemed both a source of past empires' glory and an agent of their demise, a prospect much on his mind as America's war in Vietnam foundered.

Nixon was winding down—but he was not done. He complained about San Francisco, and "not just the ratty part of town," he added. "The upper class in San Francisco is that way," as at "the Bohemian Grove, which I attend from time to time"—the secretive enclave near the city where elite men gathered, soon mocked by Armistead Maupin, who once met Nixon, in his *Tales of the City* series. "It is the most faggy goddamned thing you could ever imagine. . . . I can't shake hands with anybody from San Francisco." There probably were a few homosexuals at the Bohemian Grove, but Nixon reacted less to them than to the whole cultural shift they symbolized for him, as he had with *All in the Family*—Meathead was hardly gay, but he seemed "faggy." Like an anxious schoolboy, Nixon used taunts like "faggy" not just to identify queers but to scorn trends in fashion, sexuality, and gender that bewildered him. John Adams's opera *Nixon in China* deserves a comic follow-up, *Nixon in San Francisco*. He was more comfortable in China.

Nixon closed with gay men's grip on fashion. "Decorators. They got to do something. But we don't have to glorify it," he fumed. "You know one of the reasons fashions have made women look so terrible is because the goddamned designers hate women. Designers [are] taking it out on the women." Nixon briskly summarized what psychoanalyst Edmund Bergler belabored in an entire book, *Fashion and the Unconscious*, published in 1953, when Nixon became vice president. The woman-loving credentials of both men were suspect, maintained by projecting misogyny onto

gay men.

Nixon's rants point to an apparent paradox: how could gay men have been so important in the arts, and so defining of American identity, when America was so homophobic? As Nadine Hubbs poses the question with regard to Aaron Copland, "What might it mean that the long-awaited goal of a distinct 'American' style in serious music was realized at last by (most prominently) the Jewish, homosexual, leftist Brooklynite Copland, who rendered musically vivid an America of prairie cowboys and pioneer newlyweds?" How did queer composers "serve, during America's most homophobic era, as architects of its national identity?"[6]

This book addresses those questions. Given the range and volume of cultural work involved, my answers are not conclusive. But I can historicize the paradox by explaining how Americans at the time perceived it. I also challenge the premise involved—was mid-century America really so homophobic (a term not then in use)? Perhaps, but only if homophobia is seen not as static and unidirectional, but as brimming with contradictions and with the attitudinal push-and-pull—fascination, dismay, disgust, even admiration—that Nixon expressed.

Another paradox runs through this material, best stated in Vito Russo's study, *The Celluloid Closet*. Russo reported in 1987: "Some years ago, New York's New Museum sponsored a forum called 'Is There a Gay Sensibility and Does It Have an Impact on Our Culture? After a lot of evasive huffing and puffing about everyone from Marcel Proust to Patti Page, journalist Jeff Weinstein said, 'No, there is no such thing as a gay sensibility and yes, it has an enormous impact on our culture.' "[7] Less given to paradox, writer Edmund White once suggested that at least "we can discuss . . . the gay *taste* of any given period" and "detect . . . a resemblance among many gay works of art made at a particular moment—a resemblance partially intended and partially drawn without design from a shared experience of anger or alienation of secret, molten camaraderie."[8] I prefer to let Weinstein's paradox stand, as something more fitting for aesthetic and cultural than historical judgment. Although I provide history about that paradox, I don't propose to settle it.

Consider this the biography of an idea—that gay people have a peculiar presence in the arts arising from their sinister and pathological ways, as many mid-century observers argued, or from their peculiar talent, as others have speculated, or from their "shared experience of anger or alienation," as White suggested. Like biographies of individuals, this one does not capture all of the life it covers. I examine this idea primarily in its adulthood at mid-twentieth century, its childhood only touched on, its old age only sketched. Given the expansiveness of the arts, I hardly capture everything uttered about this idea, all the aesthetic issues that the arts present, or all of gay people's creative work. My account tilts toward those who scorned claims about gay creativity but also gave those claims more publicity than gay artists ever could have. Gay creative figures were numerous, but they had little voice in public discourse about homosexuality, and many, wrestling with the creative challenges of their fields and careers, paid less attention to claims about their creativity than those who belittled it. It was mostly others who took a low-profile idea and turned it into a major object of contention.

Although gay men's prominence in mid-century culture was recognized and argued over at the time, the subject has been little examined, in part because of an assumption, stubborn even among scholars, that homosexuality was unmentionable at the time. It "could only be discussed in whispers and almost never in print or on camera," according to one recent study.[9] Most Americans still believe that the "closet" was real, ironclad, and silencing of all talk, whereas insofar as it existed (the term was not used in the 1950s), it mainly silenced queer voices, not other voices. Homosexuality was often discussed, even shouted, in the 1950s— in Congress, by medical experts, in intellectual commentary, in scandal journalism, and even in Hollywood film, despite its ban on explicit labels like "homosexual." Insofar as gay men and lesbians shattered a silence on homosexuality in the 1970s, the silence was largely their own, not others'. Indeed their activism was, among other things, a response to the worrying, denouncing, and pathologizing that homosexuals had earlier received.

Scholars of mid-century culture have much else to attend to, of course: America's aspirations to cultural hegemony, the shift from modernism to postmodernism, and the dynamics of gender, race, and religion. But the queer presence figured in all those developments, not just as an issue by itself. Much history barely notes that gay people and controversies over them inflected mid-century culture. They go virtually unmentioned, for example, in an exhaustive recent history of the cultural Cold War, although Rudolf Nureyev is the book's title character. Even three scholars of queer history have asserted that "lesbians and gay men remained largely banished from mainstream culture of the time, which 'condemned' a significant portion of the American population to 'something less than life.'" Condemnation was indeed intense. Yet this was also when Alfred Kinsey's studies unleashed debate about homosexuality and when gay people played major roles in cultural life.[10]

8   Neglect also owes to how scholars usually scrutinize specific arts rather

than the arts generally. Although some work explores the queer presence in fields like music, dance, and Hollywood, that presence has not often been viewed comprehensively. Arts scholarship and criticism also long focused on the evolution—often seen as predestined—of artistic forms and styles like film noir and musical serialism more than on the identities of creative figures. Artists often favored that focus: the modernist ethos prized the abstract and the universal over the concrete and the particular; work grounded in traits like race, gender, and sexuality seemed provincial. In fields like concert music, biography was a robust enterprise, but it paid little attention to identities beyond composers' national aspirations and affiliations—its purpose was to locate them in (or outside) the great chain of music's evolution. More recently, a biography of Samuel Barber barely mentioned his sexuality and a sophisticated study of Aaron Copland squeezed it into one chapter, tellingly titled "Personal Affairs." Biographies of composer Virgil Thomson and writers James Baldwin and Gore Vidal, among others, avoid such compartmentalization.[11]

A comprehensive view of gay artists has also fallen victim to a division of labor between two fields: most cultural historians ignore its queer aspects, and many queer scholars overlook middlebrow and highbrow culture, stressing resistance to dominant norms—a vital story—more than the queer role in setting those norms. Studies by George Chauncey, Robert Corber, Nadine Hubbs, Philip Brett, Robert Dawidoff, Anthony Tommasini, and others are exceptions, ones influential on my work.[12]

Other challenges arise. It is troublesome to label past figures as gay if they resisted that category, understood it differently than we may, or lived lives too shifting for a static label to capture. In a history as broadbrush as this one, I have had to apply labels crudely, but I know their anachronistic, simplifying qualities. Moreover, precision about how artists' work and success related to their sexuality is impossible, especially given their multiple identities. As Baldwin argued in 1949, "people, unhappily, refuse to function in so neat and one-dimensional a fashion."[13] Barber's music and Williams's plays are no more (or no less) reducible to homosexuality than are Baldwin's writings to African Americanness (or homosexuality), Saul Bellow's to Jewishness, or Eudora Welty's to gender. Gay artists themselves differ. "The fact that homosexual people represent different, sometimes opposing, stylistic and ideological positions," Philip Brett and Elizabeth Wood note, "argues against a unified 'homosexual sensibility' in music," although there may still be a "connection" between "sexual identity and musical expression."[14] On such matters, the historian can only offer correlations and tendencies.

But the historian can capture how Americans understood the role of gay men—almost always the focus was on men—in cultural life. Why did many observers notice, often worriedly, the presence of queer people in the arts? Why did anxieties over it peak in the 1960s, in a presumably liberationist era, rather than in the 1950s, usually regarded as the high point of postwar repression? That presence was not news, after all. Many Americans could recall controversies about Tchaikovsky, Walt Whitman, and Oscar Wilde. Postwar observers might have regarded the queer presence as familiar, benign, even welcome. By and large, they did not.

Observers of today's fast-changing, international culture will recognize that one mystery addressed here—how a group gains prominence in culture—extends far beyond the case I examine. There is, for example, striking evidence of a current Finnish ascendancy in concert music—a profusion of Finnish singers, instrumentalists, composers, conductors, orchestras, recording companies.[15] Why Finland, this small country with Jean Sibelius in its past but little else that earlier caught the world's attention? That puzzle involves familiar elements of ethnic identity and national homeland, not the less obvious elements of sexual identity, yet that distinction begs a question: what made ethnicity and nationality obvious while sexuality was not? As with queer creativity, explaining the Finnish case could be an idle parlor game, but the satisfaction lies in teasing out possible answers, not in achieving conclusive ones, to be asserted only by those bolder than I am.

Readers may deplore this book's emphasis on male artists and men's opinions about them. That emphasis reflects, beyond my limitations, men's dominance of the mid-century arts and the scrutiny given to gay creativity. But gender figures in this story, most baldly in how so many observers displaced onto gay men the common misogyny of the times as they assailed the woman-hating gay male designer or dramatist. In turn, change in the gender order, including the lesbian activism of the Stonewall era, did much to break up that discourse.

My method is straightforward. I use published texts that took up or touched on homosexuality and the arts. These are numerous, scattered in prominent and obscure cultural places, and not always obvious (many books did not index "homosexuality"). I set them in the context of related currents and conflicts. I draw insights from secondary sources, but less from theoretical perspectives. All this passes through a filter of my memories and sensibilities. I burrow into unpublished sources, primarily for presidential White House conversations and for the case study of Samuel Barber, which in more detail shows the value and limits of a queer lens on cultural history. I employ shorthand on some matters. I use "the homintern discourse" for the untidy bundle of ideas and accusations about the gay creative presence. I use "queer" in order to avoid repetition of "gay" and "homosexual" and because its usage is older than many recognize, as in W. H. Auden's Christmas Day 1941 poem for Chester Kallman—"Because mothers have much to do with your queerness and mine."[16] The result is a sketch designed to provoke inquiry rather than issue final judgments.

Readers will find fools and bigots in this story, but also context for understanding them. Antigay voices constituted a skein of American conspiracy thinking, though few scholars place them in that context, in which "the enemy appears chameleon-like, pervasive, and opportunistic." Borrowing at times from other strains of conspiracy thought such as anti-Semitism, antigay voices created a distinctive strain, one often articulated by well-placed figures, not the socially or psychologically marginal types that historians once saw as prone to conspiracy theories.[17] But context can only do so much to soften the bigot label.

And my background for this? Readers familiar with three well-known memoirs will find bits of my story in them. Like Alan Helms, I was a *Young Man from the Provinces* (1995)—Indiana in both cases—although I headed to Washington University (St. Louis), not Columbia, never to become "the most famous piece of ass of my generation," as Edmund White called Helms. My age (I was born in 1945) and experience resemble Paul Monette's as recorded in *Becoming a Man: Half a Life Story* (1992), including time at Yale (for me as a graduate student), prep school teaching, and the textures of queer longings, evasions, and self-abasement.[18] Like Monette, I "came out" slowly in the 1970s through therapy, which for me had some of the dark qualities Martin Duberman recorded in *Cures: A Gay Man's Odyssey* (1991), but more of the helpful ones that Monette recalled.

Other elements in my life diverge from theirs. An amateur violinist, I was once thrilled to be in an orchestra playing Igor Stravinsky with the old man in the audience and to join a group at the Interlochen National Music Camp chatting with Aaron Copland. There was political activity, not of the heroic sort, that included starting a gay history course in the 1980s. In scholarship I've shaken my fist at American militarization, which overlapped American homophobia. I have had personal ups and downs, but as Alan Helms comments, "Everyone runs the pain sweepstakes alone, & everyone in that race is a winner, which is to say a loser, which is enough confusion for anyone for a single lifetime."[19] My partner, our children, other family members, and friends have persisted, my mother with intimidating geriatric energy and forbearance. But this is not my story. I offer a few shards of it only to suggest where I come from in telling others' stories.

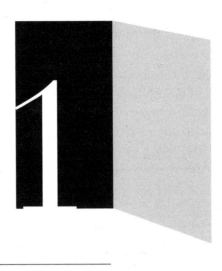

Discovery

In a flurry of comment after World War II, intellectuals, journalists, psychiatrists, and others announced their discovery of a queer presence in American culture and their dismay at what they discovered. In doing so, they helped to initiate the Lavender Scare in the arts and to make queer artists one face of the "Cold War homosexual menace."[1] William Barrett's 1950 statement of discovery was typical in its shrill, breathless quality (a quality often assigned to gay men). Reflecting in *Partisan Review* on his travels in Europe, Barrett, a leading philosopher, tugged at the sleeves of his presumptively heterosexual readers for sympathy — "by now many travelers must know the embarrassment of the isolated heterosexual in the midst of homosexual chatter" — and explained how "Italy was like a bracing air, reviving one's faith in the beautiful possibility of heterosexuality." His kind was under siege: "Apparently, the fraternity of the gay is a network as carefully organized as the American Express, and, like the latter, now takes in the whole of Europe as its territory."

Just as America's cultural Cold War against the Soviet Union was gearing up — *Partisan Review* would soon receive covert funding for its role — Barrett worried that "the Americanization of the globe, it seems, is proceeding even on this front," that of homosexuality. (Visiting Venice at this time, playwright Arthur Laurents saw homosexuality, but not as an American import: "The cruising was everywhere: it seemed indigenous to the city.") Barrett linked this latest of the "great waves of homosexuality" to an American "culture where woman has been accorded unprecedented status of equality," portending a "transition to a matriarchy" and "a society of neuters." He announced "a new chapter in the history of that traditionally corrupt image that Europe has always represented for the American." According to Barrett, "The American mother who fears that her son, drifting about Europe on the G.I. Bill, may be seduced by some European hussy, is no longer up-to-date. Mother, that boy of yours . . . has his eye peeled, not for the poor drab who winks vainly at him from the quay, but for the pretty young sailor boy of his dreams." Barrett upended that "image" in two ways: Europeans were now "seduced" by corrupt Americans, and the field of corruption was now queer. Barrett was a principal figure at *Partisan Review*, one of whose founders, William Phillips, was hailed on his death as an "editor who never let ideology triumph over common sense." But ideology did spill out on its pages. As their leftist credentials indicated, alarm about homosexuals' role in American culture was sounding across the political spectrum.[2]

Barrett sounded the main themes of that alarm. Alarmists emphasized the numbers, cohesiveness, and power of homosexuals—that "fraternity" organized like "American Express"—and their capacity to corrupt American culture and American influence abroad. Like Barrett, most focused on male homosexuality but often linked its spread to changes in women's place in American society, and they saw themselves as discovering something new in this latest "great" wave of homosexuality. And Barrett hinted at one tension shaping their alarm: the role of gay men in the cultural work of America was growing just when that work seemed to involve America's survival in a global struggle against totalitarian foes. Those boys "drifting about Europe on the G.I. Bill" were, after all, products and agents of American power. In that tension lies one answer to a question addressed by this chapter. Why did discovery of gay people's role in American culture occur in the 1940s and 1950s? Two developments, surging ambitions for American culture and swelling contributions to it by homosexuals, were on a collision course. Many observers saw danger in those contributions.

Before the "Homintern"

Postwar observers' claims to have discovered something new was more a pose designed to shock than a statement of fact, for gay people and themes in culture had long drawn comment. That comment, however, was limited as it emerged in the 1920s and 1930s. It focused on a few fields rather than the broad run of the arts, on scandalous moments more than continuing patterns, on women as much as men, and on representations of deviant sexuality as much as queer authorship. In theater, it was sharp, explicit, episodic. In fields like music, it was murky and indirect, entwined with wrangling over what constituted legitimate American art. It set the stage for postwar agitation but did not lead directly to it.

Associations of the "sodomite" or other deviant figures with the arts and entertainment were centuries old in Western life. One figure singled out by a New York City paper in 1842 "was said," Jonathan Katz reports, "to perform nightly in one of the city's 'Concert Rooms'—an early American reference to the sodomite as entertainer." Poet Walt Whitman faced puzzlement and hostility for his celebration of same-sex "adhesiveness." As John Bayley argues, "Art, aestheticism, and homosexuality made a rich trio in the nineteenth century" in Europe, as in the United States.[3]

By the early twentieth century, gossip, newspapers, and court cases frequently linked the arts and entertainment with sodomites or homosexuals, as they were coming to be called. Especially sensational was what Americans learned about Irish playwright and wit Oscar Wilde, who had toured in the United States and then was convicted in England in 1895 on sodomy charges after suing for libel the father of his lover, Lord Alfred Douglas. That case, and Wilde's very name and writing, circulated widely thereafter in the Anglo-American world as emblems of homosexuality, degenerate artistry, and—for many gay men—victimhood. A related case, also well chronicled in the American press, involved the American Maud Allen, who made a sensation in England dancing her version of Salome, derived from Wilde's 1893 work. Her performances became associated with "sodomites" who flocked to them and women who took an unseemly interest in her work, joining a "Cult of the Clitoris." *Salome* was also touchy stuff in Richard Strauss's version: New York's Metropolitan Opera ended its first production after one performance, reportedly at the insistence of financier J. P. Morgan's daughter, and in Chicago, evangelist Billy Sunday denounced it as "very sinful" and the police chief found it "disgusting." In 1918, amid wartime fears of spies and decadent artists undermining the British cause, Allen, like Wilde, made the mistake of suing for libel, taking on an editor who accused her of belonging to "a cult of high-ranking 'moral perverts'" and speaking "a foreign 'language generally used by homosexualists.'" Like Wilde, she lost her case and her career but continued to defend herself.[4]

Against the background of queer decadence abroad, American journalism, fiction, and scandal mapped homosexuality in the arts by geography and by genre in the 1920s and 1930s. Greenwich Village, Harlem, and

Hollywood were among the recognized geographic locales. Theater, the movie industry, and the nightclub scene with its "pansy craze" of female impersonators and campy entertainers were identified as institutional sites. That actors Randolph Scott and Cary Grant lived together occasioned winks and nods in the gossip press. That lyrics for Cole Porter's musicals hinted at homosexuality was hardly unsuspected. That Radclyffe Hall's lesbian novel *The Well of Loneliness* (1928) was the object of a sensational obscenity trial was standard news. "Nor did Ma Rainey's arrest in 1925 on the charge of staging a lesbian orgy in her Harlem apartment," John Loughery writes of the black singer, "alienate many of her fans, of either race or proclivity." Among followers of serious music, speculation about Tchaikovsky's sexuality was common. As a young composer, Lou Harrison later recalled, he " 'early learned' that Tchaikovsky and 'the divine Mr. Handel' were gay," and Tchaikovsky was on "The List" that one young man learned—"Michelangelo, da Vinci, Tchaikovsky, Wilde"—a list with many iterations that circulated beyond gay men (in Sigmund Freud's famous 1935 letter to an American mother, for example) as well as among them. New events updated the list: the navy removed Paul Cadmus's painting *The Fleet's In!* from a 1934 exhibit at Washington's Corcoran Gallery, not pleased with its "hectic record of shore-leave debauchery" by and between sailors.[5]

Yet by later standards, agitation about homosexuality in the arts was circumscribed. It focused mainly on theater and the popular arts, where notions of queer danger shaded off into perceptions of other evils like Prohibition speakeasies and Jewish moguls in Hollywood. Nor were authorship and product tightly linked: most controversy had little to do with recognizable homosexuals. Lillian Hellman's play *The Children's Hour* (1934) triggered alarm about her lesbian theme, not her identity. Few authors of fiction about homosexuality—most characters coming to a bad end— were gay, or at least known to be. Indeed, one strain of bluenose indignation was that authors, playwrights, and producers exploited the subject, not that homosexuals created the product. Homosexuals were mostly phantasms who haunted plays, movies, and novels, not real-life figures. Queer people, especially celebrity pansies, got notice in gossip—"Sissies Permeate Sublime Social Strata as Film Stars and Broadwayites Go Gay," announced *Broadway Brevities*—and in complaints about the "impudent sissies that clutter Times Square."[6] But they surfaced less as makers of culture than as objects of representation. The menace, for those who saw it, lay more in the texts and the people who peddled them than in homosexuals, and queerness seemed a rude intrusion into culture, not a pervasive presence in it. Notable too was how often women as creators (Hellman and Mae West, for example), performers, or audience and lesbianism as subject sparked controversy, reflecting women's major place in the arts, in contrast to male dominance after World War II.

Queer characters, especially the stock figures of the pansy and the mannish woman, appeared often on screen. Indignation among cultural watchdogs at their appearance helped force Hollywood to devise its own censorship system in the 1930s, the Production Code, which banned the representation of homosexuality (among other things), in theory if not in practice. With movies featuring so many outcasts and liminal types, it is plausible to see—or not see—a plethora of queer figures, as in director James Whale's Frankenstein films. Notable was the low-budget *Freaks* (Tod Browning, 1932), soon withdrawn because of the outcry it unleashed, with its half-man/half-woman, bearded lady, cross-dresser, pinheads, midgets, and other "monstrosities" of "nature" who live by a secret "code" in a secret world until they take revenge against the "normal" people who torment them. They appeared in a decade when *"freak* could be used as a synonym for homosexuality or other forms of sexual nonconformity." In their world, "a proliferation of erotic proclivities coexist, partners are exchanged, and heterosexuality is one among many options."[7] But if the "freaks" evoked a secret queer world, they also seemed pitied and exploited by the film's makers.

Harlem and the Harlem Renaissance illustrated the reach and limits of contemporary awareness and agitation. Male impersonator Gladys Bentley was well known as a "bulldagger," Harlem had a reputation as a sexual playground for queer people, including white visitors, and key literary figures—among them, Langston Hughes, Countee Cullen, Alain Locke, and the white novelist and promoter Carl van Vechten—were gay. "You did what you wanted to," writer Richard Bruce Nugent later recalled. "Nobody was in the closet. There wasn't any closet." Indeed, the metaphor of the closet as expressive of gay experience was not yet coined. But homosexuality hovered at the periphery of the Harlem Renaissance. It "retained an outlaw status that few blacks embraced at the time," three scholars note, and "that fewer still would have championed alongside matters of race and class." Most creative figures kept their sexuality under wraps in their output and their public lives. The waning of the Renaissance amid the devastations of the Great Depression and the tighter official control of public space ushered in by repeal of Prohibition further muffled Harlem's lived and literary queerness.[8]

Contemporary conceptions of homosexuality also shaped cultural con-   17 troversy. Although the terms "homosexual" and "heterosexual" were used by the 1920s, a sharp line between them was not yet drawn. And although hardly tidy or uniform, ideas about homosexuality, George Chauncey has explained, associated it with gender role—effeminacy among men and masculinity among women—rather than with sexual object choice. The pansy who performed queerness faced scrutiny that the male-identified "gay" man largely escaped when homosexuality was seen as gender inversion, not erotic attraction. Often associated with working-class culture, "the effeminate 'fairy,' " Chauncey notes, "came to represent all homosexuals in the public mind," and the "pansy" was the most visible deviant in vaudeville, theater, and the movies. Communist writer Mike Gold's "denunciation of [playwright] Thornton Wilder as an 'art pansy' writer of unmanly literature" captured that emphasis. Men who did not fit the "pansy" image had less to worry about. Although queer women were suspect regardless of their perceived gender role, those who embodied role inversion—the bull dyke—were more suspect, though also more titillating to some audiences.[9]

Generalized notions of homosexuals in the arts were sketchy. To be sure, many gay men sensed a link between homosexuality and the arts, and their "subcultural strategies" included lineages of creative achievement. "Claiming that respected historical figures—ranging from Julius Caesar, Michelangelo, and Shakespeare to Walt Whitman and Oscar Wilde—were homosexuals helped enhance the usually maligned character of gay men," explains Chauncey. The "possible significance of homosexuality in Plato, Whitman, or Shakespeare" was noted "in almost every gay novel published in the early 1930s." "The List" of queer artists and the euphemism "artistic"—slang for queer or gay—emphasized a connection between homosexuality and the arts, especially music. Pre-1960s "code words and phrases for a homosexual man," Philip Brett argues, included ones like "is he 'musical' do you think?" Moreover, music "represented that part of our culture which is constructed as feminine and therefore dangerous," and in that light, "all musicians . . . are faggots in the parlance of the male locker room." In turn, some gay men were proudly defiant, asking, as one historian summarizes their stance, "What do you think would be left of theater and dance, fashion and interior decoration, without us, just as we are?" Yet the affinity of gay men for the arts was more casually assumed than carefully explained, and there was no widespread perception of gay domination of the arts, only the notion of a suspicious—or welcome—queer presence in some fields.[10]

18   Scrutiny of theater and concert music suggests the extent and limits

of pre–World War II agitation about homosexuality in the arts. It also
demonstrates how little homosexuality was a freestanding concern but
instead one that overlapped other charged contexts—of gender, race, and
nation, for example.

A spike in agitation about theater came in the 1920s and focused on
the New York stage, especially on two among many plays with discernible gay characters. Adapted from a French version, Edouard Bournet's
The Captive, about "a married woman pursued by a persistent lesbian admirer," created a sensation in 1926. Even more did the pending arrival
of Mae West's "farcical representation of pansy life," *The Drag*, accompanied by her plea against "the criminalization of homosexuality" (West
preferred to let doctors "treat it like a disease"). Moreover, West planned
to use a chorus of boys publicly identified as queer—one instance of real
gay people at issue. None saw the New York stage, however, for when
police arrested her for another of her productions, she scratched plans to
bring *The Drag* to New York. Pushed by the Catholic Church, publisher
William Randolph Hearst, and others, the state legislature banned plays
"depicting or dealing with the subject of sex degeneracy, or sex perversion," a ban later extended to nightclubs and echoed in Hollywood's Production Code. A similar federal law was introduced in Congress, though
not passed.[11]

Language reflected an unsettled framework for argument about homosexuality and the arts. Critics, legislators, and others often employed the
new lingo of medical pathology, insisting that the subject of "perverts"
belonged to "the clinical laboratory" or was "the province of patholo-
gists," not the stage. But medical understandings, themselves divergent
and shifting, competed with others. One critic straightforwardly proclaimed, "Lesbian love walked out into a New York stage for the first time
last night" with *The Captive*, which, Frederick Lewis Allen soon wrote,
"revealed to thousands of innocents the fact the world contained such a
phenomenon as homosexuality." Metaphors frequently involved casting
light on dark places: in *The Captive* "one of the darker secrets of sex has
been exposed"; in *The Drag* "a calcium light has been cast on those who
will never get over to greet St. Peter"; a Chicago critic reviewing *Sin of
Sins* assailed those who "drag into the glare of the footlights a loathsome
disease from out of the psychomedical clinics": *The Captive* referred to
lesbians as "shadows," never showing its "pivotal" lesbian character.[12]

But the trope of light on darkness did not involve a metaphorical
closet. Instead it owed to muckraking journalists' relish in exposing secrets and readers' sense that sex was being discovered in their Freud-

influenced era. A smart-ass style of criticism exuded wicked delight in the revelations. Commentary mingled disgust with homosexuality, condemnation of those who exploited it, and denunciation of those who censored it. *The Captive*, with a European pedigree, drew a "gilt-edged, first-night audience" and considerable approval, even as its subject was seen as "horrible in its implications, terrible to contemplate." [13]

Still, in volume, frenzy, and bluntness, 1920s debate about theater exceeded public commentary for decades, in part because public recognition and representation of a "gay male world" peaked in the 1920s. The pansy craze in nightclubs and vaudeville, faintly echoed in film, soon followed. But the censorship that emerged from the 1920s diminished controversy, as did the general "exclusion of homosexuality from the public sphere" after the end of Prohibition—with bars and nightclubs now legal, the state could control them more tightly—and the onset of the Depression in the 1930s. "Unabashed gay self-representation," like West's chorus boys, "let alone the direct defense of homosexuality that began Mae West's *Drag*, would not be allowed on the stage or screen again for more than a generation," Chauncey argues.[14] Postwar discovery seemed fresh because earlier discovery was barely remembered. Gay representations continued but lacked their former resonance with a visible gay world. Overt censorship soon declined, but the formal closing of plays was not the only measure of censorship's grip. Censorship did provoke challenges, as when critic George Jean Nathan, no fan of "the sons of swish," argued in 1938 that given how the theater "has freely presented every other form of abnormal and perverted humanity," homosexuals "may— if treated objectively and without cheap sensationalism—be allowed their clinical place."[15] But as indicated by his outlook, which persisted into the 1960s, many foes of censorship acted out of loathing of homosexuality, seeking freer rein to expose it.

While interwar debate was sharp regarding theater, it rarely arose in many other fields. In serious music, for example, agitation about the manliness of composers dealt obliquely, at most, with their sexuality. Differences between the genres were one reason. Drama's verbal texts and staged enactments regarding gender and sexual identity were transparent. Composers did on occasion use sexually charged subjects or texts for operas, choral music, and ballets. But most concert music involved no verbal text or characters and thus no easy way to spot sexualized themes or to link them to composers' sexuality. "The ready 'abstractness' of music," Nadine Hubbs notes, "can render it unusually resistant to the mechanisms of identity labeling and regulation by which society and culture classify and control subjects." At the same time, "abstractness" made music an inviting realm for aspiring homosexual artists, at least those seeking a safe place. As Wayne Koestenbaum explains, with music "as mystery and miasma, as implicitness rather than explicitness, . . . we have hid inside music; in music we can come out without coming out, we can reveal without saying a word. Queers identify with shadow because no one can prosecute a shadow." [16]

With music widely regarded as a universal language, it was rarely judged as an expression of composers' representational intentions about sexuality. Critics instead focused on creative quality, descent, influence, and school, with much debate about which composers were major (the three "B's") and which were minor (a long list)—all male. They usually saw work by central European composers as the main trunk of music, joined by Russian and French composers in the late nineteenth century; composers elsewhere formed secondary branches. That approach drew attention to composers' national identities—after all, whole countries also were ranked for musical genius, with the ranking deeply influenced by nationalism—but less to their social milieus, politics, and personal identities. The focus on greatness did make for rich storytelling about a composer's temperament (Beethoven as stormy, Dvořák as contented), and sometimes more. Tchaikovsky was "a bachelor, except for a brief, extremely unhappy marriage," wrote Deems Taylor, who felt "great pity for . . . the mental and spiritual invalid." But even with Tchaikovsky, the main story was how his difficulties—which should not, Taylor argued, "color our view of Tchaikovsky's entire output"—inspired results to be judged in their own right.[17] American composers were further shielded from scrutiny because few were regarded as worthy of it. Despite undercurrents, sustained attention to sexualized identities and intentions came only after World War II.

Composers, scholars have argued, do manifest gender and sexuality nonverbally through harmony, melody, and other devices. "The point of recapitulation in the first movement of the Ninth [Symphony of Beethoven] is one of the most horrifying moments in music," Susan McClary claims, one that "finally explodes in the throttling, murderous rage of a rapist incapable of attaining release." But Leo Treitler wonders "where the gender-labeling is coming from"—composers and audiences at the time, or critics now? Perhaps, McClary argues, serious music "is not even viewed as sexual (let alone masculine!)" because its sexual meanings are submerged in a view of music as "absolute." More likely, although music is a gendered sphere like all the arts, its "genderization" owes to how people hear it more than to any intrinsic meanings.[18]

Tensions over gender and sexuality did inflect debate about music, however, as the fulminations of composer Charles Ives indicated. Ives excoriated many European composers as effeminate. Wagner "is a soft-bodied sensualist=pussy," and as for Chopin, "one just naturally thinks of him with a skirt on." Ives reviled "pansys," "lily-pads," "old ladies," and "pussy-boys," and asked, "Is the Anglo-Saxon going 'Pussy'?" Perhaps, Philip Brett has speculated, Ives experienced "homophobic panic." Similarly, critic Paul Rosenfeld denounced composer Edward MacDowell, who "minces and simpers, maidenly and ruffled. He is nothing if not a daughter of the American Revolution." As Aaron Copland's biographer notes, "The modernist rebellion against romantic sentimentality often took on, at the least, misogynistic overtones, even among women themselves." For some, like Ives, it also entailed an assertion of white superiority and privilege.[19]

Yet such commentary barely touched on sexuality. What riled Ives was not the same-sex attractions of composers, but his place in a world of music he saw as feminized and his rage about rejection of his music. Lambasting composers, critics, and patrons as effeminate was his way to impugn their cultural authority, not to signify their sexual orientation. As Judith Tick argues, "His name-calling was purposeful. His project was the emasculation of the cultural patriarchy," and he expressed a gender ideology that "stigmatized classical music as 'effeminate' and simultaneously defined its highest achievements as masculine." Given how "diffuse and contradictory" that gender ideology was, "the terms *masculine* and *feminine*, or *effeminate* and *feminized*, were used similarly by people of highly disparate musical orientations and taste." Gender ideology provided an unsettled language of abuse, not a settled scheme for assessing composers and musicians, and it reflected a disdain for women — one reason many women fled music in the teens and twenties — more than a homo/hetero distinction.[20]

There were queer American composers precisely when Ives was active. Well informed about the literature and politics of homosexuality in Europe, where he studied, Charles Tomlinson Griffes (1884–1920) privately documented his active sexual and social life in New York's gay world of the 1910s. His musical "impressionism" was of the sort Ives might have labeled "effeminate," but the insular Ives "did not meet any of [the] proponents of modern music and probably did not know who they were." For his part, Griffes shielded his gay life from other professionals in music in the spirit of the "double life."[21]

Still, "the language of creative musical achievement was patriarchal," as demonstrated by Arturo Toscanini as conductor of the Metropolitan Opera (1908–15), the New York Philharmonic (1926–36), and the National Broadcasting Corporation Symphony (1937–54). Ives had derided him as "Toss a Ninny," and Toscanini first worked in opera, where female voices and celebrity loomed large, but in a long process abetted by the Maestro and his promoters, he became the object of a cult of musical masculinity. His authority over musicians and his rages, philandering, public aloofness, supposed courage under fire during World War I, antifascism, and stamina in old age—these were used to define classical music as a manly arena, a quest capped by his association with American nationalism during World War II. Toscanini's celebrity suggests how American musical life was implicated in the nation's assertion of power and how gender defined discourse about it.[22]

But homosexuality less often did. Gay composers coming of age in the interwar era—among them Virgil Thomson, Aaron Copland, Samuel Barber, and his Italian American partner, Gian Carlo Menotti—met little difficulty finding their place in a gay world and forging links between their homosexuality and their creativity. Most were neither homosexuals who happened to become artists nor artists who happened to be homosexuals. Instead, those identities wound around each other like DNA strands: they became homosexuals through their creative work and artists through their sexuality. As Nadine Hubbs argues, they composed themselves. There were many variations on this theme, depending on an artist's circumstances, tastes, and moment. Composers who drew on French modernism, Hubbs shows, created different sounds and identities than Barber, who followed a more Germanic and "conservative" route. Those coming of age in the 1920s and 1930s worked things out differently from a later generation, which faced a more overtly antigay environment. Other identities also counted—Jewish and urban Copland differed from WASP and patrician Barber. But for most, their identities as queer artists emerged early, often abetted by a sense of social or artistic privilege. As Thomson's biographer explains: "His champions . . . were like-minded men who treated their varied homosexual inclinations not as shameful perversities but as curiosities to be explored discreetly. Being men of high social position, they felt entitled to indulge themselves and would not be judged by people with less intellectual accomplishment."[23]

It was a stance prewar artists could sustain partly because they faced 23 only an embryonic apparatus of journalistic, medical, and state scrutiny. The stereotype of the pansy further sheltered those like Barber and Copland who appeared conventionally manly and middle-class. Although gay men often lived a "double life," the separation of their gay lives from other facets of their social world did not reflect shame or isolation, only a practical accommodation. Barber, Copland, and Menotti experienced no agonized search for heterosexual love and no resort to disguises—separate quarters for a partner, the cover marriage, the female escort. And to a degree few nonmusicians appreciate, one label—composer—trumped all others, while also incorporating them.

Gay artists before World War II had several sources of identity and support. They tapped into European writing on sexuality and its "association of homosexuality with 'artistic attitude,'" in Havelock Ellis's phrase,[24] and they often worked, studied, and traveled in Europe, where artists and intellectuals often made less fuss about sexuality. Both abroad and in the United States, they connected with the emerging gay worlds of large cities, seeking sex, romance, or friendship. There they grasped the homosexual's presumed affinity for the arts and the arts' presumed affinity for homosexuals, coming to regard homosexuality as a benign or even empowering context of their artistic lives.

Most composers were occupied less with how to function as gay artists than as American artists, facing sharp tensions between European and American influences, a national and an international style of composition, high and popular culture, and older and newer idioms and genres. For years composers and critics debated what constituted American music, who best composed it, and whether it was even a worthy goal. Should it reflect music's nationalist history or its aspirations to be a universal language? Should composers draw on folk idioms, as European composers often had, and if so, whose? Should they capture some intangible spirit of the nation, or should they ignore any specific American aspirations? Would they compose American music, or merely be American composers?

Cultural politics in the 1930s prized the return of artists to America and their use of the culture of Americans (or "the people"), but composers and critics disagreed about what music would be authentically American. Copland wanted composers to "speak directly to the American public in a musical language which expresses fully the deepest reactions of the American consciousness to the American scene." Others wanted music transcending America in sources and appeals, thus proving that America had come of age. Both were forms of cultural nationalism, and "more so than in the other arts, a musical work did not necessarily require a distinctively American content to serve a nationalistic purpose." But the competing definitions—music *of* America or music *by* Americans—went unreconciled in the 1930s. Critic Olin Downes, for example, chided Barber's *Overture to "The School for Scandal"* (1931–32) for not being "American in flavor," claiming that it "fails to suggest race and environment." That outlook jostled with more capacious or tentative definitions. Daniel Gregory Mason, although espousing American music and disliking Jewish "ugliness," saw American life as "many-sided, nowhere nucleated, and, as a subject for art, chaotic." Marion Bauer believed that "music in order to be sincere must reflect an inner national something which comes from the life of the people."[25]

Was there at least an "American sound"—musical devices widely used by Americans, even defining of America? Virgil Thomson noted "the non-accelerating crescendo and a steady ground rhythm of equalized eighth notes." Copland pointed to "a certain vigor and a certain rhythmic impulse which are recognizably American." Composer William Schuman saw American music as "terse, sinewy, direct, sentimental." Some critics noted the prominent role of brass, often in elegiac or affirmative fanfares. Ned Rorem later asserted that Copland "brought leanness to America, which set the tone for our musical language throughout the war." Others focused on what American music seemed to express as much as how it did the expressing. Copland captured America's expansiveness, both prairie and urban, and the loneliness and alienation that expansiveness might induce—cultural nationalism, but with an ache.[26]

Critic Deems Taylor mocked this debate over "an American 'school' of music" in 1938, at its peak. Its contesting advocates, as Taylor teased them, saw such music as expressing anything from "the spirit of American independence" to "the relentless perfection of a Ford plant" and "the Ku Klux Klan and the brotherhood of man." As a basis for American music, the folk songs of one group excluded others. How do Indian songs "express anything of *us*?" Taylor asked. "We have stolen everything else from the Indian that he ever owned; we might at least let him have his own music for himself." The "magnificent" Negro spirituals "are not American—that is, in the sense of expressing the soul of the average white American." "There is no American school of music," Taylor concluded, "and I doubt if there will ever be one." He was more agitated by the carnage of World War I, in which "Europe murdered," he noted, "a whole generation of potential composers, painters, poets, novelists, play-wrights, architects, sculptors." He pointed to another goal of some composers on the eve of World War II: to prevent more such carnage. As his comments indicated, racial, ethnic, and political tensions about who or what constituted authentic American music agitated prewar debate.[27]

Sexuality was hardly irrelevant to those tensions, but it did not structure public discourse. Each composer found a way to navigate these tensions and fuse a style from them—Copland's was seen as more leftist, nationalist, and upbeat, for example, Barber's as more traditional, European, and brooding. But both were recognized as American composers. Queer composers also shared an international hybridity of style typical of musical modernism. The 1930s saw "the emergence of multiplicity and heterogeneity as vital conceptual patterns," explains Terry Cooney, despite "a powerful urge to maintain a sense of progression in Western aesthetic culture from one dominant style to another."[28]

The terms of debate largely shielded serious music from scrutiny about the presence of queer people and content. Although suspicion persisted that some American music lacked virility, the work of composers like Barber and Copland was seen as too lean or muscular to receive the "mincing" charge that composer Edward MacDowell had suffered. Barber's style was often likened to that of Sibelius, in turn viewed as "rough-hewn" and possessing "granitic strength."[29] Moreover, categorizing such music as American implicitly gendered it masculine—vital, energetic, capturing the nation's spirit—given 1930s cultural nationalism. The contributions of composers, musicians, and other artists to America's effort in World War II further coded them as masculine.

Still, there were cracks in the shield against inquiries about queerness. The Virgil Thomson/Gertrude Stein opera *Four Saints in Three Acts* (1934) was queer at every level—authorship, dramatic treatment, and music, with the all–African American cast at its premiere serving to "emblematize a queer sexual freedom associated with Harlem and projected onto black bodies." For all "its renowned abstractness," the opera was "pivotally concerned with certain tender subjects: those of the authors' own lives, loves, and work as modern queer artists." Insiders saw it as such, and hostile critics, to whom Thomson's and Stein's sexuality was no secret, attacked it as such. Olin Downes in the *New York Times* sputtered about its "foppishness," its "affected and decadent" quality, its appeal to the "precious" in the audience, words whose meaning New Yorkers could readily grasp.[30]

More palpable trouble emerged in the other arenas. In 1936, Henry Cowell, a prominent and unconventional composer, confessed to "performing oral sodomy on a seventeen-year-old male" in a case that "became fodder for the Hearst tabloids" and put Cowell in San Quentin until 1940. The Eastman School of Music purged some of its gay faculty and students in the 1930s and 1940s (accounts vary as to whether its director, composer Howard Hanson, was behind the purge). A bigger scandal came in March 1942 when New York City police and naval intelligence officers raided 329 Pacific Street in Brooklyn and arrested its owner and others on suspicion that it was a site for the sale of gay sex and the corruption of servicemen passing through the city. Rumors sprang up in the papers that Nazi agents had infiltrated the premises and that Massachusetts Democratic senator David Walsh ("Links Senator to Spy Nest") had frequented the place, though he had not been arrested. White House intervention helped to quash that rumor, but Senator Alben Barkley still had the distasteful task of denying it on the Senate floor. Among those nabbed was Virgil Thomson, the composer and sharp-tongued *New York Herald Tribune* critic who "fit comfortably into this closeted milieu" of that newspaper, his "foppish side . . . offset by his pugnaciousness." Thomson escaped formal charges and press coverage, but as his biographer puts it, "Word had gotten around." Meanwhile Thomson scrupulously maintained separate apartments for himself and his lover and ostentatiously showed up at Carnegie Hall with a female date, whereas Barber lived openly with Menotti, and Copland lived comfortably, though not conspicuously, as a gay man.[31]

Press snickering about the incident boded ill. Referring to "that musician [Thomson] mentioned in the Brooklyn house," columnist Walter Winchell raised the specter of a "swastika swishery." Suspicions of European ethnicity that poisoned American life and purged American music during World War I were becoming passé in the melting-pot ideology of this war. But homosexuality offered a fresh object of suspicion. Even before the war, "one of the best ways to characterize the vileness of Nazism" had been "to equate it with sexual perversion," including homosexuality. When 329 Pacific Street was raided, the armed forces were developing an apparatus to screen homosexuals from service, although one often ineffectual and capriciously applied. These new links in perception and law between homosexuality and national danger had few immediate consequences for most artists, though alarming ones for Thomson, and the place of sexuality remained more obscure regarding music than many of the arts. But those links were strengthened as the nation elevated the arts into weapons of American stature and power abroad—"Send me a list of ten composers you consider most worthy to represent American culture to European nations," composer Roy Harris, from his post at the Office of War Information, ordered Copland. The conjunction of heightened scrutiny of queer people and soaring demand for their creativity set up ominous prospects.[32]

So too did a growing gay presence in the arts. Individuals like Griffes had been in the arts earlier, and a collective presence in entertainment and theater was well known by the 1920s, but in high culture such a presence and awareness of it emerged later. By World War II, composers moved in social and professional circles where gay figures were numerous. Notable was the Brooklyn household over which English poet W. H. Auden sternly presided during World War II. At various times it included, among others, composer/writer Paul Bowles, stripper/novelist Gypsy Rose Lee, English composer Benjamin Britten and his partner, tenor Peter Pears, Thomas Mann's son Golo, and writer Carson McCullers. Others moved in different circles, but ones with numerous gay figures. Their collective presence, combined with the new apparatus of national security, opened the way for greater scrutiny.

McCullers critiqued that scrutiny in *Reflections in a Golden Eye* (1941), which Clifton Fadiman called, not sympathetically, a novel of "murder, lunacy, and stray hints of rape, homosexuality, and other items out of Kraft-Ebbing." If anyone deserves the label "queer," it is McCullers, who had intense relationships, mostly troubled, with men and women. To critics, *Reflections'* main characters, stranded on a backwater Southern military base, were Major Langdon and his wife, Alison, and Leonora Pemberton and her husband, Captain Weldon Pemberton, whose seething homosexuality erupts murderously against Private Williams. But Anacleto, the Filipino houseboy to the Langdons, is pivotal. He flounces about in camp style, decides to "compose" a ballet, struggles to speak French, and aspires to be artistic. His attempts were relegated, by other characters and by critics, "to the realm of 'imitation' rather than creation, in rhetoric that unmistakably pairs the cultural evaluation of work produced by African American and/or homosexual artists," one scholar explains. But Anacleto is more insightful and resourceful than the other characters, and *Reflections* subverts any notion that "a homosexual artist's lack of creativity is merely symptomatic of a more essential sexual and emotional (that is, a reproductive) barrenness." Reviewers ignored the novel's "critique of military industry and psychoanalytic medicine."

But it was another sign of difficult times for gay artists who helped to define a nation nearing the zenith of its ambitions.[33]

Postwar Agitation

Far from natural, mid-century antihomosexuality took work to develop and promote. Agitation about queers' place in culture did much of that work. Postwar agitation diverged sharply from prewar commentary, which was largely forgotten. Its purveyors were louder, more numerous, and more widely heard. They focused on men more than women because World II and the Cold War raised the stakes on masculinity and male performance. They scrutinized homosexuals as creators, not just fictionalized characters. Most of all, they emphasized a systematic gay presence in all the arts—queer people as a social type rather than eccentric individuals in a few fields. Their observations were scattered and episodic—no sustained argument was needed given the scant resistance met—but it cohered in the claim that the queer presence in the arts was large and malign. Its purveyors came from both highbrow and popular culture, cosmopolitan and provincial outlooks, and left and right politics.

Scandal journalism—its politics usually right wing and its motivation crassly pecuniary—was the liveliest source of alarm. Jack Lait and Lee Mortimer, authors of best sellers like *Washington Confidential* (1951), were consumed with the spread of homosexuality generally: "We offer as proof that America is being feminized the fact that tough and isolated Kansas is going homo." Homosexuals, they noted, believe "many of them possessed artistic traits," but "only a few of them can and do enter" the arts, "where their talents make them equal, often superior." Lait and Mortimer worried more about "where the dull, dumb deviates go"—into government service, like the "more than 90 twisted twerps in trousers [who] had been swished out of the State Department." They nonetheless hinted at links among homosexual artists, political radicalism, President Harry Truman's "Fairy Deal," and the "56,787 Federal workers [who] are congenital homosexuals." For his part, Truman had already said something similar: "All the 'artists' with a capital A, the parlor pinks and the soprano voiced men are banded together," he complained privately in 1946 as his fears of communist subversion deepened. "I am afraid they are a sabotage front for Uncle Joe Stalin."[34]

Other scandal merchants located peril squarely in the arts and in entertainment. Started in 1952, *Confidential* magazine racked up brisk sales with gossip about romance and sex, especially deviant or interracial,   29 among celebrities. "Is It True What They Say about Johnnie Ray?" an article title asked about a crooner whose sobbing style prompted adulation among teenagers. *Confidential*, noted the fledgling gay magazine *One*, "says nothing directly in affirmation of whether Johnnie is or isn't," but readers see "a host of strange rumors, suggestions, hints and quotations of 'certain well-known' people all of which sum up to one answer." For its part, *Confidential* suggested that not only Johnnie's tears but "the million-dollar showman himself be wiped away." [35]

Besides its whispers about individuals, *Confidential* took on an entire industry in an article titled "Skeletons in TV's Closet!" It reported efforts by television executives to purge "the pinkie-waving dandies swaying into [the] living rooms" of ordinary Americans and regretted that gay men took on not only "milksop" roles but manly ones as a "TV detective" and "co-hero of a 'space drama' for kids." The situation was so bad that even the "prim and proper chronicler of Broadway, Dorothy Kilgallen," had declared it "time for TV to switch from switch-hitters." *Confidential* offered typical themes about the gay threat. Queers were associated with murder — "a television actor-producer who was trussed up like a bundle of wet wash and then stabbed to death by his lover boy." They were conspiring to take over the industry — they "make no effort to disguise the fact that television has become home, sweet homo to them," and "hell hath no fury like a swish scorned," who will "exact vicious revenge" if challenged. *Confidential* noted that "queers have often possessed surprising talents as scene designers, actors, playwrights, directors and producers." But their talents only heightened their threat: as one "worried network vice president" claimed, queers are "calling our headquarters 'Fairyland,' and they don't mean Snow White's home." Similarly, *Tip-Off* magazine deplored the gay "stranglehold on the theater" and television and sexual predation by queers in those fields. [36]

Alarm reached beyond conspicuous rags like *Confidential* into obscure niches. *Physical Culture* lamented that big-name magazines failed to "run a crusade against the evils of homosexuality," perhaps because "too many publishers and editors are homosexuals themselves." Arthur Guy Mathews claimed that "Homosexuality Is Stalin's Atom Bomb to Destroy America," as his article was entitled. The enemy, through its control of publishing and entertainment, sought to turn the United States into a nation of helpless homosexuals — "cowards who shriek, scream, cry and break down into hysterical states of psychoses when they are called upon to carry arms to defend our shores." Mathews's diatribe featured a contradiction common in agitation about homosexuals—gay men were both hysterical sissies and strangely powerful, getting their "filth injected in popular reading matter" and spread about "in comic strips, on the radio, TV and in movie scripts." They would help "the commies . . . TO CONQUER US FROM WITHIN THROUGH PHYSICAL WEAKNESS." Less tawdry, *Pageant* magazine gave one issue's cover adjoining billing to "If A-bombs Blast U.S. City" and "Homosexuality Can Be Cured."[37]

Readers might have dismissed this stuff as transparently exploitative. It was "mock shock," in the apt phrase that *One* magazine applied to *Bare*, a tabloid whose claims about queers were "news to no one old enough to drink a watered martini." "Magazine Goldmine: 'Run an Article on Queers,' " as a *One* headline highlighted the pulps' crass motivations. But scandal merchants believed that their stuff sold, and they had other reasons to peddle it, *One* explained. Publishers of *Physical Culture*, which had "pictures of young men locked in naked struggle so closely approximating Siamese twins," knew "precisely who buys both magazines and pictures, yet they continue their pretense of anti-fairyism," performing "a mental strip tease in a current series of articles against homosexuality." "Anti-fairyism" could be a sham—a legal ploy to forestall U.S. Post Office agents eager to root out gay pornography. But the sham was hardly transparent to everyone. Moreover, scandal journalism's claims resembled those made, often with its bile, in other arenas where motivations seemed less crude.[38]

Pulps did not always peddle scandal. *People Today*, a pint-sized magazine whose cover blared "3rd Sex Comes Out of Hiding" in August 1954, gave a straightforward account of the Mattachine Society (a pioneering gay rights group) and *One* magazine, asking, "Will Homosexuals Try to Swing Elections?" *Picture Life* once featured a buxom blonde on its cover alongside the headline "How Broadway Handles the Third Sex," but inside it offered matter-of-fact summaries of gay-themed plays, photographs of scenes, and samples of dialogue ("He was a Sicilian boy . . . full of color, odor, savor, like a fruit," from Andre Gide's *The Immoralist*). Broadway had taken on anti-Semitism, race relations, and witch-hunting, *Picture Life* commented, but regarding "homosexuality, the Broadway searchlight has always been inexcusably dim." Now theater was taking "a giant step by lifting [the] hush-hush curtain," showing "this tragic human problem in terms all can understand." The "third sex," an older term that persisted in many pulps, was arguably a less caustic label than "perverts" and the crude medical terms used in respectable venues. Catering to less affluent and educated Americans, the pulps showed a greater range of images and opinions than higher-brow outlets, suggesting that their publishers spotted little antigay animus among working-class Americans.[39]

Still, scandal got more play, not only in published form but in gossip and folklore, recorded loosely or not at all.[40] Rumors about actors Montgomery Clift, Tab Hunter, and Rock Hudson and entertainer Liberace were common, for example. As a *Confidential* cover proclaimed, "Why Liberace's Theme Song Should Be, 'Mad about the Boy!'" Gossip and innuendo also swirled in high culture and in international circuits, given the scale of travel in the postwar arts. When Benjamin Britten was commissioned to write music for Queen Elizabeth II's coronation in 1953, rival composer William Walton and his colleagues stepped up their antigay whispering campaign. Walton "apparently believed that there was a homosexual mafia at work in the music world, led by Britten" and his partner, Peter Pears, and the Walton crowd went about "renaming Britten's work as *Bugger's Opera, Twilight of the Sods* and *Stern of the Crew*." The law also sparked rumor. When Virgil Thomson's colleague at the *Herald Tribune* was arrested for sex with teenage boys, "none of the story appeared in any New York newspaper," but Thomson (who refused to testify at a subsequent trial), *Tribune* staffers, and others knew about it. Ned Rorem's reaction to a rumor that Copland "championed mainly his gay entourage" suggested another vector of gossip. "For a gay goy like me he never lifted a finger," Rorem recalled, revealing his sense of an uneasy relationship between categories of Jewish and homosexual.[41]

In sources, language, and concerns, scandal journalism bore a close relationship to scandal politics. Unlike the localized prewar skirmishes about homosexuality, postwar scandal often played out in national arenas and hinged on presumed offenses to national power and prestige. State Department efforts to exhibit American art abroad in the late 1940s met insinuations that modernist artists might be homosexuals as well as communists. An "effeminate elite" in art, related to a "sinister conspiracy conceived in the black heart of Russia," sought to degrade the nation's image abroad, according to Congressman George Dondero, the leading foe of such exhibits.[42] The State Department, allegedly infiltrated by communists and homosexuals, was suspect as the supervising agency.

Scandals about queers in the arts and about queers in politics shared an emphasis on conspiracy. As the Washington newsletter *Human Events* maintained in a 1952 piece widely distributed in government circles, "by the very nature of their vice," homosexuals "belong to a sinister, mysterious, and efficient international." Indicting "The Homosexual Interna-

tional," Countess R. G. Waldeck saw a homintern parallel to the Communist International. Waldeck and others identified a cultural component
of the queer threat and did so in the context of national security, seeing
homosexuals as actively embracing communism or as weak-willed victims of its agents.[43]

In attacks on gay creativity, high- and middlebrow arenas differed
little from scandal journalism. *American Mercury*—the magazine H. L.
Mencken helped found, now diminished in stature and shrill in politics—
offered a vicious attack in 1951. Deploring "Homosexuality in American
Culture," as his article was titled, Alfred Towne warned not only about
individual writers but a whole system of publishing under queers' control. Their "coterie guards the door to the general public," including editors who borrowed Hollywood's "casting couch" and homosexuals who so
"dominated the 'quality fiction' scene that their preferences, by osmosis,
have permeated the thinking of many people." Moreover, the social world
of publishing featured "armies of chattering youths with soft faces, lisp-
ing critics, and certain gray flannel Brooks Brothers–suited book reviewers." As a result, the young "writer is soon sucked into a world of Queen
Bees" until he learns that "he has not entered a world, but a universe" ("a
milieu dominated by gay editors and writers," one critic a half-century
later called it). There was in New York, Towne warned, a "machinery of
success" in publishing controlled by "people who by their nature cannot experience the single biggest emotion in life." And in Hollywood a
writer would only confront "the west coast branch of the coterie," just
as abroad "he meets the whole overseas branch of the coterie, the *international trade*," a veritable "army of occupation" in Europe. The result
was a vast debasement of literature not only in "manuscripts of a swish
nature" but in work by writers like Carson McCullers, Eudora Welty,
and Jean Stafford—all "critically seduced"—and in the whole short story
genre, "increasingly shallow in content and elaborate in decor." Literary
culture was becoming "chic, artificial, and possibly effeminate," leading
to "a gradual corruption of all aspects of American culture."[44]

Towne also spotted a "flood of 'swish-comedy' on TV" and a tidal wave
of transvestism in the movies, noting examples from Milton Berle drag
routines and the masculinity-challenged characters played by Danny
Kaye to the "thinly veiled lesbian character" of the 1950 film *All about
Eve*. Towne was correct in fact if vicious in judgment. Although moral
crusaders and advertisers restricted television networks, vaudeville and
other traditions made "swish-comedy" seem tame, especially since viewers could see it as mocking queers or simply dismiss it as buffoonery.   33

Hence outrageous TV characters emerged like comedian Ernie Kovacs's Percy Dovetonsils later in the 1950s, a pansy whose lines included:

When I was a little child everyone said I was manly
I had a parakeet—a bicycle seat—and a dear little friend named
   Stanley.

Given the familiarity of such humor, *One* magazine mocked Towne: "What there is of Mr. Towne's mind is alarmingly lascivious. It must be fun for him though: think of all the filthy thoughts the rest of us miss by not looking askance at such seemingly harmless things as trench-coats and pork-pie hats. Sex, sex, everywhere! Even Milton Berle is among the depraved, as well as Eddie Cantor, Ed Wynn, and Danny Thomas." Normalizing what Towne saw as shocking, *One* got the argumentative upper hand, but Towne had the bigger audience. He used metaphors of war and disease to condemn this "new army of men dressed up like women which is invading the movie and television screens." "War, judging from the movies, breeds transvestism like trenchmouth." The "invasion" theme was common. According to Waldeck, "giggling and swishing" comedians "invade the American home via the screen." If they intend no harm, "the nauseating ambiguousness of their mannerisms, their poses, their jokes," and their "indecent dance acts" offered "moral advantages for the Communist cause."[45]

Waldeck and Towne articulated the major themes of postwar agitation: gay men covertly controlled cultural production and nurtured a culture lacking authenticity and weakening the nation. Similar themes had arisen earlier in anti-Jewish complaints, especially about Hollywood, but those complaints were now less acceptable given the racial liberalism of World War II and the record of Nazi genocide. They found a new outlet in antigay criticism, with associations between Jewishness and homosexuality connecting the old and the new—notably, many of the "swish" comics whom Towne assailed were Jewish. In both cases, the complaints addressed fears that American culture was shallow, sensational, and debauched—a mass culture whose banality and corruption gay men now served to explain. If queers were carrying out "a gradual corruption of all aspects of American culture," as Towne claimed, the threat to national vigor was large.

Other attacks were brief and arch. Critic Marya Mannes, in the middlebrow magazine the *Reporter*, skewered "Robin," a wealthy gay New York decorator, and his circle of "the most successful photographers,

painters, choreographers, composers, and writers in town, and certainly the leaders in the world of fashion." Despite "many talents," they were unhappy and superficial. They inhabited an "exquisite, tasteful, witty, and powerful stratum" but possessed "a profound discontent" that they could never "admit, for they consider themselves in nearly all ways superior to their fellows." Here was a bitter sketch of bitter queens. As *One* commented, a gay reader, "delighted to turn from the latrine-wall scribblings of BARE," a scandal rag, learns from Mannes only that he "lacks humanity, feels superior, [and] mixes Regency with modern." *One* asked "if there is a difference between the prejudices of BARE's sniggering scribe and the urbane, highly colleged cosmopolite from THE REPORTER." There is not, *One* decided: "Despite her background, Marya really writes for BARE."[46]

To be sure, indignant musings about queer people and themes in the arts appeared episodically amid other comments less hostile. When reviewers took on queer-themed fiction, some were enraged, others were puzzled or ambivalent, and a few were given to praise. Where queer themes were not obvious — still the case in much of high culture — critics and observers rarely speculated on queer content or authorship. Still, postwar indignation, though occasional, also was ugly, and it opened the way for more to come. It made claims about peril to American survival that had been absent in prewar commentary. And it was rarely contested in public, in part, so gay poet Robert Duncan complained in 1944 in the journal *Politics*, because homosexuals, rather than fighting back, retreated into a "cult of homosexual superiority," laying "claim to a Palestine of their own, asserting in their miseries their nationality."[47] Meeting little resistance, attacks on homosexuals in the arts set a tone, especially because they emerged in other venues, such as the psychoanalytic ones discussed in the next chapter. There the attacks were more frequent and sustained, providing intellectual ballast, or at least its appearance, to assertions that homosexuals endangered not just the nation's mental health and cultural creativity but even its survival.

Hollywood quickly expressed the new ideas, using watered-down analytic concepts to mark the homosexual with an artistic bent as disturbed, shallow, repugnant — or all three in Alfred Hitchcock's *Strangers on a Train* (1951). In the film and the novel on which it drew, Bruno (Robert Walker) lives in the nation's capital, enjoys decadent artistic trappings that his wealthy family can provide, boasts a tie "my mother" (a silly but suffocating woman) "made for me," and speaks French. His queer treachery is sharply sketched at the film's start when the camera zeroes in on his fluttery mannerisms and dandified wardrobe as he meets Guy

(Farley Granger), a tennis player (in the novel an architect who "left behind his volume of Plato," the author's "not-so-subtle clue that he is
latently homosexual"). Guy succumbs to Bruno's predatory homosexuality and his fiendish scheme whereby Guy will murder Bruno's father
and Bruno will murder Guy's estranged wife. On screen, the "stark contrast between [Bruno's] dark silhouette and the gleaming white marble
[of the Jefferson Memorial]" renders Bruno "a blight on the nation's political system." Bruno, a fraud as friend of Guy and as aesthete, must be
killed off, and Guy freed from his queer seductions.[48]

Queer Artists and Cultural Empire

Observers explained their agitation as a response to the growing numbers and power of homosexuals, mainly men, in the arts, an explanation hard to verify then or now. But even if homosexuals in the arts
were becoming more numerous and powerful, why was their presence
often viewed hostilely? Observers could have regarded it as familiar—
there were precedents, after all—mildly mysterious, even welcome, or
hardly worth noticing. Some did: bemused, casual, or welcoming responses grabbed no headlines and left few tracks in history's record. But
many observers saw something weird, problematical, or offensive in the
gay cultural presence, which they partly defined through the scrutiny
they gave it. Anxieties about homosexuality and the arts had existed
earlier, but why did they broaden and intensify after World War II?

Suspicion was no offshoot of timeless anxieties about homosexuality,
but instead the product of historically specific conditions. Changes in
understandings of gender and sexuality laid one foundation for suspicion. As George Chauncey argues, an earlier regime of gender and sexuality, dominated by male-female distinctions, yielded in the 1940s to
one in which a heterosexual/homosexual divide governed how Americans classified each other. Male homosexuality, once identified with inverted gender role—the sissy or fairy—was reimagined so that the choice
of sexual partner became the decisive criterion.[49] In the new scheme, a
man outwardly male in appearance was a homosexual if the object of his
desire was other men, just as a feminine woman was homosexual if she
was erotically drawn to other women. To those "who think of queers as
prancing nances," Lait and Mortimer warned that the "fairies" included
"tough young kids, college football players, truck-drivers and weather-
bitten servicemen."[50] That scheme meant that male-appearing artists
now might fall into the suspect category just like the fairies and pansies

had. The process of pathologizing and punishing homosexuals continued to draw on older language—they were still often called "sissies"—but prewar categories about gender mingled with new ones about sexual object choice. This shift also aggravated fears that homosexuals were no longer identifiable by appearance: they were an invisible, but therefore more insidious, presence that had presumably burrowed into American life, becoming a grim menace rather than a laughable but recognizable sideshow.

That shift contributed to the Lavender Scare that swept postwar America, especially the federal government.[51] Through official initiatives that rivaled those of the concurrent Red Scare, thousands of gay men and women (and others accused as such) were expelled from the military, the civil service, schools, and other institutions, usually as "security risks." They might show no disloyalty, but they were still regarded as corrosive and dysfunctional. Though sometimes accused of dangerous political affiliations, they were also suspect if they had none. No spin-off from the Red Scare, the Lavender Scare had its own dynamics. So too did agitation about queers in the arts, as timing suggests. It intensified in the late 1940s and 1950s amid the Lavender Scare, of which it was a constituting element, not just a by-product.

The arts drew special attention as an arena where homosexuals had a recognizable, sustained public presence. In other arenas—in the State Department and the civil service, among sex criminals, in large domains of urban life, especially seedier ones—they still seemed anonymous, hidden, and furtive. There were no major, recognizably gay people in government, politics, sports, religion, or other arenas, except when scandal exposed a few figures. For the most part, those purged from government service or caught in police dragnets were unknown or inconspicuous, fleetingly mentioned in the press or never publicly identified.

It was different in the arts. There the murky phenomenon of homosexuality could be connected to something familiar to readers of newspapers and followers of scandal—to actors they saw in films, composers they heard on the radio, dancers they watched in musicals. Few figures gained explicit public mention as gay, although writer James Baldwin, poet Allen Ginsberg, and entertainer Liberace, among others, effectively did by the mid-1950s. After Gore Vidal published *The City and the Pillar* (1948), his novel of queer love gone bad, some reviewers suggested his homosexuality—gay themes now seemed more traceable to gay authorship—and Vidal began his career of coyly handling such suggestions. For most artists, discretion in public—being rarely seen with partners—

protected them from the law and public ridicule, shielded gay friends and colleagues, and forestalled dismissal—routine at the time for the "Negro" composer or the "girl" musician—of their work as the product of a presumably narrow and lesser identity.[52]

But public discourse had functional equivalents of the queer designation through what D. A. Miller has called the "open secret." Its informal rules discouraged explicit labels but fostered thinly coded indications of homosexuality, as when *Newsweek* dubbed Samuel Barber and Gian Carlo Menotti "the closest of friends for 30 years." In such cases, the "open secret" operated "not to conceal knowledge so much as to conceal the knowledge of the knowledge. . . . we know perfectly well that the secret is known, but nonetheless we must persist, however ineptly, in guarding it."[53]

The "open secret" was a loose convention, not a rigid formula, and one with many variations. It revealed less about Leonard Bernstein, married and raising a family in the 1950s, than about Tennessee Williams. Barber, Bernstein, and Williams were well-known figures—others had far less publicly said about them. For some, other qualities—Baldwin's African American identity, for example—at times overshadowed their sexuality. Still, in a rough and uneven way, the "open secret" of many artists' identity was public, and within inner circles of artistic politics and society, frankly spoken knowledge was common. Just as important, even when names were not named, readers of scandal and popularized psychoanalysis could learn about queers as a type who allegedly dominated much cultural production, such as the "switch-hitters" *Confidential* portrayed as taking over television. Queer artists were not as frightening as queer sex criminals or devious bureaucrats. But as individuals and social type, they were more visible, operating in a realm to which all Americans were exposed.

They achieved a major place in American culture just when culture itself was called upon to play a new role—to underwrite America's power in its struggles against fascism and communism. Precedent for that role went far back in American history, but the stakes in the new struggles and Washington's efforts to mobilize the arts transformed the situation. Far more than before, the arts were an emblem and instrument of American power. As a result, American authorities often celebrated gay artists—as American artists—even as their presence came under suspicion, setting up the tension that structured postwar agitation about discovery.

World War II and the Cold War provoked visions of American hegemony in cultural matters, as they did in economic, strategic, and political affairs, and they likewise stirred fears of disaster if the nation failed on those fronts. In 1951 the *New York Times* deplored "America's foolish disregard of the importance of the 'cultural offensive,' " just as one congressman warned that communists "picture our citizens as gum-chewing, insensitive, materialistic barbarians." Federal sponsorship of the arts under the New Deal had fallen victim to political opposition, but it surged again during World War II and the Cold War, yielding what Jane De Hart Mathews has called "a form of 'free world' advertisement — the cultural exchange program," and much else. National security provided a less controversial yet more generous rationale for federal support of the arts, and it contributed to men's dominance of culture: except in matters like entertaining the troops, hot and cold war were putatively male enterprises.[54]

The armed forces did much of this cultural work. They used thousands of musicians, sponsored musical composition by men like Barber, and promoted the spread of American music abroad through performance by military units, support for the distribution of recordings, and programming by armed forces radio. Other federal agencies promoted American arts, artists, and intellectuals abroad as the Cold War intensified. When right-wing foes in the late 1940s challenged federal support for artists, covert and private channels provided alternative funding. "In the heyday of all this activity," Malcolm Muggeridge later recalled, "the airlines were crowded with dons and writers carrying branded culture to every corner of the habitable globe." Queer figures were among those on board. Off to West Berlin in 1950 went Tennessee Williams and Carson McCullers, for example.[55] The cultural crusade had few ideological constraints — anticommunist leftists served as emblems of freedom — and few sexual ones insofar as many queers joined it.

Tensions accompanied the state's effort to display American cultural maturity and freedom abroad. How could the arts serve as emblem of American freedom when the state sponsored them? Artists and intellectuals agonized over that question, or evaded it, for decades. It was acute but submerged when state sponsorship was covert, as with the CIA's funding of the Congress for Cultural Freedom, which mobilized European and American intellectuals and artists against communism, or its support of a Metropolitan Opera tour on the premise, CIA director Allen Dulles was told, that its "impact would be absolutely terrific in the capitals of Western Europe, including Berlin." The CIA's role involved the "sublime paradox of American strategy in the cultural Cold War: in order to promote an acceptance of art produced in (and vaunted as the expression of) democracy, the democratic process itself had to be circumvented." When the United States sponsored modernist art and music that communist nations condemned, the cultural victory was especially sweet. President Dwight Eisenhower compared "our artists," who "are free to create with sincerity and conviction," to "tyranny. When artists are made the slaves and tools of the state . . . progress is arrested and creation and genius are destroyed." But his boast sidestepped the fact that many American artists, though hardly "slaves" of the state, were its complicit or unknowing tools.[56]

State sponsorship did not alone account for the reach of American culture after World War II, for the war had cleared a path and developed a market for it. Europe's cultural resources were denuded by fascism and war, while Soviet communism both lavishly supported and savagely throttled its artists. American culture rushed into the vacuum, through a mix of state and private initiatives typical of American expansion abroad in many arenas. American occupying forces promoted their nation's culture, especially in Germany and Japan. Corporations spread American culture with new technologies like television and long-playing records. In opera, the demand ran high for American talent, especially in Germany. "It soon became obvious to ambitious Americans where the big careers beckoned," and with federal help "and any other financial assistance aspiring singers could lay their hands on, one hopeful after another crossed the Atlantic."[57] Many became mainstays of European houses; others returned to the United States with international reputations. In opera as in other spheres, America, once the great importer, now could export. But given its wealth and power, it was also a cash magnet for foreign singers, musicians, conductors, composers, and other artists and intellectuals, who joined those driven to America by war, fascism, or communism.

Americans approached the task of advancing their culture with an unsurprising mix of arrogance and anxiety. Artists were often confident, with figures like Barber, Copland, Vidal, and others nearing their peaks of creativity and reputation. Confidence got expressed in art critic Clement Greenberg's claim in 1948 that "the main premises of Western Art have at last migrated to the United States, along with the center of gravity of industrial production and political power." But cultural authorities — critics, board presidents, federal officials, and the like — also inherited a tradition of felt American cultural inferiority to Europe, a reflex that the success of Americans did not entirely dispel. In one reactivation of that reflex, some critics feared "the spreading ooze of Mass Culture," as Dwight MacDonald called it — America's cultural vulgarity, blandness, and uniformity. Formidable economic and cultural resources, and sheer desperation to prevail in the global struggle, never altogether offset such doubts.[58]

A mix of anxiety and arrogance defined the American stance toward the world in many arenas, but the nation's economic and military power had long been formidable, whereas American cultural power had been deeply doubted and less tested on the world stage. American ships, guns, soldiers, and products had reached beyond the nation's borders for most of its history. So too had American culture in some forms — in ideas and in figures like Mark Twain and Henry James who lived or worked abroad. But American arts institutions had rarely ventured abroad. Most composers, painters, and writers had gone overseas as individuals — to learn from Europe more than to teach it. And most previous efforts had lacked underwriting by the state and the urgency of global crisis. Doubt about whether Americans were up to the task was substantial.

This moment of cultural anxiety and ambition coincided with the enlarging role of gay artists and intellectuals. They served that ambition and sometimes criticized it, but they also served as objects of anxiety about it, as did others. As also the case with African Americans, the state depended for cultural prowess on a marginal group, and the tension between dependence on them and revulsion at them from many other Americans shaped much of the story, as black musicians ("jambassadors" like Dizzy Gillespie and Louis Armstrong) and opera singers (like William Warfield and Leontyne Price) were showcased abroad. But there were substantial differences. African American artists were obvious — skin color publicly marked them. They were emphatically identified with key American cultural forms well known abroad — jazz was America's "Secret Sonic Weapon," according to a front-page *New York Times* headline.[59] And incorporating them into cultural empire was driven by obvious imperatives — attacks from communist and neutral nations on American racism, the desire of American leaders to win the allegiance of nonwhite nations overthrowing colonialism, and agitation at home for racial justice. No such ideological leverage was available to queer artists: the Kremlin did not denounce homophobia, its own or America's, and most of the left in America, especially the Communist Party, vigorously practiced it. And as social type, homosexuals seemed the newest and most mysterious, a group for which languages of approval or suspicion were least settled. Their newness on the scene added to their vulnerability.

What if the task of defining and advancing American culture fell in some measure to homosexuals? That question inflected postwar critiques of creative gay men. Occasionally it received blunt expression, as in attacks on "effete intellectuals" and on homosexuality as "Stalin's atom bomb." Often the question hovered in the background. The cultural Cold War so depended on queer figures that open repudiation of them risked the enterprise. However uneasy their role made others, only a few—like Congressman George Dondero—challenged it openly. Nor was it clear whom to challenge, for the old archetype of the sissy, which many artists did not fit, yielded slowly to more expansive notions of the homosexual, and the queerness of individuals was not always apparent to cultural watchdogs. The armed forces sometimes tolerated the presence of gay men and women when there seemed no alternative. In the cultural Cold War too, gay soldier-artists were tolerated as long as the need for them persisted and their presence imposed no political costs. The untidy nature of the American state also facilitated the queer presence. Oversight was difficult, given how funding ran through a plethora of public agencies and private channels, rather than through the single ministry of culture many European nations were developing. Most of all, it was difficult to disparage figures presented to the world as emblems of American freedom. Unsympathetic observers of the gay presence in culture had no easy choice: ignoring the rot was as risky as destroying it.

Given those circumstances, anxiety about queer artists got expressed in sputtering rage, inarticulate bewilderment, or outright denial of queer talent, rather than in a coherent assault. For some, homosexuality was unleashing "a gradual corruption of all aspects of American culture," surely a threat to American power. For others, it was to be ignored, snickered at, or worried over in private. Still, a major shift from prewar discourse was under way. Gay people were now seen as a systemic presence in most of the arts, not an exotic presence in a few, and they were linked to the nation's survival and power, not just its moral health at home.

The shift was reflected in the use by antiqueer crusaders of a recently coined word, "homintern." Notions of queer power in the arts were common in Europe by the 1930s, and invention of the word "homintern" has been claimed by or attributed to W. H. Auden, Cyril Connelly, Harold Norse, Maurice Bowra, and others who presumably bandied it about in England in order to evoke a sense of secret community among queer artists or to mock others' notions of their conspiratorial power.[60] After World War II, its public use was almost wholly by alarmists warning of a threat, and it met with no significant public challenge by queer figures. Its meaning was obvious—it was a play on Comintern, the Soviet-sponsored Communist International organization that officially, if not functionally, dissolved during World War II. Its resonance came from how it evoked presumed similarities or ties between queer conspiracy and communist conspiracy. It sometimes referred to a conspiracy of homosexuals generally but often was deployed in the context of the arts. There were other terms with different connotations. "Homosexual mafia," for example, also had resonance in an America awash in stories about organized crime, suggesting an ethnic-group model—most obviously, that of Italian Americans—for describing the queer presence. But it did not convey international scale and creative ability in the way "homintern" did. As used in antiqueer polemics, it turned the defensive secrecy or discretion that gay artists thought necessary for survival into an offensive cunning by which they stuck together and burrowed into American culture.

The notion of a homintern competed with other ideas of conspiracy, given the jealousies and politics of the arts. The ugliest public vitriol against Copland was anti-Semitic, his biographer reports, and he was imagined as "heading up a powerful cabal variously populated by New Yorkers, Jews, homosexuals, Communists, Boulanger students [Copland and others had studied with Nadia Boulanger in Paris], populists, modernists, nationalists, or some combination thereof," to which might be added "fascist," given Winchell's rant about "the swastika swishery." Thomson once referred to the Copland-led League of Composers as "the League of Jewish Composers"—queers were not above seeing each other in conspiratorial terms—and black composer William Grant Still suggested that Copland was part of "an alleged racist and communist conspiracy."[61]

But that list conveys an inaccurate impression of randomness. Most categories—especially those of New Yorkers, communists, and "Boulanger students"—had associations, real or imagined, with homosexuality, as did musicality itself. That was why the League of Composers "was once dubbed the Homintern," a Bernstein biographer reports, and why composer Edgard Varèse advised a colleague, "Use your arse as a prick garage—or your mouth as a night lodging and . . . N[ew] Y[ork] is yours," adding that "it seems impossible to get help and support for something healthy and white."[62] Though not always the main object of attack, homosexuality was a common thread in the patchwork quilt of dangers imagined by conspiracy peddlers. And cries against "Boulanger students" had currency only within one field, meaning nothing to outsiders. Notions of queer conspiracy transcended those particulars. It outlasted most of the others.

Queer Artists in the Cultural Moment

However apoplectic or paranoid it often was, the homintern discourse responded to gay people's large role in American cultural life. That role was not new — Barber, Copland, and Cole Porter, for example, were established figures by the 1930s — but it swelled and gained further recognition during the postwar years. Any Rolodex of famous names would be incomplete, trite, and insensitive to the many ways in which artists understood their sexual identity, but in some fields queer prominence was striking. In composing, gay men dominated, from the mainstream of Copland, Barber, Thomson, and Bernstein to the avant-garde fringe of John Cage, and not just in a single generation, since younger composers such as Ned Rorem, David Diamond, and John Corigliano came to the fore. Many performing arts presented a similar picture. Among figures in dance and ballet was arts patron Lincoln Kirstein, founder of the New York City Ballet and major figure in the city's artistic and intellectual circles for decades. In drama, Tennessee Williams was a dominant figure, along with Thornton Wilder, William Inge, and later Edward Albee. In other fields, the queer presence was less pervasive but still notable — writers Vidal, Baldwin, and McCullers, poets James Merrill, Frank O'Hara, and Allen Ginsberg, architect Philip Johnson, and painters Jasper Johns and Robert Rauschenberg. Nor is naming those who were gay the only measure of things. According to Christopher Reed's expansive summary of the visual arts: "A catalog of all twentieth-century artists who were or were thought to be homosexual, or who documented aspects of homosexuality in their work, or who reacted against associations of art and homosexuality by aggressive displays of homophobia or heterosexuality, would come close to a chronicle of twentieth-century U.S. art in its entirety."[63] Beyond well-known names were, as critics complained, thousands of others. Judged by numbers, celebrity, reputation, and influence, mid-century figures made this a queer moment in American culture.

They succeeded in part as creators and definers of that culture, especially when more commodious definitions of "American" emerged. Musical composition is a good example. After World War II — in the glow of idealized wartime unity, Allied victory, and further successes by composers — an obvious common denominator of American music gained authority. Surveying the range of styles among composers, Virgil Thomson threw up his hands regarding the earlier debate and offered a definition that applied to most of the arts: "The way to write American music is simple. All you have to do is to be an American and then write any kind of music you wish."[64] American music could convey prairie optimism, urban energy, throbbing anxiety, and a lot else, and in many styles.

Thomson's definition sidestepped how European composers had defined American music for decades, Antonin Dvořák famously in his symphony *From the New World* (1893).[65] There were few better blues than the "Blues" movement in Ravel's Violin Sonata (1923–27) or more vernacular American operas than Benjamin Britten's *Paul Bunyan* (1941). European composers working in Hollywood invented their own American idiom, although they were sidelined in mid-century debates about serious music. And the American sound of Thomson and Copland owed much to their immersion in French musical modernism.[66] In an international arts world, drawing lines around "American" was difficult. Still, Thomson's formula helped to explain how Americans' work became emblematic of "American music" and how American creativity came to seem "American."

By the 1940s, composers had forged a music taken to be defining and representative of America. Its core came from Copland when he turned to a more accessible style—his ballet scores *Billy the Kid* (1938), *Appalachian Spring* (1944), and *Rodeo* (1942), and other works'like his *Fanfare for the Common Man* (1942). Both their subject and sound seemed unerringly American. Beyond Copland were Thomson, whose work paved a way for Copland, and younger figures, many of them mentored and loved by Copland, most famously Leonard Bernstein. Others like Barber developed a less evidently American sound but still fell within the wider orbit of American music. Most were gay, and they were the first group of serious composers to define America sonically, although individuals like George Gershwin had pointed the way and popular forms such as jazz offered other definitions. Gay composers also defined the nation in a fashion that endured—many Americans still hear their music as American, influenced by countless later uses to do so. Bypassing earlier debates about whether music should express race, nationality, or "environment," they wrote music implicitly white—whites composed it and racial or ethnic texts and idioms were few—but also inclusive because it was not marked as the music of any one group.

Its intrinsic qualities alone, however, did not define it as American. It became American due to powerful associations of text, occasion, mood, and music. Copland's ballet *Rodeo*, the American music played during World War II, the use of Barber's *Adagio for Strings* to underscore President Franklin Roosevelt's death, the music heard at the start of the "American Century," as media mogul Henry Luce called it: these connections strengthened the sense that Copland and others wrote American music, all the more so as many Americans came to regard the 1940s as the quintessential American moment. How American music coincided with World War II was key, forging specific associations for it with American loss and triumph in war—with nationalism. "*Appalachian Spring* affirmed traditional American values that were being dramatically challenged by Nazism," according to Copland and his first biographer. "Audiences knew immediately what the country was fighting for when they saw *Appalachian Spring*, even though it had no explicit patriotic theme." It helped that choreographer Martha Graham sought "to create an American 'look' in dance" and that the ballet drew inspiration from the poetry of Hart Crane, the deceased gay poet Copland had known in the 1920s, "with its mixture of nationalism, pantheism, and symbolism."[67] The result was American music because Americans chose to make it so—because artists, critics, sponsors, and audiences shared a desire to define America and because artists offered evocations of America congruent with shared understandings of the nation.

That creativity came substantially from gay artists in many fields. Did others better evoke Americans' joys and pains than Williams in *The Glass Menagerie* (1945) and *A Streetcar Named Desire* (1947) or Thornton Wilder in *Our Town* (1938)? Did they exceed Copland in evoking spacious plains, cowboys, and rural life, or Barber at conveying loss in *Adagio for Strings* (1938)? Who bettered Leonard Bernstein in his musical *On the Town* (1944) at expressing wartime exuberance and urban energy, or Cole Porter at teasing urban sophisticates in musicals and George Cukor in film comedies? Who embodied the vulnerable man better than Montgomery Clift in *Red River* (1948), *A Place in the Sun* (1951), and *From Here to Eternity* (1953), or a more confident manhood than Rock Hudson in *Giant* (1956)? And who better reflected on American traditions than F. O. Matthiessen and Newton Arvin, pioneers of American studies who revived figures like Herman Melville and Walt Whitman and wove them into American history? Who else, that is, did so well at making art from American words, sounds, images, histories?

The answer of course is that others contributed as much or more. In Hollywood, Jews and others—some also gay, of course—established a distinctive American idiom and industry. In opera, no one surpassed Gershwin's *Porgy and Bess* (1935), and in crossover works of jazz, blues, and symphonic music, Duke Ellington reigned supreme. In drama, Eugene O'Neill and Arthur Miller rivaled Williams. In musical theater, Richard Rodgers and Oscar Hammerstein began their collaboration with

Oklahoma! (1943). For every Rock Hudson or Montgomery Clift, there was a Burt Lancaster or Marlon Brando. Black, working-class, ethnic, and immigrant Americans also forged the new, definably American culture, as Michael Denning has shown. Ellington, Billy Wilder, Elia Kazan, and others formed "a new generation of plebeian artists and intellectuals"— though some were well born—rooted in the Popular Front politics of the 1930s and linked to the rise of mass culture. But their social identities were more visible at the time, and some, like Marc Blitzstein and Aaron Copland, were also queer, an overlap Denning fails to acknowledge.[68]

Just as important, success often involved collaboration between queer and nonqueer figures: Rodgers with librettist Lorenz Hart ("the song-writer whose lyrics define what America means by romantic love") before Hart's death in 1943, Copland and Barber with choreographer Martha Graham for their ballets, Bernstein with Betty Comden and Adolph Green for *On the Town* and with Lillian Hellman for *Candide* (1956). Too, gay contributions were greater, or seen as such, in some fields than others. Fiction by McCullers, Vidal, Williams, Baldwin, and Truman Capote lacked status as great literature, often instead typecast as "new fiction" or "Southern gothic"—provocative, but "too 'morbid' (i.e., homosexual) to be acceptable to the dominant critical establishment." Also "marginalized" was Christopher Isherwood, the Englishman who lived much of his life in California and who was usually noted for "being one of the first significant gay writers but never [for] his literary contributions." No scorecard of queer-versus-straight achievement is possible or desirable, yet the success of gay figures was stunning. The queer moment, far from being diffuse or generic, had specific content: gay artists helped create the sights, sounds, and words of modern American culture.[69]

Insofar as gay artists defined America, it was not because they alone grasped its essence, if it even existed. Copland's "prairie cowboys," Bernstein's sailors, and Porter's sophisticates no more defined America than Southern racists, industrial moguls, poor African Americans, or lonely housewives. Gay artists did tackle some of those matters—composer Marc Blitzstein in *The Cradle Will Rock* (1938), for example. His leftist politics were one reason he never fully gained American credentials (when murdered by queer-bashers in 1964, he was setting the Sacco and Vanzetti story). But many of these subjects were taken up more by other artists. And novels with evident queer themes remained few and were routinely purged of queer content when filmed: Charles Jackson's *The Lost Weekend* (1944) about a queer alcoholic writer emerged on-screen (1945) minus the queerness; Richard Brooks's *The Brick Foxhole* (1945) about the murder of a gay soldier became a tale of anti-Semitism as *Crossfire* (1947); James Jones's *From Here to Eternity* (1951) was bleached of homosexuality as film (1953). Just when gay people were accused of "passing"—of hiding behind a conventional gender mask—their work endured passing under Hollywood's censorship.

Gay artists' work converged on no single meaning or dimension of America. Copland's America was not the same as Barber's, or Wilder's as Williams's. In music alone, the range was large. Mid-century scores by Copland brimmed with American referents—tunes, words, situations—and seemed affirmative in message. Barber's *Adagio for Strings* was somber and lacked evident Americanness; only later, as it was performed and broadcast after the deaths of Franklin Roosevelt, Albert Einstein, Robert Taft, John Kennedy, and other notable figures, did it come to mean something American (and more, given its use outside the United States) and funereal. Barber's partner Menotti provides another case in point. His opera *Amahl and the Night Visitors* (1951) made use of·Italian folklore, a Puccini-esque musical style (as critics heard it), a story related to Christ's birth, and a Catholic religiosity. Yet, commissioned for television's *Bell Telephone Hour* and highly popular within (and beyond) the United States thereafter, it became an emblem of American culture, in part because it coincided with the postwar ascendancy in the United States of Catholics and Italian Americans.[70] American music— American culture—was defined by such artists as eclectic and diverse. Convergence on a single meaning of or idiom for America, an impossible task anyway, was hardly intended. Artists worked in too many fields and from too many sensibilities for that to happen, and no system existed to impose convergence.

Hence gay artists, although working at a nationalist moment, did not always celebrate the nation. Williams's plays, so very American, nonetheless critiqued much that was American. Barber and Bernstein were by the 1950s sharply satirical about elements of American life. At mid-century, an adversarial stance toward America could still be an American posture for artists to have. Indeed, Matthiessen and Arvin placed an adversarial consciousness at the center of America's literary past. Mid-century artists and writers succeeded in defining America because they grasped its heterogeneity, not because they divined some singular essence.

Gay artists also succeeded through their ability to reach audiences and cross divisions of culture and genre. Williams's plays quickly made it to Hollywood, Copland composed for films, and Barber dabbled in jazz and blues. The rapid movement of creative products across the permeable boundaries of high, mid, and popular culture was one source of the anxiety they aroused. It was a characteristic of the period, not just for queer artists—Gershwin, F. Scott Fitzgerald, and William Faulkner worked in Hollywood—but gay artists possessed it in abundance. Their ability to find large audiences and cross boundaries informed the suspicion they aroused—it was evidence to some that they produced superficial work, pandered to mass culture, and lacked modernist rigor.

Despite the carping, most queer artists were modernists, and they succeeded by heeding the modernist moment as well as the nationalist impulse. They had a knack for capturing, advancing, and popularizing modernist idioms, sensibilities, and aspirations: they made modernism lyrical and accessible while sustaining its excitement and broadening its range. Copland, for example, differed from serial Viennese composers like Arnold Schoenberg (transplanted to the United States) and his American followers, whose severe modernism seemed less appealing to audiences. In the 1940s and 1950s, the divide between serial and tonal composers sharpened, and by association between straight and gay composers: "I hear that you are homosexual," Virgil Thomson reportedly said to the younger composer Ben Weber, and "I hear you're a twelve-tone composer," and when Weber agreed with both statements, Thomson added: "You can't be both. Now which is it?"[71] Copland, Barber, and other tonal composers were often tagged as insufficiently modernist or as throwbacks to romantic traditions, and the policing of modernism's boundaries was intense. Yet performers and audiences recognized that Barber was not Brahms, Menotti not Puccini, Copland not Debussy, Cole Porter not Rudolph Friml, and that Williams, McCullers, and Baldwin were fresh voices. Modernism was capacious enough to contain numerous variations. Many gay figures are best seen as lyrical or expressive modernists.[72]

Queer artists also contributed to other strands of modernism, pushed beyond it, or never embraced it. In design, the visual arts, and architecture, many gay artists, collectors, and audiences resisted modernism's juggernaut, preferring Victorian and other older styles, and were scorned for doing so. "The love that dared not speak its name had learned to scream through decor," as Herbert Muschamp puts it. After the high-water mark of lyrical modernism in the 1930s and 1940s, other modernist strands, less representational and more cerebral, gained critical favor at its expense. Composer John Cage; his partner and collaborator, choreographer Merce Cunningham; and painters Johns and Rauschenberg may have—scholarly debate is fierce—protested homophobia through the silences and dense coding that abstract modes allowed. Cage's "inclusion of silence" perhaps affirmed what "was silenced in society—homosexuals and others who did not conform to the mainstream"; and "the secretive, gay-coded art of Johns and Rauschenberg became, by the end of the 1950s, the most celebrated artistic expression of a culture intrigued by well-kept secrets." If so, however, few probably got the message at the time. And for all their presence across the range of styles, gay men were especially prominent in fields—serious music, theater, prose—where lyrical, accessible forms of modernism were widely taken as defining of American culture.[73]

Gay artists' contributions to American modernism had major implications for discovery of them at mid-century. Queer creativity had long been recognized but was usually regarded as an individual achievement: Michelangelo was simply a great artist, Tchaikovsky a great composer. Modern queer creativity, however, was too collective in authorship, large in impact, and specific in content to be treated only as a matter of individual greatness. The achievements by so many figures made discovery a fraught enterprise—the discovery of a social type playing a major role in defining American culture at a nationalist moment.

These qualities of gay people's creativity were not fully evident at the time. Homosexuality, modernism, and Americanism were moving targets, not fixed benchmarks, and who fit them was unclear given the "open secret," individuals' prudence or uncertainty about sexual identity, and artists' varied roles and styles. But queers' role in culture was an unsettling matter to many, vaguely felt or deeply suspected but hard to pin down. They thought they glimpsed something disturbing that demanded explanation. Their explanations occupy the next chapter.

Explanation

Discovery prompted explanation, just as explanation spread the word of discovery. "Do Homosexuals Have Special Artistic Gifts?" psychoanalyst Edmund Bergler titled his article in 1957. An affirmative answer had circulated for years. "The fact that homosexuality is especially common among men of exceptional talent was long since noted by Dante," Havelock Ellis claimed decades earlier.[1] But the question gained urgency after World War II as people like Bergler tried to explain why, or deny that, gay men were numerous and talented in the arts. Most observers located queer creativity beyond the bounds of psychological, political, social, or cultural normality. The notion of queer artists' outsiderness was not new, but the vigor with which it was now asserted was striking. Experts presented gay artists as both pathological outsiders to American life and consummate insiders in the arts. They usually failed to explain how such artists could be both, except through trickery and conspiracy. They nonetheless strengthened an enduring image of gay people as outsiders. They also showed how antihomosexuality served as a vehicle for venting the anxieties of the age.

Contemporary inquiries were muddled and overlapping. Medical experts, intellectuals, journalists, and others borrowed freely and often carelessly from each other and substituted repetition for cumulative inquiry. Few posed a counterquestion: Why shouldn't gay men be powerful in the arts? Most presumed something wrong or weird, as if the queer presence violated a natural distribution of social groups in the arts. Partly in response, some gay men naturalized the queer presence as the product of a timeless queer talent for the arts. One explanation that later become dominant maintained that gay artists thrived because as outsiders to the dominant culture they could better perceive, define, and transform it. They could, argued Donald Webster Cory—the pseudonym of the major gay authority on homosexuality—"see this stream of humanity, its morals and mores, its values and goals, its assumptions and concepts, from without."[2] Although a more sympathetic argument than most, it still had problems.

Critics of gay artists also faced a paradox. How could queers be so influential at such a homophobic moment? Critics knew the prevailing stigma against homosexuality—many endorsed it. How, then, did queer artists thrive despite it? The paradox was more apparent than real. The queer ascendancy began before World War II, and the flood of suspicion came after—it was more a response to gay creativity than a preceding condition. Suspicion also preoccupied observers more than artists themselves. It was commentary *about* them, rarely by them. Most avoided the public fray and stuck to their work. Although sensing a relationship between sexuality and creativity, queer artists rarely belabored it. Others did.

Pathological Outsiders

The most sustained and pernicious commentary on gay artists came from psychoanalysts and other medical experts. Like many of them, Edmund Bergler denied that gay men had special talent for the arts—their malicious conspiracy accounted for any success they had. He was the era's most visible denier, his views widely circulated in his many books, articles, and radio appearances. He was "the most important analytic theorist of homosexuality in the 1950s," Richard Lewes claims, "an extreme figure" who still captured "the general psychoanalytic consensus" at a time when analysis had great intellectual and popular influence. He "provided a whole bestiary of homosexual monstrosities," contending that homosexuals were crippled by medical and moral maladies, which he listed at great length and in scathing tones. Their pathology, he insisted, made them outsiders to American life.[3]

Bergler feigned objectivity, but his questions—one of his books was titled *Homosexuality: Disease or Way of Life?* (1957)—had only one, obvious answer. After all, "there are no happy homosexuals," whose propensity to fraud, thievery, espionage, child molestation, and murder Bergler emphasized. He condemned Alfred Kinsey's reports on the frequency of homosexual behavior as explainable only because Kinsey "became the voluntary or involuntary dupe of the highly efficient homosexual propaganda machine," whose existence Bergler asserted without evidence. Worse, Kinsey's claims "will be politically and propagandistically used against the United States abroad, stigmatizing the nation as a whole in a whisper campaign." Bergler also linked homosexuality to fascism and communism — "the *capos* in Hitler's concentration and extermination camps were only too frequently recruited from the ranks of homosexual criminals" and "the setup" behind the Iron Curtain likely "is similar."[4]

Analysts often ascribed homosexuality to deep flaws in relationships between children and parents. An engulfing mother made her proto-gay boy fear intimacy with women, while a remote father deprived him of a healthy role model. A "supportive, warmly related father *precludes* the possibility of a homosexual son," Irving Bieber wrote. Roughly the reverse befell the vulnerable daughter. Wounded offspring — angry at, fearful of, or overidentifying with the opposite-gender parent — sought intimacy with others of their gender and doomed themselves to emotional immaturity, a horrible condition that Bergler and others still promised to cure. For Karen Horney, male homosexuality arose from "the desire to escape from the female genital, or to deny its very existence," yielding men who "debase women." To Bergler, the gay man "is not a rejector of women but a fugitive from women. He is in deadly fear of women."[5]

Within that broad framework, analysts took on gay men in the arts. Insisting that they lacked special talent, Bergler argued that even "if a homosexual is a great artist, this is so *despite*, and not because of his homosexuality." In his chilling words, any homosexual who became a "great artist" did so only because "a small autarchic corner has been rescued from the holocaust of illness." Turning a homosexual's words against his own kind — a common ploy — Bergler tapped writer Somerset Maugham's comment (picked up by others from Bergler's account) on gay artists' "ability to ornament, decorate, and embroider." But Bergler saw in that ability only "the very defect that mars all of Maugham's writing: superficiality." He argued that the sexuality of artists who propagated queer themes should be publicly exposed so that their "corroding, flippant attitude" could be understood and rejected — in the 1950s, the push for queers' visibility usually came from their foes, who wanted to break a "conspiracy of silence" in order to protect the nation's moral and martial virtue.[6]

For all that some analysts scorned queers' talents, they visited the subject repeatedly, as if in asserting queers' failure they feared their success. Bergler spilled much ink on the matter, including an entire book on queers in the fashion industry, where the homosexual's "*unconscious hatred of women*" was "responsible for some of the dress absurdities of the last half-century." The result was "the paradoxical fact that women are dressed by their bitterest enemies." In fashion as in more serious arts, queers' work was a sick joke inflicted on unsuspecting women and an unsuspecting culture. "The influence of homosexuals in certain professions is great," Bergler lamented, especially "theater and the entertainment world," plus "fashion and interior decoration" and "the academic world," along with "writers"—a long list indeed. How could homosexuals have such "influence" if they were failures as artists? Bergler never fully addressed that question, instead simply raging at their influence: "*Power misused, malice exaggerated, cynicism pronounced, subtle systems of emotional blackmail perfected*—these elements combine to make the *working method of some homosexuals*."[7]

Critics poked fun at Bergler's sensationalism but not his substance. Writing in the *New Leader*, *Time* editor Gilbert Cant noted Bergler's "great need for the hotter Klieg lights of personal publicity" and wondered "what intimate psychodynamic need Bergler satisfies by his all-out attack on homosexuality." But he embraced Bergler's claims because "homosexuals have . . . launched a drive not only to be accepted as the equals of normal men, but honored as a special breed, the repository of most of the world's artistic talent." Cant did not document this "drive," for there was little to document. ("Driven into defiance," one gay essayist noted, many homosexuals did find "something intrinsically superior in homosexuality.") As for "the worst offender in this obscene propaganda drive," Cant singled out "a confused Madison Avenue pervert who hides behind his wife's skirts and the pseudonym Donald Webster Cory." Cant recognized Cory as "intellectually gifted" but appreciated that Bergler went "against Cory and his ilk—who are now coming out of the woodwork with increasing insolence." "We need join in no witch hunts," but "neither should we let" deviants "deceive us and gain license to seduce more of the innocent."[8]

Bergler had no monopoly on this subject. Some experts ignored it, offered less strident views, disagreed on specifics, or deemphasized pathology. For D. J. West, homosexuals were "ordinary human beings, neither specially gifted nor specially evil," and "the discovery that all these great men"—West cited a standard list—"were sexual deviants is worth about as much as a discovery that they all had fair hair," given gay people's distribution "in all walks of life." Although "homosexual coteries and homosexual literature provide compensation" for society's "contempt," West argued, the "dreariness of cultivated artificiality" among many gay men diminished their contribution to the arts. In *Great Men* (1956), Edward Hitschmann stressed Johannes Brahms's ties to his mother and Clara Schumann, his effeminacy, and his piano playing at age thirteen in seedy bars where sailors "half-naked sang their obscene songs to his accompaniment" and "enjoyed awaking his first sexual feelings," experiences "momentous in their consequences." Departing from reigning analytic bias, W. David Sievers offered a massive, nonjudgmental *History of Psychoanalysis and the American Drama* (1955), treating work by Tennessee Williams and others sympathetically and claiming that the audience for Andre Gide's *The Immoralist* indicated "the psychological maturity of the Broadway theatre by the mid-fifties." For him, "maturity" was not a trait homosexuals lacked, but one play-goers needed.[9]

Still, views like Bergler's prevailed among medical experts, and after he died in 1962, others carried the torch. Charles Socarides regarded homosexuality as "filled with aggression, destruction, and self-deceit. It is a masquerade of life." Harry Gershman brushed aside Sigmund Freud's pithy remark—"Before the creative artist, analysis must, alas, lay down its arms"—to insist that since the homosexual is sick, his creations can only entail "rebelliousness" and "sterile narcissism." Although a gay writer "may have an uncanny ability" to depict "the destructiveness of man," a homosexual's boasts of creativity were usually like "his pseudo-facade of 'gaiety'"—only "a disguise for his deep hopelessness, depression, and resignation." Irving Bieber endorsed Gershman's challenge to "the widespread notion that homosexuals are more artistic and creative than are heterosexuals"—a notion that people like Bieber spread, then claimed to debunk. Lawrence J. Hatterer, citing findings from his New York patients in *The Artist in Society* (1965), found that while some gay men functioned well as artists, most pursued their careers for destructive or shallow reasons, especially in fields with a close "relation to wealth and social position," which offset their "feeling discredited and outcast." The homosexual's "work tends to become fashionable, stale, and lacking in emotional commitment," given his "restless, transitory nature." Many analysts, Richard Lewes concludes, "insisted that . . . artists were creative and productive despite their homosexuality, not because of it"—or simply aside from it—and saw it "as inimical to true creativity."[10]

Common also in other venues, the depiction of queer artists' work as shallow and sterile was a staple of medical judgment. How, after all, could genuine creativity arise from gross pathology—from the homosexual's *"great internal conflict, which like a sponge absorbs all inner energy,"* as Bergler put it? Even experts professing "tolerance," Lewes notes, believed "that the homosexual 'is ill in much the same way as a dwarf is ill — because he has never developed' " — and that gay people had " 'petrified patterns of living' " which made them " 'atrophied.' " The homosexual artist as sick person drew more attention than as artist, as if a product was bad simply because a queer produced it.[11]

Those who did examine the product — and many analysts saw themselves as expert in cultural, not just individual, pathology — usually regarded it as destructive, as did Bergler with fashion and Frederic Wertham with comics. Wertham, a senior psychiatrist for New York City's Department of Hospitals who testified in court about segregation's damage to black children, scorned the comics' creators and condemned their impact on youth. He spotted, among many dangers, how Batman and Robin displayed a "psychological homosexuality," one phase of *The Seduction of the Innocent*, his 1954 book (with reproductions of sample lurid comics), which he outlined for a congressional committee. Their "Ganymede-Zeus type of love relationship," set in "sumptuous quarters, with beautiful flowers" and bulging genitals on display, is "like a wish dream of two homosexuals living together." Such comics "softened up" youngsters for "homosexual childhood prostitution." Wonder Woman gave Wertham no peace either, given her " 'psychologically unmistakable' lesbianism." He was hardly paranoid. The homoeroticism he spotted seemed transparent even to some young readers. (Batman, Alan Helms recalled of his childhood fantasies, "untied me, gently stroked my hair & caressed me, & that's when I came. Night after night.") Given that transparency, when *Batman* became a TV series in the 1960s, ABC decided to "forestall" the "overtones" and "put Aunt Harriet into his house." And queer men and women did help create comics. But Wertham's indignation drew on more than his unsurprising observations. It also tapped into the shift whereby the invisible, straight-acting gay man — Batman was certainly butch — displaced the laughable, less sexualized gender invert. Amid the postwar sex crime panic, it was a small jump to suggest that if gay men preyed on America's youth, so did cultural images of and by them, corroding the nation's moral and masculine fiber.[12]

Analysts' antigay stance arose in part, Lewes suggests, among émigrés, often Jewish, from war-torn Europe. Just when World War II raised the stature of psychiatry, they sought respectability, patriotic credentials, and professional power in their new land by attacking a despised group and linking it to erstwhile fascist or newfound communist enemies. "It is as if psychoanalysis, having found refuge in a new homeland, EXPLANATION sought to demonstrate its relief, gratitude, and worthiness by subscribing to . . . American values and institutions." Freud had offered complex, shifting views, at times criticizing hostility to homosexuality, which he regarded as no more pathological than many conditions. Many later analysts abandoned his complexity for a more coarse, singular view, in a process Lewes variously labels a "progressive rigidification of psychoanalytic attitudes toward homosexuality," the "vulgarization of psychoanalytic ideas," "their moral brutalization," and the "Americanization of psychoanalytic discourse." [13]

Some refugee analysts were working out their demons. That they attached to homosexuals the stereotypes inflicted on Jews was a grim irony compounded by the fact that many queer artists were Jewish. Their "frequent ignorant portrayal of the sad and desperate lives of practicing homosexuals," Lewes asserts, derived from "vicious stereotypes" that "found their models in anti-Semitic and racist propaganda." Moreover, Lewes adds, it was "remarkable how many times in the postwar period homosexuals were compared to Nazis, when quite the opposite comparison could as easily have been made." Abram Kardiner commented in 1954 "on the similarity of the Nazi's hatred of Jews with the homosexual's 'notorious hatred of women.' " A quarter-century later, Kardiner still compared gay men "to Hitler's Jew-baiters" and linked them to trends that he damned in "everything from atonal music and *Sesame Street* to the late work of Picasso and women's liberation." No wonder Bieber maintained in 1967 that "homosexuals were underrepresented among Jews" — otherwise, the logic was that Jews might be Nazis. Striking to Lewes was "the repeated use during this period of the chilling phrase *a solution to the problem of homosexuality*." Some analysts, he suggests, found a scapegoat for the fate of Europe's Jews and a role as Cassandra warning of a similar fate for their new land. Analysts also regarded themselves as protectors of a European high culture in ruins in its homeland and devalued in their new land ("I was 'educated in Vienna,' " Bergler boasted). By accusing queers of subverting American culture, they could attack it without being un-American or challenging postwar racial liberalism — when, two intellectuals observed, "homosexuality becomes a much more feared enemy than the Negro." [14]

That said, Lewes's take needs context. As he acknowledges, if analysis was a fraught endeavor in the 1950s, so is analysis of the analysts now. Jews, refugees, and medical experts were not alone in seeking status by beating up on a more despised group. Many Catholic leaders, for example, pushed their antigay animus as the status of Catholic Americans (Irish, Polish, Italian, and others) rose. The influence of medical experts can easily be exaggerated, and they hardly created the broad anxiety about national security that antigay polemicists exploited.

But the convergence of psychoanalysis, the arts, and the media on New York City, the capital of all three during this period, magnified the alarm they sounded. With analysis peaking in appeal, some gay men readily found their way to the analytic couch. New York therapists then often took what they heard (or chose to hear) from patients as normative for all time and geography, believing that they had identified pathology common to all gay people. Given their cultural status and their access to the media, their views in turn easily found their way into New York's media, and were in turn broadcast to the nation. That their clientele was atypical of gay artists or gay people generally occurred rarely to any parties, any more than did New York's atypicality. Analysts' claims were not entirely fanciful. Troubled gay people saw shrinks who in turn saw pathology, which some ascribed partly to the hostility gay people faced. But therapists usually endorsed that hostility, leaving patients to deal with therapists' "certitudes about the hopelessness of homosexual life," as some have testified.[15] Analysts often complained that queers justified their lives as driven by the hostility they faced. By adding their hostility, analysts energized the queer presence they derided.

Analysts' influence went beyond a generalized cultural impact. They influenced other medical and mental health practitioners as well as artistic and academic venues, shaping how deans handled students and straight people viewed queer acquaintances. Their work did have consequences besides the obvious repressive ones. Protected by their status, medical experts wrote about sexuality with an explicitness unusual in postwar America, thereby stirring debate they could not fully control. Like others' efforts to stigmatize homosexuality, theirs also inadvertently promoted it since gay people could develop from their work a heightened consciousness of queerness, including its place in the arts, and reject or embrace the pathology experts attached to it. Some experts questioned the new orthodoxy, adhered to older Freudian or other traditions, and helped gay clients. But the inadvertent consequences of analytic discourse surfaced slowly. In the 1950s, its scornful portrayal of queer artists held sway.

Although problematic, analytic ideas were nonetheless widely popularized. Despite Hollywood's prohibitions on representing homosexuality, queer sterility and predation came together in the murderous char-

58

acters of major releases such as Alfred Hitchcock's *Rope* (1948) and
Strangers on a Train (1951). Less harsh was *Tea and Sympathy* (Vincent
Minnelli, 1956), based on a Robert Anderson play and one of many films
whose queer content caused hand-wringing among its makers, censors,
and reviewers. At a boys' prep school, shy, artsy, long-haired Tom (John
Kerr) is taunted as "sister boy" by the crew-cut crowd. *Tea and Sympathy*
criticized McCarthyite bullying and defended Tom's right to *appear* gay,
but not to be gay. Tom eventually finds his writing talent and his heterosexuality when they are nourished by the love-starved, motherly spouse
(Deborah Kerr) of a brawny athletic coach (Leif Erickson), whose fum-
bling fondness for boys and Bach makes him a contemptible queer figure
by the end. Presenting masculinity as performative, even contrived, *Tea
and Sympathy* urged viewers not to confuse men's external packaging
with their internal state, but it divorced homosexuality from creativity,
available only when Tom finds straight love. Its message resembled one
that screenwriter Arthur Laurents saw in *Gentleman's Agreement* (1947),
in which a Gentile pretends to be Jewish—the "moral was Be nice to a Jew
because he might turn out to be a gentile." While experts like Wertham
feared media culture, movies often warned against homosexuality.[16]

More lurid were the films of some of Tennessee Williams's plays. In
Suddenly, Last Summer (Joseph L. Mankiewicz, 1959), poet Sebastian—
unseen in the release print, as if too horrible (and queer) to be shown—
is locked in a sick relationship with his formidably disturbed mother
(Katherine Hepburn). Abroad, he preys on Mediterranean boys until
("suddenly, last summer") they turn on and devour him, an awful fate
revealed after a psychiatrist (Montgomery Clift) and Sebastian's cousin
(Elizabeth Taylor) slowly claw their way to the truth. Here in Southern
Gothic psycho-horror was what analysts said about gay artists—Sebastian is a mother-fixated, predatory, doomed artist—as uncovered by an
analyst and as written by two queers: Williams, author of the original play
and rumored to have been pressed by his psychiatrist to condemn homosexuality, and Gore Vidal, largely responsible for the screenplay (though
the script had many hands, including censors').[17]

Cinematic representations, it is true, can be read many ways. Viewers of *Suddenly, Last Summer* clued into Hollywood gossip, for example,
might identify not with Sebastian—unseen anyway—but with gay actor
Montgomery Clift, whose psychiatrist displays wisdom, authority, and
little romantic interest in women. Multiple readings were possible also
with *Cat on a Hot Tin Roof* (Richard Brooks, 1958), based on a Williams
play. In that film, Brick (Paul Newman), an alcoholic ex–football player

tortured by the death of his beloved football buddy, resists the sexual demands of his wife, Maggie (Elizabeth Taylor). He finally makes peace with his dying father, Big Daddy (Burl Ives), an overbearing patriarch, and with Maggie, who seeks to ensure their place in Big Daddy's empire by having a child. *Cat*, at least its stage version, also challenged capitalist patriarchy, or so Robert Corber asserts. Williams, Baldwin, and Vidal "treated homosexuality as a subversive form of identity that had the potential to disrupt the system of representation underpinning the Cold War consensus."[18] That subversiveness helps explain the "bad time of it Tennessee used to have," in Vidal's recollection, because "the anti-fag battalions were everywhere on the march. From the high lands of *Partisan Review* to the middle ground of *Time* magazine, envenomed attacks on real or suspected fags never let up."[19]

But the popularity of Williams's work suggests that his subversive message was murky, that audiences failed to get it, or that if they did, the "Cold War consensus" was hardly hegemonic. Most likely, all those possibilities have merit. The "anti-fag battalions" spotted *something* subversive in Williams's work, if not what Corber later saw, but they scored no complete victory, or else his work would not have appeared so widely. And reactions did not only fall along "anti-fag" and pro-"fag" lines. In the lesbian magazine the *Ladder*, Florence Conrad praised Williams's "unfailing artistry" but was "repelled by the ugliness and horror" and the "predatory" theme in *Suddenly, Last Summer*."[20]

Some analysts sought to contextualize rather than deny queer creativity. Even Bergler acknowledged that although all homosexuals were sick, so too were many heterosexuals. The notion of creative people as weird, disturbed, or crazed was old and continuing. Had not Van Gogh sliced off his ear, Tchaikovsky entered a doomed marriage, and F. Scott Fitzgerald drunk too much? Seen this way, sexuality less exclusively explained the queer artist. William Phillips, in *Art and Psychoanalysis* (1957), duly noted "some significance in the large number of homosexuals peopling the intellectual and artistic professions," but after all "only certain kinds of neurotics" — he viewed homosexuals as one kind — "are able to make the break with the community necessary to enter the unstable world of the arts." The compiler of *Homosexuality and Creative Genius* (1967) saw homosexuality as just one of many neurotic wellsprings of creativity, though he condemned "converting homosexuality into a virtue."[21]

The nod to neurosis was simple enough to require little elaboration, but its very obviousness deprived it of traction. That artists were neurotic was a commonplace notion, yet what did it say specifically about queers in the arts? It sidestepped the claim that, although pathology was common, it was uniquely crippling to homosexuals. And linking homosexuality to neurosis and alcoholism hardly took queer artists off the hook. Medical experts saw alcoholism as a sign of homosexuality and an escape from it. They mapped homosexuality and alcoholism onto each other and onto related traits of narcissism and immaturity, all traced to the burdens on a boy of a distant father and a smothering mother. That the gay bar was the most public queer institution perhaps strengthened these associations.

They were expressed in Charles Jackson's 1944 novel *The Lost Weekend*, in which Don is a narcissistic, alcoholic, queer writer. Placing Don in psychiatric treatment, the novel captured developing ideas about the nexus of booze and queerness but also challenged them by emphasizing the psychiatrist's failure to treat Don effectively and Don's effort to flee an analytic framework. Ending on "a double note of defiance and desperation," *The Lost Weekend* both reflected and resisted the conflation of homosexuality and alcoholism. And like many queer-themed novels of the period, it set its troubled gay figure in a web of flawed straight characters. Don was on a spectrum of trouble, not beyond its pale, as were the queer characters in John Horne Burns's *The Gallery* (1947), a novel about baffled and embittered American servicemen in wartime North Africa and Italy, which warned against "the bright psychiatrists who try to demarcate clearly the normal from the abnormal." But the subtle ideas of *The Lost Weekend* were overshadowed by the powerful images of alcoholism and were mostly erased in Billy Wilder's Academy Award–winning 1945 film.[22]

In the dominant mid-century view, homosexuals might have talent, but it would go nowhere if they stayed queer, whether or not they conquered alcoholism — which, in the circular reasoning, they could only do by overcoming their perversion. The alcoholic straight writer had a problem with booze, not sexuality. The drunken queer writer was in trouble on both scores. That reasoning also informed national policy, which identified "the loquacious, the alcoholic, and the perverted" as "security risks." But "it was only the pervert who was always a security risk. The other two categories involved qualifications — not all those who talk but those who talk too much, not all those who drink but those who drink too much. But even one homosexual encounter qualified someone as a security risk, making it perhaps the easiest such offense to prove."[23] Likewise, analysts regarded alcoholism and homosexuality as both bad, but the latter as worse.

Among maverick analysts, Robert Lindner, whose *Rebel without a Cause: The Hypnoanalysis of a Criminal Psychopath* (1944) was the loose basis for the 1955 James Dean film, took on the topic "Homosexuality and the Contemporary Scene" in *Must We Conform?* released in 1956, the year he died. Lindner ranged widely. His list of gay groups from Europe to Indonesia showed "the world-wide movement to organize homosexuals." Here was fodder for alarmists imagining a homintern, a movement he regarded with sympathy though it was "doomed to failure." Lindner argued that "a sex-denying," "sex-confused," "sex-hating" culture operated beneath the veneer of modern sexual liberalism. Homosexuality was "adopted by certain individuals as their solution to the conflict between the urgency of the sexual instincts and the repressive efforts brought to bear upon sexual expression by the reigning sex morality." It "is a form of rebellion," one that Lindner judged "commendable" but in the end "negative" since homosexuality brings "immense quantities of unhappiness" for many queers. He offered "hope that it can be eradicated," but not by punitive or therapeutic measures. Instead, destruction of the entire "sex-denying" culture would make it unnecessary. The demise of homosexuality would not be a means to social health but instead its product, as inevitable to Lindner as the disappearance of social classes to Marx.[24]

Lindner shifted homosexuality from individual to social pathology, linked it to common worries about conformity, and lauded how queers' resistance revealed the repressiveness of culture. If not agents of rebellion, they were at least its beacons, glimmering in Sal Mineo's character in *Rebel without a Cause* (Nicholas Ray, 1955), his revolt "doomed" though "commendable." But in some ways Lindner was conventional. Gay men might be the revolution's forerunners—like bourgeois rebels before the class revolution—but other men would lead it and women would have little role.

As Lindner's observations suggest, postwar commentary bore the imprint of the era's gender norms. To be sure, most commentators presumed they were simply describing the natural state of gender. Unusual was one analyst's suggestion that treating "cultural patterns as the expression of an ultimate truth concerning masculine and feminine must be combated." Even Lindner, who grasped the constructed nature of sexual regimes, seemed oblivious to it regarding gender. But the gendered features of commentary were striking. The blame heaped on engulfing mothers—the distant father's sin more one of omission—for causing male homosexuality was one feature. At a time when " 'mom'-bashing gained industrial strength," no harm inflicted by "momism" was worse than homosexuality, sapping the nation's moral and military prowess, while lesbianism was "biological and psychological treason," as military psychiatrist Edward Strecker called it. And there was the simple fact that men wrote most expert commentary, and wrote mostly about men. Those addressing lesbians differed little in outlook, and some women matched men's viciousness, but the gender imbalance in both authorship and objects was striking.[25]

It owed partly to "lesbian invisibility," whereby gay women received (and perhaps pursued) less public scrutiny and recognition than gay men.[26] For one thing, lesbians were fewer than gay men, ran the prevailing view. And as one analyst explained, gesturing to a lingering tradition of female romantic friendships, "Women in general are permitted greater physical intimacy with each other without social disapproval than is the case with men."[27] Less affluent than gay men, lesbians less often entered psychoanalysis, and hence analytic writing. Having less access to public spaces of sex and sociability, they more often avoided the legal snares that led some men to treatment and helped shape experts' views of them. Men's domination of the postwar arts also rendered lesbians less obvious, despite rumors that some prominent women were queer.

Analysts featured distinctive sources of gender imbalance and bias. Their "failure in dealing with homosexuality" stemmed, Lewes suggests, partly from an "initial gynephobic stance." They saw gay men "as deeply flawed and defective because they shared certain psychic characteristics with women"—both women and gay men were regarded as "people who would forever remain incomplete," doomed by "the conviction of being castrated." Although that gynephobia was later "purged from the theory of femininity," it "found refuge in the theory of homosexuality." Many analysts "were also protesting that they themselves suffered no taint of a condition that impugned their masculinity." They displaced male hostility toward women onto gay men, attacking them as woman-haters even as many analysts angrily condescended toward women. Analysts assigned similar traits to both women's and gay men's creativity—shallowness, decorativeness, shrillness, and lack of authenticity. In their harshest vitriol, gay men, like women, produced only an angry or pathetic burlesque of the culture made by real men. As Barbara Ehrenreich notes, postwar "sanctions" against gay men and "failed" heterosexual men rested on "contempt for women," with all three groups portrayed as trapped in emotional immaturity. Since gay men were " 'aspirants to perpetual adolescence,' " immaturity had to define their cultural products. As they aged, they could only create stale, imitative, or downright sick work.[28]

The conflation of women and gay men drew strength from the coding of the arts as feminine and of queer men as gender inverts. Gay men might appear masculine, but analysts spotted an interior psychic femininity, as if gender inversion had gone into disguise and gay men into drag—mimicking not women, but real men. While gay men might "have extraordinary talent," Kardiner conceded, "they cannot compete. They always surrender in the face of impending combat" and fail "to fulfill the specifications of masculinity." (Never mind analysts' fear that queer artists competed all too well.) Their masculine drag seemed a deceit even when regarded as a mechanism shielding them from hostility. "This was perhaps the most despicable thing about them: They *looked like* men, but they weren't really men," Ehrenreich notes of images of "failed" men.[29] In this reasoning, the queer man's interior femininity made his artistic work feminine in superficiality and artifice. Analysts offered no small hint that gay men's hostility toward women was only the tip of an iceberg of pathology: underneath was their failure to master women as true men did. As failed men who could mock but not master women, queers could not produce an authentic, masculine culture.

These gendered themes overlapped concerns about the masculine robustness of American culture. The older fear of a feminized culture expressed by figures like Charles Ives was updated for an age of global struggle. Critics sought to restore a manly order in the arts, or, for those despairing that America ever had that order, to create it. How else could the United States compete with Soviet culture and dispel what was "whispered" about America, as Bergler worried, after Kinsey's reports? That urge to construct a masculine culture was hardly confined to straight men. At least to many of its champions, the music of Copland and Bernstein was robustly masculine. The swift rise, multiple roles, and outsized theatrics of Bernstein—composer, pianist, Broadway star, New York Philharmonic conductor, husband, father—rendered him an embodiment of the heroic musical masculinity once attributed to Toscanini. Rock Hudson and Montgomery Clift performed masculinity on film. That queer men embodied masculinity in realms as diverse as the New York Philharmonic's high culture and Hollywood's mass culture struck many as insulting and insidious, proof that fake men were replacing real ones. Many observers were not about to cede masculinity to gay men, yet these men so marvelously impersonated it that expelling them from the arts threatened the rickety edifice of cultural masculinity. Hence a tone of exasperation: many observers felt hamstrung from pursuing expulsion, leaving containment the only option. Hence they often preached exposure—a common goal of American moral crusades—a truth-in-packaging regime to guide naive cultural consumers and promote vigilance about queer artists' work.

Gendered attacks on gay men also expressed concerns about masculinity among other men. Analytic and intellectual commentary belittled the queer artist, but it also hinted that the homosexual man was a stand-in for the failing heterosexual male. Traits assigned to gay men—narcissism, immaturity, staleness, lack of competitiveness—had seeped into men's lives generally, critics worried, in an era of mass culture, conformity, and female power, producing a "flight from masculinity," as analyst Kardiner called it.[30] Queers were flogged for failures that other men suffered or were blamed for them because of their insidious influence. But they were also treated like canaries in a cultural coal mine—the first to succumb to a miasma imperiling all men, as Lindner suggested.

Much like white people's attacks on blacks, attacks on gay men betrayed envy as well as fear. As "the image of the homosexual loomed over the manhood discourse," one scholar notes, the gay man "appeared to have what many male critics . . . seemed ultimately to desire: freedom from marital commitment, ease of sexual relations, and a kind of power over his life that conventional male roles precluded."[31] Never mind that law, custom, and antipathy constrained that power: in private and creative realms, he seemingly had insider power and freedom to rebel. Gay men embodied both the failures other men feared and the freedom they wanted, a paradox resolved only by attributing special advantage to them: unburdened by family and sexual constraint, moving in stealthy cliques, they had freedom and power, but rarely used them well.

In addition to its gendered concerns, inquiry by analysts and other experts also had an unsurprising class and racial focus. Many people in the arts had the white middle-class status and cultural outlook to seek help from analysts, themselves solidly white and middle class. Although observers portrayed gay men as found at all rungs of society, they gave the lower rungs less attention, reinforcing notions of queer affluence and saying little about queerness among minority groups. By implication or assertion, those groups—including Jews, some analysts claimed—were relatively free of queers, even though they featured well-known examples. For their part, minorities were hardly eager to add queerness to the burdens they faced. The analytic style further erased social differences. Writing about an unnamed clientele, analysts were bent on describing a unitary homosexuality and its pathology. Differences among queers were less important. Homosexuality was marked as white, affluent, and male. The urge to force it into one mode was strong.

Writing for fellow homosexuals in response to psychiatric discourse, David Freeman, for one, protested in 1955 that most homosexuals are "not jumping off cliffs on the French Riviera or committing suicide with jeweled sabres in the Taj Mahal or nurturing delicate neuroses at elegant cocktail parties on Park Avenue." Instead, they were "very like their neighbors—working at dull jobs with inadequate wages, struggling to meet the payments on furniture from Sears," and coming "from places like Rockford, Illinois, or Minot, North Dakota."[32] Despite his assimilationist outlook—"very like their neighbors"—Freeman captured the diversity of gay people that psychiatrists often ignored.

Political Outsiders

Intellectuals and politicians often depicted queers as purveyors of political pathology and cultural decadence—outsiders to American life. Intellectuals' ideas resembled medical experts' views, but while analysts examined homosexuality at length, intellectuals usually did so in a brief, snide fashion reflecting their awkwardness with the subject. And with antihomosexuality facing little opposition, it required little exposition.

In *A Generation of Vipers* (1942), Philip Wylie, a Princeton dropout and successful writer, presaged postwar commentary. The book was too iconoclastic to define any mainstream—*Vipers* excoriated liberalism, communism, and conservatism and was banned from U.S. Information Service libraries after the war as anti-American. It was nonetheless influential in its biting tone, ideas about "momism"—he coined the term—and claims about homosexuality, with which Wylie had a hard-to-classify fascination. Unusual among mid-century writers, he mentioned "female homosexuality," "[which men regard] only as a shady and inscrutable washroom joke." Nodding to Freud and others, Wylie viewed male homosexuality as a form of developmental immaturity abetted by mothers. He predicted that World War II would "inaugurate a new spread of homosexuality in America," as "every war" does. He was among the first to disparage State Department diplomats as "sissies." But he thought it "silly" to treat homosexuality "as a fiendish manifestation, like ax-murdering," although "male ignoramuses . . . stand ready to slug nances on sight and often do so." Besides, much in America was sham: "The [Chris-

66

tian] cross . . . hangs around the necks of thousands of harlots in the whorehouses of these United States," "thousands of American flowers of womanhood are whores," and "millions of noble American men get in bed with them." Sham—about sex, religion, patriotism, humanity—was Wylie's target. Few postwar intellectuals threw the barbs so sharply, but many agreed that homosexuality marked a failure to mature.[33]

Arthur Schlesinger Jr., a leading young historian and intellectual, demonstrated as much in *The Vital Center* (1949), his influential call to arms for a tough, liberal anticommunism. Totalitarianism "perverts politics into something secret, sweaty and furtive like nothing so much . . . as homosexuality in a boy's school," he observed, and homosexuals resemble communists: "They can identify each other . . . on casual meeting by the use of certain phrases, the names of certain enthusiasms and certain silences," just as in a "famous scene in Proust" when two characters "suddenly recognize their common corruption." Schlesinger made no direct comment on queer creativity. But he was writing at the time when attacks on leftists like Aaron Copland began and he implicated homosexuals in his portrayal of progressives as "soft, not hard," with a fatal "weakness for impotence," contributing to the nation's impotence. He made queers suspect on three counts—their "soft" leftism, cliquishness, and lack of mature manliness. Such deficiencies undermined a "vital," "hard"—Schlesinger liked phallic phrasing—political and cultural life. He lashed out at Soviet authorities who condemned Prokofiev, Shostakovich, and Stravinsky because, as Schlesinger quoted them, their music " 'extols the eroticism, psychopathic mentality, sexual perversion, amorality, and shamelessness of the bourgeois hero.' " But as he failed to note, agitation about "psychopathic mentality" and "sexual perversion" also informed attacks in the United States on artists.[34]

Like Schlesinger, politicians also melded cultural and political concerns. Senator Joe McCarthy lampooned Secretary of State Dean Acheson as the "Red Dean of Fashion," fusing communism, homosexuality, and privilege in one label for the patrician diplomat, with his "lace handkerchief," "silk glove," and "Harvard accent." Using "fashion," McCarthy linked Acheson to an industry queers presumably dominated and to affluent gay men's style. Perhaps McCarthy had in mind the much-rumored fate of the patrician Sumner Welles, the undersecretary of state whom Franklin Roosevelt fired after complaints that Welles brazenly approached men for sex. "If you want to be against McCarthy," the senator said, "you've got to be either a Communist or a cocksucker."[35]

Beyond McCarthy's casual swipes, ugly public episodes linked politics and queer creativity. In "the overheated atmosphere of the counter-subversion and counterperversion purges" of the early 1950s, charges were rife about the perversity of officials who had worked for FDR and Truman. Innuendo, score-settling, and turf battles occurred among FBI agents, squeals with a grudge, politicians, reporters, and psychiatrists consulted by various agencies. State Department staffers became suspect because someone had " 'just a funny feeling about him' " or because of " 'her mannish voice, her odd-shaped lips, and her friendship' with other women."[36]

Homosexuals did hold government positions, but what propelled the charges was not their intermittent accuracy. Charges of perversion served conservatives seeking to oust liberals and Democrats from power, and they tapped fears of sexual decadence stoked by J. Edgar Hoover's FBI, by the GOP's right wing, and by some liberals, often no more accepting of homosexuality. The Lavender Scare later faded from memory due to McCarthy's minor role in it, liberals' discomfort with their part in it, and historians' neglect of it.[37] But it rivaled the Red Scare in scale, and some GOP leaders preferred it because exposing perverts seemed easier and likelier to generate headlines than exposing communists. Liberals, too, deployed antihomosexuality, in self-defense as they saw it, charging that the antiperverts were perverted and promoting whispers about Roy Cohn, Senator McCarthy's sidekick, and the bachelor McCarthy. Columnist Drew Pearson asserted that McCarthy employed a "sexual pervert," eliciting a physical attack from the senator, and the *Las Vegas Sun* dubbed the Wisconsin senator, after a then-famous beer, "the queer that made Milwaukee famous." Such charges, especially against Cohn, figured in McCarthy's downfall during the 1954 Army-McCarthy hearings, when army lawyer Joseph Welch "lavender-baited the red hunters."[38]

In this swirling milieu came the charge that figures like diplomat Charles Thayer were "at the center of a cosmopolitan, international network of bohemian sexual and political misfits." That circle was said to include the oft-married Russian émigré composer Nicolas Nabokov, writer Vladimir's cousin. Nabokov and Thayer worked for a time at the federally funded Voice of America and allegedly roomed together, and Nabokov served in the cultural Cold War on both sides of the Atlantic, his CIA ties helping him survive his connection to Thayer. Their circle included " 'French artist[s] and musicians, among whom it was the practice for the men to sleep together,' " one report read. Such reports knit American and European decadence together, with both in turn linked to privilege: Thayer had gone to St. Paul's School and West Point, and he hobnobbed with East Coast patricians in key agencies. As countersubversives saw it, queer artists worked hand in hand (literally, it seemed) with political subversives while their decadent art undermined America's cultural offensive.[39]

These suspicions went public in 1953 after President Dwight Eisenhower, for once defying the McCarthyites, nominated Soviet expert Charles "Chip" Bohlen, Thayer's brother-in-law, to be ambassador to Moscow. Bohlen "symbolized everything the 'primitives' [McCarthyites] detested," argues Robert Dean. He was a member of the "imperial brotherhood," having been groomed at St. Paul's and Harvard, and he had a place at the 1945 Yalta Conference beside Alger Hiss, leading countersubversives to regard him an appeaser of communists. As Thayer's brother-in-law, he was tied to a circle of allegedly queer artists, aesthetes, and subversives. The "primitives" assailed Bohlen's nomination. Like most paranoia, theirs had some basis. Bohlen, Thayer, George Kennan, and others had served together in the 1930s at the American embassy in Moscow amid a " 'carnivalesque atmosphere' " of homoerotic camaraderie and affairs with Russian ballerinas. As Thayer wrote in 1940, suggesting his own queerness, it was hard to find "a gal in the Russian hordes. . . . It's almost enough to turn you pansy (there are plenty of partners in the diplomatic corps)."[40]

Despite his ladies' man reputation, Bohlen faced insinuations he was queer. He "walks, acts, and talks like a homosexual," claimed one Moscow veteran, and he "associated with sexual perverts," which was bad enough. Amid rumors in the press and the Senate, Eisenhower and Secretary of State John Foster Dulles nervously stood by Bohlen. They prevailed by sacrificing Thayer "to the congressional wolves"—forced to resign, he begged the State Department to publicize the "girl charge" against him, not the "charges of another and much less savory kind." They prevailed too because the "imperial brotherhood" included Dulles and his brother Allen, the CIA director, and Ike's party controlled the Senate, where right-wingers fought each other as well as Eisenhower. Still, there were blackmail attempts, ugly scenes in the Senate, where code words now competed with frank talk of "homosexuals," and stern White House orders to Bohlen to fly off to Moscow with his wife much in view. The stain on him of association with decadent artists and dangerous Soviets persisted. And the administration continued the pervert purge, avoided in Bohlen's case only because he seemed in the clear and the president's authority was at stake. Nor were victims free of prejudice: Thayer sneered at the Catholic agents of Irish and Eastern European origin who helped bring him down (it was galling, David Caute later wrote, that "Fordham men now decided whether Harvard men were fit to work").[41]

Queer scandal, or the threat of it, erupted repeatedly in the 1950s. Well-known in Washington as gay, prominent journalist Joseph Alsop survived a Soviet effort to blackmail him into spying for Russia—secret police photographed him in Moscow "during a sex act with a male Soviet agent provocateur." He was protected by his staunch Cold War politics, rich connections in Washington, and good sense to report the blackmail effort to friends in the CIA, where insiders fixed the matter, although the White House quietly used the incident against Alsop. Other patricians, Republicans and Democrats, faced swipes from the lavender brush— Henry Cabot Lodge Jr., for allegedly bedding a "former page boy in the United States Senate." Most alleged offenders were also aficionados of the arts. Elite connections and anticommunist politics helped many escape damage, but some endured more—the FBI's Hoover helped circulate rumors about Adlai "Adeline" Stevenson, the Democratic presidential nominee in 1952. Homosexuality was a volatile rather than absolute category—suspect less in itself than as tracer to a dense web of finely spun connections. Scandal was also grist for fiction's mills: elements of the Thayer/Bohlen story appeared in Allen Drury's novel *Advise and Consent* (1959), Gore Vidal's play *The Best Man* (1960), and the films (1962, 1964) based on those texts.[42]

In the Thayer/Bohlen affair, queer conspiracy, dishonesty, and superficiality resounded. Shallowness and artifice, regarded as hallmarks of queer cultural production, also were spotted in diplomats' effete ways, associations with artists, and naive embrace of communism. In both politics and the arts, lavender-hunters claimed, one could be tough, or queer, but not both (unless, as with Cohn and Hoover, one's queerness was hidden and politics were conservative). The purge of diplomatic perverts linked queer creativity to subversion and disloyalty, and to national fitness in looser ways. Political and religious leaders saw anticommunism as a moral as well as political crusade. Terms like "morals" and "morality"—or McCarthy's term, "immoralism"—had many meanings, from sexual virtue to the amorphous moral toughness needed to resist communism, from "morals" to "morale." To their foes, queers failed on all counts—inclined to favor an alien ideology, leak secrets, face blackmail, promote decadence, endanger family, and undermine religion. Contemporaries noticed how McCarthyites fused "the image of the homosexual with the image of the intellectual," to which should be added the artist. The political, cultural, and moral were entwined.[43]

The Thayer/Bohlen affair had the episodic quality—consuming one moment, gone the next—typical of American "moral panics," as all-Monica-all-the-time in Bill Clinton's presidency demonstrated. "Each new panic develops as if it were the first time such issues have been debated in public and yet the debates are strikingly similar," notes one scholar.[44] Because queerness involved especially weighty elements of furtiveness, shame, and revelation, the episodic pattern was more striking, as each eruption gave way to silence, followed by another, seemingly disconnected, sensation. That pattern also reflected how wariness about a queer presence jostled with dependence on it. Public silence after each tumult tacitly permitted dependence to continue. As in the cultural realm, a wary containment was more tenable than outright expulsion.

After the Thayer/Bohlen affair came another, more localized, fracas that began in 1954 when the *Philadelphia Inquirer* asked readers to suggest names for a new bridge across the Delaware River.[45] One option was poet Walt Whitman, who had resided across the river in New Jersey later in his life. His presumed "homosexuality" or "homoeroticism" spurred debate, as it did in literary circles throughout the century. Opposition to Whitman's name arose especially from Catholic clergy and laypeople, who saw both his poetry and his sexuality as dangerous. According to the Reverend James Ryan, Whitman's poetry was "delicate" but steeped in "pathos" and his "ideas were destructive of usual ethical codes" and marked by "destructive egotism," a failure to achieve "maturity of thought," and the embrace of "sub-animal conduct." Ryan, notes the episode's historian, listed failures by Whitman—"anal eroticism ('baser, irreverent passages'), narcissism, and immaturity," and emotionality and fragility—similar to those often attributed to gay men. Added to that list was superficiality, for Whitman "possesses the depth of a saucer." His "revolting homosexual imagery," Ryan wrote, "permeates the fetid whole."

Some proponents of Whitman distrusted the church's power ("we don't need advice from Rome or Moscow") and condemned it for hiding its own dirty secrets—"homosexuality amongst the celibate clergy, and lesbianism in the nunneries"—by attacking Whitman. Most, however, stressed Whitman's creativity and sidestepped his sexuality. They won in the end, Marc Stein concludes, by sounding more "negative about same-sex sexualities" than Whitman's "detractors" and by steering those "sexualities" away from Whitman and to the church, as when one suggested that "Father-of-What?? get married to some nice girl instead of acting like an old lady."

Given how claims about Whitman's sexuality collided with charges of Catholic homoeroticism, debate got complicated, but at its core it posed stark alternatives: if Whitman was creative he could not have been queer, and if queer he could not have been creative. To defend Whitman meant denying his apparent sexuality; to attack that sexuality meant denying his creativity. In a tenuous middle ground, some saw his sexuality as irrelevant or pointed to Benjamin Franklin — no paragon of sexual virtue — whose name was also proposed. As the conservative intellectual Clinton Rossiter argued, "Whitman may have been a queer bird in many ways, but what does that have to do with the fact that he is America's greatest poet." *One*, a gay magazine out of earshot of most in the debate, suggested a positive linkage: His "greatness was not in spite of, but specifically because of the nature of his love for man." A few went further, finding queers in a long history of creativity — in the church no less. If Whitman's foes prevail because he was "abnormal sexually," wrote one Whitman proponent, "their next job is to remove Michelangelo's statue from the Vatican, tear down St. Peter's Basilica and throw out all copies of Leonardo's Last Supper." Meanwhile, *One* published a lengthy "Study of Walt Whitman."[46] Homosexuals, Stein suggests, could be proud that Whitman's name prevailed even if victory owed partly to "strategies that encouraged hostility toward same-sex sexualities."

In other episodes, queerness figured less overtly. Aaron Copland was suspect for his leftist, anti–Cold War politics, especially after he attended the 1949 World Peace Conference. Apparently in reaction, Republican Party leaders cancelled a scheduled performance of his *Lincoln Portrait* (1943) at the 1953 inaugural concert for President Eisenhower, despite Copland's stature as musical nationalist. Party leaders ignored Copland's sexuality, or so most contemporaries and historians have maintained. But Copland had already suffered an attack "drenched in anti-Semitic and homophobic innuendos" in a 1949 radio broadcast: Arnold Schoenberg, the great atonal composer now residing in America, "had named Stalin and Copland in the same breath, as would-be agents of artistic degeneration" — a category easily implying queerness — "and restriction on artistic freedom, including particularly Schoenberg's own." And Congressman Fred E. Busbey, who instigated dumping *Lincoln Portrait*, suggested that Copland's "questionable affiliations" would cause offense "at the inaugural of a President elected to fight communism, among other things." "Among other things" was an elastic phrase, and possibly a gesture to the open secret of Copland's sexuality.[47]

In response, Copland and his defenders steered clear of sexuality, appealing to national pride and security: as the League of Composers pro-claimed, he had advanced "the reputation of American culture through-out the civilized world" and the GOP's action "will hold us up as a nation to universal ridicule." Critic Paul Hume hinted at GOP anti-Semitism after Busbey suggested putting Copland's music off-limits for armed forces en-sembles, like Jewish music had been in Nazi Germany. Bruce Catton, his-torian and political columnist, teased the GOP for its relief at avoiding the "brooding" words of Lincoln used by Copland—for a party abandoning its black constituency and courting the white South, race was probably another reason to scrub *Lincoln Portrait*. More than "communism" both-ered Copland's foes, but they let code words do the work on the other fronts of sexuality and race.

Behind the scenes, more went on. Queer composers like David Dia-mond were grilled about their sexuality and their politics and pressured to reveal or spy on others, and some endured blacklisting. An unsigned letter to Scott McLeod, McCarthy's hatchet man in the State Department as head of its Bureau of Security and Consular Affairs, warned against men "who have gotten married since 1950 when McCarthy began his reign of terror" and against "deviates who are hiding behind marriage.... And how is it you allow one of the biggest homosexuals in New York to repre-sent the US in the music section of UNESCO? Samuel Barber." The Bureau followed up, with unclear results. There were likely more complaints like this one, located in a closed file that archivists inadvertently showed to a researcher. Its dispatch in April 1953 suggests that the inaugural flap and the accession of a GOP administration aggravated complaints that went well beyond artists' leftist politics.[48]

Copland's rough times continued. Watched by the FBI, he was hauled before McCarthy's subcommittee in a closed session on May 26, 1953. In a familiar routine based on what investigators handed them, senators questioned him in harsh but formulaic fashion about his alleged past ties to communist-front groups, insinuating that they tainted his work as a State Department–sponsored lecturer. When Copland pointed out that he had only been connected to one group before the attorney gen-eral cited it as subversive, McCarthy responded that "the date of the cita-tion . . . is no more important than the date a man was convicted of rob-bing a bank. The question" was whether "you participated in robbing the bank." McCarthy threatened perjury charges, since "you have what appears to be one of the longest Communist-front records of any one we have had here." For his part, Copland often pled naïveté or forgetfulness. "I spend my days writing symphonies, concertos, ballads, and I am not a political thinker," he maintained. "My impression was that my political opinions, no matter how vague they may have been, were not in question as far as the Department of State was concerned." His testimony was perhaps less heroic than lore has it. He never emphatically stated the belief that he committed to his diary—that "my conscience was clear—in a free America I had a right to affiliate openly with whom I pleased, . . . and no one had the right to question those affiliations." He did deny that he had been a communist.

The subcommittee made no allusions to Copland's sexuality, a dog-that-didn't-bark problem confounding to historians. The senators likely knew of Copland's sexuality or could have readily found out, given the FBI's open door to the committee, and they would hardly have assumed that queerness among artists was so taken for granted that publicizing it would have caused no stir. Instead, calculations of risk and reward, of the sort politicians usually make, likely held them back. Perhaps committee members believed that drawing attention to Copland's sexuality would have no effect in a secret hearing, but they readily leaked damaging information to the press when they wanted to. Perhaps they thought that publicity about Copland's sexuality would have little benefit, but politicians had already reasoned otherwise by assailing perverts in government. Perhaps they regarded naming names as beyond the pale— something so scurrilous or tasteless that it might give offense—but given the rumors circulated in the Thayer/Bohlen affair, that too seems unlikely. More likely, McCarthyites calculated not that the rewards were few but that the risks were high, especially by 1953. In charging people with communist proclivities, conservatives had no fear of a boomerang, for they had no leftist background to haunt them. But queerness was a less tangible—provable or disprovable—trait, and for bachelors Hoover, McCarthy, and subcommittee chief counsel Cohn, the backlash was already coming by 1953. Flagging Copland's queerness was risky, a task best left to others like Busbey who made the accusation vague enough that it did not have to be proved or traced to McCarthy and his allies.

Oddly, it was Copland who stumbled close to the subject. Pressed about his connection to "various organizations," he insisted that it "was the direct outcome of the feelings of a musician. . . . Musicians make music out of feelings aroused out of public events" and "out of emotions and you can't make your music unless you are moved by events." Senator Karl Mundt objected to Copland's murky attempt to move from politics to "emotions" and place composing in some ethereal realm. "Emotions are part of everyone's personality. . . . I think musicians have to go by the same code as governs other citizens." Copland's appeal was risky—emotionality was often attributed to gay artists like Tchaikovsky. But the committee, baffled by Copland's appeal or tiring of a witness too evasive to gain it headlines, ended proceedings and never called Copland for public testimony.[49]

Copland faced trouble after the inaugural flap and after his testimony (the facts of it, not the specifics, were well publicized). The State Department barred his music from American information libraries abroad, passport problems curtailed his promotion of American music, and some of his stateside appearances were cancelled. But as the McCarthy moment receded in the late 1950s and Eisenhower got nervous about others seeing America shackle its artists, Copland's troubles receded. He was too important to be expelled for long from the cultural crusade. By the early 1960s he was conducting on the White House lawn and in 1964 he received the presidential Medal of Freedom. Cultural preening about Copland replaced cultural vigilance against him.

Meanwhile, in several essays, Schlesinger revisited issues of homosexuality and national power. He dubbed Whittaker Chambers's *Witness* (1952), the ex-communist's account of subversion and his testimony against Alger Hiss, "one of the really significant American autobiographies," and labeled the "whispering campaign" about Chambers's homosexuality "one of the most repellent of modern history." He also took it unkindly that charges of effete softness, which he had earlier made against leftist progressives, were turned back on his own kind. Foes of presidential candidate Adlai Stevenson had tagged him an "egghead"—someone, Schlesinger explained, "feminine" and "supercilious" and "a self-conscious prig," who would usher in "Communism, crookedness and psychopathic instability." Such words insinuated queerness, but Schlesinger cordoned off that insinuation: Adlai's foes simply expressed "hatred of the intellectuals"—after all, "anti-intellectualism has long been the anti-Semitism of the businessman." Schlesinger protected intellectuals from the taint of homosexuality (only their "intellectualism" was under attack), linked "anti-intellectualism" to anti-Semitism, and occluded homophobia, leaving it legitimate, unlike hostility to intellectuals and Jews.[50]

Schlesinger also took on queerness in the arts, reviewing Englishman John Osborne's controversial play *Look Back in Anger* (1956). Schlesinger saw its central character as a woman-hating homosexual who showed "repulsive tenderness" to a man described oddly in the play as "a sort of female Emily Bronte." He found the play troubling for its homoeroticism and its hold on audiences. "Its contrived mixture of hysteria, sadism, and self-pity fascinates audiences already fascinated before they enter the theater by the homosexual anxiety, that increasingly prevalent obsession of our theater, if not our age." It was a murky passage: What was this "homosexual anxiety," and who felt it—and about what? It was likely Schlesinger's anxiety, about homosexuality (clearly the audience's "anxiety" did not keep it away). Perhaps he took comfort that Osborne soon denounced queers for producing "bad, narcissistic art," as his views have been summarized, and seemed in the vanguard of virile writers reclaiming the British stage.[51]

"What has unmanned the American man?" Schlesinger asked in 1958, postulating a timeless past when the American man "seemed utterly confident in his manhood" and "sense of sexual identity." Now, "men design dresses and brew up cosmetics." Perhaps "what has unmanned the American man is the American woman," but if so it means "that the American man was incapable of growing up." "Masculine supremacy," after all, "like white supremacy, was the neurosis of an immature society." Instead, what unmanned men was the void they lived in—"the great vacant spaces of equalitarian society," the "centralization" and uniformity of corporate capitalism, and "the prefabricated emotional cliches" of mass culture. No wonder people "are no longer sure what sex they are." Schlesinger identified causes of devalued masculinity so vast that they defied solutions, although he proposed more highbrow culture and "a virile political life." Key to his reasoning was his equating of a "crisis in masculinity" and a loss of sexual identity—people not "sure what sex they are." That equation suggests that he viewed homosexuality as gender inversion and regarded it as one cause, or at least one sign, of the "crisis." "Lurking beneath the crisis in masculinity," one scholar comments regarding Schlesinger, "was often the specter of an expansionist homosexuality," including its expansion into culture. Schlesinger bewailed that expansion— cultural work by or about gay men traded in sensation (*Look Back*) and superficiality (designing dresses). So did others: for critic Hilton Kramer, artists Jasper Johns and Robert Rauschenberg offered "the window decorator's aesthetic."[52]

Critic Edmund Wilson was less exercised about these matters, but not mute. He ruminated about "the strong pressure" that young composers faced "to become twelve-toners," who had become a "cult." "A friend" (perhaps Wilson's euphemism for himself) had told him that this "pressure" was "almost like the pressure of a homosexual group—though he didn't mean to imply that there was any connection between homosexuality and serial music. Except, of course, that they're both *culs de sac.*" Indeed, there was little connection; most "twelve-toners" were straight and most composers of tonal music were gay. The comparison of a specific compositional style to the entire phenomenon of homosexuality was oddly gratuitous. To see both as "*culs de sac*" reinforced an image of gay artists as cliquish (another "pressure" group), aesthetically blocked, and emotionally sterile. Wilson's comparison also vaguely backed his claim that "Anglo-Saxons are no longer a musical people" like Germans, Italians, Russians, Negroes, and Jews. Wilson knew gay artists and praised composers Benjamin Britten and Aaron Copland. Hounded by the law about his own obscenity and tax problems, he supported gay scholar Newton Arvin after his arrest in 1960 on sex and obscenity charges. But those actions coexisted with his casual assumption that homosexuals were locked in a "*cul de sac,*" aligning him, more than perhaps he realized, with the deniers of queer creativity.[53]

Gay artists took flack not only from Cold Warriors but also from critics of Cold War culture. Leslie Fiedler regretted that "The Un-Angry Young Men" (as his 1958 piece was entitled) in American letters, arriving after World War II and amid prosperity, had no voice, only anger borrowed from an older generation, a weakness nourished by American largesse. "Scholarships and fellowships abound," failure "becomes increasingly difficult," and if a young writer "is momentarily in Paris (or Athens or Rome), he is there to give a series of lectures under the auspices of the State Department." Fiedler lamented how the Left's weakness enabled queer writers (he identified Truman Capote, Carson McCullers, and James Baldwin) to become "the staunchest party of all," "the last possible protest against bourgeois security," and the exponents of "a politics to be flaunted." Fiedler had uncovered a tradition of homoerotic American fiction in his 1948 essay "Come Back to the Raft Ag'in, Huck Honey!" but he had dismissed Gore Vidal's *The City and the Pillar* and its "incipient homosexual" author. Queer themes were one thing, queer writers another—their challenge was superficial and misdirected. Fiedler felt that "they come so fast, the new homosexuals, queen treading on queen," and they get swept into "a world of chic" and become "eager to read the latest effete exploitation of . . . the Faulknerian themes of dissolution and infertility." Still, he offered grudging admiration, for perhaps "homosexuality is the purest and truest protest of the latest generation," even if it yielded bad writing. And he gave an explanation for creative queers: they occupied territory that real men were vacating, just as critics feared that real men were vacating American life generally.[54]

Max Lerner, a prominent journalist and intellectual, had a different outlook. He criticized Washington's purge of the perverts, approved Tennessee Williams's work, and became "a close friend" of Edward Albee. He touched on homosexuality in his massive study, *America as a Civilization* (1957), placing gay people among those "on the margin of the culture." Most Americans ask only that homosexuals "pursue their eccentricities privately. They provide them with a reluctant neglect" while retaining an "obvious and continuous disapproval" of them. The phrase "reluctant neglect" captured conflicting desires among some liberals—"to cut down to a minimum the growth of homosexuality and the harshness of social attitudes toward it." Lerner also spotted similarities between America and imperial Rome—"the succession of ever bigger wars, enriching the nation yet draining its resources," the rise of a spectatorial and "depersonalizing" culture, and "the exploration of deviant and inverted forms of behavior." But he was not perturbed by those "forms" or their effect on America's cultural power: he was skeptical anyway that "movies or jazz or literature" could be a " 'weapon' in the international struggle." Lerner was distinctive for his cautious tone, skepticism about the Cold War, and avoidance of pathologizing language for homosexuality.[55]

Among varied women's voices on these matters, the most famous, Betty Friedan's in *The Feminine Mystique* (1963), resembled that of most men. If she sensed that women and homosexuals—she hardly recognized that women could be queer—faced similar stigmas, she responded by jettisoning the queer baggage burdening her feminist agenda. Smothering mothers, Friedan argued, produced sissy sons who undercut national strength—behavior by American POWs in the Korean War indicated a troubling " 'new softness' " and homosexuality was "spreading like a murky smog over the American scene." But she shifted blame from mothers to a "feminine mystique" that "glorified and perpetuated in the name of femininity a passive, childlike immaturity which is passed on from mothers to sons, as well as to daughters." That allowed her a pitying sympathy for "sad 'gay' homosexuals," who "may feel an affinity with the young housewife sex-seekers." On a resort island, Friedan found the "sex-seekers" drawn to "a colony of 'boys' right out of the world of Tennessee Williams." "Perhaps, these housewives and their boyfriends recognized themselves in each other. For like the call girl in Truman Capote's *Breakfast at Tiffany's* who spends the sexless night with the passive homosexual, they were equally childlike in their retreat from life." Sex-starved housewives and sad homosexuals also shared an "implacable hatred for the parasitic women who keep their husbands and sons from growing up."

That hatred left "male homosexuals" doomed to be "Peter Pans, forever childlike, afraid of age, grasping at youth in their continual search for reassurance in some sexual magic."

Eager to release women's creativity from captivity, Friedan assumed queers had little to be released. She judged Williams's *Suddenly, Last Summer* "a flagrant example" of "the retreat of American playwrights and novelists from the problems of the world to an obsession with the images of the predatory female." It was a curious complaint, since Friedan deplored "parasitic women" no less than *Suddenly* did. But Friedan dismissed "all" of Williams's plays as "an agonized shout of obsessed love-hate against women." Giving queers brief, smirking treatment, she saw them as products of pathology — superficial, immature haters of women differing little from the creatures Bergler imagined.[56]

Many intellectuals understood gay people much as analysts, journalists, and political demagogues did. Those who doubted that homosexuality directly threatened national security still usually saw it as a form of failed heterosexuality whose sterile creations weakened the nation; genuine creativity occurred only despite queers' sexuality. Although Newton Arvin received, his biographer writes, "the unanimous support of the elders of the literary left" after his arrest, they defended his professional stature and personal integrity, not his sexuality, rendered a thing apart from his creativity. Some themselves queer, intellectuals did often praise the work of queer artists, but mostly when it seemed distant from their queerness. Since much commentary dealt with the queer artist as generic category, it was possible to praise individuals while deploring the type. Donald Webster Cory asserted that "deepgoing sympathy" for homosexuals existed "in intellectual and artistic circles," but if so, it was mainly private. "The hostile majority," Cory admitted, "tends to disparage the achievements of homosexuals, finding them sick, perverted, immoral, neurotic, degenerate, and disgusting." "Intellectual and artistic circles" differed less from "the hostile majority" than Cory claimed.[57]

Social Outsiders

Anthropologists and sociologists also regarded homosexuals as outsiders, but the outsiderness they imagined was more benign. Relativism went with their territory, since their job was to compare social groups. Their leaders were also less concerned about the Cold War, cultural or otherwise, and were often female, with Ruth Benedict (who died in 1948) and Margaret Mead, themselves deeply attracted to women, still influential. Like them, many social scientists saw queerness—often subsumed under categories like "sex roles" and "deviants"—as harmless or at least understandable. But they also linked it to the exotic, giving it a whiff of something odd in an American context.

Mead asserted that sex roles were hardly uniform. Concepts of masculinity and femininity varied among cultures, making silly "the habits of lumping all males together and all females together and worrying about the beards of the one and the breasts of the other," as she put it. In turn, "deviants" in modern societies were often products of "the contradictory influences of a heterogeneous cultural situation"—those who failed to adapt to rigid sex roles. Though "culturally disenfranchised," they might make valuable creative contributions. Mead and Benedict moved homosexuality from individual to social pathology, and others attributed it to numerous modern ills, as John D'Emilio has noted them: "depression and war, the generalized anxiety of the nuclear age, intense competitive demands placed on males, pressure to conform, the rapid pace of technological change, shifting roles and increased expectations of American women." Yet the lengthier that list the less it explained, since everyone endured the burdens listed. The turn to social pathology still marked queers as damaged, if through no fault of their own. Like Lindner, Mead suggested that if that pathology were curbed, homosexuality might diminish. Many in her field regarded queer sexuality as authentic in primitive contexts, where it arose out of natural patterns of adaptation, but unsettling in modern settings, whose pathologies it reflected. Their achievement was to see queerness in the full range of human experience, but its uneasy implication was that homosexuality belonged in exotic cultures, not "advanced" societies.[58]

Sociologists of deviance—Erving Goffman, Howard Becker, Edward Schur, and others—insisted that deviance meant difference, not dysfunction. By noting similarities between homosexuals and jazz musicians, they linked queer deviance to creativity, attained by outsiders looking in on their culture. But seeing homosexuality as deviance also linked it to groups that many Americans regarded as exotic or downright dangerous —Schur compared "drug users, women who sought abortions, and male homosexuals." In a more benign comparison, Martin Hoffman urged a "solution to the problem of homosexuality . . . modeled on the solution to the problem of religious difference," while Becker championed lesbian and gay rights by the mid-1960s. But deviance retained an aura of weirdness or criminality rather than simple difference. Putting queers with deviants gave them company, but of mixed repute.[59]

Social scientists' diffuse ideas were vaguely echoed in postwar culture. Americans' fascination with the exotic was intensified by the spread of American power in World War II and the Cold War. Millions of men and women, in and out of uniform, went abroad. Millions more at home wondered what they were encountering and how they were changing. Postwar culture was awash in tales of Americans in war-torn Europe, Asia, and the Pacific who often resorted to gender-bending, as Cary Grant did in *I Was a Male War Bride* (1949). It also drew on the tradition outlined in Fiedler's 1948 "Huck Honey" essay of imagining homoerotic (often interracial) bonds and gender-bending behavior at or beyond the periphery of American life, where characters penned by James Fenimore Cooper and Mark Twain, or Tonto and the Lone Ranger and Batman and Robin in the 1950s, found inspiration.

In unusual locales, Americans were more freely imagined as queer and creative. Congresswoman Frost (Jean Arthur) in Billy Wilder's *A Foreign Affair* (1948), mannishly dressed and frosty indeed toward men, carries her political talents into the rubble of postwar Berlin. Sebastian seeks his muse in the Mediterranean in *Suddenly, Last Summer*. And David in Baldwin's novel *Giovanni's Room* (1956) pursues creativity and finds queer sex in France. Suspect at home, intense bonds between girl-less men and motherless boys also flourished abroad cinematically. In *The Search* (Fred Zinnemann, 1948), set in postwar Germany's wreckage, Steve (Montgomery Clift), an American officer without apparent interest in women, rescues a shattered Czech refugee from Auschwitz, and he and his housemate (Wendell Corey) gaze on the child like proud parents. Steve dresses him, has his hands all over him, moves into an attic with him, teaches him to speak again, plans to adopt him and take him to the states — mothers him — until chance brings him to his real mother. In *The Geisha Boy* (Frank Tashlin, 1958), set in the "exotic beauty of colorful Japan!" as posters blared, Jerry Lewis plays "The Great Wooley," a magician who tries to revive his career by entertaining American troops and adopts an orphaned Japanese boy. Tashlin, a veteran director of gender-bending films, and Lewis, the film's producer and later the star of Tashlin's *Cinderfella* (1960), meant "geisha boy" to refer not to the orphan but to Lewis. As Paramount instructed theater managers, "It's pronounced GAY-SHA with the accent on GAY . . . THE JERRY LEWIS WAY!" Lewis's film shtick was a boyish cluelessness, especially about women, in an era when immaturity was tied to homosexuality, while his live act — "smutty material with an emphasis on homosexuality" — left critics appalled about its "pansy theme." In *Geisha Boy*, his emotions run to the orphan, not to the women who court him. In Japan, he finds himself and revives his magician's creativity.[60]

In the end, most celluloid queers in foreign locales find either homosexual damnation or heterosexual redemption. Many return to "normal" sex roles, America, and less creative pursuits. Congresswoman Frost falls in love with an American officer, trades her mannish clothes for frilly frocks, loses interest in politics, and returns to Iowa. "The Great Wooley" finds love, at least a mother for his orphan. Queer creativeness is a transitory product of exotic or ravaged places. As Vito Russo noted of American film at this time, "Homosexuality was still something you did in the dark or in Europe—preferably both."[61] Asia would do as well.

The association of queer creativity with foreign locales operated in the lives of many gay figures, not just in the cinematic imagination of them. For decades, writers, composers, and other artists had found mentors, inspiration, refuge, or money abroad, with the Red and Lavender scares adding more incentives in the postwar years. Among them were Baldwin in France, Barber and Menotti in the latter's Italian homeland, and Audre Lorde in Mexico (where "I stopped feeling invisible").[62] Time abroad was a familiar pattern for American artists, queer and nonqueer alike. But it reinforced the impression films cultivated that queer creativity was "something you did in the dark or in Europe," the product of exile and exoticism—not authentically American.

Although some observers located queer creativity abroad, others placed it in urban geography at home, and usually in urban pathology. With gay men linked to urban arts—entertainment, theater, fashion, interior design—civic authorities had long connected them to the city, including its tawdry realms of prostitution, alcohol, and other vices. "The discourse of urban degeneracy," as George Chauncey calls it, was well developed in New York by World War I, justifying "surveillance" of public spaces where homosexuals were conspicuous. Postwar scandal merchants renewed the agitation. Others more calmly observed a "distinct tendency for homosexuals to gravitate to certain places and fields of interest," especially the arts. "To remain in one's own small town might lead to exposure and ridicule; therefore, many leave for the metropolis and its accompanying cloak of anonymity." That aspiring gays might head for the "metropolis" for reasons beyond a cringing fear of "ridicule" went unremarked.[63]

The *New York Times* placed queer life in the pathology of the city and the social type. As a front-page headline from 1963 claimed, "Growth of Overt Homosexuality in City Provokes Wide Concern"—at least among overt heterosexuals ("psychiatrists, religious leaders and the police"— and editor A. M. Rosenthal). The *Times* dwelled on street and bar life and the sexual underworld, and it drew on doctors who "exploded" the idea that homosexuality is "incurable." "Sexual inverts have colonized three areas of the city," it reported, especially "the creative and performing arts and industries serving women's beauty and fashion needs." But the *Times* disputed "the old myth fostered by homosexuals" that they "tend to have superior intellect and talent." Instead, not finding acceptance "in more prosaic" fields, they "naturally gravitate" to the arts, where "introspective behavior" flourishes. This was silly—introspection was no hallmark of the fashion and beauty trades—but the effort to find hidden power prevailed. Queers' presence in theater is "self-perpetuating" because they hire their own whenever possible, noted the family-controlled paper.[64]

In contrast, Englishman Bryan Magee simply noted "a marginal tendency for homosexuals to drift into those occupations which are more tolerant of homosexuality." Apparently referring to John Gielgud, he noted that "an actor can be known by everyone to be a homosexual—he may even, like one of our greatest actors, have been convicted in a court of law for a homosexual offence—and this does not appear to damage his career or his reputation with his colleagues." All this bothered Magee little. Despite his complaint that "queers . . . think everybody's queer," his own List ranged from Socrates, Plato, and "the Old Testament story of David and Jonathan," through Tchaikovsky, Wilde, "and many more."[65]

If cities like New York were "tolerant"—an oft-used word—then other places presumably were not, but that was not quite the case. "Texas has symphony orchestras as well as Stetsons," one intellectual felt compelled to remind his peers.[66] Frank Hains, arts editor of Mississippi's *Jackson Daily News*, offered explicit and sympathetic "de-Coding" of code-era gay-themed films, and his writing style and persona hardly disguised his queerness.[67] If the ambitious often left them, smaller cities still had cultural ambitions buoyed by postwar affluence, local boosterism, and growing colleges. When I grew up in Muncie, Indiana, in the 1950s, Ball State Teachers College boasted new faculty in the arts, including a lesbian prominent in the art department. The social circles of my parents, musicians in the local symphony, included queer figures, and the "open secret" operated. Local papers were oblivious to anything queer, despite scandal: in 1962, the Indiana State Police probed charges that older members of the city's storied high school basketball team "forced" younger ones "to remove their trousers for indecent acts of degeneracy."[68] But through magazines and movies, metropolitan discourse reached the city.

Meanwhile, major artists and groups still barnstormed provincial places like Muncie (big names had not yet priced themselves out of such markets): Lawrence Tibbett and Sergey Rachmaninoff before World War II, for example, and Isaac Stern, Aaron Copland, and Igor Stravinsky after it. Little in this setting occurred to me as explicitly gay, or perhaps I just did not register it, but it was there.[69]

Edmund Bergler, *Confidential*, Arthur Schlesinger, and *Partisan Review* knew little of such places, which did not fit their template of urban decadence, alien ideology, and queer conspiracy. Not that small-city America was more queer-friendly: witch hunts erupted on occasion, notoriously in Boise, Idaho. But neither was it more provincial by some wide margin. Moreover, the idea—then commonplace, now quaint—of music as a "universal language" (inscribed at the entry to Muncie's concert hall) discouraged suspicion of the identities (queer, Jewish, "foreign") of local figures and visiting dignitaries. The stakes in the arts were also different: in Peoria or Fresno, it sufficed for the orchestra to tackle an unfamiliar score or accompany a visiting star; the fate of American culture was remote. In New York, that fate seemed to tremble in the balance, fueling scrutiny of the queer role in it. Anxieties that stirred the big city echoed only faintly beyond it.

Reflecting and shaping the big-city view of the big city, Hollywood also offered versions of queer urban pathology. *Rope* (Alfred Hitchcock, 1948), loosely based on the Leopold and Loeb murder case of the 1920s, with a screenplay by gay writer Arthur Laurents, gave urban pathology an urbane twist. The educated, dandified killers share pretensions to creativity (one is a pianist) and a tasteful upscale apartment, a Manhattan skyline prominent in the background. *Rope* stamped its queer characters as fraudulent aesthetes, able to concoct an artful murder and talk smartly about the arts but oblivious to the truths the arts offer.

All about Eve (Joseph L. Mankiewicz, 1950) offered another version of queer urban pathology. Addison DeWitt (George Sanders) is a venomous theater critic interested in aspiring actress Eve Harrington (Anne Baxter) only for purposes of controlling her, his sexual interest in women at best warped. Eve, often read as a proto-lesbian, courts and uses men, but it is women who fascinate her—above all, veteran actress Margot Channing (Bette Davis), who nurtures Eve only to be betrayed by her. Eve captures the surface of her stage and real-life roles, whereas Margot earthily grasps the substance of both—she accepts getting too old for some roles and settles into marriage with her playwright husband. DeWitt and Eve are predators of the theater, but the healthy heterosexuals finally elude their clutches. Gay viewers understandably have been more drawn to Davis's bitchy humor and outsize performance as Margot the "all-wise queen."[70]

Where *Eve* featured the arts' creative center, *Sweet Smell of Success* (Alexander Mackendrick, 1957) dwelled at its tawdry fringes. J. J. Hunsecker (Burt Lancaster) is a powerful, predatory critic, gossip columnist, and television personality who trades in rumors about celebrities and parades fake patriotism, anticommunism, and concern for the people. Sleazy public relations flack Sidney Falco (Tony Curtis) feeds Hunsecker gossip, curries his favor, and does his dirty work, especially when J. J. gets enraged at a romance between his kid sister Susie (Susan Harrison) and jazz musician Steve Dallas (Martin Milner). *Sweet Smell* was a sharp film about the arts, entertainment, and scandal, with a script by Clifford Odets and Ernest Lehman, an edgy sounds-of-the-city score by Elmer Bernstein, and fine work by Lancaster (also a coproducer) and Curtis. It was the urban jungle to the third power: a gritty film about gritty urban journalism covering the gritty city.

Sweet Smell's makers and actors apparently never saw its main characters as gay, and commentary then and later regarded Hunsecker as based on Walter Winchell, the preeminent, and increasingly right-wing, gossip columnist and womanizer. Yet J. J. never womanizes as Winchell did, and in both the film and its making, men were bent on proving their sexual power to each other more than to women. Lehman recalled that when he met Lancaster, the actor walked in "zipping up his fly and smiling proudly, saying, 'She swallowed it.' " The studio "was rife with womanizing," Lehman remembered, but men were its audience. Odets, Curtis recalls, "used to call me 'boychick,' right from the start."[71]

Falco and Hunsecker are perverse, spitting out one bitchy quip after another. They have no interest in women except to manipulate and control them, while fearing dependence on them. As J. J. tells his sister, "Don't ever tell anyone, Susie, how I'm tied to your apron strings"—a twist on the familiar line about sissy boys and their mothers. If, as critics suggested, J. J. has incestuous designs on his sister, those hardly mark him heterosexual or preclude his being queer. Falco and Hunsecker are drawn to each other, Sidney pretending to address J. J. as "sweetheart." Trying to resist J. J.'s bullying, Falco shoots back, you don't have "the cards to blitz me. . . . Almost a year ago I did you a certain favor. It was a thing—well, I never did such a dirty thing in my life." Perhaps the "dirty thing" involved violence or sex with women, but a "dirty thing" in postwar film could usually be named or inferred unless it involved queer sex, which became identifiable precisely as the one "dirty thing" that could not be named. J. J. and Sidney are sick predators on women and the arts—J. J. can't even spell Picasso—scheming in a cesspool of blackmail, police corruption, political fraud, and violence. Girl-lessness—queerness—is key to their sickness.

In contrast, musician Steve Dallas embodies wholesome, creative manliness—not for nothing is he named Dallas. He is the only character called an "artist," and a genuine one at that: rejecting mass culture, he is into progressive jazz. J. J. and Falco smear Steve as a marijuana-smoking pinko and have the cops beat him up because J. J. can't stand his authentic love for Susie and his authentic creativity. As the film ends, Susie attempts suicide but then breaks from J. J., who is left alone, as cinematic queers often were. As she returns to Steve, the music shifts to uplifting Coplandiana, further signaling that a heterosexual paradigm in life and art has been reestablished and that queers' insidious influence in both realms has been purged. *Sweet Smell*'s queer undercurrents—too buried to challenge, too powerful not to register at all—were perhaps one reason the film bombed at the box office, but they document the era's antiqueer impulses.

However menacing their queer figures, films, novels, and news accounts that placed them in urban pathology loosely reflected some realities. The institutional nature of the arts and entertainment rendered solitary creativity less viable in the twentieth century and favored urban locales. Gay artists, like others, often settled in cities, where a wealth of jobs emerged, from copy editor to writer, from stagehand to playwright, from carpenter to composer. Communities of identity had advantages in these settings, as Jews and African Americans also found out, allowing members to trade information, carve out paths others would follow, and sustain identities in the face of pressures to assimilate or hide.

Moreover, most gay men faced fewer demands of family, at least offspring. Arthur Laurents, indignant when producer David Merrick publicly complained that "homosexuals are taking over the theatre," secured an explanation from Merrick: "It's only for publicity. I wouldn't have anyone on my staff who wasn't homosexual. They have no one to go home to so they work late and don't complain." Laurents may have been imprecise in his memory or Merrick disingenuous in his explanation, by whose logic gay men with "no one to go home to" would have seized every job in capitalist America. But others offered similar explanations: gay activist Hal Call told a San Francisco radio panel that "homosexuals are no more gifted or talented than any other group, but perhaps the homosexual has more opportunity . . . since he doesn't have the economic pressure of providing for a wife and family."[72] Whatever the truth of such claims, their circulation invited gay men to look to the arts. They had advantages, real and perceived, though hardly ones produced by conspiracy.

Some observers described both the city and its queer presence in neutral rather than pathological terms. Gay people simply found shelter and opportunity at Times Square or Carnegie Hall, where prostitutes and playwrights had a live-and-let-live attitude. That outlook informed William J. Helmer's take on "New York's 'Middle-Class' Homosexuals" —a "barely known community"—in *Harper's*. Helmer found that many gay men (as usual, lesbians were barely mentioned) take "refuge in a separate homosexual community which possesses its own customs, social structure, ethics, argot, organizations, and even business establishments." Implicitly rebuking experts like Bergler, he cited Freud's "Letter to an American Mother" and noted Evelyn Hooker's challenge to "the theory that homosexuality and pathology are inherently related."

But Helmer did not stray far from prevailing views. Gay "folklore" presented homosexuals as "specially gifted in the creative arts," but Helmer found little evidence for that view, although social hostility "may well increase one's sensitivity and perception." "Quite naturally, however, homosexuals tend to be attracted to creative fields, which are traditionally tolerant"—what was "natural" and "traditional" went unexamined except that "a young single man . . . can better afford the risks and financial insecurity of an artistic career." Gay men especially enter "gay trades" like "clothes designing, window dressing, decorating, modeling, and hairdressing." But "homosexuals of the gay community are not notably successful people," whereas the lives of "gifted" queers "will seldom center in gay society." Helmer correlated creative success with detachment from the "gay community" and failure with immersion in it, where "conformity, phoniness, and lack of individuality" prevailed and not "much depth of personality" was found. He pointed to the stunted, superficial qualities among queers that others also claimed to find.[73]

Not only did queers gravitate *to* the arts, manly men shied away from them, observers worried, depriving American culture of the muscularity needed to prevail against communism. That "an undue interest in the arts is likely to bring on a boy the stigma of being a 'sissy'" was such a commonplace notion that it needed no proof.[74] It reflected old concerns about the arts as a feminized domain, but also social reality. As many biographies and memoirs attest, mid-century parents often did tell boys—not girls—that the arts were for sissies. The Cold War added incentives and pressures for young men to avoid the arts: conscription pushed them toward schooling in technical fields earning them draft deferments, good jobs, or tickets to the officer corps. A system that equated manliness with science and war left it up to "sissy" boys—and to girls— to enter the arts.

Muscular warriors of the arts had to be taken where they could be found. Cold War logic operated: federal officials passed up sending a ballet company to the Soviet Union "because American ballet is not up to the Soviet level," preferring the Philadelphia Orchestra, "which is far better than any the Russians have." One unplanned triumph was Van Cliburn's at the 1958 Tchaikovsky International Piano Competition in Moscow, although Cliburn, who had already won several competitions, was not the flash in the pan the media made him out to be. *Time* regarded his victory as an "American sputnik" to counter the Soviet triumph of orbiting the first manmade object in 1957, and others viewed it as countering "the impression that the U.S. is backward culturally." As ecstatic Soviet responses to Cliburn and American responses to visiting Soviet artists suggested, this was no idle game: cultural prowess mattered in nations' jockeying for position and in peoples' hopes for peaceful contact. That Cliburn came from Texas and could sport a cowboy hat aided celebration of him. But he was also fey, unmarried, and deeply attached to his mother—perceivable, that is, as gay. Enlisted in the cause, their peculiarities winked at, such figures did not erase concern that the arts attracted sissies.[75]

Cultural Outsiders

Most observers saw queer artists as outsiders to American culture, but few offered much analysis of their relationship to culture. In particular, the notion that they derived insight as outsiders got little development. It had no disciplinary home as ideas about pathology had among analysts, and its sympathetic view of gay creativity cut against the prevailing grain. Usually it received only passing mention. "We are two-sided, [and we] often understand others better," one lesbian casually observed. "Many of us are artistic, can act or write."[76] The List of great artists long kept by some gay men had not assumed those artists' marginality to their cultures. Michelangelo had been a favored artist of the church, the dominant institution of the age. Tchaikovsky had triumphed in the central institutions of Russian music and helped to open Carnegie Hall in 1891. Since their cultures had not recognized a homosexual identity or had only begun doing so, their sexuality did not define them as marginal. Oscar

Wilde's trial and imprisonment suggested a new environment in which gay people seemed to occupy a more marked and marginal place, and by the 1950s a few figures offered lengthier explanations of gay creativity as the product of cultural outsiderness.

James Barr did so in his novel *Quatrefoil* (1950), gay authored and popular among gay readers. Phillip and Tim are manly officers who fall in love while facing antiqueer intrigue in the U.S. Navy. Their wisdom about human nature and the arts is signaled by Phillip's French name (Devereaux), their facility with French words, their taste for ballet and opera, their aristocratic origins, and their deep bond with each other. "My grandfather once met [Andre] Gide in Paris," Phillip tells Tim, and Tim instructs Phillip, "We constantly pass into and out of states of being as we develop. Few people even recognize them. Fewer learn to master them." Tim and Phillip are among those few, their superiority over queer "degenerates" as well as ordinary straight folks defined by class and lineage as well as sexuality. It was a posture struck in real life too. A Columbia University student in the 1950s, Alan Helms believed that he and his Swedish lover "were the only two men in the world the way we were — masculine men who loved men," and he reveled in his taste of high culture — "one of my classmates was John Corigliano [who became a leading gay composer], whose father was concertmaster of the New York Philharmonic. John had an autographed photograph of Toscanini on his desk in the dorms. That was culture, & that's what I wanted."[77]

Phillip and Tim display class snobbery, distaste for American provincialism, and misogyny. Phillip admires working-class women "as he might admire an exhibit of prize brood mares," regards his fiancée as "rather like a spaniel," and views Tim's wife as "a whore, no better and no worse than a million of her sisters." But Phillip understands that "his superiority complex hid something that was terrifying" to him, his attraction to Tim. He and Tim come to lead "dual lives," not closeted ones, embarking on marriage for dynastic, financial, and child-rearing reasons but forging a relationship apart from the conventions of ordinary life. Likewise, their wisdom about the arts derives from a cultural space above and apart from America — Europe's high culture — not from a closet causing pain and affording acuity.[78]

Just after Barr's novel appeared, Donald Webster Cory used pain to define the cultural outsiderness of gay people and the creativity they possessed. Cory — Edward Sagarin when not using the Cory pseudonym — was a middle-aged, homosexual, New York teacher, married with two children, a complicated man who clung to the medical model of homosexuality to the point of estrangement from gay activists in the mid-1960s, when he wrote a sociology dissertation "scathing" in its treatment of New York's Mattachine Society. Nonetheless, he was well informed about the arts and social sciences, and among lengthy examinations of homosexuality during the 1950s, *The Homosexual in America* (1951) was the most sophisticated and sympathetic. Other books followed, including *The Lesbian in America* (1964).[79]

Cory tackled contradictions in contemporary perceptions. Given the common notion that gay men were everywhere—found across occupational and class spectra—how then could they be so numerous in the arts? Perhaps, Cory suggested, "one tends to notice the unusual" in the arts, whereas among "chemists and physicists" it may be that "the sexuality of the homosexual goes unnoticed."[80] It was a sensible observation. Most visible gay people—perverts prosecuted in courts or purged from jobs— were anonymous or briefly notorious, but the queer presence in the arts received ongoing attention and had famous names attached to it. Cory discouraged exaggeration. But he hardly denied queer creativity. Offering his list of great figures, he attacked deniers of that creativity and the tricks of translation, deletion, and logic they used. He cleverly skewered Newton Arvin for dismissing Whitman's sexuality, noting that "lest the reader confuse Whitman with the homosexual stereotype, Arvin adds (in manner reminiscent of those who know 'a good Jew' or, worse, 'a white Jew') that 'Whitman was no mere invert, no mere "case": he remained to the end, in almost every real and visible sense, a sweet and sane human being.' . . . And this characterization is made by an astute critic—not a mere heterosexual!"[81]

Cory saw queer creativity partly as compensation for pain. "Each moment of chagrin, each instance of humiliation, each act of rejection awakes a rebel spirit which is seldom antagonistic to society, but only to society's offensive and unjust attitudes." (As Ned Rorem later explained his drive to compose, "Much of it came from 'I'll Show Them,' those ignorant admired bullies who whipped me in grade school.") Indeed, the gay man "frequently reacts to rejection by a deep understanding of all others who have likewise been scorned because of belonging to an outcast group." Outsiderness thus nourished a moral capacity, "a sympathy for all mankind," that also served "as a form of self-protection." Too, the homosexual is likely "a skeptic and an iconoclast" because "he is forced to reject an attitude which he finds so universally taken for granted by others." Cory later added that "creativity" often results from "an intense fantasy life begun in early childhood," especially "if homosexuality results from frustration and traumatic experiences in early childhood."[82]

Cory traced homosexuality to trauma and pathology, but he turned the psychodynamic model against its advocates by seeing pathology as nurturing creativity rather than crippling it. The homosexual's position "on the sidelines," he observed in 1963, "enables him to see this stream of humanity, its morals and mores, its values and goals, its assumptions and concepts, from without." "As a member of a minority group, the homo-sexual is often on the outside looking in—not at the heterosexual condi-tion, but at the human condition"—and "aware of many nuances of that life that most people take for granted."[83] Cory explained queer creativity much as it was explained for other minorities. Marginality as a wellspring of artistic insight was a common notion. The novelty of Cory's work lay in applying it to gay people, a group he helped constitute as a distinct "minority."

But there were differences. Cory saw queer outsiderness largely as a place of emotional and social pain. Jewish, African, Italian, and other identity groups were seen as coming from somewhere, bringing their tra-ditions into America's culture. For Cory, the queer margins were mostly blank, defined by no specific cultural tradition beyond The List of great gay figures. His approach left unexplained what was peculiar in queers' marginality beyond the painful fact of it, and what they could contribute if their marginality diminished.

But Cory helped open an inquiry, which a few others also pressed. Writing for *One* in 1954, Arthur Kroll pointed to the limits of the mi-nority group model. For the young heterosexual, "the tribal wisdom is at hand, even in the crassest film or fiction, to help him discover his nature," but "the homosexual has no such guidance," especially in "romantic lit-erature" or "suitable biographical literature." Although Kroll overlooked the "guidance" homosexuals provided each other, he identified the felt lack of tradition. "The Negro or Jewish individual does not stand alone; he is guided by group tradition and linked in warm human relationships. The homosexual finds no bond between his love feeling and the familiar values about him." For Kroll this was why "We Need a Great Literature," and for *One* it was reason to reprint large hunks of Shakespeare, Whit-man, Wilde, Cavafy, and others.[84]

Set against dominant opinion, the notion of homosexuals as creative outsiders barely made it to the silver screen, but Plato (Sal Mineo) in *Rebel without a Cause* vaguely reflected it. His name implying both homosexuality and creative ambition, Plato is an outsider to American life and his tough high school, who with Jim (James Dean) and Judy (Natalie Wood) briefly fashions the family he otherwise lacks. Plato is the most imaginative and colorful of the lot, but also the one doomed to die, his potential never realized. Queer marginality sometimes appeared on screen, but rarely the creativity it presumably nourished, except when the films were comic and the artists insubstantial. Hollywood did offer Kirk Douglas as Van Gogh in *Lust for Life* (Vincent Minnelli, 1956), but Van Gogh's sexuality was so obscure in the film that Douglas, answering a critic's charge that his portrayal "lacks virility," claimed that the critic had "hit upon the core of Van Gogh's problem as a man—a tremendous homosexuality problem," which he tried to evoke "with some taste and delicacy." [85] Approaching Cory's model were the wounded dreamers, women and men, queer and not-so-queer, of Williams's films. If most succumb (Blanche to the asylum, Sebastian to the carnivores), before their demise they express insights about art, beauty, and human nature.

The marginality imagined by Cory was an abstraction—one reason that it resisted realization on screen—unspecified as to time, place, and circumstance and unanchored in cultural tradition. Where were the "sidelines" from which homosexuals looked at the "stream of humanity"? Cory offered few visible cultural and social locales. His queer artist was solitary, aloof from not only the general "stream of humanity" but from his own kind.

Spaces for gay artists did exist, but whether they were "sidelines" is debatable. They were found in professional, social, and personal networks—in Virgil Thomson's New York apartment, the home shared by Barber and Menotti, the gay bars people frequented, the baths that Newton Arvin nervously entered, the circles and matings chronicled by Ned Rorem and Alan Helms, the arts-rich colleges, the communities like Provincetown, and more ordinary towns and cities. These "sidelines" varied according to the success, field, identities, age, and other factors of the people involved. The space for Barber and Copland, older composers in rich networks of performance and patronage with deep roots in European culture, differed from those for Williams or Baldwin, writers less indebted to Europe. The "sidelines" for wig makers in opera houses or piano teachers at small colleges differed from those for elite figures. No common "sidelines" existed, unless defined as a place of pain common to all.

But pain, fear, and ostracism, felt acutely by some like Arvin, enveloped others little or only in select spheres of their lives. As Alan Helms recalled his Hoosier adolescence, many boys heard "that Chuck Stengel liked to give blow jobs. Guys in the know talked about it, but in an amused non-judgmental way, as if they were talking about an eccentric but harmless appetite, like the Habsburgs' for dwarfs." The notion in Helms's youth that boys went through a "phase" provided them protection from self-doubt and social ostracism about their sex play. Helms had bad experiences, but they involved family dysfunction, not sexuality. And for Helms as for many, moving into New York's artistic circles was an exuberant if troubled experience — hardly on any sidelines, he reached the center of where he wanted to be.[86]

The place of gay men in the arts was one of intense creative connections and energies, a place where they often were insiders. Since their queer identity was often indistinguishable from their artistic identity, they had little sense that one was at odds with the other. Queer artists came in such varieties of personality, identity, and artistic style that their outsiderness, such as it was, is insufficient to account for all their contributions to American culture. Often, the pain they did encounter owed to critical disapproval or disinterest, as when tonal composers were eclipsed by exponents of serialism. Sexuality was relevant to that eclipse — tonalists, most gay, faced off against serialists, most straight — but hardly its sole determinant.

Just as the sidelines resist definition, so do the main lines they abut. What were gay artists outside of? To what mainstream were they marginal? Any culture has dominant values, and World War II and the Cold War exacerbated the pressures in America for conformity to them. Yet those pressures were intense in part because shared values were hard to discern in a raucous, polyglot nation. On the sidelines, the main lines rarely appeared tidy. Gay people did seem marginal to the mainstream of marriage and family. But all did come from families; some, like Leonard Bernstein, married and raised children; some kept close ties with parents or other relatives; some, like Copland, were mentors to younger men; many made a version of family with partners (Barber with Menotti, Britten with Pears, W. H. Auden with Chester Kallman) and other gay people. They were hardly outside of family, only differently positioned with respect to it. Nor were they marginal to American institutions. By definition, those who succeeded — who got orchestras to play their music, theaters to mount their plays, movies to do their scripts — were insiders. Some kept their sexuality private, but it was rarely a secret from others in those institutions, often queer themselves.

But it was largely a secret — or an "open secret" — in public discourse.   93

For all the rumor, encoded revelation, and stereotyping of certain fields, individuals were rarely identified publicly as queer. What Arthur Laurents wrote of Hollywood applied to most of the arts, though no other art was so carefully controlled: "Image was all. . . . nobody was concerned so long as the studio could keep whatever it was out of the papers and whoever did it out of jail."[87] Here marginality was evident—in public silence about individuals' sexuality and their absence from public debate about queer creativity. Marginality lay in the ether of public discourse, where it had no locale, no visible "sidelines." It might cause pain, but most figures accommodated it.

They also had other identities. Copland and Laurents regarded their Jewishness as creative wellspring and object of suspicion. Williams typecast himself as much as a Southerner and a drinker as a queer, although those categories could merge. Some addressed homosexuality in their work—Britten and Williams, who perhaps best fit Cory's model of viewing the "stream of humanity" as pained outsider—but were also thereby among the least closeted figures. For none was queerness the sole identity. For many, another category—artist—was a source of marginality, since artists were widely seen as weird regardless of their sexuality. "In twentieth-century America," Nadine Hubbs argues, "to declare oneself musical was to claim membership in a special class or even a secret society." For many, identities as queers and artists emerged in tandem— each consolidated the other, a pattern throughout the century. Paul Monette wrote of his experience in the 1970s: After years of "self-hatred" —felt more acutely by his generation than an older one—the "breakthrough to my queer self happened to the writer in me as much as it happened to the man."[88]

James Baldwin illustrates how an artist's many identities might interact. Although ever-conscious of writing as a Negro, Baldwin, his biographer notes, "set himself apart from the school of 'Negro writing' which came before him, and aligned himself with mainstream American literature," and literature generally. He also wrote as a homosexual—but did not see himself as a homosexual writer. By giving "a homosexual content to his writing," Baldwin "pre-empted the shame which was usually attendant upon a homosexual life in those days." He "was never a closet homosexual; nor did he make his homosexuality into a political stance." Barbs came his way—his one-time mentor, Richard Wright, complained publicly of "a kind of unmanly weeping" in Baldwin's writing and privately of his "disgust" at Baldwin's sexuality—but such complaints did not define him.[89] Baldwin's "pre-empting" stance was unusual, but his sense of broad aspirations, into which particular identities were folded without being erased, applied to most queer artists.

Queer artists' marginality, then, was partial, varied, and elusive, in contrast to the stark model of it that Cory and others later proposed. The difficulty of applying it is apparent with the period's most famous queer creation, the musical *West Side Story* (1957; film, Robert Wise, 1961). Moving Shakespeare's story of Romeo and Juliet to the landscape of New York's youthful gangs, *West Side Story* was the product of Leonard Bernstein for the music and some lyrics, Stephen Sondheim for other lyrics, Arthur Laurents for the book, and Jerome Robbins for direction and choreography (and Ernest Lehman for the movie script). Charles Kaiser, though lauding the "rebel" and "outsider" in New York's "gay metropolis," finds no queer inspiration, rebellious or not, for *West Side Story*. "None of the collaborators (or their 1950s contemporaries) ever suspected there was anything gay about their heterosexual love story," he reports, and he accepts Laurents's claim that *West Side Story*'s makers attributed its "sensibility" and "passion against prejudice" to their Jewishness, a claim Laurents restated in 2004.[90]

But *West Side Story* shows the difficulty of measuring creative work on a binary, queer-or-not (or Jewish-or-not) scale. Laurents's own account suggests that for the musical's creators, sensitivity to anti-Semitism blended with awareness of antihomosexuality. His autobiography, often keenly specific about anti-Semitism, turns generic in describing *West Side Story* as "establishing a world of violence and prejudice in which the lovers try to survive," and it interweaves the story of creating *West Side Story* with the story of his love-for-keeps with Tom Hatcher under the subtitle "West Side Story, Gypsy, and Tom," as if the two developments were hardly coincidental. The creators bonded through many shared traits—Jewishness, politics, and ambition—but also queerness. Laurents also knew the cruel taunts that Robbins, though queer, inflicted on a gay dancer ("Can't you move like a man, you faggot"!). And if there was nothing "gay" in *West Side Story*, why did "thousands of gay Americans fell in love" with it, as Kaiser claims?[91]

But what would something "gay" have meant? Was it the stylized, boy-bonding exuberance of the dancing, the gay identities of some of the cast, the slim-hipped hypermasculinity of Bernardo (George Chakiris in the film), the proto-lesbian figure named Anybodys, the relationship between Riff and Tony, the over-the-top musical passion, the satire on psychoanalytic explanations of juvenile violence and sexuality, the story of outsiders hostile to authority and love doomed by prejudice? Those familiar with the stereotype that male dancers were gay or with gossip about the creators' identities had further reasons to read queerness into the musical. Given how much musicality was culturally coded as homosexuality, simply the symphonic and operatic nature of the score provided a reason. The Puccini-esque, faux-Catholic religiosity of the song "Make of Our Hands, One Hand" was an opera queen's delight. And there was the genre-crossing nature of the whole affair—its blending of opera, jazz, popular music, Broadway musical, ballet, modern dance, and dramatic tragedy: the sort of modernist hybrid at which queer artists seemed adept. Was *West Side Story* queer even though its creators (according to Laurents) did not see it as such? Or was queerness less an intrinsic or intended quality than a characteristic in beholders' eyes, in which case it makes sense that "thousands of gay Americans" loved the musical? Such questions hardly exhaust those that can be asked of *West Side Story*, or other creations. They resist easy answers, but that is the point—the difficulty of tracking relationships among artists' identity, marginality, and product.

Casual extrapolation of a "closet" back to the 1950s may further skew assessment of that marginality. Although repression was frightening, it was not then imagined as creating a "closet," a term not yet used, for frightened queer inhabitants. When the gay magazine *One* tackled "Coming Out" and asked "Out from where? Out into what?" in 1962, it mentioned no "closet," instead identifying "coming out" as "our slang phrase for coming from a majority and going to a minority." *One* knew the need for " 'wearing the mask' " in a "hostile world" that taught "the evilness of homosexuality." But "the absolute necessity for secrecy from the majority" was something "you learned quickly" *after* coming out— a protective device, not a place of hiding.[92]

Made retroactive, the "closet" becomes today's place to hide a complex past. Recalling the world of arts and celebrity in 1950s New York, Alan Helms, then "becoming the most celebrated young man in all of gay New York," stressed his fear of being spied on by authorities at Columbia, the desperation of some men to see shrinks and " 'go straight,' " the threat of "arrest or blackmail" or "a gang of fagbashers," the abuse of alcohol and drugs, and "a kind of concentration camp mentality." "Save for a few artists & hairdressers & decorators & dancers, we were all terrified of being found out," and "group loyalties crumbled" when threats arose. A "sense of shame . . . was pervasive in our lives," Helms wrote. "You can still see it in the timid gestures toward self-exposure of a John Ashberry [the poet] or a Jasper Johns [the painter], & in the furtive, guilty cruising of gay men in their fifties & sixties."

Yet "sex was everywhere" and remarkably "out in public," and Helms encountered many figures, such as the "conspicuously nelly" Arthur MacArthur, "a living affront to his father, the General [Douglas Mac-Arthur], which was surely the point." Helms's list of famous folks he met included Noel Coward and John Gielgud and all "the *West Side Story* crowd" and ended with "Jackie Kennedy & the Dalai Lama. (I'm name-dropping, yes, but how else can I make the point so neatly?)" And there were "the most closeted parties of all, attended by diplomats & politicians, heads of corporations, top military brass, the gay men most terrified of exposure." It was an exuberant world: "With so much fear & danger hedging our lives, it's no wonder we were a wildly romantic bunch." White male privilege fostered exuberance for Helms, but writer Audre Lorde, a poor black lesbian, also felt it in 1950s New York. In his memoirs, Helms invoked the "closet" but records no contemporary use of the term. As Cory and others suggested, queerness involved a sense of being cast out of society, not trapped *in* something. If it applies at all to this era, the "closet" had a door that swung open as often as it slammed shut.[93]

When the terminology of the "closet" did arise in the 1960s, it had sources and meanings soon forgotten. "Homosexuality is, and for too long has been, a skeleton in the closet of society," proclaimed a Florida legislative committee report in 1964. It placed the *subject*, not homosexuals, in a "closet," whose door it wanted "thrown open" so that "the light of public understanding" would be "cast upon homosexuality." The "closet" was nonqueers' ignorance; the outsiders were exasperated inquisitors who wanted to know what went on inside. Hence the committee's photographs of half-naked men illustrating "fetish appeal." Hence its rich "Glossary of Homosexual Terms and Deviate Acts," from "Puppy's Lunch" ("Not as bad as a dog's lunch, but still unattractive") to "Reaming Queen" ("fairly well self-explanatory") and "come out" ("The time one admits he is a homosexual and adjusts himself to that life"). Prurient, like most sexual inquisitions, the report built a closet of its own, not queers', imagination.[94]

The question may be less how a marginal group played a major cultural role than how the group came to be perceived as marginal. The *perception* of gay artists' marginality, not some measurable fact of it, is the key matter. Marginality was less the source of creativity than an idea fashioned in response to it. At least since Oscar Wilde's time, some gay men

97

had regarded themselves, and others had regarded them, as solitary or outcast geniuses. But in the postwar era, that idea gained new resonance and application—to an entire social type rather than occasional individuals. Seeing a rising tide of queer creativity, a rising chorus of observers insisted on that marginality—psychological, ideological, geographical, sociological, cultural—in order to contain or deny the creativity. That is, they constructed that marginality, which figures like Cory refashioned as the wellspring of creativity.

Perhaps the notion of gay artists as outsiders was covertly appealing, for it harkened back to the imagined romantic artist of the past, a solitary explorer of beauty, truth, and humanity. Now the arts were institutionalized, industrialized, incorporated, and deployed by the state. Universities hired them, corporations underwrote them, Washington funded them. In turn, the artist's diminished individuality became a major lament. In the 1930s it had been "possible to commit one's self to a great human cause," Stephen Spender remembered, but by the 1950s "the painter Robert Motherwell wrote that the modern states as we have known them have all been enemies of the artist," while, Randall Jarrell complained, the critic spoke "a jargon as institutionalized as that of a sociologist." Some responded to the artist's shrunken autonomy by defiantly celebrating "an art which refuses to serve ends other than itself," in Clement Greenberg's formulation. "Who Cares If You Listen?" was the title given a *High Fidelity* piece by Milton Babbit, who favorably compared serial and electronic music to the complexity of modern physics. Others, equally defiant, excoriated the art-for-arts-sake crowd: "You guys are just afraid of being emotionally involved in anything bigger than yourselves," painter Ben Shahn declared. Schlesinger complained that manly autonomy was being crushed by "centralization," capitalism, and "the prefabricated emotional cliches" of mass culture. Fiedler lamented that writers had succumbed to "bourgeois security" and Lindner that "sex-denying" culture imposed "conformity." Against supposedly spirit-crushing, homogenizing forces, the queer artist imagined as neurotic outsider had appeal. Many observers scorned him, but almost wistfully, sensing that the artist as outsider and rebel was a disappearing type. It made little difference whether the queer artist really was marginal and rebellious: he was an abstract type covertly admired if overtly vilified.[95]

In modest ways, some gay artists fit the ideal of creative independence. Many queer composers, for example, avoided long-term posts in the academy, arts organizations, or corporations, relying on commissions, royalties, commercial success, temporary teaching, or their own wealth.

In contrast, exponents of serial and electronic music, most of them self-consciously straight men, often affiliated with universities. Writers like Laurents, Merrill, Williams, Baldwin, and Vidal also stayed clear of the academy, even as some dipped nicely into Hollywood's treasury. They were not institutional outsiders, but they were semidetached freelancers. Moreover, their appeal to audiences was notable at a time when alienation from the crowd seemed a virtue to some, and they were artists who made American culture. Had they been exponents of truly alien cultural forms and themes—real outsiders—they would have been less noticed or more completely demonized. They were often demonized, but too shrilly to disguise envy.

Although few observers acknowledged envy, they reflected it in their striking failure to offer healthy heterosexual alternatives to the queers they cast to the margins. No reader of Bergler would have learned who might create healthier women's fashions. Critics rarely proposed worthy straight artists to replace the gay ones they bemoaned. By their silence on that score, they suggested their fear that queers were often the best of the lot.

Psychologist Albert Ellis, who introduced Cory's 1951 volume, belatedly grasped the problem. There were "no objective studies" regarding "much speculation about homosexuals being more artistic or creative than heterosexuals," he wrote in 1959. To assess "creativity," Ellis compared "sixty-six individuals with severe homosexual problems and 150 exceptionally heterosexual psychotherapy patients." But he stacked the deck. Did "severe homosexual problems" mean subjects who were severely homosexual—mirror images to the "exceptionally heterosexual" —or those who had severe problems, or was homosexuality itself a "severe" problem? What did "exceptionally heterosexual" mean? Ellis noted that "with clinical diagnosis held constant," "neurotic" heterosexuals were "not statistically different" in creativity from neurotic queers. But he bypassed that finding to conclude that homosexuals by nature were crazier and less creative, especially the queerest—those with "sex role inversion."[96] Speaking publicly about his work, Ellis maintained that "homosexuals in our culture are almost invariably neurotic or psychotic," and so "the only legitimate control group" for them would be "emotionally disturbed individuals." Their reputation as creative owes to "notorious characters . . . more easily remembered than the outstanding heterosexual creators who may be leading a quiet home life." Gay artists cannot "devise new solutions to artistic and scientific problems," explained Ellis, and are "the most imitative, most conventional, and most acceptance-demanding people in our ultra-conforming culture." No wonder that a few years later, when Ellis told a gay activists' convention that "the exclusive homosexual is a psychopath," the retort came: "Any homosexual who would come to you for treatment, Dr. Ellis, would *have* to be a psychopath!"[97]

Ellis left queer creativity a marked, pathologized category requiring little comparison to its heterosexual counterpart. Indeed, no one carefully counted queers in the arts—an improbable task given how hard it was to define and ascertain who was "homosexual," but possibly a revealing one. A study of sexuality and the arts envisioned by Alfred Kinsey might have corrected that imbalance—it surely would have avoided Ellis's splenetic stance toward queers—but it did not go forward before Kinsey's death in 1956.[98] That imbalance left unclear the standards by which queer failure was measured. To be sure, worriers had an implicit escape hatch: straight designers, writers, and composers had been squeezed out by scheming queers or never nourished by the infertile soil of American culture. But vagueness about robust alternatives to the gay artist revealed anxiety about their paucity. Perhaps it was assumed that people would naturally set the record of queer creativity against a presumptively larger one of straight achievement. If so, it is surprising that no one said so, though Ellis's reference to "heterosexual creators . . . leading a quiet home life" lamely suggested the point.

Did observers really feel the envy of queer artists surmised here? I deduce it from the structure, content, and silences of their claims more than from direct expression—a tricky, speculative technique, though one employed by scholars who detect envy in, for example, whites' denunciations of black sexuality. Those skeptical of this old-fashioned, analytic technique may, in postmodern fashion, cast envy differently—as less a felt emotion than a constructed trait of discourse. Pragmatic historians see it as operating, partially and raggedly, in both dimensions.

A similar approach may help explain the "master trope of excess" in commentary about homosexuals.[99] Gay men were seen, and sometimes saw themselves, as given to florid gestures, emotional extravagance, hyperbolic language, and uncontrolled sexuality, qualities spotted in their everyday behavior and their creative output—the fashions they designed, the plays Tennessee Williams wrote, the music tonalists composed. Their excess was in turn linked to their immaturity. Just as adolescents' expressiveness might be captivating, so might gay men's, but both lack self-reflection and discipline. Just as adolescents are driven by impulses they poorly control, so are gay men, their excess manifest in predatory behavior toward youth or the mannerisms of men fluttering like women. Adolescents mature into adulthood, but perpetual adolescents never do, so gay men's work never matures: it only becomes empty, showy, burnt out. It never achieves the maturity evident to many observers in the tough-minded adherents of serial music.

The perception of gay artists as prone to immature excess played awkwardly off of Americans' boastful penchant for bigness. They had the biggest economy, bombs, cars, and ambitions, although the Soviets threatened them in some categories, and American culture prized bigness in artists' ambitions, arts' budgets, and arts palaces. A sense of America as a youthful nation, different from a tired Europe and a backward-looking Asia, further underwrote bigness. But exuberance now competed with the disciplined restraint seen as necessary for the United States as a global power. American leaders often positioned their nation as a mature tutor to adolescent learners—Germans and Japanese discovering democracy, non-Western peoples modernizing their economies. America, it was thought, had grown up in World War II, assuming new burdens for stopping bullies, aiding the unfortunate, and managing the world. In their cultural life, too, many authorities expected mature discipline. That Americans were given to excess was both a chronic boast and a chronic worry. "Our expectations," Daniel Boorstin observed, "are excessive." Listing examples (among them, "new heroes every season, a literary masterpiece every month, a dramatic spectacular every week, a rare sensation every night"), he concluded, "We are ruled by extravagant expectations."[100]

Americans had many ways to navigate the tension between adolescent bigness and mature restraint. Anxious commentary on teenagers was one way—would reckless teenagers mature into responsible adults? Queer people were another locale for addressing these tensions. Prized as artists of exuberance, they were also damned for lacking disciplined maturity. On them, as on the adolescent, were displaced anxieties about whether American culture was maturing sufficiently to shoulder new burdens. Rebuking them offered reassurance that the nation's penchant for excess resided with an odd, alien group incapable of growing up.

So the historian can speculate. As with seeing envy of gay artists among those who ridiculed them, seeing anxiety about maturity employs a psychoanalytic technique. No one said: "Let's displace onto gay men our fears about maturity." Displacement lay in the interplay between repeated assertions of gay men's adolescent excess and chronic worries about American maturity. It was another way in which their outsiderness was less a reality than an imagined trait used to explain and contain their creativity.

Convergences

So why did gay men play such a large role in America's mid-century arts? Most contemporaries attributed their role to conspiracy rather than talent and saw it as alien to an authentic America. Celebrants like Cory also posited queer outsiderness, but as a source of creativity rather than its poisoned well, an explanation later common among queer artists, critics, and scholars. As Tennessee Williams put it in the 1970s, homosexuals are more artistic "because they have greater sensibility, and because they've *had* to develop a greater sensibility because they have been rejected. . . . They look deeper into themselves and deeper into the human spirit." Recently, Philip Brett and Elizabeth Wood have seen music as "a lifeline to those whose basic emotions are invalidated." "Most homosexuals internalized their oppression" and musicians often "combined such internalization of oppression with some manner of protest." Among examples, they cite "the insider allusions in the songs of Cole Porter and Noel Coward" and John Cage's "dual embrace of both noise and silence within music"—practices that may indicate "both an accommodation to as well as subversion of the pervasive fact of the closet." Other versions of the outsider model appear in chapter 5.[101]

Beyond problems with that model already noted, its application to so many groups saps its explanatory power. Writing in 1971, Dennis Altman, though "somewhat suspicious of those who would glorify the outsider," thought it "true that one does see certain things more clearly from outside. Homosexuals have been important in our literature for the same reason as Jews and Southern women." But as Altman acknowledged, much the same has been said of so many other groups as to leave unclear what group is left as the insiders to be observed. At best the problem is soluble only by claims that one group's outsiderness is more onerous than another's: mine is bigger than yours. The outsider model also presumed an unvarying "closet"—"arguably the most important attribute of 20th-century homosexuality," asserted Brett and Wood—operating on all queer artists regardless of age, circumstance, or other identities.[102]

How else might historians account for queers' role in mid-century American culture, if the outsider model is inadequate? In such a matter, historians attend usefully to convergences more than causes. As C. A.

Tripp suggested in 1975, "There are indefinable lines of 'connective relevance' between the homosexual matrix and what a number of occupations in Western society happen to require."[103] Queer men excelled in the arts in part because men generally were more valued than women. Cultural nationalism—the drive to make America the imperial center of culture—rewarded those who could distill, transform, and disseminate defining elements of American life and the world beyond it. Those tasks were performed in settings that meshed well with gay men's patterns of living, mobility, and minimal encumbrances. Many showed talent as jugglers of multiple identities and trends, a talent valued in America's expansionist culture. Queer artists were not solidly ensconced in one identity, instead moving among many. Copland was Jewish, leftist, queer, nationalist, and modernist—and a Hollywood composer, Red Scare target, lover to younger men, conductor, writer, and, finally, grand old man of American music. If one category momentarily shunted others aside, all the categories together defined a multiplicity of roles that Copland juggled. In an era of American cultural ambition and international traffic in the arts, multiplicity was valuable—dizzying for some, but the best, like Copland, sustained the juggling act.

A perch on the sidelines undoubtedly sharpened some gay men's acuity, but outsiderness was less the cause of their creativity than the way in which it was understood. Most creative figures are both insiders and outsiders: wholly insiders, they may simply replicate a culture; wholly outsiders, they may not grasp it. Outsiderness is a historically contingent, shifting, partial, and imagined condition. Gay artists moved through too many categories for a singular outsiderness to define them. "Inbetweenness," while an awkward term, better captures their historical position.

That might be said of many artists at many moments, but social groups vary in when they find their cultural moment. White Protestant men did so in the nineteenth century, and African Americans more in the twentieth. Jewish Americans were finding their moment at roughly the same time as gay Americans, many also Jewish, an overlap that charged the effort to grapple with how the two identities related to each other. Queers' achievements suggest that their moment came at mid-century, when global struggles uprooted them and when queer communities were consolidating and drawing scrutiny. Those communities were essential to their success. But without them, a queer identity, had it emerged at all, would have defined them less as a social type than as odd, isolated individuals. With communities came networks of friendship, knowledge, patronage, and rivalry—networks that allowed others to see collective menace.

Queer identity, mobility, community, talent, scrutiny, and opportunity converged at mid-century. Did gay men have the "special artistic gifts" that Bergler derided? Yes, insofar as circumstances fostered those gifts and abetted the process of identifying them, if often to be scorned, as queer. Many Americans wanted to celebrate their creativity and see it as cosmopolitan. Not alone, gay artists helped them do so by making modernism lyrical, accessible, and expressive of mid-century America.

Dyspeptic explanations of queer creativity yielded little that was persuasive—no surprise, since most authors wanted less to explain than to disparage. With no other commanding explanation, the field was open to the lowest common denominator—the notion of queer conspiracy, adamantly expressed in the 1960s. Creative queers, rendered as outsiders in most ways, were also portrayed as consummate insiders scheming for power. That combination of images was hardly novel. It was a staple of American anticonspiracy thinking about imagined subversives, from Jewish bankers to fascist fifth columnists, from pinko intellectuals to right-wing nuts—such thinking knew few ideological boundaries. Its application to others made it no less pernicious in this case.

3

Frenzy

Agitation about homosexuals in the arts became more frenzied and conspicuous in the early 1960s. It also seemed less guarded and euphemistic, its explicitness sometimes equated with tolerance. But Vito Russo's claim about film's treatment of homosexuality—"the dirty secret of old emerged on the screen in those newly enlightened times as a dirty secret" —to a degree applied generally. "The much vaunted sexual permissiveness of our times," Dennis Altman worried in 1971, "may replace being largely ignored with a prurient voyeurism" regarding gay people, or with "the patronizing tolerance of liberals, or what [Christopher] Isherwood has referred to as 'annihilation by blandness.' "[1] Greater license to discuss homosexuality often meant greater license to loathe it. In particular, hostile observers regarded gay secrecy as a threat to the nation's cultural and political vitality. In the 1970s, they became indignant that queers came out of the closet. In the 1960s, they were indignant that queers apparently hid in it.

Inventing the Closet

Indeed, those hostile inquisitors helped to invent "the closet"—that imagined place where gay people, they charged, hid their identities and practiced their wily ways. A key step in that invention was Jess Stearn's *The Sixth Man* (1961), a best seller unencumbered by expert jargon and backed by Stearn's credentials as a former *Newsweek* editor. Stearn's survey of male homosexuality "dripped with venom and contempt," John

D'Emilio later noted, for all its pretense, unquestioned by most reviewers, of objectivity and compassion. Stearn claimed that despite all his "research" he "had yet to meet a truly happy homosexual." Gay men, he found, were deceitful, unstable, confused, hateful to each other, and prone to "excess" and masquerade. "And nobody grows older faster." Their menace, however, involved more than the specific traits, most long alleged, that Stearn identified. It derived also from how gay men were beyond comprehension by others—Stearn billed one chapter "Origin of the Species," casting himself as Darwinesque discoverer of something nonhuman. If they were fathomable at all, it was as bearers of the decadence that corrodes nations and empires. The problem of homosexuality, as Stearn approvingly quoted one psychiatrist, " 'bears comparison . . . to the decline and fall of Rome.' "[2]

Little in Stearn's account was new, but it was packaged as if it were— "A Startling Investigation of the Spread of Homosexuality in America!" the dust jacket blared. It resembled earlier rants that were among the "many tons of pulp and slick paper," as One magazine had complained, full of "malignant scribbling" about homosexuality. Stearn nonetheless claimed to reveal the secrets of a "growing homosexual population," one "far more considerable than I would have thought possible," including "whole beaches and entire community areas." More "research" made him "accept the homosexual's own estimate of the over-all homosexual population—one out of every six adult males!" He cajoled readers to share his supposed shock: "Inevitably, the revelation of homosexuality hits an unsuspecting community like a succession of shock waves." The pose of shock erased past moments of discovery and presented queerness as surprising and sinister. In that vein, R. E. L. Masters claimed to overcome "the pornographic, the obscene, and the tasteless" talk about homosexuality in order to reveal the gravity of the situation, in The Homosexual Revolution (1962).[3]

That pose—what One had called "mock shock" in 1953—had deep roots and wide usage. The author of City Crimes, an 1849 American novel that inveighed against a "miserable sodomite," explained: "It is an extremely delicate task for a writer to touch on a subject so revolting, yet the crime actually exists."[4] After World War II, the slow revelation of a dangerous secret was a standard narrative device in fiction and in films exploiting the Production Code's slow demise. Story line, visual narrative, and sound track worked together in movies to unlock the sordid secrets of homosexuality: in Advise and Consent (1962), the camera, to the music of urban decadence and Frank Sinatra's woozy crooning about the "secret voice" and the "loser's song," enters a New York gay bar ("Club 602"), its patrons returning the camera's gaze. The language of revelation about a secret life was common.

Aided by that language, accounts like Stearn's did much to construct the closet, a way of viewing the place of homosexuals emerging in the 1960s. The closet is often seen as a regime of silence, but silence was the obligation of homosexuals, not others. "More space about homosexuality has not necessarily meant more space *for* homosexuals to present their position," gay writer Dennis Altman noted in 1971. No doubt some men spoke to Stearn about the furtive nature of queer life, yet given that "they were only too happy to talk to me," not to mention the "entire community areas" he found, their secrecy was more Stearn's invention than their practice. Homosexuals faced repression, but the closet was less the space they already occupied than one to which others now consigned them— Stearn referred to " 'closet queers' " — and then presumed to reveal. As a reviewer of Stearn's book complained, this was an "exercise in Peeping-Tom-Foolery," one that helped invent the closet and then pry it open.[5]

Stearn offered gay artists as a disturbing sign of queers' designs, for "in the theater and the arts they find tolerance and acceptance, just as prostitutes and other characters would, and can show themselves openly." Although "the subject was once theatrically verboten, it has lately become fashionable"—Stearn cited the usual suspects (*Tea and Sympathy, Compulsion, Suddenly, Last Summer*) and claimed that gay playwrights created distorted, malign portraits of women and marriage. But worse than the work of individuals was queers' collective power. Stearn identified "the homosexual clique dominating the style world," who forced female models to diet to the point of emaciation, and the "vast conspiracy" in the entertainment industry—ballet, theater, film, and television—where homosexuals dominate "not only as performers or playwrights, but as producers, directors, composers, choreographers," even financiers. As for television actors, " 'these casting directors look at you [if you are straight] as though you're a carbuncle on the seat of progress,' " one source told Stearn. In drama and film, "the homosexual playing a heroic role . . . walks, talks and makes love like a man" and is perhaps better at the " 'gutsy, two-fisted' role" than straight actors, Stearn suggested. Although it did not fool other queers, his "burlesque . . . hoodwinks a nation."[6]

The idea of queers as dangerous tricksters in the arts had completed its move out of specific venues like analytic writing into general view. It surfaced in many fields: a magazine for art museum executives complained about "the covert influence of homosexual in-groups"—people "well-trained and extremely competent" but with "a tendency to weed out colleagues who 'don't fit'" ("If you're not gay, you can't stay!" as the *Ladder* summed up the article's complaint). It circulated in middlebrow commentary: "Many of our unhappy geniuses defend homosexuality," according to critic Joseph Wood Krutch. "From that we are sometimes prone to assume that homosexuality is what has made them geniuses. Perhaps it is only what has made them unhappy."[7]

If a gay "vast conspiracy" already ruled much of culture, then it might, Stearn implied, soon seize the whole nation—precisely how a "vast conspiracy" operates. If analogies to ancient Greece and Rome held, queers endangered not only cultural empire, but empire in any form. That reasoning drew attention to the arts: queer dominance there was a stepping-stone to further conquest. After all, the New York Academy of Medicine claimed, "the homosexuals seem to have become more formally organized, with a central office and a magazine of their own."[8]

What transformed scattered and often obscure alarms about queers into the high-profile frenzy of the 1960s? Its purveyors, though exasperated at queers' secrecy, pointed to their swelling numbers and assertiveness. "Homosexuals Proud of Deviancy," a *New York Times* headline announced, making pride appear alarmingly new, although it long had been denounced. Examining "The Third Sex on Stage," *Show Business Illustrated* found that "the legal and societal hounding of the misfit has fallen with a dreadfully heavy hand on the homosexual," but "to a degree" he was "asking for it out of exhibitionistic, narcissistic, guilt-ridden masochism." *Time* asserted that "homosexuality is more in evidence in the U.S. than ever before." "This social order," *Life* claimed, "has forced itself into the public eye."[9]

Yet the media did most of the "forcing." *Life*'s claim was oddly dissonant with how its cameras and reporters pushed into queer settings and peered at what they observed. As skeptics noted, no evidence showed that gay people were more numerous relative to a growing population. Ritually invoked to justify scrutiny, media pressures were illustrated by anecdotes, often recycled more than documented. It was unclear anyway how people facing intense hostility—stressed and endorsed in most accounts—could do much "forcing," although queer disguise and conspiracy (their "central office") were cited. An uptick in gay political activism during the early 1960s still left it on a small scale. Insofar as a gay street presence was more "overt," it represented a return to the forgotten prewar state of things. The gay presence in the arts was not measurably larger in 1964 than in 1954, and few figures were more willing to address homosexuality in their creative work and public discourse. Much evidence for queer "pressures" was self-referential: observers construed others' notice of homosexuality as a sign of its swelling presence, and they equated the growth in talk *about* queers with growth in talk *by* them. Homosexuality was "more in evidence," as *Time* put it, in good part because the media called attention to it—"not to condone it," *Life* made clear, "but to cope with it."[10] If anything, gay activism was as much a response to growing condemnation as its cause.

Film also called attention without condoning. Because censorship unraveled when homophobia was peaking, Hollywood treated queerness more viciously as well as more explicitly. In fact, one reason censorship unraveled was to allow viciousness fuller expression, as well as to make money by exploiting homosexuality. Reviewing the changes in 1966, *Tangents*, a new magazine spun off from *One*, doubted that old "prejudices" were disappearing on-screen. "The impact of this emancipation upon Hollywood has been fairly predictable: more bedroom scenes, torrid rapes, adultery, inter-racial conflicts, abortion, etc., all strung together in the most unlikely and tasteless fashion" and most were calculated to "appeal primarily to the average man" and his prejudices. At best, "many Hollywood directors find homosexuality a fashionable touch." Some movie goers saw, as did scholars later, complexity in 1960s cinema or registered gratitude for any treatment—even viciousness was better than invisibility, as they saw it. Nor were all films vicious: two 1960 English movies offered sober, frank portrayals of their subject (*Oscar Wilde* and *The Trials of Oscar Wilde*). But one English film with a sympathetic view of queer life found few outlets and much scorn in the United States. *Victim* (Basil Deardon, 1961) starred gay actor Dirk Bogarde as a gay character, a rare choice for a movie star. Early scenes suggested liberal pity for a beleaguered homosexual trapped by blackmail, but *Victim* also endorsed his refusal to stay beleaguered. *Time* worried that the film failed to show that homosexuality "attacks the biological basis of life itself." Pauline Kael sniffed in apparent disapproval that it treated homosexuals "seriously, with sympathy and respect, like Negroes and Jews." *Victim* was an exception to prevailing cinematic trends.[11]

Queer Resistance

No transformation in queer life prompted frenzy, but modest changes were unfolding. There were the Broadway plays widely discussed and often denounced, for example, and poet Allen Ginsberg's *Howl* (1956), whose denunciations of Cold Warriors and passages about men "fucked in the ass by saintly motorcyclists" generated a national sensation, especially when police in San Francisco seized copies of it. Commentary in queer magazines was another barometer of change. They were few and their readership small—"a little two-bit magazine," *One*'s editors labeled their new publication in 1953—and they had limited impact except as fodder for alarmists warning of a "vast conspiracy" and postal inspectors making a bust. But they tracked a rising resistance.[12]

The *Ladder*, produced by and for lesbians, showed gendered differences in responses to agitation over queers in the arts. Since many gay women and men felt a common bond of oppression, and since gay men's portrayal of women was often at issue, the *Ladder* hardly ignored the agitation. But with women's place in the arts—and in the imagined queer takeover—publicly discounted, the *Ladder* paid less attention to the agitation than did publications for men. Treating literature and the arts, it stressed great women of the past (from Sappho to Radclyffe Hall) more than living figures and it offered straightforward reporting to fellow homosexuals more than snappy back talk on their behalf. The *Ladder*, that is, reflected an insular lesbian community that both suffered and benefited from its place at the margins of public furor, and it incorporated middle-class norms of respectability, including deference to male authority, devoting more space to men's contributions than male-oriented magazines did to women's. "Is the Lesbian Being Portrayed Realistically by the Mass Media?" a panel at the 1962 Daughters of Bilitis convention was asked. "Is the Lesbian Being Portrayed at All?" its moderator— a man—responded. As that exchange suggested, where gay men fought against pernicious recognition, lesbians struggled for any recognition, and welcomed it from men. The *Ladder* judged Jess Stearn's report on lesbians, *The Grapevine* (1964), "a far better book" than *The Sixth Man*, showing his "indefatigable determination" and "brave plunge into icy and unknown waters." Except for the praise men's magazines gave a few women, like psychologist Evelyn Hooker, who challenged the sickness model for homosexuality, there was no male counterpart for this deference to the opposite sex's authority. More assertive currents emerged in lesbian fiction and in the *Ladder* by mid-decade, but deference shattered only late in the 1960s, leaving lesbians often pitted against gay as well as straight men.[13]

Magazines like *One*, written mostly by and for men, relished snappy back talk. They ranged widely over political developments, medical views, police busts, and the like, but they treated cultural figures and products—the famous actor, the scholarly book, the Broadway play, the composer's score, the twists and turns of censorship—with special zeal. A running joke was Irving Stone's popular novel heterosexualizing Michelangelo, *The Agony and the Ecstasy* (1961), a title ripe for puns and jeers, and Hollywood's film of it (1965), starring Charlton Heston. Hollywood was a preoccupation, but a scorecard mentality—which films were homophobic or sympathetic, evasive or explicit—was joined by insightful essays and by attention to foreign films seen as more sympathetic and clever—as when one character in *The Knack* (1965) "answers to, 'Are you a homosexual?' with 'No, but thanks just the same.'"[14] As much as their tiny staffs permitted, gay magazines tracked anything in culture about homosexuality, effectively indexing it (far more than standard sources did) and starting a practice still carried on by gay periodicals.

They did more. At its start, *One* promised that "every article will be equally bright or misinformed within certain surprisingly confined limits," and that whimsical spirit had persisted. In deadpan fashion, *One*'s Dal McIntire noted that "Race-baiter John Wilson Hamilton, . . . Editor of *The White Sentinel*, was arrested & charged with sodomy . . . in connection with [a] 15-yr-old boy." Officials of the magazine "*Modern Man* were fined $50 each . . . for desecration of the flag by publishing a photo of a nude partially flagdraped," McIntire reported, but not for "selling obscene literature," having argued that "their nude photos were comparable to those painted by old masters." Tracking little squabbles that defined culture as much as big ones, McIntire reported that Beverly Hills police ordered an art store to remove a "replica of Michelangelo's statue of David" from its window, but "the owner protested that Europeans bring their children hundreds of miles to see these statues, which stand in the streets." That is, the magazines showed how battles over queerness pivoted on race, gender, and history, not on some freestanding homosexuality alone.[15]

Like their antagonists, gay magazines' editors and writers viewed culture as a vital battleground. The "average" homosexual's "basic problem . . . is not his conflict with the law, but his conflict with prevailing community ideals," *One* maintained. That claim reflected a comfort with the law that many men lacked and a disdain for "sickly irresponsibles who live the schizoid life of promiscuity." But it gave *One* reason to address culture astutely and extensively. Unlike antagonists who saw cultural decline in censorship's demise or optimists who saw inexorable progress, *One* spotted "a precarious freedom" hardly "yet near the freedom that permitted Shakespeare to dedicate love sonnets to a youth." It did not take progress for granted—it had to be fought for. It shrewdly refuted its enemies' accusations, among them that homosexuals sought "to filch a little vicarious glory or simply to excuse their own 'nasty habits' by counting many of the great in on the fraternity." All groups search for heroes, *One* observed. "Need Americans feel ashamed of admiring Jefferson, Washington, Lincoln, etc.?" *One* ridiculed both those who disparaged and those who exaggerated queer creativity. An FBI agent, it reported, found that " 'one rather definite index of homosexuality' is that 'almost without fail, all of them, both male and female, are exceptionally brilliant people.' " "Not just brilliant. Exceptionally brilliant!" *One* added. It suggested that stereotypes about gay creativity owed to others' anxiety.[16]

One's playful combativeness informed its response to a diatribe against "sissy" composers that captured the queer-baiting frenzy. Writing for *Fact*, a short-lived magazine from porn publisher Ralph Ginzburg, "female concert manager" Anna Frankenheimer offered "A Much-Needed Upbraiding of Long-Hair Music" and an "intriguing explanation of why American concert music has become sissified." Citing the 1948 arrest for sodomy of *New York Herald Tribune* critic Jerome Bohn, Frankenheimer also fingered English conductor Sir Eugene Goossens and American composer Marc Blitzstein as gay. For her, "homosexuals—by definition—possess infantile, unstable personalities" and "form closely-knit, powerful cliques in the professions." Frankenheimer proffered a standard list of fields "they succeed in penetrating." In concert music they maintained a "world-wide fraternity 'the homintern,' " which included critics Virgil Thomson ("a confirmed bachelor"), the *Times*'s Harold Schonberg ("an unusual critic—he is married"), "nasty, bitter old women like [the *Chicago Tribune*'s Claudia] Cassidy," and *Musical America* editor John Ardoin. As for concert managers, their "fluttering enthusiasms . . . their constant little excitements, and their current favorites among the artists dominate their actions." Among unhealthy results was stardom for pianist Van Cliburn, whose success in the 1958 Moscow competition she attributed to Soviet manipulation, claiming that Russian cellist Mstislav Rostropovich "said to an American colleague, 'We knew Cliburn was no great talent, but we thought it would be politically opportune to show that we can be friends.' " Frankenheimer also restated familiar contradictions. It was unclear how "infantile, unstable" people operated "powerful cliques" or how neutered "sissies" did so much "penetrating," a word implying phallic potency.

More baldly than most who deplored the homintern, Frankenheimer held queers responsible for the alleged shallowness and artificiality of the American arts. The "homintern," she argued, "has created an atmosphere of loose integrity and distorted values, and has severely sabotaged the position of serious music in America." Somehow, it was responsible for the fact that America "has the lowest per-capita attendance of classical music in the Western World," even though "the public rejects the hoaxes foisted on it by the homintern." Homosexuals may be "talented" and should be "free to practice their talents," but with an exception. "We do not intentionally appoint homosexuals as principals of boys' schools. . . . By the same token, and with as much vigilance, they should be prevented from entering fields in which they can affect the fate of others—like music criticism." But not just critics disturbed her. She was also alarmed "that 10 of the 12 leading American composers of serious music are homosexual."[17]

"And who in the hell are the 2 odd ones?" quipped *One* in response. So well understood was gay dominance among American composers that no extended response was necessary to "a silly article" by a woman "screaming hysterically," except to point out correctly "that U.S. music has never before been rated so high by the world. And what would it be rated WITHOUT the 10?" *Fact*'s articles drew virulent responses. About a piece on Barry Goldwater, one reader fumed to Ginzburg: "You irresponsible kike. . . . If I had you on my ranch, I'd castrate you like I do my pigs." A rejoinder to Frankenheimer pointed to "all the nonsense going around about the Commie conspiracy, the Negro conspiracy, and the Jewish conspiracy," and added that "we are *not* a 'we.' One homosexual cannot always, or even usually recognize another." Another reader dismissed "so minor a field . . . as serious music, when the power of the 'homintern' in *every* field is so great," endangering national security and reminding him of how "the well-known proverb of the Infantry goes, 'It's not who you know, it's who you blow.' " By those standards, *One* occupied the high ground.[18]

The *Fact* fracas reflected changes that stoked the frenzy about queers in the arts. One change was a sharpening politics of identity, most manifest in African American activism but also among other social groups, including gay people. A more raucous style also characterized public discourse, prompted in part by resurgent conservatism—climaxed in 1964 by Goldwater's run against Lyndon Johnson for the presidency—and a fissuring liberalism facing the pressures of black activism and war in Southeast Asia. And although the great power conflict remained intense, the hunt for communists at home diminished, leaving queers more alone to face the anticonspiracy strains of American life, especially since left-ists, liberals, and conservatives alike still embraced antihomosexuality.

The Politics of Authenticity

Frenzy in culture owed a good deal to frenzy in politics, with the two realms more enmeshed than ever. Under presidents John Kennedy and Lyndon Johnson, liberals conducted no antigay campaign on the scale of the Lavender Scare waged mostly by conservatives. But their antigay animus ran deep and their hold on power was fragile — Kennedy was elected by a tiny margin, a conservative GOP–Southern Democratic coalition still ran Congress, and liberals' success as Cold Warriors was contested. In response to those challenges, liberals portrayed right-wingers as sexually perverse fanatics, a tactic as telling as it was dangerous. Politics gave new urgency to the theme of queer duplicity and disguise.

Antigay activity surged in the early 1960s. Although Washington, D.C., featured a legal and political challenge to federal antigay practices of hiring and firing, it yielded few results. At the state and local level, the picture was also bleak despite a few changes like Illinois's repeal of its sodomy law. Police raids on bars and arrests of queers on sex or "indecency" charges swelled, a predictable response to media alarm about the "Growth of Overt Homosexuality," as the *Times* had put it. The Florida legislature launched an inquisition into homosexuality, and in the South generally, queer-baiting of civil rights activists flourished, unleashing an overt politics of homosexuality where it had scarcely existed. Politicians continued to froth about homosexuality, pressing, often in alliance with religious groups, for municipal and statewide cleanups. On the far right, the American Nazi Party's George Lincoln Rockwell asserted that "Hitler had trouble with the same kind of filth and had to shoot [Ernst] Roehm, the leader of the gang. When it can be done legally, I will not hesitate to do the same thing."[19]

Major films reflected dominant liberal attitudes. A notable instance was Otto Preminger's *Advise and Consent* (1962), based on a Pulitzer Prize–winning novel (1959) by Allen Drury, a *New York Times* reporter and probably a gay man. Plodding in prose, tedious in detail, endless in length, the novel and the movie were dismissed by some highbrow critics as melodrama. But both commanded large audiences, captured elements of contemporary politics, and became reference points for real-life controversies.

The film had to depart sharply from the novel to work as a liberal tract.

In both, young Senator Brig Anderson (Don Murray in the film) harbors a
secret — his World War II love affair with another man — learned by black-
mailers, who are angry that he opposes Senate ratification of the president's nomination of Robert Leffingwell to be secretary of state. In the
novel, Leffingwell and other liberals collude in the blackmail of Anderson, driving him to suicide. In the film, casting Henry Fonda as Leffingwell lent him a dignity missing in the novel, and liberals' collusion in
blackmail shrinks largely to the single character of Senator Ackerman, a
cartoon lefty, while others utter lofty sentiments, their stance toward Brig
merely pitying. The film ends by emphasizing the majesty of the Senate
and the presidency, shunting aside Brig's story and his death. Compared
to the novel, it let liberals off the hook of homophobia, repositioned them
as enlightened, and recast homosexuals as troubled and self-loathing.

Brig was therefore also changed. In the novel, he is a married father
with a handsome face the cameras love, but he is no self-hating queer.
His deception about his queer past plays off against Leffingwell's deception about his communist past, and Drury makes clear that Leffingwell's
deceit endangers the nation, but Brig's is merely a practical necessity.
The film shows Brig recoiling at what he sees inside Club 602 in New
York, suggesting that his shame as a homosexual leads to his suicide.
That scene is absent from the novel, which instead attributes Brig's suicide to his impossible personal and political situation. In print, Brig, far
from repudiating his wartime romance, remembers it warmly. "For four
weeks he was happy, and he was unsparing enough in his honesty with
himself to realize that it was a perfectly genuine happiness." Although
marriage gave him satisfactions, he recognized "that the happiness he
wanted would never come with Mabel." Brig "was a good father, a good
if temporarily troubled husband, a good servant, a good Senator, and a
good man; and central to all this, in a way he understood thoroughly in
his own nature, was the episode [with his lover] in Honolulu." That episode, far from impeding his later success, was the very source of it, and
"he did not regret that it had happened." When his wife finally learns
the truth and protests "such a horrible thing," Brig responds, "It didn't
seem horrible at the time . . . and I am not going to say now that it did,
even to you." As his suicidal gun goes off, "he realized that it was not
only of his family that he was thinking as he died. It was of a beach in
Honolulu on a long, hot, lazy afternoon. The waves crashed and he heard
for the last time the exultant cries of the surf riders, far out." The prose
lamely echoed the Burt Lancaster–Deborah Kerr Hawaii beach scene in
From Here to Eternity (1953), but it also stoutly defended queer love. Al-

though the obligatory suicide occurs, it is triggered not by Brig's shame but by his stubborn pride in that love—roughly the opposite of the film's groaning plot mechanism.[20]

Advise and Consent also linked homosexuality to the nation's empire, but again the film departed from the novel. Politicians often suggested that queers threatened American empire, but in Drury's novel the threat arises not from Brig's sexuality but from others who cannot deal with it or who choose to exploit it. Brig is the honest figure—true to himself and his past—even though he has a secret. The film, making Brig's suicide the product of his revulsion at his own kind, shifts the balance from Brig to others who must deal with his "tired old sin." Hollywood earlier had erased or obscured queerness, but *Advise* pumped it up (albeit using euphemisms—"tired old sin"), wrapping antipathy to it inside a thin veneer of pity for it. It thereby distanced liberals from overt antihomosexuality, while sanctioning its practice, and endowed them with tolerance, rationality, and virility.

Doomsday films, some made in collusion with the White House, pitted level-headed liberals against perverse right-wingers who endanger national sanity and safety. Popularizing intellectual theories of authoritarian McCarthyism and cultural associations between fascism and homosexuality, these films traced right-wing fervor to the sexlessness or perversity of pivotal characters. John Frankenheimer offered the most complex version of Hollywood sexual liberalism. At once satire, warning, and thriller, *The Manchurian Candidate* (1962) placed a devouring mother (Angela Lansbury) at the center of a nefarious plot, manipulating her brainwashed son (Laurence Harvey) and scheming with both communists and her corporate mogul husband to assassinate the president and take over the nation. It was hard to tell whether the film spoofed "momism" or invited dread of it. In a more straightforward style, *Fail-Safe* (Sidney Lumet, 1964) showed a seething, girl-less military officer (Fritz Weaver) ordering an American nuclear assault on the Soviet Union. Staunch liberals avert further disaster by agreeing to nuke New York City in return for Moscow's incineration. They are good married men who make gutsy decisions: the president (Henry Fonda) sacrifices his wife, who is visiting New York, to world peace. Right-wing crazies risk destroying the republic and the world. Heterosexual liberals save both.

Seven Days in May (1964), another Frankenheimer film, located danger higher up the chain of command. The villain is Air Force general and Joint Chiefs of Staff chairman James Mattoon Scott (Burt Lancaster)—one prototype was General Curtis LeMay, who commanded the bombing

of Japan in World War II and served as Air Force Chief of Staff in the early
1960s. Scott schemes with the other Joint Chiefs and assorted civilians to
overthrow the republic and initiate nuclear war with Russia. Their osten-
sible motivation: President Jordan Lyman (Frederic March) has secured
a nuclear disarmament treaty with the Soviets that Scott claims will dis-
arm America, much as President Kennedy had secured a modest 1963
treaty limiting nuclear weapons tests. Casting Lancaster as Scott made
him larger-than-life and formidably masculine, but he is also girl-less and
sexless—he is never pictured with a woman, although he is married. The
film hints at a dark secret about a failed affair he once had with Eleanor
Holbrook (Ava Gardner)—"He really never felt anything," Holbrook recalls. "Everything was calculated"—leaving his perversity unspecified.
Viewers see Scott seated before models of U.S. rockets—symbols of phallic power but not the real thing, which, the scene suggests, Scott lacks.
His passion is not for women but for fanatical patriotism.

Set against Scott are Colonel "Jigs" Casey (Kirk Douglas), a robustly
heterosexual hero who uncovers Scott's plot, and bourbon-swilling senator Ray Clark (Edmund O'Brien), who has a heart of gold, an eye for
girls, and fierce loyalty to President Lyman. The senator offers the most
striking moment in the film's sexual politics when he tells one officer,
"right now the government is sitting on top of the Washington Monument, right at the point"—an odd image of both precarious balance and
Scott's impending queer rape of the Republic. To underline right-wing
girl-lessness, a boozy broad in a Texas bar laments that the guys at a
nearby base that Scott secretly established never show up: "All those men
sitting up in the desert seeing no girls" makes her wonder what the world
has come to. Finally confronted by the president, Scott charges, "you're
a *criminally* weak sister" for cozying up to the Russians. But the president has the nerve to crush the coup, his own weak sisters abandon Scott,
and the sexually psychotic patriot—a "strutting egoist" in the president's
phrase—abruptly gives up.

Grounded in perverse sexuality, cinematic right-wingers' patriotism
was shrill, histrionic, and insubstantial. It was dangerous, but also pathetic once its affectations collapsed and its sick inner core was exposed.
It was the sort of patriotism, some liberals believed, that made Goldwater
the GOP presidential nominee in 1964 and LeMay the running mate of
George Wallace on their third-party ticket in 1968. It was not so much dishonest as unhealthy—lacking genuine understanding of the Constitution
and nuclear war—in part because it derived from sexual ill health. Liberals were psychologically and sexually healthy, and therefore politically

virtuous. They were like Kennedy and his advisers in the Cuban missile crisis, who presumably averted nuclear war by making nail-biting decisions and staring down the Soviets. Earlier, *Vital Center* liberalism had associated homosexuality with progressivism and communism. 1960s cinematic liberalism attached it to the right wing. The constant was in figuring liberals as virile men who had the country's interests at heart.

Stanley Kubrick's *Dr. Strangelove or: How I Learned to Stop Worrying and Love the Bomb* (1964) was so wicked a satire on these stock types that it disrupted Hollywood liberalism. Once again a perverted officer—General Jack D. Ripper (Sterling Hayden), obsessed with his "precious bodily fluids" and pawing at Colonel Mandrake's knee—launches a nuclear attack on the Soviet Union. Once again, Washington ponders how to prevent all-out war. But this time all parties are sexually weird and politically dangerous. No cool-headed heterosexual offsets the deluded general: the president (Peter Sellers) is a neutered blank, General "Buck" Turgidson (George C. Scott) confuses the "blast-off" of rockets with the "blast-off" of sex, and Dr. Strangelove (Peter Sellers again), a crippled former Nazi scientist, regards nuclear Armageddon as the ultimate orgasm, his arm given to sexually ecstatic salutes to the Führer. *Dr. Strangelove* can be read as suggesting that American (and Soviet) technological madness derived from sexual madness—from passions that men displace into fantasies of nuclear orgy. Just as plausibly, however, *Dr. Strangelove* mocked the liberals' claim that danger lay with perverse right-wingers and mocked the very effort, fashionable in the 1960s, to trace nuclear danger to unruly sexual passions. Given that demented sexuality defines all the film's characters, it either explains everything or nothing.

Like all Hollywood constructions of masculinity, the 1960s liberal version seethed with tensions. Right-wing fanatics are disturbingly girl-less, but virile liberals are often contemptuous of women. Rabid patriotism is frightening, but cool rationality still leads *Fail-Safe*'s president to destroy New York City. And as if liberal rationality was a tough sell, filmmakers spiked it up with earthier types—Edmund O'Brien's boozing senator and Kirk Douglas's jut-jawed officer in *Seven Days*.

Antiqueer politics surged not only in film but in reality during 1964. In June, *Life* examined "Homosexuality in America," and, although noting various voices, it peddled familiar antipathy and familiar contradictions: queers are hard to detect yet are "openly admitting, even flaunting their deviation." They disguise and distort—gay men make a dishonest claim to masculinity—but also reveal themselves. They live in a "sad and often sordid world" yet possess remarkable power. "Do the homosexuals, like the Communists, intend to bury us?" asked *Life* writer, Ernest Havemann (he suggested that few probably did).[21] Goldwater added to the frenzied sexual politics. Addressing fears of Soviet rocketry and Kennedy's decision to send Americans to the moon, he declared, "I don't want to hit the moon. I want to lob one into the men's room of the Kremlin and make sure I hit it."[22] Seen one way, this was a conventional conservative stand, promising victory rather than mere containment in the Cold War. But the odd image suggested more: the Kremlin men's room as site of a dangerous sexuality and source of rockets that could now "penetrate," the era's operative verb, U.S. defenses. Good heterosexuals must destroy it and weak-kneed liberals flinched at rooting it out, Goldwater suggested.

Amid liberals' efforts to locate perversity on the lunatic fringe and following Goldwater's attempt to put it in the Kremlin men's room, the Walter Jenkins scandal exploded.[23] Jenkins, a Catholic married father of six children and devoted chief of staff to President Johnson, was arrested on 7 October 1964, in a Washington, D.C., YMCA men's room on charges, which he did not contest, of performing "indecent gestures" — having sex with another man. Quickly hospitalized, he resigned. The White House explained that he was a loyal family man and national servant who succumbed to stress and exhaustion, not to intrinsic queerness.

Like earlier queer scandals, this one arose at a tense moment in the Cold War — just after the Tonkin Gulf incidents that justified escalation of the American war in Vietnam and days before Nikita Khrushchev's overthrow in the Soviet Union. But unlike past scandals, this one erupted with no preparatory rumor-mongering, during a bitter contest for the presidency, and with the president's closest confidant involved. Only rumors had swirled around Charles Bohlen, but uncontested facts attached to Jenkins: he had sex with other men. The Sumner Welles matter had been kept quiet, but this one was glaringly public. Liberals suddenly found perversity in their camp. And the line between politics and culture remained permeable — Jenkins, *Newsweek* reported, had invested $900 in a stage production of *Advise and Consent*.[24]

Suspicions were lavish. LBJ and his confidants suspected that political extremists had set up Jenkins for arrest, as if they believed the plots of cinematic thrillers. Perhaps Jenkins's sexual partner was a communist agent, GOP trickster, or dupe in a Goldwater scheme. This "could have been a big frame-up, big lie by fascists and neo-Nazis," Tommy Corcoran, a veteran Democratic wheeler-dealer, eagerly suggested to Johnson. LBJ suspected Goldwater: "They framed him [Jenkins]," he told one publisher; Goldwater "is a whole lot more evil than McCarthy. You just wait." The FBI also suspected a setup. But efforts to unearth one from the right or the left came to naught.[25]

Jenkins's authenticity obviously was in doubt—had he lived a lie, a queer man disguised as a loving father and friend? But White House conduct also raised questions. By presenting Jenkins as a lapsed heterosexual —and apparently a lapsed Catholic—it sought to counter any notion that it had harbored a real queer, but what was heterosexuality if Jenkins could fake it? The official claim that Jenkins was a troubled heterosexual was widely doubted and Johnson's honesty, morality, and virility widely mocked: LBJ's campaign motto, "All the Way with LBJ," reappeared as "Either Way with LBJ"; "LBJ for Moral Decay" signs appeared on the campaign trail; and wags wondered if LBJ would stand "behind" Jenkins. Suspicion readily slid from Jenkins to Johnson. Stern advice to LBJ to appear in public with Lady Bird and their two daughters in tow, embodying the "American family," revealed fears that the president looked vulnerable, as if what Betty Friedan called the "murky smog" of homosexuality now enveloped him.[26]

Although scripted for publication, the claim that Jenkins had succumbed to stress was also fervently believed in the White House. "I guess we've all been tired in our lives," Johnson opined to one publisher. "I've had a few drinks in my life and [then] I want to call up *my* girlfriend." Lady Bird told Lyndon that the incident "can only be a small—a period of nervous breakdown." Abe Fortas assured LBJ, "I just think the man went off his rocker."[27] They were desperate to believe that Jenkins had not fooled them. Their affection for "Walter" was genuine. But their public use of stress to explain Jenkins's behavior risked backfiring. During a cold war and against the background of doomsday films, the notion that an important figure could succumb to stress was hardly comforting: was not that, the films instructed, what crazy right-wingers did, not cool-headed liberals? And was not all of Washington under stress, in which case who else might go berserk? "It is startling to me that dedication and overwork in behalf of our Nation could lead to perversion," read one letter to LBJ, citing World War II leaders who "were pushed almost beyond physical and mental endurance during the great War. Yet they emerged with integrity and moral fibre beyond reproach." "Most of us are constantly subjected to tremendous pressures and overwork. Does this give us license to commit illegal acts?" asked one woman.[28]

Excess—of appetites, mannerisms, effeminacy—had long been attributed to homosexuals, but now, Lee Edelman suggests, it haunted LBJ. He already had a well-earned reputation as a man of towering rage, will, and appetite. Had Jenkins—who "would walk 'on his hands and knees on broken glass to avoid giving President Johnson any problem,' " as *Newsweek* quoted an FBI report—succumbed to excessive devotion to Johnson, or to LBJ's excessive demands?[29] A private measure of Johnson's excess was his intense fear that the Jenkins affair might cost him the election.

That excess got blurted out before TV cameras. "I was shocked," LBJ commented about Jenkins, "as if someone had told me my wife had murdered her daughter." In this "loaded act of cross-gender figuration," as Edelman calls it, LBJ did remarkable cultural work in remarkably few words.[30] He likened Jenkins to his wife, suggested the homoerotic closeness of a relationship that he wanted to downplay, and compared Jenkins to a murderer, inflating Jenkins's misdeeds and calling up the stereotype of the homosexual murderer even as he was denying that Jenkins was queer. He also made women the ultimate culprits, suggested his wife's betrayal (privately, she defended Jenkins), and disowned his own daughter ("her daughter"—his wife's—not his). All this as the White House tried to promote LBJ's "American family"! To be sure, Johnson was trying to convey his "shock" and his ignorance of Jenkins's awful secret. But in that effort he got ensnared in a web of significations. What was his own heterosexual authority if his chief of staff was like a wife to him and his family so dysfunctional that his wife could murder her daughter?

Most likely, his fears of his legitimacy as president fueled this bizarre statement. He worried that others saw him as an illegitimate president for having gained office through JFK's assassination and for lacking JFK's cool grasp of politics, policy, and ideas: for being a fake JFK, at a time when fakery was routinely assigned to homosexuals and Jenkins seemed guilty of it. Questions about Jenkins so much slipped into ones about Johnson as to panic him. No moment better exposed how allegations of queers' fraudulence displaced fears of fraudulence among others.

Like most queer scandals, the Jenkins affair waned quickly. The affair left few traces amid the exaltation over LBJ's crushing election victory and the rush of decisions for war in Vietnam over the winter of 1965. If fraudulence had slipped from the homosexual to the heterosexual—from Jenkins to Johnson—the slippage soon reversed: LBJ had his presidency legitimately and showed his manly determination to take on the commies, if not in the Kremlin's men's room. But it had been a near miss.

Concerns about authenticity evident in the Jenkins affair had long vexed Americans, but they surged in the mid-twentieth century, partly in reaction to technological changes. Daniel Boorstin suggested as much in

The Image: A Guide to Pseudo-Events in America (1961), which he prefaced with Max Frisch's definition of technology as "the knack of so arranging the world that we don't have to experience it." The filters between self and experience—"the thicket of unreality which stands between us and the facts of life," as Boorstin put it—seemed to make the self harder to discern. Modernity fractured and occluded it in dizzying ways.[31]

Anxiousness about that fragmentation was measured by frequent use of the terms "authenticity" and "artifice." Those terms defined much cultural work in the 1960s, as Howard Brick argues, and the key role in American life played by queer people, as George Chauncey suggests. At play, Brick notes, were both "devotion to the ideal of authenticity—of discovering, voicing, and exercising a genuine whole personality freed from the grip of mortifying convention—and fascination with the ways of artifice, with the calculated techniques of image making or 'the games people play.'" The quest for genuineness "implied an anti-institutional animus," an "assertive individuality," and "a view that aesthetic conventions" hid real-life truths. But applying such criteria was difficult, since what one person claimed as genuine another might see as fake, and artifice might express something genuine.[32]

In a use particularly applied to, and sometimes by, queer people, "authenticity" meant the transparent alignment of public and private selves —a refusal to disguise the latter with the former. That meaning was often found in the popular arts: "Main forms of popular music—jazz, folk, blues, and rock'n'roll—all conveyed an ethos of authenticity," Brick observes, "resting on the idea that musicians expressed feelings deeply rooted in themselves." Divining the hidden "feelings deeply rooted" in others seemed a burden especially imposed on subordinate groups. As James Baldwin wrote about the black man's efforts to see the hollowness of white liberalism, "In order to save his life, he is forced to look beneath appearances, to take nothing for granted, to hear the meaning behind the words." Gay men and women often employed a similar strategy of survival, Donald Webster Cory had suggested, their antennae decoding others' words and stances.[33]

Several circumstances fueled anxiety about authenticity at mid-century—depersonalizing technologies, racial conflict and civil rights activism, and postwar affluence. Critics worried that mass-produced goods and images were cheapening American life, erasing social distinctions, debasing America's image abroad, or luring Americans away from fundamental values. The Cold War gave this anxiety much of its specificity and intensity: a tawdry mass culture hardly seemed likely to win

Americans the respect of others. To be sure, American affluence was another weapon to be deployed, as Vice President Richard Nixon did in Moscow in his "kitchen debate" with Premier Nikita Khrushchev in 1959. But Nixon's bragging risked defining America by homogenized affluence and soulless technology, whereas the Cold War put a premium on displaying a more deeply rooted American culture.

Seen as the transparent alignment of public and private selves, authenticity bore the imprint of analysis and psychology, which instructed Americans to see much simmering and scheming beneath the surfaces that people displayed. Commentary about queers was one vehicle for that instruction: experts promised to strip away gay people's disguises and expose their interiors. Those experts believed that difficulties arose for individuals who ignored or defiantly defended the rupture between private and public self—who failed to be true to the self. In mild forms, that rupture included the "other-directed" person, explored by critics like David Riesman, who might not even recognize an inner self, or the young person groping for an "identity," as Erik Erikson explained, or the housewife who feigned contentment, as Betty Friedan pointed out. Experts stressed the costs of trying to "fit in" and "get along"—the splitting of public and private selves.

Homosexuality was a rich playing field for contemporary concerns about that splitting. Queer people were portrayed as peculiarly prone to disguise, deception, and trickery—to masks, above all the mask of gender. Jews, blacks, and other social groups also elicited suspicion, but their presence seemed at least familiar, and gender was not the main realm of their imagined trickery. Homosexuality functioned as a blank screen on which to project all manner of artifice—from the showy emptiness of women's fashion to disturbing trends in prose, music, painting, and theater—under the simple logic that unwholesome people produced insubstantial creations. Their power helped to explain why American culture often seemed to lack the muscle, integrity, and seriousness to impress the world. The problem was no lack of intrinsic American strength, but subversion of that strength from within. The notion of a homintern emphasized queers' alien nature, echoing contemporary notions of organized crime (*The Enemy Within* (1960), in Robert Kennedy's formulation) and communism.

Queers served another projective purpose: by implication, they subverted civic equality and melting-pot liberalism. The concentration of social groups in various fields of work and business—Jews in physics or Hollywood, the Irish in politics or police work—was an utterly familiar aspect of American life, but one rendered peculiar and dangerous regarding homosexuals in fashion or the arts. Postwar culture and politics portrayed the ethnic enclave as an "affront to consensus" and "an anachronism" being dissolved by "assimilation and upward mobility."[34] But unlike virtuous ethnics, homosexuals, it seemed, refused to assimilate or were incapable of doing so, sticking instead to their stealthy cliques. In that way they resembled ethnic mobsters of organized crime — one reason that "homosexual mafia" gained resonance. That impression rendered melting-pot liberalism otherwise faultless and exempted other groups from failing to live up to it.

Queer people were also agents of debate, not just objects of projection. For one thing, they struggled with each other over these matters. Did rebellion or respectability reveal the true homosexual? Did cross-gender behavior express genuine queer distinctiveness or hide the genuine self? In the language of authenticity, "homosexual men and women everywhere" were enjoined "to throw off their fears and 'become real men and real women, as is our right,'" as one group was told before setting off to Europe on "the first all-gay excursion ever to be undertaken."[35]

As artists, gay people were inevitably engaged in defining authenticity, sometimes sweepingly. For Baldwin, nearly all Americans lacked it. He was "struck, in America, by an emotional poverty so bottomless, and a terror of human life, of human touch, so deep, that virtually no American appears able to achieve any viable, organic connection between his public stance and his private life."[36] For those attacked as purveyors of artifice to claim to define authenticity infuriated others. It roiled the waters further that some queers relished artificiality in the campiness of their lives or their creations. More visibly queer than his contemporaries, Pop Artist Andy Warhol, who gained enormous attention in the 1960s, produced repetitive images of artifacts like Campbell's soup cans that seemed to their detractors to be the epitome of artificiality. What if, such artists seemed to ask, genuineness was easily faked and "artifice had its own authenticity," as Howard Brick writes of Pop Art?[37] And what if its inventors' very lives were performed, contrived? To those who wanted culture embedded in the immutable — of gender, sexuality, religion, patriotism, or other qualities — the performative character of queer lives and creations was maddening.

But queer artists of almost any aesthetic were attacked as creators of the twisted and the artificial. Many observers disparaged the entire type. Anna Frankenheimer dismissed all the disparate "sissy" composers. Artists given to flamboyant artifice in personal demeanor and creative product—Truman Capote or Andy Warhol—were not necessarily even the most disturbing. They could be seen, after all, as practicing a perverse honesty: they were creatively true to their insubstantial selves. Queers who defined apparent fundamentals of American life—the nationalism of mid-century concert music, ballet, and dance, for example—were at least as vexing, for they seized the core of culture while others only staked out its fringes, and their appearance, often conventionally manly, disguised their hidden selves. In eliciting exasperation, the fact that queers did the defining was as telling as the definitions they offered, which might be quite conventional (as Baldwin defined masculinity, "a man without balls is not a man").[38] They were magnets for anxiety over America's cultural authenticity, with their presumed penchant for artifice and disguise of their true selves evidence of their fraudulence.

Frenzy in the Arts

Frenzy about queer artists erupted in the context of these rising concerns about authenticity. In commentary that peaked at mid-decade, major arts critics and others judged those artists, especially in the theater, to be untrue to themselves, subversive of cultural vitality, and bent on controlling the arts. Their attacks brought the homintern discourse to a climax, but the variety of the voices involved also signaled its impending disruption.

Changes in Cold War cultural competition played a key role. Soviet-American competition initially had been an indirect one for the allegiances of peoples wavering between the superpowers. By the late 1950s, with the Cold War stalemated and the arms race accelerating, leaders in both powers promoted direct competition—each sending its artists and artifacts into the other's homeland—while the waning of McCarthyism removed one obstacle on the American side to cultural exchange. Proponents of exchange were divided about whether it was another way to wage the Cold War or a new way to settle it through mutual peace and understanding. But either way, it seemed preferable to the brushfire wars already raging or the nuclear war that might break out. Both views of cultural competition informed the U.S.-Soviet Cultural Agreement of 1958, regarded by its historian as "one of the most successful initiatives in the history of U.S. cold war diplomacy."[39] Both views surfaced again at the American National Exhibition in Moscow in 1959. The space race also showcased competing cultural and technological systems. Satellites, tractors, scientists, musicians, even the kitchen sink in Nixon's case during the "kitchen debate," were thrown into the new battle, with large meanings attached to Van Cliburn's victory in the 1958 Tchaikovsky contest, the American visits of Soviet musicians, and trips to Russia like Aaron Copland's in 1960.

Eisenhower was largely responsible for the shift to direct cultural exchange, but Kennedy got credit for it. Despite stereotypes about Ike's cultural tin ear and JFK's cultural savvy, federal support for tours abroad by U.S. orchestras "dropped away under the Democrats," Leonard Bernstein's biographer notes. Eisenhower defended the U.S. exhibit at Moscow against fierce criticism that it included art by "pro-communists," as Senator Strom Thurmond called them. Given American criticism of the Soviet ban on the Boris Pasternak novel *Doctor Zhivago*, Ike hardly wanted "the Pasternak thing in reverse."[40] Eager to show that Harvard produced better cultural Cold Warriors than West Point, the Kennedy White House welcomed performers and artists, celebrating American creativity and its own youthful vitality. Eisenhower was eager to show off America to the world, Kennedy to show off to America.

In this new stage of cultural struggle, Americans still displayed a familiar mix of confidence and anxiety. They trumpeted their apparent freedom. Compared to what they learned of Soviet repression, "U.S. culture didn't look so bad," as one historian notes. Turning artists into emblems of freedom, "Cold Warriors promoted avant-garde art because they saw in the work the expression of the 'unique and rebellious life' that distinguished the 'free world' from the Communist world." In this new mood, the black singer/actor/activist Paul Robeson found the ban on his international travel lifted, while Copland, blacklisted in Washington early in the 1950s, found a welcome in the Kennedy White House. Anxiety did persist that New World culture fell short of Old World sophistication, or, among right-wingers, that cultural exchange was a communist trick. Soviet authorities were also ambivalent about such exchange; the music critic for *Sovetskaya Kultura* condemned Bernstein's 1959 Moscow lecture and concert on modern music—music that the Soviet Union banned—for "putting on a show called 'Leonard Bernstein Is Lifting the Iron Curtain.'" But to leaders in both countries, much seemed to hinge on what Americans or Soviets displayed, whether to their enemies or to their own citizens. In that spirit, in 1962 Samuel Barber became the first American composer to attend the Congress of Soviet Composers (he also lunched with Khrushchev). Speaking to the group as a Cold War liberal, Barber found common ground in the challenge they faced but warned "that there could never be a five-year plan for talent." Especially in music—the richest field for Soviet-American exchange—gay figures played leading roles in the intensified competition and incipient thaw that now marked the Cold War.[41]

Gay artists met no fatal challenge to their role as cultural ambassadors and exemplars insofar as they served as American artists, not gay ones, but suspicion continued. "When the Russian dancers toured here," *One* magazine noted, "several butcho press hacks emphasized that these male dancers, unlike our own, were real males." Sydney Harris, in his widely syndicated column, claimed that "many spectators were surprised at the virility of the [Russian] male dancers . . . ruggedly masculine, and no non-sense about it. American and English dancers, on the contrary, are notoriously lacking in the masculine virtues: with very few exceptions, they are frustrated ballerinas." As Harris viewed it, "The cultural patterns of a nation determine which activities are taken up by what sort of people." In Russia, there is "nothing at all 'sissified'" about dancing, but in America dance attracts "merely the 'sensitive' and willowy young men." Harris expressed typical anxiousness about Americans' ability to compete with the Soviets. "We get the kind of arts we invite," ones "crowded with men of dubious gender, because as a nation we are making a false separation between every-day living and the arts." As a result, "virile young men are shamed out of their early interest" in the arts and "the vacuum" gets "filled by the deviates—some of them with talent, but more of them merely seeking to create a closed and comfy society of their own." Harris tied American insufficiency to queer effeminacy and conspiracy. *One* offered several rejoinders, among them that "if Mr. Harris thinks virility can be judged from a distance, he should investigate the sexual proclivities of the wrestlers, actors, marines, marlboro men and football players who set the pace of this masculinity jazz."[42]

A rejoinder of a different sort came a year later, in 1961, with the sensational defection in Paris of Soviet ballet star Rudolf Nureyev. The Western press heterosexualized the moment, citing "romance" and "a red-haired girl" as key to his defection. American dancers might be suspect, but no refugee from Soviet oppression was to be queer, and Nureyev's ballyhooed dancing partnership with Margot Fonteyn after his defection helped preserve the illusion. But Fonteyn was twenty years his senior and the Soviet government knew otherwise, as Nureyev hinted in his ghosted 1962 autobiography. Soviet authorities had condemned his "'irresponsible' way of life" and "dangerous individualism"—code, for the knowing, about his homosexuality.[43]

Another complaint, about audiences rather than artists, also arose.

127

Writing in 1958 for the *New Republic*, Patrick Dennis found the characters in Tennessee Williams's *Something Unspoken* and *Suddenly, Last Summer* "woefully unpleasant and decidedly from the wrong side of Queer Street," making for "an evening of unrelenting horror." Dennis was the married but privately queer author of *Auntie Mame* (1955), and in one judgment "the first American writer to popularize High Camp," but he deplored not only Williams's version of camp but the "distressingly large percentage" of the audience "occupied by unescorted young men who protest sibilantly that Tennessee Williams is really writing about the norm." Perhaps his complaint reflected a growing queer presence in audiences, or perhaps it provided an outlet for his indignation about the plays or for his private struggles.[44]

A rash of complaints soon raised the profile of themes emerging since the 1940s. As earlier, scandal journalism and trade magazines often retailed these complaints. In 1962, for example, *Show Business Illustrated* lamented queer influence on the content of plays and urged "that it is time to speak openly and candidly" about the matter.[45] Entering the fray, the *New York Times* pretended that its critics were discovering the problem. *Times* critic Howard Taubman offered the standard pose of discovery and shock, promising in 1961 to write "openly and candidly" about a subject given to "sly whisperers and malicious gossips," which was "the increasing incidence and influence of homosexuality on New York's stage—and, indeed, in the other arts as well." Taubman praised playwrights, such as Williams in *Cat on a Hot Tin Roof*, who "did not dissimulate" and portrayed homosexuals "without meanness and snickers." But he disliked plays in which a "homosexual motif gets [a] heterosexual guise," as his article was subtitled. The "dissembling" that involves "the safe way of smuggling a touchy subject onto the stage by heterosexual masquerade" makes the audience sense "rot at the drama's core." Though not naming names, Taubman probably had in mind some of Williams's work, Noel Coward's, William Inge's, and Edward Albee's. The complaint was solely about men. Lorraine Hansberry, for example, who wrote the play *A Raisin in the Sun* (1959) and contributed to the *Ladder*, escaped notice in this context, with her race and gender, not her lesbianism, the object of attention.

Authenticity lay at the core of Taubman's complaint. Queer playwrights were untrue to themselves and deceiving to others—they "dissimulate." An absolutist view of the homosexual/heterosexual divide underlay that claim: those of one identity had nothing to say about the other—or, more likely, Taubman believed that queers only were disabled in this regard—and shared no common ground that they both might illuminate. Queers who crossed the divide were either poaching on territory they did not understand or smuggling their queer themes onto the stage. Either way, public self was misaligned with private identity. It was a strikingly literal view of that alignment, oblivious to how dramatists often imagined characters removed from their experience. And although attacking disguise, Taubman cared no more for the transparency of the novel *Advise and Consent*, whose "sympathetically described" gay senator "was a facile dramatic device, used without compelling force or overriding need." The language of authenticity suffused Taubman's complaint. Not only were queer dramatists suspect, but because of their "influence," the theater generally.

Ostensibly, Taubman condemned "the insidious result of unspoken taboos" against representing homosexuality, but his was a mixed message. Hardly "unspoken," the taboos had once been enforced by legal action and by critical disapproval splashed across New York's newspapers: Taubman was inventing a silence he now claimed to break. He deplored the "taboos," yet his language—"the infiltration of homosexual attitudes" yielded bizarre "intrusions" and "insidious" results—suggested his worry that their removal would yield something unpleasant and dangerous. Although calling for honesty by and about homosexuals, Taubman was prepared to judge the results sternly according to his ill-defined criteria about "compelling force or overriding need."

Since "there can be no blinking the fact that heterosexual audiences feel uncomfortable in the presence of truth-telling about sexual deviation," Taubman wanted an end to ambiguity, a truth-in-packaging rule: a play should be unequivocally about homosexuality, or not about it at all. The "taboos" would be lifted in order to ensure that homosexuality was labeled and contained. Taubman restated demands made by Bergler and others in the 1950s for surveillance that would not overtly silence queer dramatists but would clearly label them. What he wanted, as he wrote a few years later, was "Helpful Hints to Tell Appearances vs. Truth," as his article was titled. Most of the time it was fine that "the theatergoer is on his own," but there are "exceptions. Homosexuality this season, for example." Perhaps truth-in-packaging would help "uncomfortable" theatergoers avoid not only queer disguise but the gay audiences Dennis had scorned. Taubman did not acknowledge that being "uncomfortable" might be valuable for, even sought by, audiences.[46]

Commentary critic Wilfred Sheed laid out the themes of exposure and containment baldly in 1965. "It is obviously better to have this [homosexual] sensibility out in the open where we can see it" and help stanch any "heterosexual backlash." Sheed disliked two plays (one was Terrence McNally's *And Things That Go Bump in the Night*) whose "real story," as he saw it, found "the homosexual protagonist" inflicting "terrible vengeance on the square world," whose representative is "treated like a prisoner of war, who must pay personally for every atrocity real or imagined that his side has ever committed." Like Taubman, Sheed worried that queer themes emerged "in heterosexual guise." But the bigger problem was that homosexuality "has become part of the prevailing style" in drama and is "absorbed with barely a trace; certain homosexual mannerisms have become part of the reigning style (as they do at some English boarding schools, where you may find the captain of rugby flopping around like Oscar Wilde) with no one quite sure how it got there." Sheed repeated an old claim: queer influence was so pervasive that heterosexuals were unwittingly absorbing it and curiously powerless to resist it, as if too stupid to see the line or as tempted to cross it. Sheed wanted the line clearly drawn. He preferred having "the homosexual sensibility asserted openly in one play rather than sneaked into twenty. It would, if nothing else, leave a cleaner smell." For the gay "playwright to declare himself . . . would clearly be suicidal," but suicide was the price to pay for clarity.[47]

By the time of Taubman's "Helpful Hints" piece and Sheed's essay, Albee's *Who's Afraid of Virginia Woolf* (1962) had appeared, and, along with other Albee plays, it exacerbated critics' ire. Its famously bickering couple was often seen as a straight burlesque of the queer couple Albee really had in mind, an interpretation Albee heatedly rejected and one that sidestepped an obvious possibility: the play's George and Martha, after all, had the names of the nation's founding father and mother. *Who's Afraid* was a play about authenticity attacked for its alleged lack of it. George and Martha play many games and wear many masks and claw their desperate way beyond them, trying to discover some emotional truth about themselves and their sexual failure, whose only issue is an imagined child. The play could be glossed as having its own mask—queer characters in straight disguise—but it hardly had to be, and just as disturbing to some was Albee's cheek in thinking he could render heterosexuals. Fittingly, its movie version (Mike Nichols, 1966) starred the queen of queer-authored movies, Elizabeth Taylor, moving from Williams to the new gay star in drama.[48]

Taubman and Sheed were trying to implement surveillance too late in the game. Legal and informal censorship was crumbling, though not for want of efforts by the U.S. Post Office and often the courts to keep it in place, and the box office indicated that many theatergoers—who, of course, included gay women and men—were disinclined to avoid queer playwrights' work. Nor did suggestions by Taubman and Sheed that theatergoers were fooled by the playwrights' "disguise" ring true: there was too much talk about what lay behind the "disguise" for many to have been unsuspecting. Likewise, Taubman was rankly speculating—or projecting his discomfort—when he asserted "that heterosexual audiences feel uncomfortable in the presence of truth-telling about sexual deviation." Those audiences were diverse, with many reasons to seek "truth-telling"—morbid curiosity, prurient interest, eager puzzlement, or simply belief that a play was nifty. A sharp line between homosexual and heterosexual was no more possible in theater's audiences than in its content.

Critics nonetheless kept trying to draw the line. In the new left-liberal journal, the *New York Review of Books*, novelist Philip Roth furiously attacked Albee's *Tiny Alice* for "its tediousness, its pretentiousness, its galling sophistication, its gratuitous and easy symbolizing, its ghastly pansy rhetoric and repartee." Once again, disguise was the issue. "How long," Roth pleaded, "before a play is produced on Broadway in which the homosexual hero is presented as a homosexual, and not disguised as an *angst*-ridden priest, or an angry Negro, or an aging actress; or worst of all, Everyman?" The question itself erected a disguise: Roth gave no sign of interest in such a play.[49]

Similar themes appeared in Stanley Kauffmann's much-noted 1966 piece for the *Times*, "Homosexual Drama and Its Disguises," whose ambiguous content, like the reactions it generated, reflected the trouble contemporaries had with the subject. Some letter writers and later critics deemed Kauffmann's piece a homophobic rant, but it met guarded approval from *Tangents*, the new gay magazine, while apparently offending *Times* matriarch Iphigene Sulzberger for its subject and its prominent placement in the paper, probably contributing to Kauffmann's dismissal months later.[50]

Kauffmann restated old complaints, but with less vitriol and more complexity. "Because three of the most successful American playwrights of the last twenty years are (reputed) homosexuals"—readers could guess that the unnamed three were Williams, Albee, and Inge—"and because their plays often treat of women and marriage, therefore, it is said, postwar American drama presents a badly distorted picture of American women, marriage, and society in general." Kauffmann accepted the charge of distortion, thereby infuriating some gay artists: he has echoed "the commonly held untruth that since homosexuals hate women they can hardly be expected to write compassionately about them," Ned Rorem complained to his diary. "How can heterosexual comportment be, to the homosexual playwright, 'a life he does not know' . . . when he has been free to observe it openly since birth?"[51] But Kauffmann argued that "the homosexual dramatist is not to blame in this matter," for "he has no choice but to masquerade. . . . If he is to write of his experience, he must invent a two-sex version of the one-sex experience that he really knows. It is we who insist on it, not he." Kauffmann wanted such dramatists freed to treat what they knew; with every other "neurosis" dramatized, the "taboo" on homosexuality made no sense. It made "homosexual artists, male and female, tend to convert their exclusion into a philosophy of art that glorifies their exclusion," and to indulge other habits long criticized—to "exalt style, manner, surface," and to seek "an instrument of revenge on the main body of society."

Kauffmann wanted to unchain homosexual artists, but in order to contain them. His was a typical liberal stance—yank off the closet door less to free those inside than to allow " 'normal' " people full view of them. "I do not argue for increased homosexual influence in our theater. It is precisely because I, like many others, am weary of disguised homosexual influence that I raise the matter." He showed no interest in what "homosexual dramatists" might say—were already saying—or in the possibility that they had a fresh angle on heterosexuality. Pressed in a flurry of letters to the *Times*, Kauffmann grudgingly admitted, *"An author does not have to murder in order to write of murder."* But he asserted "a cosmic difference between a homosexual's writing about marriage, if he chooses, and a homosexual's being forced to disguise his own experience as marriage in order to write about it." He made no apparent effort to learn whether gay playwrights in fact felt "forced." Quick with the pen, Kauffmann had other rejoinders: *"A play should be judged on its merits, not by its author's sexuality.* With this thundering truism, who would disagree?" He closed with his own thundering assertion: If "liberty" for gay dramatists seems "too much for us to contemplate, then at least let us drop all the cant about homosexual 'influence' and distortion: because we are only complaining of the results of our own attitudes."

Kauffmann wrote gay dramatists out of American culture even as he seemed to invite them in. Their work lacked gravity, honesty, humanity—it was "style, manner, surface." Blaming "our own attitudes" for those failures was an earnest but empty gesture, for in lumping homosexuality with other "equally neurotic, equally undesirable" traits, Kauffmann sanctioned those "attitudes." Queer dramatists could reenter American culture only if they stuck to their own "neurosis." Kauffmann echoed earlier reactions by many Euro-Americans to the artistic output of African Americans: they might have something to say about their own kind, but not about others, or about matters beyond race. He also restated dominant responses to gay men's role in culture, ones that fearfully exaggerated that role while seeking to contain it by branding its products superficial, artificial, hateful, and alien.[52]

Authenticity was key. Critics remained infuriated by gay men's apparent misalignment — queer actors who excelled in "he-man" roles (or caricatured those roles, as Rock Hudson did in his 1960s comedies), playwrights who addressed marriage, designers who dressed women. They called on such men to get the alignment right: the queer dramatist's personal identity and artistic product had to be synchronized, so others could resist an insidious influence. But it was an uneasy call in several ways. As critics acknowledged, drama involved license, not literalism. Artifice, distortion, and imagination were its essence. Few playgoers expected photographic reproductions of reality, and to assail only some plays for artifice was silly. Kauffmann implicitly acknowledged as much but insisted: "All that we ask for is conviction." And no one proposed to curb heterosexual dramatists from creating gay characters, while gay playwrights who offered queer characters might, Kauffmann noted, unleash fury against themselves. "It is," *One* pointed out to Roth with campy hyperbole, "like asking a Jew why he didn't march right up to Hitler with prayer shawl, skull cap, the Torah in one hand, a flaming menorah in the other, his fly open and flaunting his circumcision."[53] The call for honesty among gay playwrights came out of concern not for them but for a cultural vitality seen as undermined by their misalignment.

Insistence on one form of alignment might also have called other forms into question — what fidelity did a creator owe to a certain gender, to national, ideological, or aesthetic identity, or to personal experience? Deception, transmutation, and escape came in many forms. Richard Rodgers, grinding out his last hit, *The Sound of Music*, in the early 1960s, offered paeans to heterosexual romance and wholesomeness when, as insiders knew, he experienced a series of tawdry affairs with chorus girls, bouts of enormous drinking, and episodes of hospitalization for depression. Did Rodgers deceive any less than his former lyricist, Lorenz Hart, "that drunken little fag," as Rodgers reportedly called him? For that matter, did private pain, often regarded as a motor of queers' creativity, drive Rodgers any less?[54] Rodgers's saccharine later work met criticism, but not for some rupture between the man and his musicals. Queer figures bore the brunt of anxiety about a chasm between artists' private identities and public creations, but critics risked opening a can of worms in which others might be found. It had not opened far as of mid-decade, but denunciation of queer dishonesty was under strain.

The strain was sufficiently latent, however, to allow *Time* magazine, ever the follower rather than the leader, to summarize the outlook of two decades in a 1966 piece appearing days before Kauffmann's. Examining "The Homosexual in America," as its article was titled, *Time* avoided one cliché—that homosexuality was an unknown topic—noting that it "is freely discussed and widely analyzed." But the article employed others. Like most mainstream coverage, it all but ignored lesbians—that gay men were woman-haters (although abandoned wives and "rich dowagers" seemed oddly fond of them) further erased lesbians. Despite a pose of objectivity and sympathy, the essay reeked of contempt for gay people. Gay men are "psychic masochists" prone to "superciliousness, fake aggression and whimpering," as Edmund Bergler was quoted. Homosexuality, *Time* concluded, "is a pathetic little second-rate substitute for reality, a pitiable flight from life" that deserves "fairness, compassion, understanding," but "above all, no pretense that it is anything but a pernicious sickness."

What could pathetic men create? Little, *Time* predictably claimed. It found that "increasingly, deviates are out in the open, particularly in fashion and the arts." But despite "the considerable talent" of "the Leonardos and Michelangelos," *Time* leaned to the views of psychiatrist Edward Stainbrook, who argued that "homosexuals are failed artists, and their special creative gift a myth." Likely borrowing from Bergler, *Time* embraced writer Somerset Maugham's claim that queers lacked "deep seriousness" and had only "a wonderful gift for delightful embroidery." *Time* echoed Bergler's notion of queers' "superciliousness," of which " 'pop' " art and " 'camp' " provided new evidence. "Fake aggression" also governed gay artists, or perhaps real aggression: *Time* spotted among them "a vengeful, derisive counterattack" on the straight world, including "attacks on women or society in general."

Gay artists' power heightened the danger. *Time* asserted that in Hollywood—where "you have to scrape them off the ceiling," as producer David Merrick was quoted—and in "theater, dance, and music, deviates are so widespread that they sometimes seem to be running a kind of closed shop. Art Critic Harold Rosenberg reports a 'banding together of homosexual painters and their nonpainting auxiliaries.' " What *Time* first called homosexuals' "considerable influence in the arts" shifted to "homosexual mafia" and "Homintern." *Time* admitted that "spiteful failures looking for scapegoats" might exaggerate the "Homintern," but nonetheless embraced the label. Responding, *Tangents* used history: "We seem to remember that Hitler blamed the decadence of art on the Jews, and condemned jazz as degenerate because of its Negro origin."[55]

Notions of queer creative shallowness and conspiracy, once confined mostly to obscure venues and cranky voices, now had *Time*'s blessing as conventional wisdom. CBS Reports' "The Homosexuals," aired on 7 March 1967, added television's tamer blessing, with reporter Mike Wallace noting "talk of a homosexual mafia in the arts." CBS's treatment was regarded by some as a breakthrough simply for being shown (with Gore Vidal and others appearing) but by others as standard (and lesbian-erasing) homophobia, ending with familiar words: "At the center of his life, he remains anonymous. A displaced person. An outsider."[56]

Although authenticity remained a dominant ideal, by the mid-1960s its definitions and embodiments were changing. The state was under attack as Johnson's war in Vietnam floundered and his sprawling "Great Society" programs sparked distrust among urban blacks, disaffected liberals, and antistatist conservatives. Acting on impulses rising in the 1950s, aggrieved Americans rejected the top-down bureaucratic systems of education, business, and the state and the affluence and environmental degradation they caused. Many Americans, soon lumped under the term "counterculture," celebrated living communally and circumventing the mediating forces between society and self. Others viewed rebelliousness as self-indulgence, and around them emerged a sort of counterauthenticity, recognized by LBJ but attached by Nixon to the "silent majority," prizing emotional restraint and loyalty to work, family, and the state. Often oversimplified as a generational split, the struggle involved ragged social, cultural, and political divisions.

In queer matters, one shift appeared in an unlikely arena. Even in the 1950s pulp publications had showed diversity. In the 1960s they often departed from highbrow discourse. In cheap, badly spelled books like *America's Homosexual Underground* (1965), the exposé of queers in the arts included soft-porn stories of gay romance, offering the alluring alongside, or in the guise of, the condemnatory. Sometimes courting gay men and penned by them, pulp treatments mocked stereotypes that mainstream accounts peddled. In "An Intimate Edition," *Faggots to Burn!* (1962) countered the "*rumor*: homosexuals are trying to take over the world" with the "*truth*: most homosexuals are trying to hold on to the lease for their apartments," according queers the blessing of ordinariness. On its cover, *Faggots* promised "what the newspapers don't dare to print" about "the alarming spread of homosexuality," asking, "Is the 'Third Sex' taking over Hollywood?" But its answer was defiant—the "third sex" had taken over long ago—and exuberant: "Hollywood is probably the homosexual capital of the world." "And Norman Mailer . . . remark[s] that in some shows even the audience is queer!" *Faggots* summarized the expert view of homosexuals as immature but also gave far more space to gay voices, including women's, than middlebrow accounts did and avoided their tolerant pity for the afflicted homosexual. And the pulps, now widely available in airports, drugstores, and the like, may have had more readers. At the top end, *The Half-World of the American Homosexual* (1966) plumbed history, language, and the arts to some depths, celebrated queer freedom, replaced the "homintern" in the arts with "the Gay Renaissance," and thundered: "The still-static believer must face the ultimatum that to condemn homosexuality per se is to condemn every note and melody of Tchaikovsky."[57]

Shifts were also marked by highbrow voices. Leslie Fiedler noted how camp, despite its self-mocking quality, had a different literary potential. As with the "hearty stage-Irishman," the "hand-wringing Jew," the "blue-eyed dependent girl," "the faithful black servitor crying 'Yassuh, massuh!'" so also "the mincing wrist-flapping fairy": who knows when they might discard "the humble roles in which they have been cast and begin to exploit those roles subversively."[58] More famous was Susan Sontag's 1964 essay, "Notes on Camp." Sontag defined camp—famously hard to pin down—as a "sensibility that, among other things, converts the serious into the frivolous." She did not claim that only homosexuals produced camp, or that they produced nothing else, but "homosexuals, by and large, constitute the vanguard—and the most articulate audience—of Camp." The qualities she found in camp—its "artifice" and "stylization," its responsiveness to "the markedly attenuated and to the strongly exaggerated"—were ones critics had for years condemned in queer creativity. Sontag seemed to find them virtues—artifice had its own authenticity.[59]

But she did so ambivalently. For most of the essay she avoided the term "homosexual" or similar words, leaving queers in the shadows. Her attitude toward them was opaque but perhaps implied in her acknowledgement: "I am strongly drawn to Camp, and almost as strongly offended by it." Sontag located camp's origins in Europe—in its artists and aristocrats, its "dandy" fashions (camp is "dandyism in the age of

mass culture"), and, of course, Oscar Wilde—in sources many Americans regarded as alien or exotic. And she made a strained comparison. As
with "Jewish liberalism," camp's function was "self-legitimization. . . .
The Jews pinned their hopes for integrating into modern society on promoting the moral sense. Homosexuals have pinned their integration into
society on promoting the aesthetic sense." To compare a political sensibility—"Jewish liberalism"—to an aesthetic one was awkward, and it
overlooked Jews who promoted an "aesthetic sense" and queers who addressed "the moral sense."

Sontag offered a sophisticated restatement of ideas about queers prone
to decorative artifice—as lacking the depth to address "the moral sense."
Like others, she also saw homosexuals as a powerful, coherent group that
could somehow decide they had "pinned their integration . . . on promoting the aesthetic sense." Sontag was describing a sensibility that was
likely real among gay men she knew in New York's arts circles, but her language was extravagantly generalized about "homosexuals" and strikingly
specific about what they had decided. Charting how gay people seized
artifice to claim authenticity, Sontag still left that authenticity in doubt.
Defending queer creativity, she deployed an idiom rooted in attacks on
it. It was, of course, a defense *of* them—on their presumed behalf—not
by them.

Many declined to follow whatever lead she offered. In the *Village Voice*,
Vivian Gornick judged Sontag's claims mostly "nonsense." Under a headline stating the obvious—"It's a Queer Hand Stoking the Campfire"
—Gornick assailed *One* magazine for offering "garish hysteria," then
offered her own. For her, style and "sensibility" were less at issue than
the simple fact that "popular culture is now in the hands of the homosexuals," whose "taste" controls "style, story, statement in painting, literature, dance, amusements, and acquisitions for a good proportion of the
intellectual middle class." Gornick added fresh items to the enemies' list:
Hubert Selby's novel *Last Exit to Brooklyn* (1964) and the selling "of cast-
iron lamps shaped like roses to sophisticated schoolteachers." Camp was
"a malicious fairy's joke" but also—somehow—"pure and simple self-
hatred." She granted the homosexual's burden—he, "like the Jew and
the Negro, always lived as an outsider," walking "in the shadows of Western privilege." But whereas Jews and Negroes successfully confronted the
challenges they faced, queers only came up with the shallow, self-hating
rituals of camp—she barely noted other forms of queer creativity. The
homosexual emerged with "nothing more than a brutal caricature of the
femaleness he so violently rejects," becoming "the women he despises, in

a form grotesquely frivolous and vicious." Gornick found sad evidence of this on "Fire Island beaches" and in a homosexual literature "frightening in its steely-eyed slickness, its language of surfaces, its heartlessness, its unbearable loathing of humanity." She exempted novels like Baldwin's *Giovanni's Room*, whose "protagonists are men in passionate search of their manhood; quite another matter, altogether," she wrote, if not approvingly. She chalked up acceptance of camp to "a time in which the spirit of self-belief is profoundly on the decline."

Frenzy peaked at mid-decade, especially in liberal and leftist circles, as Gornick's piece suggested. In the politics of authenticity, queers were fakes, found wanting compared to Jews and Negroes. In the politics of gender, gay men were blamed for misogyny, with other men off the hook. Although Gornick deplored how "middle-class intellectuals" embraced camp as hip—as indeed some did—it was also telling that she found it hip to deplore camp, and homosexuals generally. Just when the spirit of liberation was rising—in black protest, a new feminism, antiwar activism, the counterculture—its extension to queers was resisted.[60]

Ramparts added its voice to that resistance. The new magazine built a well-earned reputation for challenging the American Cold War by digging up official lies and secrets. Its journalists were attacked, in a *Human Events* article likely planted by the CIA, as " 'snoops, 'eccentrics,' ventriloquists,' and 'bearded New Leftniks' who had a 'get-out-of-Vietnam fixation.' "[61] In April 1967, *Ramparts* reported on covert CIA funding of the cultural Cold War. But as it prepared that article, one of its writers ranted about "getting damned tired of all the art being campy and all the plays being queer" because of "the homosexual cultural takeover." The takeover included "almost any part of the culture," except for "the relatively virile jazz and rock fields," fields presumably mounting the counteroffensive against queer "takeover." That takeover was "turning a society that was sexually sick to begin with into a pathological horror." The author had no more relish for "pseudo-Lesbians like the Barbara Stanwyck role in [the television western series] 'The Big Valley.' "

The author was Gene Marine, a name oozing male authority, and the article's title, "Who's Afraid of Little Annie Fanny," offered an obvious swipe at Albee. "I really, honestly, truly don't care what you do with your spare time, but if you are homosexual will you kindly let somebody else play with a piece of the culture for a while?" Marine mockingly pleaded. Embracing Stanley Kauffmann's brief, Marine rolled out familiar charges. "Yes, a lot of playwrights are homosexual, but no, that's not the point. I wouldn't give up Oscar Wilde for the world." But their influence is insidious: even if not queer, "more and more playwrights write plays as though they were." And they portrayed women viciously, as in *Virginia Woolf*: few critics pointed out that Albee's play also portrayed men viciously, instead posing as defenders of women under attack by Albee. Women "are as badly stereotyped as any racial minority" and gay men were responsible—Marine blamed them for "the shift from a simply male-dominated society" guilty only of "affective indifference" to women "toward one that holds its women in faggoty contempt." And gay artists prompted Marine's personal concern, it seems: "I don't want my daughter to grow up thinking that men want a Playmate." Varying a some-of-my-best-friends-are-gay line, Marine noted that he liked "a lot of camp humor, and I probably would have had a good time at Truman's [Capote's] party." But "I want heterosexual artists to hang in galleries *too*." The idea of a "homosexual cultural takeover" reached across the ideological spectrum, now deployed in struggles over feminism by men echoing Betty Friedan and professing women's rights (Marine soon wrote *A Male Guide to Women's Liberation* [1972]).[62]

Commentary about "the homosexual cultural takeover" remained New York–centric—generated by New Yorkers about New Yorkers, or by others observing them. But other sources, tracked by magazines like *One* and the *Ladder*, also emerged. The *Tulane Drama Review* condemned plays pandering to the "morbidity and sexual perversity which are only there to titillate an impotent and homosexual theater and audience." The *Toledo Times* observed, "Today, the third sex dominates the seven lively arts, it has a strangle-hold on the theatre, and a dominant place in modern literature." Broadway's old formula has been "revised to 'boy meets girl (ugh!), boy meets boy (ah!), boy gets boy.'"[63]

But by mid-decade there were also signs that the homintern discourse faced disruption. One sign was *The Boys of Boise* (1966), by journalist John Gerassi, which examined that city's antigay witch hunt from a decade earlier. Like others, Gerassi offered a discovery discourse, but it revealed the secrets of antigay persecution as much as homosexuality. He traced persecution not to the behavior of gay men but to the political economy and culture of a backward region. Idaho's moguls manipulated Boise's panic about queer sex in order to beat up political enemies and to resist urban liberalism, embodied for them in efforts to bring mental health services to Idaho, especially for victims and perpetrators of queer activity. "Well, we don't want fairies—or mental health. We don't want Boise to change," insisted one local executive. "Mental health is a Communist plot," as Gerassi summarized the local view. His account oozed big-city condescension toward small-town America and uneasily deployed a medical framework for homosexuality. But it also defied prevailing wisdom by showing teenagers as the predators more than the prey of adult men and by arguing that Boise's panic owed to political and economic interests more than the moral concerns trumpeted by local leaders. (Reissued a quarter-century later, *Boys* again stirred up a hornet's nest, including among scholars.)[64]

Gerassi made Boise the antithesis of "liberal" New York, "where homosexuals are rarely arrested (except in shakedowns), where young men and even teen-age boys freely drag the streets in make up and wigs." He did not grasp the dangers that New York queers still faced and showed them the same condescension he showed benighted Idaho. But he did endorse their freedom from harassment and he saw no cultural threat from them, construing Kauffmann's piece to mean simply that "the fuss made over 1966's 'homosexual playwrights,' both in defense and attack, would disappear if the laws were changed." More striking, he took on the armed forces' antigay policies. Although "the Army found that homosexuals topped the average soldier in intelligence, education and rating," it "proceeded to kick such homosexuals out of the service despite the fact that many 'performed admirably.'" Gerassi repositioned queers as the victims of corporate, cultural, and military empire rather than threats to it. His work signaled that liberal consensus about homosexuality, as about much else, was ending.[65]

Sharper resistance to charges of gay cultural conspiracy also emerged in queer circles. At the 1965 meeting of East Coast Homophile Organizations in New York, Gregory Battcock, in his speech, "Homosexuality and the Arts," maintained that critics—he singled out the *Tulane Drama Review* piece—and others "perplexed by the new art, who feel left out by it, look around for a scapegoat and have found one in the homosexual." Often arts criticism "by-passes the art itself and hits catch-all targets such as homosexuality." Battcock, a New York City artist and college instructor, overlooked how the scapegoating involved conventional work, not just daring "new art." But he made explicit an argument about scapegoating that had long hovered on the fringes of debate.[66]

Alongside this change in attitudes—modest and hard to measure—came change in forms of debate, a change queers did much to further. The List long had been a tool of debate about queer creativity. Some gay outlets now questioned its politics. Reviewing *The Gay Geniuses* (1965), by W. H. Kavy, M.D., *Tangents* quoted Dodo in *Alice in Wonderland*: "Everybody has won, and all must have prizes," adding, "Dr. Kavy appears to believe everybody in history was homosexual and deserves the prize of being written up in his catalogue," which *Tangents* found "stupefying." "The harsh fact is that most of us cannot gain the respect of our fellows by means of outstanding accomplishments in the arts, science, politics, war. Few homosexuals are Caesars, Leonardos, Wagners, Prousts. Applause is not what today's homosexual needs. He needs acknowledgement of his right to respect as a human being. Contentment with the accomplishments of famous homosexuals of the past—and present—will cheat him of this end."[67] For *Tangents*, "respect" was still a goal, but a class-and-culture tactic that erased most queers was a bad means to it. *Tangents* shunted the List, and much that went with it, to the sidelines.

In the mid-1960s, agitation about the homintern in the arts reached its peak. As chapter 4 shows, the effect of that agitation on individuals was often less direct and more coded than the blunt public rhetoric would suggest—but still damaging. Yet the agitation also faced disruption, as did America's Cold War, foundering in Vietnam. The timing was not coincidental. Upheaval in the Cold War crusade hastened disruption of the homintern discourse. Gay people were widely portrayed as dishonest poseurs who should align their public and private selves. To a degree, the injunction to "come out," as the act of aligning the two would be called, first came from those suspicious of gay people. But it offered queers a chance to reposition themselves: by coming out, they could undercut their foes' foremost argument.

Aaron Copland (left), Samuel Barber (center), and Barber's partner Gian Carlo
Menotti (right) in 1945, three of the leading mid-century American composers.
(Photograph by Victor Kraft; Aaron Copland Collection, Music Division, Library
of Congress, box/folder 479/3; reproduced by permission of Mrs. Rheba Kraft and
the Aaron Copland Fund for Music)

Tennessee Williams, whose
plays and movies met with great
success but also denunciation
for their sexuality and queer
themes. (Photograph by Foto-
Life; Photography Collection,
Harry Ransom Humanities
Research Center, University of
Texas at Austin)

MAGAZINE GOLDMINE:
"RUN AN ARTICLE ON QUEERS!"

You and a little two-bit magazine have much in common. Far from being something you just pass the time with waiting for a haircut, the popular mags are potent opinion-formers from way back. None of them merely present news as news any more than the general press does. All of them have their special slant; they only vary in the subtlety with which they present it. For instance, Life is highly circumspect in its pro-Catholic attitude and leans over backward trying to appear unbiased on the subject. Actually no apology is necessary yet Life, as do most magazines, wishes to attain a reputation for objectivity and disclaims all religious and political bias. This is hardly possible and their editors are naive to either wish for it or hope to **appear** unbiased. Their contents strip them bare. ONE, on the other hand, is the first to concede its own bareness. It has plenty of bones to pick. Many of them concern other monthly magazines.

On the following pages are summaries of articles on deviation as printed in representative magazines. The selection is in cross-section ranging from the quality mag down to the filthy cheapy all of which wield great influence with their many readers. It is interesting to note that tables of contents are generally quite consistent; the magazine which expresses prejudice in one direction will be found to be prejudiced in others as well. In addition, levels of appeal are strictly adhered to: every article will be equally bright or misinformed within certain surprisingly confined limits. Seldom do you find a brilliant article in an issue containing foolishness elsewhere, nor outstanding stupidity amid wisdom. Where ONE fits into this analysis is up to its readers.

Early gay magazines, like One *in this 1953 piece, tracked and challenged how the mainstream media exploited homosexuality and disparaged the queer presence in the arts.*

Stephen Sondheim (left), Leonard Bernstein (center), and Jerome Robbins (right) in 1956, who, along with Arthur Laurents, formed the queer Jewish team behind the musical West Side Story. *(Photograph by Alfred Eisenstaedt; Time & Life Pictures/Getty Images)*

Samuel Barber the composer, Gian Carlo Menotti the librettist and director, and Eleanor Steber the soprano star of Vanessa, *which premiered at the Metropolitan Opera in 1958. (Archives of the Metropolitan Opera)*

Librettist and director Franco Zeffirelli (left), conductor Thomas Schippers (center), and composer Samuel Barber (right), three of the queer team behind Antony and Cleopatra, *whose 1966 premiere at the new Metropolitan Opera House coincided with the climax of the homintern discourse. (Archives of the Metropolitan Opera)*

*Choreographer Alvin Ailey, another member of the queer team
behind* Antony and Cleopatra. *(Archives of the Metropolitan Opera)*

Leontyne Price as Cleopatra at the Met, whose costuming was criticized as another sign of the opera's excess. (Archives of the Metropolitan Opera)

A Much-Needed Upbraiding
of Long-hair Music

By Anna Frankenheimer

A leading concert manager offers an intriguing explanation of why American music has become sissified

On April 28, 1948, Jerome Bohm, one of the New York *Herald Tribune*'s music critics, was arrested at his home in Westchester and charged with sodomy and with impairing the morals of a minor. At the time, Mr. Bohm had just completed his 28th year on the *Tribune*. He was one of the most influential music critics in the world.

Mr. Bohm's homosexuality was no secret. He lived openly, even ostentatiously, with a male "friend," a dress designer, and had a reputation as a Don Juan among the more flowery young musicians. It was widely known among professional musicians that in order to get a good review in the morning *Tribune* a male performer should find ways to become intimately acquainted with Mr. Bohm, while a female performer should order her gown from his close friend, the dress designer. These facts did not seem to outrage any of the higher-ups at the *Tribune,* and it was not they who prompted the police department to arrest him—it was sheer accident that brought about Bohm's downfall: A boy (who did not even have the excuse of being a budding performer) suffered a rectal injury in a sexual encounter with Mr. Bohm and confessed to his father, who sicked the police on the busy critic.

It was a scandal of sorts at the time, but since Mr. Bohm was not a government official, it hardly made a sensation. It simply joined the long succession of other cases of homosexuals in the music world who were unfortunate enough to get nabbed by the police, including such luminaries as conductor Sir Eugene Goossens and composer Marc Blitzstein. And the Bohm story is not being rehashed here in order to beat a dead horse, but because it reflects the corruption that permeates the entire field of serious music.

This article is not an attack against homosexuals in the music world. There is nothing corrupt about being a homosexual per se. I don't give a damn—and I don't think anyone should —about what they do in their private lives. As for the injured boy (who was seduced rather than raped) and his outraged father, I believe that his parents were more responsible for his aberration than the seducer. But the undeniable clinical facts are that homosexuals—by definition—possess infantile, unstable personalities. They are emotionally and sexually more promiscuous than heterosexuals, their perversion plays a central role in their lives and colors everything they do, and—perhaps because they feel discriminated against and persecuted—they form closely-knit, powerful cliques in the professions they succeed in penetrating, and tend to favor their own kind. This is glaringly obvious in the dress-designing industry, in the ballet, and in many areas of the theater, publishing, and

The short-lived and sensational magazine Fact *published this essay, one of the most inflamed attacks on gay composers and musicians, in 1964. (General Research Division, The New York Public Library, Astor, Lenox and Tilden Foundations)*

Susan Sontag in 1966, whose influential 1964 essay "Notes on Camp" both reflected and disrupted earlier commentary on queer creativity. (Photograph by Bob Peterson; Time & Life Pictures/Getty Images)

Hey, lover, dig the old Jack Oakie poster.
Or: Isn't the fine art spread in the Christmas Playboy a *scream*?
Or: Really, Harry, *nobody* has a room in Chinese Modern.
Or: I'll have what you're having, but make mine with Metaxa.
Or: Who's afraid of Virginia Woolf?
People, I have had it. I really, honestly, truly don't care what you do with your spare time, but if you are homosexual will you kindly let somebody else play with a piece of the culture for a while?

LET ME PUT THINGS STRAIGHT (my God, even the language) for you and the libel lawyers. I don't absolutely know for certain the names of any famous homosexuals, though I probably make the same guesses you do, and if I did know any for certain, I wouldn't tell you. As far as I know, Edward Albee is a square family man, Andy Warhol is afflicted with satyriasis and California has no homosexuality south of the Santa Ynez River. I couldn't care less.

All I know is, there is a thing that men and women do together which, besides being necessary to the continuance of the species, is regarded by a lot of Americans, possibly even a majority, as a lot of fun. I have begun to doubt whether an anthropologist from another planet, here on a short visit, would ever figure that out.

When I was 14 or so I read James M. Cain's *Serenade*, including the part where the guy explains to the girl that we all have five or ten per cent of "that" in us, and I gave a huge sigh of relief and quit worrying about it. I don't mean that all the hangups went away; I, too, grew up in a culture that told me to be a man, son, and sock the kid back. No doubt there are still things going on underneath my consciousness that I don't know about, but I find a kind of wry humor in heterosexual types being afraid to write about homosexual types for fear they'll give something away about themselves. If you're big on long-distance second-hand psychoanalysis, have at it; you have as much right as Freud had to psychoanalyze Wilson, though probably not the skill.

Anyway, I have at least reached the point at which, when I see a friend I haven't seen in months, I can put my arms around him without glancing about to see who's watching. I have held another man in my arms to give him comfort in sorrow, and been held in sorrow of my own. I can feel, and admit to feeling, the sexual attraction of other men as well as the next cat.

But there are two things. One: I like women. Not like

"I like girls," with a snigger; I like women. And two: I write things down and bitch a little about how things are, but I don't shape culture.

I wish I did. I'm getting damned tired of all the art being campy and all the plays being queer and all the clothes being West Fourth Street and the whole bit. *Some* I don't mind, but it's getting too close to *all*, and I have the feeling that there are healthier bases for a culture.

Kindly save the letter about your brother-in-law the interior decorator who is absolutely straight and has three lovely children. The only playwright I know really well is so virile that I don't know when he has time to write, and he has a play running in its second year in New York. The heterosexual artists I know have trouble getting into galleries, but I'm sure you know one who doesn't.

But really. Take a look around, at anything. Say "homosexual influence" to a very square solid citizen and he will of course come up with long-haired hippies and rock-and-roll and paisley belts on men's trousers, which will only prove that he doesn't know much about hippies or rock-and-roll, and he isn't paying attention to who's wearing the paisley belts (he'll be wearing one next year). Aside from noting that hippies are more influenced by than they influence the culture, I'll just say that the Greenwich Village scene and the Haight-Ashbury in San Francisco are not what I'm talking about—such negative comments being necessary to an approach to what I *am* talking about.

If you need a key to what I am talking about, take a look at the whole American culture, and focus on the portrayal, the image, the treatment, the presentation of women. I'm going to make a distinction later on among ways of putting down women—the homosexual way and the simple, male-dominated, male-chauvinistic way—but for the moment let's just say that there's a difference between affectionate indifference and a few male stereotypes on the one hand, and absolute contempt on the other.

When was the last time you saw a more or less con-

by Gene Marine

THE HOMOSEXUAL IN AMERICA

IT used to be "the abominable crime not to be mentioned." Today it is not only mentioned; it is freely discussed and widely analyzed. Yet the general attitude toward homosexuality is, if anything, more uncertain than before. Beset by inner conflicts, the homosexual is unsure of his position in society, ambivalent about his attitudes and identity—but he gains a certain amount of security through the fact that society is equally ambivalent about him. A vast majority of people retain a deep loathing toward him, but there is a growing mixture of tolerance, empathy or apathy. Society is torn between condemnation and compassion, fear and curiosity, between attempts to turn the problem into a joke and the knowledge that it is anything but funny, between the deviate's plea to be treated just like everybody else and the knowledge that he simply is not like everybody else.

Homosexuality is more in evidence in the U.S. than ever before—as an almost inevitable subject matter in fiction, a considerable influence in the arts, a highly visible presence in the cities, from nighttime sidewalks to the most "in" parties. The latest Rock Hudson movie explicitly jokes about it, Doubleday Book Shops run smirking ads for *The Gay Cookbook*, and newsstands make room for "beefcake" magazines of male nudes. Whether the number of homosexuals has actually increased is hard to say. In 1948, Sexologist Alfred Kinsey published figures that homosexuals found cheering. He estimated that 4% of American white males are exclusively homosexual and that about two in five had "at least some" homosexual experience after puberty. Given Kinsey's naive sampling methods, the figures were almost certainly wrong. But chances are that growing permissiveness about homosexuality and a hedonistic attitude toward all sex have helped "convert" many people who might have repressed their inclinations in another time or place.

Homosexuals are present in every walk of life, on any social level, often anxiously camouflaged; the camouflage will sometimes even include a wife and children, and psychoanalysts are busy treating wives who have suddenly discovered a husband's homosexuality. But increasingly, deviates are out in the open, particularly in fashion and the arts. Women and homosexual men work together designing, marketing, retailing, and wrapping it all up in the fashion magazines. The interior decorator and the stockbroker's wife conspire over curtains. And the symbiosis is not limited to working hours. For many a woman with a busy or absent husband, the presentable homosexual is in demand as an escort—witty, pretty, catty, and no problem to keep at arm's length. Rich dowagers often have a permanent traveling court of charming international types who exert influence over what pictures and houses their patronesses buy, what decorators they use, and where they spend which season.

The Homintern

On Broadway, it would be difficult to find a production without homosexuals playing important parts, either on-stage or off. And in Hollywood, says Broadway Producer David Merrick, "you have to scrape them off the ceiling." The notion that the arts are dominated by a kind of homosexual mafia—or "Homintern," as it has been called—is sometimes exaggerated, particularly by spiteful failures looking for scapegoats. But in the theater, dance and music world, deviates are so widespread that they sometimes seem to be running a kind of closed shop. Art Critic Harold Rosenberg reports a "banding together of homosexual painters and their nonpainting auxiliaries."

There is no denying the considerable talent of a great many homosexuals, and ideally, talent alone is what should count. But the great artists so often cited as evidence of the homosexual's creativity—the Leonardos and Michelangelos—are probably the exceptions of genius. For the most part, thinks Los Angeles Psychiatrist Edward Stainbrook, homosexuals are failed artists, and their special creative gift a myth. No less an authority than Somerset Maugham felt that the homosexual, "however subtly he sees life, cannot see it whole," and lacks "the deep seriousness over certain things that normal men take seriously . . . He has small power of invention, but a wonderful gift for delightful embroidery. He has vitality, brilliance, but seldom strength."

Homosexual ethics and esthetics are staging a vengeful, derisive counterattack on what deviates call the "straight" world. This is evident in "pop," which insists on reducing art to the trivial, and in the "camp" movement, which pretends that the ugly and banal are fun. It is evident among writers, who used to disguise homosexual stories in heterosexual dress but now delight in explicit descriptions of male intercourse and orgiastic nightmares. It is evident in the theater, with many a play dedicated to the degradation of women and the derision of normal sex. The most sophisticated theatrical joke is now built around a homosexual situation; shock comes not from sex but from perversion. Attacks on women or society in general are neither new in U.S. writing nor necessarily homosexual, but they do offer a special opportunity for a consciously or unconsciously homosexual outlook. They represent a kind of inverted romance, since homosexual situations as such can never be made romantic for normal audiences.

The Gay Subculture

Even in ordinary conversation, most homosexuals will sooner or later attack the "things that normal men take seriously." This does not mean that homosexuals do not and cannot talk seriously; but there is often a subtle sea change in the conversation: sex (unspoken) pervades the atmosphere. Among other matters, this raises the question of whether there is such a thing as a discernible homosexual type. Some authorities, notably Research Psychologist Evelyn Hooker of U.C.L.A., deny it—against what seems to be the opinion of most psychiatrists. The late Dr. Edmund Bergler found certain traits present in all homosexuals, including inner depression and guilt, irrational jealousy and a megalomaniac conviction that homosexual trends are universal. Though Bergler conceded that homosexuals are not responsible for their inner conflicts, he found that these conflicts "sap so much of their inner energy that the shell is a mixture of superciliousness, fake aggression and whimpering. Like all psychic masochists, they are subservient when confronted by a stronger person, merciless when in power, unscrupulous about trampling on a weaker person."

Another homosexual trait noted by Bergler and others is chronic dissatisfaction, a constant tendency to prowl or "cruise" in search of new partners. This is one reason why the "gay" bars flourishing all over the U.S. attract even the more respectable deviates. Sociologists regard the gay bar as the center of a kind of minor subculture with its own social scale and class warfare.

As André Gide pointed out long ago from personal experience, there are several varieties of homosexuals that the heterosexual world lumps together but that "feel an irrepressible loathing for one another." Today in the U.S., there are "mixed" bars where all homosexuals, male and female, are *persona grata*; "cuff-linky" bars that cater to the college and junior-executive type; "swish" bars for the effeminates and "hair fairies" with their careful coiffures; "TV" bars, which cater not to television fans but to transvestites; "leather" bars for the tough-guy types with their fondness for chains and belts; San Francisco's new "Topless Boys" discothèques, featuring bare-chested entertainers. San Francisco and Los Angeles are rivals for the distinction of being the capital of the gay world; the nod probably goes to San Francisco.

This 21 January 1966 essay in Time *magazine shows that the conspiratorial ways and superficial products of gay artists were by then staples of middlebrow commentary.*

President Richard Nixon, whose secretly taped tirades about gay men are far less known than his fulminations against other "enemies." (Library of Congress Prints and Photographs Division)

Midge Decter in 1987, who showed in her infamous "The Boys on the Beach" in 1980 how antihomosexuality was becoming more exclusively a right-wing phenomenon. (Photograph by Cynthia Johnson; Time & Life Pictures/Getty Images)

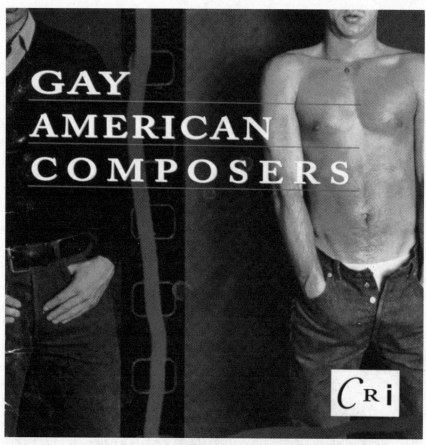

GAY
AMERICAN
COMPOSERS

C R i

The CD "Gay American Composers" (1996) illustrated the more explicit public identification of many artists as gay late in the twentieth century but also revealed confusion about what that identification meant. (Gay American Composers used by permission of New World Records, compact disc #721, ℗ 1996, © 1996 Recorded Anthology of American Music, Inc., <www.newworldrecords.org>)

Barber at the Met

Samuel Barber's life shows how the categories of gay, American, and composer intersected without cohering. His life likewise illuminates the homintern discourse, whose arc coincided roughly with the arc of his career. Barber succeeded despite that discourse, and much else shaped his career, but it threaded its way through his life — after all, he did set the words "every day another version of every known perversion" to music.

Ascent

Growing up in a maturing arts culture, Barber (1910–81) drew on the cultural currents of his era, but at arm's length. "Moral and cultural conservatism" marked West Chester, Pennsylvania, near Philadelphia, where he grew up in a family of local gentry.[1] But cosmopolitan connections started early: his uncle, Sidney Homer (1864–1953), was a respected composer; his aunt, Louise Homer (1871–1947), was a leading contralto at the Metropolitan Opera, singing in its first efforts at American opera.[2] The first opera Barber saw featured her opposite Enrico Caruso in *Aida*. He watched her at Victor's recording studio, and she later sang his music at Carnegie Hall and on tour, sometimes with her nephew accompanying. The family cultivated Barber's ambition and his entry into Philadelphia's Curtis Institute of Music in 1924. Success as organist, pianist, singer, and composer came fast; the Philadelphia Orchestra premiered his *Overture to "The School for Scandal"* (1931). In Rosario Scalero, his Italian American composition teacher, and Leopold Stokowski, the Philadelphia's conductor, he met versions of musical manliness that Arturo Toscanini also embodied. As song composer he had to decide what he dared represent — he read poetry by Langston Hughes, the gay black writer, setting his "Fantasy in Purple" to music. He was within earshot of the furor over queerness on Broadway.

Barber also sensed early that his sexuality and his music were linked. He wrote his mother ("and *nobody else*") at age eight or nine that "I was not meant to be an athlet [*sic*]. I was meant to be a composer. . . . Don't ask me to try to forget this unpleasant thing and go play football. — *Please*."[3] The notion already existed that an aversion to sports and an attraction to the arts were a gay boy's traits, and Barber opened his note by announcing "my worrying secret." In a family that nourished his interests, his ambition to compose could not have seemed "worrying" — instead, he was signaling its connection to his homosexuality.

Soon he made an apparently easy entry into a gay life. At Curtis he met, sheltered, and fell in love with Gian Carlo Menotti, one year younger, just arrived from Italy, and "a mama's boy," as his biographer paraphrased Menotti. Each became the love of the other's life, despite later difficulties, and both moved in an artistic gay world. In this dimension, Barber reflected his temperament, social class, and times. Serious, conventionally manly, patrician in style, he hardly fit the stereotype of the effeminate fairy (an acid wit came closer); instead he was "queer" or "homosexual." Middle-class gay men often lived a "double life," but compartmentalizing their gay life rarely connoted shame or isolation. Barber was private but not secretive — social privilege furthered his sense that his sexuality was no one else's business, as opposed to something to hide. Without labeling his relationship with Menotti, he called attention to it in rhapsodic letters to his family ("He is quite perfect") and in public — he and Menotti allowed *American Home* magazine to feature in 1946 the home and life they shared. Nor did he use disguises — the cover marriage, the female date.[4]

Only later generations saw men like Barber as in "the closet." "How can the modern queer imagine what it would have been like to have lived as a homosexual in the 1930s, 1940s or 1950s?" John Gill has asked regarding Benjamin Britten, Barber's contemporary. "Britten and I might just as well have lived on different planets," especially given Britain's laws against gay sex. "Homosexuality," Gill claimed, "had a wholly different meaning then than it does now." But he undercut that claim: Britten and tenor Peter Pears had a "one-to-one relationship akin to many gay relationships today," "made no secret" of their shared bed "among their friends," and survived "the oddly public nature" of their "marriage" (perhaps odder to Gill than at the time); and composer Michael Tippett "was saying, in effect, we're here, we're queer, get used to it." Britten was "either happily unaware, or careless, about allowing queer themes to surface in his work," Gill argues—unconvincingly, given how Britten let such themes surface. The dangers facing Britten's generation should not be rendered as unfathomable to our own.[5]

Like other queer composers of his time, Barber focused on how to be an American artist more than a gay one. He faced divisions between America and Europe, between traditional and modernist modes, and between high and popular culture. Earlier Americans offered little guidance. Ambitions for American music's escape from Europe's shadow had run high at the turn of the century, when America's imperial success stirred visions of its cultural ascendancy as well. But most composers were "nationalists by quotation" who grafted vernacular music onto a familiar idiom, with results neither very new nor very American. Visiting the United States during the 1890s, Antonin Dvořák urged the use of African American and Indian music, and his "example focused a debate [about music] that had grown vigorous, sophisticated, and dense." But Dvořák employed American idioms more creatively than Americans, some of whom rejected his advice: "Purely national music has no place in art. What Negro melodies have to do with Americanism still remains a mystery to me," argued Edward MacDowell, a leading composer. After World War I, however, young composers like Aaron Copland, Virgil Thomson, and Roy Harris used modernist techniques learned in Europe to fashion music expressive of America. Although influenced by modernism and nationalism, Barber did not pursue so consciously a fusion of the two. Less a teacher and polemicist, he sidestepped quarrels over music's direction and forged his own style.[6]

Barber handled those matters differently in part because he experienced them differently. Copland and Thomson studied with Nadia Boulanger in Paris early in the 1920s. Barber's European ties came later and mainly from Italy, with Menotti as his guide. His first trip "awakened a romance with European society and culture that continued for the rest of his life." Barber favored composers of classical forms like Brahms, though he was a fair-minded judge of modernists. Too, the European-American divide was hardly neat. The "German-Austrian musical complex" often loomed larger—it was, Thomson complained, like "an international cartel operating through the familiar techniques of 'price-fixing, dumping, and pressures on the performing agencies.' " Barber was less burdened — or inspired — than others by a sense of sharp choices between Europe and America, or between older and modernist influences.[7]

Barber forged an "international" style, as he called it, or "no identifiable style," as composer Ned Rorem claimed. It still defined him as a composer of American music, and his 1936 *Symphony in One Movement* entered the informal sweepstakes for the "great American symphony." But his music usually lacked the American texts and idioms found in Copland's work. He used jazz and blues cleverly but not often and shared some of Britten's "capacity to assimilate other composers without merely imitating them."[8] He rarely created "Amurhican" music, as he wrote in jest in the 1930s — music that evoked the nation's values, history, or people. Even *Knoxville: Summer of 1915* (1947), setting a James Agee text for soprano and orchestra, was too personal (written as his father and Louise Homer were dying) and bittersweet to be standard Americana. His *Adagio for Strings* (1938) — the most performed, recorded, and played piece of American concert music ever written — lacked any American text, program, or vernacular sound. "Skyscrapers, subways, and train lights play no part in the music I write," he commented in 1935. "The universal basis of artistic spiritual communication . . . is through the emotions." His international style seemed confirmed by how often his work was performed, and sometimes premiered, in Europe, on occasion as the first American piece heard in a venue, and by his debt to Brahms and Sibelius. Toscanini's patronage added confirmation. Through Menotti, Barber met Toscanini in 1933, and in a 1938 broadcast Toscanini conducted the *Adagio* and his first *Essay for Orchestra* (1937). It was a mutually satisfying bargain. Barber got Toscanini's Old World imprimatur. Toscanini answered charges that he neglected American music.[9]

Because of how Barber's music meshed with the times, however, it became identified as American almost as much as did work by Copland and others. Nationalism in the 1930s prized both music that sounded American and American-composed music that sounded international, thereby carrying American prestige abroad. Barber spoke more to the second, or confounded any divide. He could display a light touch, but works like the *Adagio* and the *Essay* were somber. Their darker quality appealed because it suggested that American music could be serious, even tragic — it had come of age — and because Americans sought expression of the somber moods aroused by depression and war. Music and mood meshed when the *Adagio* was played for Franklin Roosevelt's funeral (and on radio broadcast) in 1945, on its path to becoming what Barber's friend Charles

Turner called America's "national funeral music." Heard upon the deaths of Albert Einstein, Princess Grace, John F. Kennedy, Robert Taft, and many others, it later figured in films such as *Elephant Man* (1980), *El Norte* (1983), *Platoon* (1986), and *Lorenzo's Oil*, (1992). Adapted from his String Quartet (1936), the *Adagio* was also arranged by Barber for chorus as *Agnus Dei* (1967) and by others for organ and various instrumental groups, and other composers echoed it in film and television scores. With that piece and in his career, he succeeded in being both international and American.[10]

He less easily finessed the fault line between modern and traditional. Barber never escaped criticism that his music was stodgy, and in a sense he never sought to. To detractors, his music got stuck in the rut of its unadventurous start. To sympathizers, consistency was a virtue, a sign that he knew what he wanted and resisted fashion. He continued to evolve his idiom and explore new texts, moods, and occasions and few exceeded him in range of genres — vocal, chamber, operatic, and symphonic music. Critic Nicolas Slonimsky, always generous in judgment, summed him up as one "whose patrician style in composition was etched with fierce romantic lines and yet stamped with an unmistakably modernist imprint." As a critic recently wrote, Barber's 1949 Sonata for Piano shows "how an unlikely amalgam of materials — Schoenbergian tone rows, Bach-like counterpoint, bravura piano writing out of Rachmaninoff, joyful riffs of Gershwin-style jazz — coheres into a convincing whole." No wonder that some scoffed at Barber's music as outdated even as others spotted something "ultra-modern."[11]

Complaints about his stodginess were themselves tradition-bound. Arts criticism, steeped in nineteenth-century notions of progress, valued work that seemed to foreshadow the next wave — Beethoven ushered in romanticism, Wagner pointed toward modernism, and so forth. In such criticism, Barber had little standing — he stormed no barricades. He and Copland were among those denounced in 1948 by Kurt List for catering to a "mass audience" familiar only with "descriptive narrative," indulging "romantic cliches" scarcely disguised by "mannerisms from [Arnold] Schoenberg," and failing to see how "atonal polyphony" was music's destiny.[12]

Detractors also saw Barber as stuck in an insular, high-culture position, but that accusation caused him less trouble. He accepted, without boasting, that he was a product of high culture. Patronage mattered: heiress Mary Curtis Bok, who founded the Curtis Institute, underwrote Barber's early career and helped Barber and Menotti purchase their home,

"Capricorn," near New York City. Unlike Menotti, he did little work for film and television, but he did not disdain their audiences. As he told listeners of a 1935 national broadcast of his music, "Too many composers today write with one or both eyes on small snobbish audiences in the larger cities, and then wonder why their music spreads no further." And he avoided toadying to elites; he disliked how "art had become . . . 'the after-dinner mint of the rich,' " just as he disliked "sensationalism, banality, and shoddiness." Such comments testified to the flexibility of his high-culture stance.[13]

Faulted for his high-culture position, Barber was also disparaged for appealing to large audiences. The two charges could coexist because their makers believed that a reactionary, banal high culture promoted unchallenging music — what they saw in Toscanini's American career, in radio broadcasts of the "classics," and at times in Barber's music. As Theodor Adorno and the Frankfurt School, relocated to the United States, fiercely maintained, the Toscanini cult was the apex of an "affirmative" culture that masked the corruptions of capitalism and sedated opposition to it. "The ruined farmer is consoled by the radio-instilled belief that . . . an order of things that allows him to hear Toscanini compensates for low market prices for farm products; even though he is ploughing cotton under, radio is giving him culture." Toscanini's "rule" as conductor reminded Adorno "of that of the totalitarian Fuhrer." Foreigners also neglected American music, as Roy Harris complained, "denying American creative musicians the right to speak to American people." Complaints like those bore down on Barber given his ties to Toscanini. "Mr. Barber's [Adagio] was 'authentic,' dull, 'serious' music — utterly anachronistic as the utterance of a young man of 28, A.D. 1938!" argued a letter to the New York Times. "What chance" had adventurous composers "in the forward march of the followers of David against the Philistines?" In such complaints, his music was at once too backward, too European, too high-toned, and too popular.[14]

Barber rarely spoke directly to such charges, but Menotti did. In 1938 he "presented Barber in a postmodernist light," according to Barber's biographer. "Must there be in art one 'modern idiom? . . . Because there is a Gertrude Stein, must we condemn a Thomas Mann? . . . Isn't it high time that a young David appeared and struck on the forehead that inflated monster which still parades under the anachronistic name of modern music?" Menotti captured an emerging "notion of heterogeneity as central to an understanding of modern culture" and suggested that it was hard to decide who was David and who Goliath, despite Adorno's certainty. But in the sharp arts politics of mid-century, the "notion of heterogeneity" was tenuous. The charge persisted that Barber's music was outdated.[15]

Barber's position was ambiguous in another way. He did not champion leftist or antiwar causes, yet *A Stopwatch and an Ordnance Map* (1940), a Stephen Spender poem about Spain's Civil War set for male chorus and kettledrums, echoed antiwar politics:

> At five a man fell to the ground
> And the watch flew off his wrist
> Like a moon struck from the earth.

But the echo was faint enough that a U.S. Army chorus performed *Stopwatch* during the war, or perhaps this "sinister music, with a threat of disaster in every measure," as a critic put it, spoke to wartime foreboding.[16] Barber's serious but nonpartisan temperament meshed well with the times.

Issues of gender and sexuality provided only grace notes to Barber's career in the 1930s, despite insinuations that some American music was effete. Besides the apparent muscularity of his music, his tie to Toscanini protected him: "Toscanini's masculine imagery" suggested that virile men now directed America's music. Composers' service to the American cause during World War II further enhanced their masculine stature. Poet Robert Horan did suggest in 1943 that Barber's first *Essays for Orchestra* (1937, 1942) were " 'music of disenchantment,' like the writing of Andre Gide"—a provocative comment given Gide's well-known homosexuality, but it caused no fuss. But Barber knew of troubling developments—composer Henry Cowell's arrest, the wartime raid on 329 Pacific Street in Brooklyn—and he moved in a more visible community of queer artists. As WASP as they come and distant from politics, Barber lacked vulnerabilities that the Jewish, leftist Copland had. But he did not altogether escape trouble.[17]

During World War II and the Cold War, Barber's career became shaped by the entwined currents of empire and sexuality. He was a prime example of how America's cultural empire depended on gay men. Many artists had doubts about their role in that empire or, like Copland, met others' resistance to it. Barber's difficulties grabbed no headlines, but as a gay artist he had them.

Drafted into military service like many gay men, Barber acted on that mix of patriotism, ambition, and circumstance that guided Americans during World War II. He wanted the armed forces to use composers "for propaganda" and heeded the advice of *Modern Music* that composers "make their abilities known" while being "good soldiers." Adept at making contacts in high places, he got the air force commander, General "Hap" Arnold, to commission his Second Symphony (1944), dubbed "Flight," and the Boston Symphony's Serge Koussevitsky, a champion of American music, to conduct it. The air force urged Barber to "write this symphony in quarter-tones" (he did not), helped him get electronic equipment from Bell Labs, and promoted the symphony's broadcast in Moscow, London, and other allied cities. But Barber kept distant from martial glory: he took a "rather dangerous" flight in a B-24 bomber, talked to veterans in a psychopathic ward "about their various mental problems and fears," and saw his work as capturing the "dynamism" of flight, not the destruction U.S. bombers unleashed.

The result was not wholly successful. Virgil Thomson derided the symphony as "Hamlet-like backward yearning toward the womb of German romanticism," albeit "Hamlet in modern dress," and as "a work glorifying the Army Air Forces," foreshadowing Barber's later regrets about the piece. Still, the symphony was novel by Barber's standards and reflected wartime ambitions for music. Boston critics saw it as "good American propaganda in the best sense of the word"—music to enhance the "morale" of U.S. forces and "introduce fittingly the American spirit and the American musical genius to peoples of other lands." Seen as a "good war" by many Americans, World War II also seemed good for American culture.[18]

Although no chauvinist, Barber enjoyed representing his nation in Europe, where as conductor and composer he found more success. Amid wartime amity, his music was "extremely popular in Russia," *Newsweek* claimed in 1944, as it remained to a degree in the Cold War. Barber found Europeans, especially Russians, "crazy to know about American music," and delighted in an invitation to Leningrad. "Diplomats are always suspicious and artists quickly bridge frontiers," he believed. Soviet-U.S. musical exchange soon suffered from the Cold War chill, but Barber found rich venues elsewhere in Europe, and he was eager to be there anyway, often with Menotti. He also grasped the politics of conducting his music in West Berlin in 1951, realizing that "several years ago these people were my 'enemies' and that my personal position in conducting them was, to put it lightly, somewhat precariously 'superimposed.' I suddenly recalled while conducting the Second ['Flight'] Symphony that this work was composed while I was nominally in that Air Force which was technically responsible for those square miles of desolation and rubble in the middle of their particular city!" Talent brought about the success abroad he and others had. But as he knew, music does often follow the flag — and wave it.[19]

These developments affected Barber's career, but not his music in any obvious way. Although an astute observer of people, events, and trends around him, he rarely acknowledged that his music reflected them, although others claimed that he rewrote his Cello Concerto (1945) in reaction to the atomic bombing of Hiroshima.[20] His work displayed the tensile quality of much mid-century American music, but while Leonard Bernstein called one of his symphonies *The Age of Anxiety* (1949), Barber did nothing comparably indicative of 1940s angst. His output issued slowly but steadily. Barber produced *Capricorn Concerto* (1944); his Cello Concerto; a ballet score for Martha Graham, *Medea* (1946); *Knoxville: Summer of 1915* (1947); the Piano Sonata that Vladimir Horowitz championed; a song cycle (*Melodies passageres*, 1950–51) to Rilke poems; *Hermit Songs* (1952–53), reflecting "his love affair with Ireland"; *Prayers of Kierkegaard* (1954); and lighter works.[21]

Conservatives still faulted him for modernist traits that progressives nevertheless found lacking. Depending on a listener's vantage point, he pursued modernist influences either less courageously than others or more subtly, as in using "twelve-tone procedures in [a] thoroughly tonal context" in *Nocturne* (1959).[22] Barber's modernism seemed pale compared to rigorously serial music, and his work retained a lyrical, though often troubled, sound. And amid composers' growing attachment to academic culture, he avoided even short-term teaching posts, triggering resentment of him as the rare composer whose income came from writing music.

In the 1950s, Barber's creativity and stature enabled him to withstand attacks, which others also suffered (Copland was "too popular to be a great composer" and his music "too triumphant"). It did not hurt that many avant-gardists disdained popularity. Oliver Larkin wrote in 1960 about the split between art-for-art's-sake insularity and art-as-engagement vitality: "Between these two conceptions lies all that was daring, obscure, sensational, stirring, compassionate, hateful, sharply intellectual, violently expressive, or warmly fraternal in the art of the Cold War years." Barber too fell "between these two conceptions," another reason that many audiences and critics embraced his music. Leonard Meyer, for one, questioned serial music's inevitability, seeing a future "characterized, not by the cumulative development of a single style, but by the coexistence of a number of alternative styles" that would "grow side by side—[Pierre] Boulez and [John] Cage as well as Barber." Meyer doubted that Western music was reaching a dead end, even if "a certificate of death is issued from Princeton or Darmstadt," two places where avant-gardists concentrated.[23]

Meanwhile, the drive for American music, which Barber never fully joined, faded. The search for national traits was "a game that quickly wears thin," Elliott Carter noted. To Roger Sessions, it was "a formula too facile" to solve "our musical problems." With America a colossus, being American sufficed for a composer; sounding American was less urgent. When Leonard Bernstein asked TV audiences, "What is American music?" in 1958, his answer popularized the theme of heterogeneity arising since the 1930s. "We've taken it all in: French, Dutch, German, Scotch, Scandinavian, Italian, and all the rest, and learned it from one another, borrowed it, stolen it, cooked it all up in a melting pot." As Barber said of his opera *Vanessa* (1957), "An opera need not have an American setting to be an American opera. Besides, art is international, and if an idea is inspired, it needs no boundaries."[24]

Vanessa's fate showed that boundaries remained, but at issue now was whether Americans wrote good music, not American music. Commissioned and premiered by the Metropolitan Opera, *Vanessa* was greeted "as if the honor of the nation as well as the health of the box office depended" on Barber, critic Howard Taubman wrote, especially since the Met had avoided American opera for years. After approaching Thornton Wilder and Stephen Spender and rejecting Tennessee Williams's *A Streetcar Named Desire*, Barber had Menotti write a libretto and direct the Met production, with lavish sets by Cecil Beaton. "At last, an American grand opera!" cheered its conductor, Dimitri Mitropoulos—gay, like the others heading up the production—approving Barber's refusal to be "contaminated by different kinds of contemporary experimentation." It was, wrote a British critic, "romantic opera in the best old traditions, not an adventure into the unknown but a fresh expression of already established taste." Americans praised *Vanessa* "almost as a matter of national pride," Barber's biographer notes—"the best U.S. opera yet staged at the Metropolitan." Barber wrote "music of such haunting beauty and cumulative power that it echoes in the ear long after the performance is over." A Pulitzer Prize followed.[25]

Nationalism like that was a double-edged sword, however. When *Vanessa* became the first American opera mounted at the Salzburg Festival, some critics dismissed it as dated ("a chromaticized Puccini, plus a few ounces of Wagner, Strauss, and Tchaikovsky and a shot of Debussy") compared to work by living European composers. In response, Taubman deplored how "some Europeans resented our achievement in an area that has been a European province" and parodied their reactions to *Vanessa*: "Isn't opera a European invention, and shouldn't creativity in this field by materialistic Americans be suspect?" Americans' music, if no longer "American music," remained contested. Especially among Europeans fearing decline in their cultural influence, one scholar explains, "American composers like Aaron Copland, Virgil Thomson, and George Gershwin were dismissed as mere popularizers" cheapening "the modernist experiments of an Igor Stravinsky or an Arnold Schoenberg." Americans defended *Vanessa* against what they saw as Europeans' snobbery, pointing to the "fine line that divides 'legitimate' from 'illegitimate' eclecticism (the former is usually described as 'influence')." Where Europeans posited a single vector of progress and assumed that "since (in their opinion) 'Vanessa' was a calamity, all American art is equally calamitous," *Saturday Review* pointed to America's "conglomerate culture."[26]

Vanessa retained a tenuous place in repertory, certainly more of one than most European operas of this period or the other nineteen American operas premiered at the Met as of 2000. Few others left *Vanessa*'s large traces — selections continued to be performed and recorded — or had premieres followed, as Ethan Mordden recalled of *Vanessa*, by "the humming of falling sevenths up and down Broadway as the audience scampered homewards." Its queerness, offered at the opera queen's Valhalla, the old Met house, helped its success — it was one of "the encoded queer operas of the age," James McCourt claims, "the pink-tea queen's fantasy of betrayal," whose star, Eleanor Steber, was "a great gay icon right down to the 1970s" when she "sang to the men in the then-regnant Continental Baths."[27]

Steber's role points up Barber's eagerness to collaborate with women. Many composers wrote for the female voice, but Barber went beyond convention. Men dominated the upper reaches of instrumental careers, but he chose two women, Raya Garboursova and Zara Nelsova, to champion his Cello Concerto. In commissioning *Knoxville*, Steber was the first American singer to seek a work for orchestra and voice, and she advanced her career by performing American music like *Vanessa*. Working with Leontyne Price, Barber took the unusual step of allying with a black and not fully tested singer; Price chose his *Hermit Songs* for her 1954 New York recital debut.

Meanwhile, there were complications in Barber's life, such as his jealousy over Menotti's success. Menotti too was accused of writing dated,

second-rate music. Still, in operas like *The Consul* (1950) he sought political relevance that most composers shunned, especially amid the Red
Scare. He also had success where few others did, in commercial theater
and television (famously with *Amahl and the Night Visitors* in 1951), and
won a Pulitzer (for *The Consul*) years before Barber did. In Menotti's
recollections—which Barber endorsed "with a charming sense of humor"—Barber wished him success but also "considered my very music
an enemy," apparently for its popularity, and "the friendship could get
very stormy." Barber sometimes privately dismissed Menotti's music, for
all that he sought his role in projects like *Vanessa*.[28]

Music and personal life meshed intricately in these lives. The two knew
many gay men, friendship sometimes spilling into intimacy. By 1958, the
young conductor Thomas Schippers "had been Menotti's companion for
eight years," according to Menotti's biographer. The reserved and sometimes acidic Barber seemed jealous, even though he had parallel relationships, as with flautist Manfred Ibel, to whom Barber and Menotti deeded a
portion of the Capricorn property in 1973. Although not a recluse, Barber
tired of the hectic social life Menotti preferred and resented his easy way
with others, women or men. When actress Tallulah Bankhead and others
arrived at Capricorn, "Sam locked himself in the bathroom to wait out
their visit," Menotti recalled, but "they stayed for eight or nine hours. . . .
We had to get food to him through the outside window." "Sam considers
every friend of mine a threat," Menotti said in 1978. The demands on
Menotti of his festival at Spoleto, Italy, where Schippers often presided,
added strain.[29]

None of that was tabloid fodder in the 1950s, but public accounts,
which Barber appears to have endorsed, revealed a good deal about Barber and Menotti. A 1954 biography featured Barber's "Dear Mother"
letter in its first paragraph and noted his ties to Menotti. The two, *Newsweek* told readers in 1958, "have been the closest of friends for 30 years"
and share "a rambling country home with two studios." *Newsweek* also
prominently quoted from "Dear Mother." Barber was labeled an American composer but implicitly also a queer one. The two identities wove
together—a case of the "open secret" about homosexuality, in D. A.
Miller's phrase.[30]

By letting so much be publicized, Barber and Menotti were as out,
to use a later term, as anyone in serious music circles, except those un-
willingly exposed—Henry Cowell arrested in the 1930s, Marc Blitzstein
murdered by sailors in 1964 "in response to his sexual advances," as a
later account put it. As a couple, only England's Britten and Pears let

so much appear. Barber was a far cry from Bernstein, with his decades-long agony over being gay and married, or Thomson, with his concealed gay life. Perhaps Barber's openness fed Bernstein's animosity toward him (returned in courtly fashion by Barber): Bernstein was "conductor of one of the greatest orchestras in the world," but part of his identity "was as a composer and as a homosexual," Joan Peyser comments, "and in both of these arenas Barber seemed to do better than he."[31]

Critics on occasion hinted at Barber's sexuality. Though queer, Thomson sounded like Charles Ives, the scourge of "pansy" composers, in his patronizing praise of Barber's *Medea*: he heard "a Samuel Barber freed at last from . . . mincing respectabilities. . . . Once more the theater has made a man out of an American composer." In a savage review, the *New Republic* explained *Vanessa*'s "fatal weakness" by claiming that Barber had "repressed his own stylistic individuality and instead favored an imitation of Menotti's musical mannerisms," as if the two had succumbed to a fatal enmeshment.[32]

Gay composers also remained vulnerable because of their wide appeal. To be sure, boundaries between serious and popular music long had been crossed — by Gershwin and Duke Ellington, for example, and in "the contemporary fad of jazzing the classics."[33] Opera stars like Maria Callas, Lily Pons, and Leontyne Price warbled on TV variety shows in the 1950s. But insofar as "serious" composers crossed boundaries, queer tonalists did much of the work. Bernstein was the protean figure, above all with *West Side Story* (1957). Notable too were Copland's film scores, Menotti's operas, and Barber's *Adagio*. Popularity invited scrutiny and criticism that such composers cheapened music by pandering to the masses.

Queer composers were likewise vulnerable because their tonal style was deemed retrograde, while "complexity boys" (Thomson's term) gained critical favor and academic underwriting.[34] Unlike Barber and Menotti, many "complexity boys" were also enamored of science and distant from religion. And like Abstract Expressionist painters, their work was forbidden in the Soviet Union, making them emblems of Western freedom. To be sure, not all queer composers were tonalists, not all tonalists were queer, and no grand edicts about a queer/straight divide were issued. But associations of queerness with tonality and manliness with complexity did inflect much commentary. "The straight boys claimed the moral high ground of modernism and fled to the universities," Susan McClary has stated, "and the queers literally took center stage in concert halls and opera houses and ballet," with music "that people are more likely to respond to." In Nadine Hubbs's subtler formulation, "the ideology of the time linked tonality . . . with homosexuality and defined it by contrast to nontonality or atonality—especially of dissonant and serial leanings—and masculine heterosexuality." Barber "loathes the imputations of the serial elite," Rorem noted in 1950, and Menotti scoffed at assertions that serialists embodied progress and at "artists who say, 'Well, it satisfied *me*!,' as art should be an act of love and not a form of masturbation."[35]

For Barber and Menotti, issues of queer identity and artistic content spiked in 1959 when *Saturday Review* critic Irving Kolodin assessed Menotti's new Spoleto festival. Menotti's "Festival of Two Worlds" involved "what might be called the three sexes," he wrote, and its opera fans included "those who have, for queer reasons of their own, become camp-followers of this peculiar art." Kolodin bewailed the festival's "reputation" as "the happy hunting ground of the 'boys' who have previously made the ballet their particular, bloodless passion," whose presence may "keep away as many as it attracts." He deplored their "preciosity" and "prejudices" and sought " 'open' and 'closed' performances, with the former set aside for what used to be innocently called a 'mixed' audience, but now has a significance unthought of previously."[36]

It was a stunning tirade far afield from Kolodin's usual style and the reviewer's usual stance (review the art, not the audience). He made no direct attack on Menotti and Barber, but his sniping at operas appealing to those with "queer reasons" certainly referred to their new piece. Menotti's recollections suggest something Kolodin did not acknowledge. "The Italians just couldn't bear the idea that it [the festival] was a success," he recalled, and "I was accused of having a festival of and for homosexuals. A very well known Italian stage director and a stage designer hired a plane and dumped obscene leaflets on Spoleto," ones that "showed a bull with a huge erection, saying something like 'We *real* men salute the Festival.' This was only one of many Italian sabotage maneuvers against us." So much for the idea that Europeans were more accepting than Americans of queer artists. Perhaps, too, Kolodin projected onto the audience his reactions to the prominent queers at Spoleto in its early years, such as Copland, Wilder, W. H. Auden, and Robert Rauschenberg. Barber and Menotti surely read Kolodin's comment, soon recycled in Jess Stearn's *The Sixth Man*.[37]

Their offering at Spoleto was *A Hand of Bridge* (1959), a biting, jazzy chamber opera in which two couples desperately sing secret thoughts while playing bridge. Both subject and music were departures for Barber, who usually avoided topical material. He had entered the crowded field of commentary on suburbia's woes, but the pungent brevity of *Hand* stood out in this field, as did its mix of sexuality, class resentment, and adultery. As the opera climaxes, David sings his yearning for "twenty naked girls, twenty naked boys, tending to my pleasures," with "every day another version of every known perversion, like in that book of Havelock Ellis hidden in the library behind the 'Who's Who.' To whip a lovely Nubian slave for fun; or better still, Mister Pritchett [David's boss], the bastard!" Fury over failing marriages and mean bosses was hardly new, but giving it a queer edge was striking.[38]

Kolodin's comment on the audience suggests that the closet—"closed" performances for queers—was now being imagined. The opera's expression of same-sex desire stood out from other American music of the period. That two male partners wrote it added to its force, as did its derisive comment on concealing same-sex desire—"Havelock Ellis hidden in the library behind the 'Who's Who.'" This opera, like the openness of their relationship, suggests that by the standards of the time Barber and Menotti let others know a great deal. In *A Hand of Bridge*, they tugged at the conventions of the open secret by implicitly connecting their private identity to their artistic product, and they mocked the newly forming closet.

In Empire's Capital

Nowhere did imperial ambitions for American culture swell more than in New York City, where Barber's role in those ambitions flourished and then failed. Long apparent, those ambitions soared further when World War II damaged Europe, drove many of its artists and intellectuals to America, and enlarged American power. "The fall of Paris as the bastion of European modernism cleared the way for New York's rise to cultural preeminence," according to Leonard Wallock, in *New York: Culture Capital of the World*.[39]

The arts both disguised and expressed its ambitions. Since "New York had become so thoroughly cosmopolitan, the art that it inspired proved neither provincial nor nationalistic," one scholar argues. New York artists "devised a new language of expression: abstract in form and international in aesthetic" and "a modern *American* art that transcended its own culture."[40] That art included experimental composers like John Cage and Morton Feldman, while Copland and others moved from overt nationalism to a more abstract Americanism. Composers tended to insist, as Barber did, that "art is international." Bernstein conducted Ives and Copland alongside Haydn and Mahler, making the natives as international as they were American. But the boast that New York's art was not nationalistic was itself nationalistic—a heady assertion that the city was the world's cultural capital. The claim of universality also sounded like one of superiority.

Opera rode the tide of America's surging wealth and ambition. "The 1950s was the greatest period of growth in American operatic history," marked by the Met's plans for a new house, the renewal of grand opera in Chicago, and new regional companies. Opera also changed. The ties of audience, performers, and repertory to ethnicity diminished and audiences became more democratized insofar as "money and money alone," not social lineage, mattered, and skyboxes in sports stadiums soon displaced opera boxes "as a symbol of privilege." Amid these changes, Met general manager Rudolf Bing combined ambition with artistic and social conservatism.[41]

Advancing that ambition was Lincoln Center for the Performing Arts, centerpiece of the Lincoln Square Urban Renewal Area project announced in 1955. Diverse impulses lay behind it. As carried on by empire-builder Robert Moses, urban renewal "promised to revitalize the city's traditional urban fabric by destroying whole sections of it." For others, the project was "a heroic and definitive attempt to refute the accusations of both outsiders and New Yorkers that the city, and with it the United States as a whole, was too focused on the bottom line to be a significant player on the international cultural stage." Circumstances lured key players. The New York Philharmonic feared that its home at Carnegie Hall would be razed; the Met wished to vacate its creaky 1883 house. The cooperation of competing institutions was "startling," Alan Rich wrote, "as if Macy's had gone into partnership with Gimbel's." Civic moguls like Moses, John D. Rockefeller III, and Governor Nelson Rockefeller secured funds and agreement from private, federal, state, and local sources.[42]

Imperial motifs ran through the creation of Lincoln Center. As the City Planning Commission claimed, it "will almost certainly make New York the musical capital of the world now and for many years to come." New York, promised a corporate chief, would become "the cultural center of the world." One historian later asserted, "You'd have to run the clock back to a Medici palace in Renaissance Florence to find the kind of complex of culture that had now seized the imaginations of six pioneering men in New York."[43]

Of course, not every ambition for Lincoln Center was imperial, nor should everything uttered in order to pry money from wallets be taken at face value. Companies exploited the moment. "There's more than money in New York," Bankers Trust announced; Lincoln Center proved "New York's culture mindedness." Just as Lincoln Center was "alone in its world," so the "Lincoln Continental, too, is alone in its private world," proclaimed Ford Motor. Postwar affluence could support expanded public services: as "a community responsibility," Lincoln Center president William Schuman argued, the arts "should be placed alongside the already accepted obligations for health, welfare and education." President Kennedy's arts adviser stressed the nation's vitality, not its hegemony.[44]

Still, Lincoln Center's backers often sounded grandly imperial. "We're building something that will be here for 500 years," one announced. Some Europeans apparently agreed. "Up to now, music has had two capitals: Milan and New York," La Scala's director told John D. Rockefeller. "After your center is built, there will be only one—New York." The project also advanced the city's dominance at home—in music it "exercised a hegemony over the rest of the country that it had not previously attained and could not subsequently retain."[45]

Like most imperial visions, those for Lincoln Center were at times defensive, designed to counter fears that Europe's culture was paramount, America's second-rate, and Russia's gaining the upper hand. Critic Howard Taubman hoped the Center would "show that democracy has the determination and power to devote itself to things of the mind and heart as well as to creature comforts." Facing Soviet Sputniks and musicians, the United States had to get beyond cars with giant tail fins for its cultural muscle to win the Cold War. Skeptics thought that an extravagant bricks-and-mortar project expressed rather than disproved American materialism, but they were brushed aside. As "the cultural capital of the world," New York "deserves a monumental focus as criterion of free world music, art, theater and dance," backers argued. The *Times* put the point gently: "It will be a beacon to the world, revealing that Americans know how to build the life of the spirit on its material bounty." As John D. Rockefeller worried, a lack of cultural leadership "has been a handicap in our relations with other peoples and, for that reason, it is my hope that Lincoln Center may become a symbol before the world of America's cultural development."[46]

An imperial mood surfaced in other ways too. Gifts from West Germany, Austria, Italy, and Japan seemed like tribute from defeated nations to the victor. As Edgar Young, a key figure in the Center's creation, said, "It was ironic that foreign gifts came only from former enemy countries." Rudolf Bing warned that the United States "simply could not *afford* to build a new opera house that looked old-fashioned and cheap next to the new theaters of Europe and Russia." Nor could it afford to include the New York City Opera at the Center, though he lost this fight: "The rest of the world and indeed the less knowledgeable parts of the United States will find it difficult to distinguish between two opera companies within the Lincoln Center." Here also was empires' impulse to show off in order to awe others or reassure themselves. America, John Dizikes notes, had become "a centralized imperial state of colossal wealth and power. Naturally, the nation wished to celebrate itself." It did, but anxiously. "Have We 'Culture'? Yes—and No," an article by William Schuman was titled.[47]

Empires are usually manly and militaristic, and so was this one, with race, class, gender, and empire linked. In the Center's creation, women were rare among decision makers, secondary in publicity, ignored in commissions and programming, and few among performers except as singers. Many Americans had asserted that a robust culture would be men's work—almost always white men's—and imperial culture valued men's achievements. Empires also need armies, and the Center had one: "The tasks of organizing and constructing the vast cultural complex began to resemble a military campaign," and "military personnel figured prominently in the growing Lincoln Center bureaucracy," especially retired General Maxwell Taylor—"the *cultured* war hero"—the Center's head until recalled to government service. As Taylor's role indicated, imperial culture required male authority within it, not just in its stance toward other cultures. While the Center was touted as a monument to democracy, most authorities regarded democracy as antithetical to the operation of the arts. "A symphony orchestra is not a democratic institution," William Schuman insisted. It "must be an absolute monarchy—the conductor is king."[48]

Imperial ambitions and Cold War fears underwrote public assistance. Federal funds and leverage enabled the purchase and leveling of the Lincoln Square area. In Washington, the 1958 Cultural Center Act, positing that "cultural enrichment is a vital part of our nation's well being," created what became the Kennedy Center, its land given by the federal government and its board appointed by the president. After private giving faltered and Kennedy was assassinated, Congress funded construction in an effort to turn "the sleepy southern town . . . into Rome-on-the Potomac."[49] In foreign policy, American leaders preferred an informal empire that relied on private-public partnerships, eschewed the brutalities of conquest, and finessed the nation's anti-imperial traditions. In cultural affairs, too, they preferred to dominate through example rather than conquest. They saw American power as benign, creating a "free world" in culture as in politics. They insisted that the United States pushed universal values, not its own. Empires talk that way. Speaking at the Center's groundbreaking, President Dwight Eisenhower, who often bristled at the bellicosity of other Americans, stressed "common contact with the performing arts" and "a true interchange of the fruits of national cultures," which would "develop a mighty influence for peace and understanding through the world."[50] Ike also promoted cultural exchange with the Soviets. Amid an unstable mix of intense competition and incipient thaw in the Cold War, artists, orchestras, and ballet companies were lobbed like harmless missiles into the enemy's heartland. In that spirit Barber went to Moscow in 1962 as an emblem of American freedom.

As Barber's role indicated, cultural empire relied in part on gay men. Although cultural moguls rarely acknowledged that reliance, they understood it when they offered Barber three commissions for Lincoln Center's inaugural—two for Philharmonic Hall and the sole one for the Metropolitan Opera House. Their choice owed not to approval of Barber's sexuality but to familiarity with gay artists' role, confidence that the open secret would stay intact, desire to expand America's empire in the arts, and Barber's stature.

Now at its peak, that stature made him an obvious choice to create a new opera for a new house, a task Bing first pressed on Barber in 1959. There was no doubt an American would do the job—how else could Americans celebrate their maturity? And there was little competition. Copland, to some minds Barber's superior, had limited success with *The Tender Land* (1954) and did not see himself as an opera composer. Bernstein's biting *Candide* (1956) seemed as much musical theater as opera and gained critical approval slowly, and it would have been too cozy for the Philharmonic's new director also to do an opera. Others lacked Barber's stature. A revival—*Porgy and Bess*, for example—would have flunked the test of doing something new. Barber had a Pulitzer for *Vanessa*, wide-ranging compositions for voice, a "tonal and lyrical" style pleasing to "conservative Met audiences," and a feel for the European/American divide.[51] Self-crowned monarch of world culture, the United States still had to be heir to something worthy, and the debt to Europe in opera was especially large. Yet it had to do something fresh, not a cheap imitation of Old World culture. Although Europeans sniped at it, *Vanessa* showed Barber up to the task, if any American was. Even family history helped: Louise Homer had been a star at the Met.

New success by Barber confirmed the Met's wisdom. His Piano Concerto (1962) premiered at the new Philharmonic Hall—John Browning, junior member of the Barber-Menotti circle, was soloist—and marked his career's "high point." Likened to Russian concertos such as Prokofiev's in its mix of propulsiveness and lyricism, it still featured Barber's idiom. It garnered instant approval, his second Pulitzer, a popular recording by Browning, who played it widely in Russia and elsewhere, and a place in the repertory. As an official at Barber's publisher recalled, "There was no one else, he was our most popular composer—our best." But his second commission—*Andromache's Farewell* (1962) for soprano and orchestra, later choreographed by Martha Graham—met criticism, which suggested that fashion was "beginning to turn away from the lyrical, Romantic style" Barber used, his biographer notes—or that such criticism was finding more favor, since it was hardly new. Barber was in a tight spot. Critics would pounce on anything *Vanessa*-like, but audiences might spurn anything novel like *A Hand of Bridge*.[52]

Opera was, in any event, a perilous undertaking, especially in the United States. Many composers produced clunkers before achieving success, but the expense of opera in America gave composers few chances to find their voices or revise their work, one reason that no "national opera tradition" existed to guide Barber. As Ethan Mordden notes, "The praiseworthy American works respond less to tradition and continuity than to the one moment . . . that they themselves create." The absence of an American tradition freed Barber but also denied him guardrails. At the same time, the long European tradition of opera could seem confining. As Noel Coward once quipped, "The trouble with opera is not that opera isn't what it used to be, but that it is." Barber sagged under such burdens until others forced his hand, doing the new opera only "because I realized none of my friends would speak to me if I didn't," he later said.[53]

Challenges of occasion compounded those of genre. The opera would appear in a house untested acoustically, technically, and in other ways, yet would have to show it off. For the double premiere of an opera and a house, much hinged on the opening run, indeed on the opening night. It had to buttress an imperial occasion yet rise above mere imperial self-congratulation.

Barber seemed well suited for this balancing act, yet his fit was less easy than it appeared. Although he lived near New York, Barber was not a New York artist—he did not identify with the city or grasp its pulse as Menotti had. Though cradled by elite institutions, he was no court composer. Patrons' support had come so easily that it seemed natural to him—deserved, not bought. Not trying to shock, he also was not trying to flatter. Even *Vanessa* had forbidding qualities — a Gothic tale of love and abortion, with debts to Isak Dinesen and Chekhov, set to music that was harshly whirling in some passages, deeply lyrical in others. Barber had long nodded to fashion but also kept it at arm's length, as he now would in the imperial mood enveloping Lincoln Center's debut.

He also showed discomfort with the American imperium. It was a "rather sad and unenthusiastic" Barber who in 1953 told Ned Rorem of Copland's ordeal before Senator Joe McCarthy. *A Hand of Bridge* challenged Cold War antihomosexuality. In 1964, Barber visited his publisher and, "with a gusto that increased our admiration for him from one torn page to the next," destroyed copies of his Second Symphony ("Flight") and withdrew it from publication (it was reconstructed, performed, and recorded after his death). Barber's vague explanation — "it is not a very good work" — hardly accounted for the ferocity of his action.[54] He could simply have let the little-performed piece fade into oblivion. Perhaps weighing on him were his tribulations in composing a new opera, the symphony's commission by an air force that bombed enemy cities, and Virgil Thomson's jab about "a work glorifying the Army Air Forces." Barber did not rebel against American imperialism. No major American composer did, though Bernstein offered satire in *Candide* and celebrity gloss later for radical causes. But judging by *A Hand of Bridge*, Barber was bitter about the increasing antihomosexuality and conversant with critiques of America's Cold War. If not rebellious, he was disquieted. Composing for an imperial moment was both the culmination of his career and an awkward task.

Barber's tortuous path to a story and libretto indicated as much. He considered several gay authors and texts with homoerotic themes. Tennessee Williams, whose *A Streetcar Named Desire* Barber had rejected earlier because it "leaves no room for music," only offered an unsuccessful play. James Baldwin seemed uninterested. Barber approached Thornton Wilder, and Stephen Spender suggested Henry James's *The American*, "but Sam thought it too close to Puccini (with the convent ending)" — an unwelcome prospect given how Menotti's operas were ridiculed as Puccini-esque.[55]

The most arresting possibility was Herman Melville's *Moby-Dick*, which, in Italian translation, Barber had once considered for an oratorio. The Met, perhaps knowing his interest, now suggested it, and Barber took it seriously enough to transcribe passages.[56] Then he backed off — "an opera that had a lot of whales and water, but no soprano, had a doubtful future," he supposedly explained, or in another version, "Too much water for an opera, and too much wind." Those words reflected his sense of tradition—grand opera usually showcased female voices, and Barber was committed to using Leontyne Price for his new opera. They also reflected his fondness for wry comments to fend off tough issues. Opera composers had latitude, and Barber might have changed the story to introduce a soprano role. But then he would have abandoned his commitment to textual fidelity, a trait that may not serve opera composers well. *Moby-Dick* was also an intimidating text of American literature, and it would have compounded the Americanness of the occasion.

And there was *Moby-Dick's* homoeroticism—known to scholars, too obvious for Barber to have missed, and alluded to in his "no soprano" comment.[57] What would he do with this famous passage? "Squeeze! Squeeze! Squeeze! all the morning long; I squeezed that sperm till I myself almost melted into it. . . . let us all squeeze ourselves into each other; let us squeeze ourselves universally into the very milk and sperm of kindness." He might have done something splendid, but he chose not to try.

Perhaps Barber thought Benjamin Britten had a corner on this market. Britten had excelled in nautical operas since *Peter Grimes* (1945) and had staked out Melville's homoeroticism with *Billy Budd* (1951). He showed a knack for American vernacular in *Paul Bunyan* (1941) and for American high culture in *Billy Budd* and *The Turn of the Screw* (1954). Britten also showed what a gay composer faced on imperial occasions. His commission for Queen Elizabeth II's coronation, which yielded *Gloriana* (1953), met "a vein, undeniably, of homophobia," including composer William Walton's complaint, "There are enough buggers in the place already, it's time it was stopped." Britten's problems with others stemmed from his relationship with Peter Pears, his music's allusions to same-sex love, and his pacifism—his *War Requiem* (1962) premiered while Barber worked on his new opera. "Throughout his life," notes Alex Ross, Britten "met with loud applause at the front and murmurs from the back." And not just the back—concerning *Turn of the Screw*, a Paris critic noted "the composer's customary intense preoccupation with homosexual love." Barber had cause to avoid Britten's example.[58]

Yet he did not set aside *Moby-Dick* out of fear of antiqueer reactions. His approaches to gay writers suggest little queasiness on that score. Nor did creative caution seize him, since his final choice, Shakespeare's *Antony and Cleopatra*, presented its own hurdles. It did not put him outside Britten's shadow, for the Met scheduled Britten's *A Midsummer Night's Dream* (1960) for the same season. Shakespeare resisted treatment, as many composers had learned and not a few people had warned

Barber. He had never set Shakespeare, and he realized it had "tongue twisters" such as "You have broken the article of your oath which you shall never have tongue to charge me with."[59] There was also no sure success in mining Cleopatra's story, as several dozen failed operas suggested, including one by the American Henry Hadley at the Met in 1921.

Temperament, not timidity, led him to *Antony and Cleopatra*. It seemed a natural choice for someone steeped in literature and at the peak of his powers. If it bowed to conservative tastes among audiences and patrons, his treatment could still challenge them. If the occasion was imperial, the story hardly was triumphant. Barber knew his opera was about "world politics," as he put it, and just when America's empire was facing strain. Writing Bing about scheduling problems, Barber joked, "Are we, as Mme Nhu says, so powerless?", referring to Madame Ngo Dinh Nu, notorious sister-in-law of murdered South Vietnamese Premier Ngo Dinh Diem.[60]

But judged by his descriptions, full of passive verbs, *Antony* happened as much to as by him. "After Vanessa," Barber commented, "it was suggested to me that I write another opera." He approached Baldwin and Williams. "Nothing happened. I gave up. Then I was reminded" of his interest in "my favorite of Shakespeare's plays. And everyone thought Cleopatra would be a wonderful role for Leontyne," just as it suited racial sensibilities to have a black singer take the role.[61]

These were not the words of someone who seized the occasion. Grand operas, the *New York Times* opined, "involve large sums of money and the talent, brains and brawn of hundreds of people," and Barber's idea "has grown into a behemoth with a thousand arms, legs and tongues." Even the Met's choice of Franco Zeffirelli as librettist and director was something "Barber says he was not aware of until he had read it in the newspapers." As Zeffirelli noted immodestly, "I was concerned with shaping the whole opera," as if Barber merely composed the sound track. "Working with Sam was very congenial, almost too much so. He loved all my ideas so much that in the end I have to serve as my own critic." Adding strain was a rehearsal schedule of "exactly 24 working days—and three weeks is barely enough time to prepare a new product of a standard opera." Barber "spoke with assurance about his opera" but also "as though the music had been written by someone else," a telling comment given the forcefulness of Zeffirelli and Bing ("Underneath this cold exterior beats a heart of stone," Bing said of himself).[62]

Barber astutely managed his career, but he was no veteran of industrial-scale arts except for *Vanessa*, more a family affair, given that Menotti was librettist and director. "Physically he resembles a successful businessman," noted one observer, but he was "probably the only living composer who does nothing but compose," *Saturday Review* reported. "He does not perform, he does not lecture, he writes neither newspaper reviews nor books, he does not organize music festivals, he is not at the helm of an opera company or a symphony orchestra. He is no professor nor a 'composer in residence' anywhere." Though witty and vivacious with others, he preferred solitude over systems, his muse over others' ideas.[63]

Personal burdens also weighed on him. His sister's death in 1961 "put him into a depression that noticeably affected his ability to work for a long period." Much of *Antony* was written amid visits to his ailing mother. The Met's decision not to use Menotti as librettist or director produced "perhaps the only moment of bitterness that actually ever existed between Sam and me," recalled Menotti, who "was dying to write another libretto for Sam." Barber kept his discipline, but at a cost to his opera and himself. Lee Hoiby recalled that in 1966 he was "soaring on some kind of magical energetic field," but in publicity photos he looked worn and wary while others in the production smiled beside him.[64]

As Barber labored over his opera, commentary about gay artists swelled. After *Time*'s January 1966 attack, composer Ned Rorem offered his *Paris Diary*, the first of his books featuring his sharp wit, storytelling, and name-dropping. Rorem rejected the rules of the open secret, though how deliberately was unclear since he wrote compulsively about everything, and his anecdotes about gay people were merely sprinkled about the book, whose focus was Rorem. But he surely knew he was up to something: he shifted discourse about gay men in the arts by being its author rather than its object and by writing about serious music, heretofore mostly off-limits. His "unabashed accounts of his homosexual life made the book a succès de scandale," Thomson's biographer notes.[65]

Barber, Rorem recounted, once said that in Italy "you'll find the Italians acquiescent. But even when they say I love you they still want to be paid. A friend of mine was hiking in the most remote region of the mountains above Torino when he came across a peasant boy who'd never seen the city. They made love. After which the boy asked for money." As Rorem later noted, "That's all" that *Paris Diary* offered about Barber in this context and almost any context. While the two moved in similar circles and wrote comparably lyrical music, their contact was often frosty and "colored—at least for me—by a certain rivalry," Rorem later wrote. "I never quite cared for the person, nor did I need the music; both were too rarefied, unpredictable, neurotic, and well, too *elegant* for me to deal with," remembered Rorem, who also was "assailed by contradictions. . . . For what reasons have I kept over the years those dozen letters [by Barber] I now reread, finding in each a generosity somehow mislaid?"[66]

Entries like the one on Barber in *Paris Diary* "caused a flurry—so innocent now it seems!—among those in the closet," Rorem later recalled. "Thomson was unhappy about his presence in such an explicitly 'queer' book," his biographer writes, so he excised Rorem from his own memoirs. "Sam was outraged," Rorem apparently learned from Barber's intimate friend Charles Turner, according to Rorem's memoirs, which ascribed the "flurry" to his challenge to "the closet." But "the closet" was a term he did not employ in 1966, one anyway that better applied to Thomson than to Barber, who understood that his sexuality was well known. "Sam was outraged," but over the details more than the fact of disclosure. If Rorem had described the Barber-Menotti relationship, Barber might not have objected. But he broke the rules by discussing sex— especially sex for hire and with a minor—leaving readers free to wonder if the story Barber attributed to "a friend" was his own. And Rorem was a fellow gay composer, not a nasty critic or prying journalist, compounding Barber's sense of betrayal. Rorem "transgressed the gay honor code by which Copland and Thomson had lived their lives," Nadine Hubbs argues. Barber's social privilege and reticent manner had fostered his sense that private matters were no one else's business—to be revealed as he alone chose (in his own way, in *A Hand of Bridge*). Rorem had stolen what he owned. Outrage was not the terrified reaction of a closeted figure to a liberated one. It was fury that Rorem exploited Barber's privacy.[67]

Perhaps Barber did not worry about public reactions since reviews of Rorem's book were not numerous and not all favorable: "Almost continually with Rorem, while one side of the mouth condemns, the other side drips honey," one review ran, and the gay periodical *Tangents* observed, "Ned Rorem is beautiful. Ned Rorem is AWARE of this fact. Ned Rorem is told this quite frequently, my dear!, by practically everyone."[68] Reviewers did not dwell on homosexuality, although they stressed the sadness and alcoholism that Rorem described. In Rorem's sea of names, Barber's floated unnoticed by most reviewers. But reviews did appear in the summer of 1966, in the wake of *Time*'s "Homintern" essay and Kauffmann's articles on theater and on the eve of Barber's premiere, and the "flurry" included gossip not in print.

Rorem's book added to the currents buffeting Barber's opera, for which a queer creative team had been assembled: Barber, Zeffirelli, conductor Thomas Schippers, and African American choreographer Alvin

Ailey, an admirer of Barber's music and beneficiary of state sponsorship, whose "ideal of interracialism" fit the opera's content and the integrationist ideals of national leaders.[69]

An avalanche of publicity preceded the 16 September debuts of the opera and the opera house. This was the twilight of an age when major media treated high culture as central to American life and power. *Newsweek* devoted dense coverage to the occasion, *Time* put Rudolf Bing on its cover, and newspapers around the country sent representatives to Gotham. Critics did not expect an aesthetically transformed Met. "It is a superb museum," noted Alan Rich, "at its most valuable when it takes one of its holdings out of its glass case, dusts it off, and displays it in the best possible lighting." Rudolf Bing defiantly agreed: "The Met is a museum," he insisted, "not an avant-garde theater or a place for tryouts." Still, Barber's opera and others in the new season — Britten's *Midsummer* and Martin David Levy's *Mourning Becomes Electra* (1967) — would put fresh items in the case.[70]

Lincoln Center was hailed for its technological wonders, but this technology also caused concern. In 1964, William Smith had attacked the soullessness and sound of Philharmonic Hall as "the result of the moonshot syndrome, an infection which affects our society in many of its interests and occupations. The infection is rooted in the belief that in this insecure world, truth and integrity can be found only in science and technology." Alas, the new hall "was a hi-fi set that simply would not hi-fi."[71] The new Met avoided its neighbor's acoustical bad rap, but Smith expressed concern that bigger might not be better — as assumed when the Center was designed — whether in the arts, the war in Vietnam, or the space program.

The grand scale, corporate nature, and technocratic focus of places like Lincoln Center drew growing skepticism. As *Newsweek* noted, "The new Met triumphs as a container for a vast and supermodern theatrical technology." But the container seemed "a kind of magnificent hybrid, as if the Louvre were equipped to fire a Polaris missile."[72] The ebullience felt in the 1950s about the Center's creation now met countercurrents that lasted for decades, prompting criticism of its aloof modernism, costly schemes to reinvent it, feckless efforts to remodel it, and in 2003 a New York Philharmonic decision — soon reversed — to return to Carnegie Hall.

Advance promotion of the Met's new house nonetheless worked the twin themes of imperial grandeur and American triumph. The new Met was "remindful of Gothic in its pull upward, reminiscent of Romanesque in the roundedness of its arches," with a "gloriously golden contour curtain," all to be revealed "in the opening of one of the world's greatest opera houses and in the world premiere of a galagrand opera." "Enormous is the proper way to describe it," Bing's assistant said of *Antony*, "probably the largest single production New York has ever seen." As "the most expensive production" in the Met's history, it had "no fewer than thirty solo parts, an oversize chorus, [and] a vast orchestra," plus "land battles, sea battles, dances of jugglers and slave girls, a drunken revel, and even an apparition or two."[73]

Publicity also stressed the American nature of the occasion. Zeffirelli was the rogue figure, but being Italian linked him to obvious operatic tradition, and he had American credentials, directing Verdi's *Falstaff* at the Met in 1964 and working in Hollywood. Otherwise, it was Americans at the top of the billboard: Barber, Ailey, Price, other Americans singers, and Schippers—the "youngest American ever to conduct at the Met" and now the "first American ever to conduct a Met opening."[74]

No publicity spelled out that the creative team was gay. To a degree, "American" functioned to displace "gay," as the Jewishness of *West Side Story*'s creators earlier had. But queerness leaked out, so obvious as to hardly require mention. Opera once had been dominated by strutting heterosexuals like Wagner, Verdi, Puccini, and Toscanini. Now many of its Anglo-American composers were queer—Thomson, Britten, Menotti, Barber, Bernstein—and on this occasion its conductor, choreographer, and librettist-director as well. As if more taken for granted, opera's queer attributes did not elicit the open suspicion shown drama. Drama had some mandate to represent reality; opera did not, and its meanings lay in subjective responses to its nonverbal core as much as to its plot and text. Queer "masquerade" disturbed theater critics, but grand opera had no masquerade because it was masquerade—an outsized burlesque of reality, rarely more than with *Antony*. To flag it for queerness perhaps seemed like noting a horse has four legs. *Antony* as an American creation coincided for the moment with its implicit status as a queer concoction.

Descent

On 16 September 1966, the right people showed up for the opening of "the world's largest opera house set in the world's largest cultural complex," as *Time* billed it. Adding suspense, the musicians threatened to strike, only reaching a new contract between acts of *Antony and Cleopatra*. Present were "our own Lady Bird J" (President Lyndon Johnson's wife) "glowing with Culture and precious gems"; imperial clients like Philippine president Ferdinand Marcos; Governor Rockefeller, Senators Jacob Javits and William Fulbright, Defense Secretary Robert McNamara, Henry Ford, and their wives; the Kennedy brothers, the Vanderbilts, and other monied folk; and "rafts of diplomats and fashion plates" providing "a show-stopping spectacle of animated finery." It was "Massive Everything," *Time* sniffed. "The wife of Met Tenor Jess Thomas, for example, was decked out in a black dress that was drenched in 15 lbs of floor-length gold chains (while a flack followed breathlessly, tossing out mimeographed press releases)." And on stage, Leontyne Price as Cleopatra "was so heavily costumed . . . that she looked like a junior-sized pyramid" in the hands of "Cecil B. de Zeffirelli," *Time* noted, referring to Cecil B. DeMille, the director of film epics. "Perhaps," *Life* archly observed, it "actually was the single biggest theatrical event in all of human history." This tone also was heard in the audience, *Newsweek* reported: " 'No doubt about it,' drawled a bored matron with tired eyes and a $900 gold lame evening dress, 'this is quite possibly the greatest social event since the Nativity.' "[75]

Reviews of *Antony and Cleopatra* varied from mixed to damning, many faulting the music, libretto, and direction but praising the performers. "Disaster," claimed *Newsweek*. "Much of what went on was a truly operatic disaster," observed *Life*. "The music is banal; an obeisance in the direction of modernity does not make one a modern composer, and the score is basically Hollywood material," complained a radio critic. *Variety* was savage: "It proved an almost uninterrupted bore, of little musical and no sexual conviction," followed by "nearly total and most embarrassing silence from the audience after the first act and hardly much more at any point. Seldom have singers . . . so hastily fled the chill." The summit of Barber's career, *Antony*, also started its descent.[76]

But the opera's failure was not universally proclaimed upon first hearing. After all, new music often flounders at first, and then gains traction. Critics also struggled to ascertain *Antony*'s value amid glaring technical glitches that owed to Zeffirelli's grand demands and the house's teething problems. Most assailed Zeffirelli's direction, though one deemed him a victim of "nebulous" music—"Even he cannot make bricks without straw." Miles Kastendieck sometimes "felt that Barber's score existed only as a means to achieve the producer's end"—Zeffirelli's—but praised his "lyric gift." To the *New Yorker*, "Barber's sensitive, retiring temperament seems out of its element in a spectacle of such grandiose proportions," but the production "would have killed it" anyway because it was "appallingly pretentious, appallingly arty, and in most respects destructive." Still, one critic found that the score provided "thrills and glamour," echoing Richard Strauss and Hans Werner Henze. Here was "choral music of striking power and range; martial music with fanfare," and for once a composer "keenly aware of the effectiveness of the human voice." Many admired the "beautifully composed" score, finding it, like *Vanessa*, strong after a slow start.[77]

But while Barber's effort did garner some critical approval, it was more and more judged a failure in the months and years after its premiere, which came to be regarded as the greatest disaster in American operatic history and the benchmark for all later efforts at American opera. Perhaps that judgment stuck because *Antony* indeed was a failure in conception and music, not just in Zeffirelli's overwrought production. But even if so, that does not explain why failure was so loudly proclaimed and seen as so damaging to Barber.

Whatever the opera's shortcomings—still debated—it also fell victim to anxieties about American culture and its queer elements. That *Antony*'s creative team was gay did not alone cause it to be deemed a failure—most likely, no new opera would have fulfilled the occasion's grand expectations, and if antigay hostility had been all-consuming, that team would never have been assembled. But its queerness did affect how—and how much—failure was assigned.

Anxieties about American culture were evident in how virtues trumpeted before 16 September became defects after. "Gala-grand" became grandiosity. Spectacle became pomposity. Extravagance became excess. The *New York Times*'s Harold Schonberg vacillated between hip humor and highbrow outrage regarding opening night: "It was quite a spectacle, situated on the cosmic scale somewhere above the primeval atom that caused the Big Bang, and somewhere below the creation of the Milky Way. . . . It was a big, complicated package; big, grand, impressive and vulgar; a Swinburnian melange of sad, bad, mad, glad; rich and also nouveau-riche; desperately aiming for the bigger and the better." And the singing? Glorious in sound, but the "cast tended to enunciate, most of the time, like an untalented myna bird on an especially bad night." An imperial culture, it seems, was yielding vulgarity and bloat. "Americans have turned toward art as the final justification of our society," *Life* summarized critic George P. Elliott, believing it " 'might help fill the spiritual vacuum accompanying our material affluence.' " But the new Met, like its new opera, "suggests that art stubbornly refuses to play the role we have assigned for it."[78]

As the Met's new house acquired "the patina of age,"[79] the distressing qualities spotted in many dimensions of opening night became linked more tightly to Barber's opera. Just as the new Met, *Time* claimed, was "neither really modern nor really traditional, neither daring nor conservative," Barber's score was "neither fully traditional nor fully modern," in Schonberg's view — "skillfully put together but lacking ardor and eloquence." "Neither daringly modern nor cleanly classical nor sweetly romantic," the *Wall Street Journal* judged. This time Barber seemed to displease all camps, his music too astringent for traditionalists yet too tame for modernists. Just as the house was judged a modernist hybrid of dubious taste, so was the score. Critics and audiences still wanted categories clean. Barber had not complied, or had provided no convincing hybrid. One critic heard "snatches of Americana . . . a hint of Puccini . . . reminiscences of Richard Strauss, and moments of Barber's soaring lyricism," all in a "passionless, uncommitted, Meyerbeerian spectacle." It seemed less hybridity than *kitsch*. Nor was it sufficiently American, whatever that meant. Although *Newsweek* dubbed it a "brand-new pointedly American opera," its creators hardly saw it as "pointedly" American. Other qualities first attributed to the house—mammoth, spectacular, showy—became linked largely to Barber's opera and Zeffirelli's treatment.[80]

That link owed partly to *Antony*'s apparent resonance with Hollywood, another site of excess, queer and otherwise, which established expectations that Barber never intended to satisfy. The resonance was obvious in references to "Cecil B. de Zeffirelli" and the like and to Barber's score as "Hollywood material."[81] If such criticism suggested tawdry Hollywood influences on the opera, it also pointed to how Hollywood was a benchmark for evaluating it: Was *Antony* too much like the movies, or disappointing in light of them? Films set in the ancient Middle East were enormously popular in the 1950s. Made on an imperial scale, epics like DeMille's *The Ten Commandments* (1956) underwrote America's imperial oversight of the Middle East, featured male heroes and temptresses subordinate to them, and offered tales of affirmation and triumph.[82] Such movies stoked expectations that the Middle East's past would be treated in "galagrand" fashion and simple, transparent prose.

But except as directed by Zeffirelli, *Antony* offered little of this. Shakespeare's words sounded awkward or archaic, not transparent. The music was often moody and gnarly, even in triumphal passages. The central figure was no Moses, Jesus, or Spartacus, but a woman who met disaster and helped a man meet his. Barber's opera cut against film's affirmative, imperial, gendered assumptions about the Middle East. Hollywood set a garish standard that *Antony* failed to meet yet was also tarnished by.

Hollywood also set a specific standard for measuring *Antony*. It had told Cleopatra's story several times, but the 1963 *Cleopatra* (Joseph L. Mankiewicz), starring Richard Burton and Elizabeth Taylor in the longest film Hollywood had ever released, was a notoriously expensive flop. By the time *Antony* entered production, Zeffirelli was finishing another Burton-Taylor Shakespeare movie, *The Taming of the Shrew* (1967), during whose filming Leontyne Price, as she prepared for *Antony*, visited Taylor. And opening night for *Antony* resembled a grand Hollywood premiere. Just as the bloated historical epic was collapsing on screen, so too was its operatic cousin. The cultural traffic between Cleopatra the movie and Cleopatra the opera offered contemporaries reasons to judge the opera a failure and to understand why it was: it flopped like *Cleopatra*, for similar reasons of excess.[83]

The impulse to fit *Antony* into a Hollywood framework showed in complaints that its music was overwrought like a movie score, even as it was faulted as being coldly restrained. A sense of resemblance was understandable. Barber's music had some of the lushness and orchestral effects found in film scores, especially in those by the Italian Nino Rota. But it was also true that film composers often sounded lush and lyrical like Barber sometimes did. Critics saw a one-way street: Barber had succumbed to Hollywood. They thereby reprised an old criticism: Barber pandered to the masses, this time unsuccessfully. It was a familiar tactic in arts criticism—guilt by association with mass culture.

Antony also suffered by comparison to Verdi's grand opera *Aida*. Barber had no intention of doing anything *Aida*-like, but the common geography of the two operas and Zeffirelli's treatment—the grand sets, horses, and camels, though not the elephants he wanted—invited comparison, as Zeffirelli intended. Seen that way, *Antony* was a bad American imitation of what the great European had done.

Excess was the theme of reactions to 16 September—seen in the opera, the direction, the house, the occasion, the Center, the bloated apparatus of American culture. Where was blame for it to be laid? It fell ever more on Barber. To blame the house, its technology, or Bing's punishing rehearsal schedule ran against lingering hopes for American opera, and when operas falter their composers usually get the blame despite the responsibility others may share. Barber was more disposable than the Met. Besides, the Met's problems were presumably correctable—its technology would get unsnarled; Bing would retire.

In the opera, empire goes awry and imperial leaders die, but no one assessing *Antony* compared Shakespeare's imperial tragedy to America's imperial troubles. To hear the opera as a dark comment on imperial excess rather than a sad example of it would have been tough—there was only a weak tradition of seeing political content in high musical culture. Such comment might have sounded if the opera had appeared later, amid escalating dismay over American imperialism. As it was, responses to *Antony* barely hinted at it.

Nor did most observers label this an American failure. Hailed in advance, the American identity of most creators and performers faded after the opening except for the applause heaped on Leontyne Price. Often singled out as the "Negro soprano," she became the residual repository of American virtue, not only for her singing but for her race, just as America was implicitly applauded for its racial progress in making her a star. For the *New York Times*, her race imposed a "burden of responsibility," one she accepted regarding "my people, every Negro in America." She was cause for white self-congratulation and black pride. The work of another black American—Ailey's choreography—was barely noticed or judged "deplorable," but he had gotten little advance hype.[84]

Antony's failure did yield familiar laments about American opera—"dealt a severe blow," Alan Rich opined, by Barber's "slick, chic fashionable opening-night opera." A London critic questioned American culture, pointing to "an uncomfortable resemblance between the plushy sub-modern architecture of the new auditorium and the neo-romantic idiom of 'Antony and Cleopatra.'" But issues of American creativity were usually muffled by stressing Barber's debt to European traditions and Zeffirelli's role as the opera's "creative spirit." A Peabody award–winning program, "The New Met," broadcast 20 November on NBC's *Bell Telephone Hour*, did hint that hubris drove the new opera and new house. The opening-night failure of the stage turntable—a plot line in "The New Met"—seemed to capture the excesses of a big-bucks American effort to recreate European grand opera. But "The New Met" stopped short of attacking American hubris. Instead it closed with individuals—Zeffirelli, Barber, and Schippers holding hands and bowing, Bing absent, and Zeffirelli walking into the city's night, "running away to Rome from the creature he created," the voice-over intoned.[85]

As the creators' Americanness slid from view, their queerness came nearer the surface, suggesting that failure owed to something alien. Harold Schonberg, reviewing Zeffirelli's direction of Price, lamented "the queer ideas current these days in certain circles of the Metropolitan

Opera." This was "artifice masquerading with great flourish as art," he wrote, making the distinction between art and artifice that often found queer artists on the wrong side. Stanley Kauffmann, fresh from his musings about queer drama, also saw sterility in this occasion. Beyond judging Barber an "unmemorable operatic talent," he faulted "the very idea of commissioning an American opera." He lamented that "this major event was prepared *without conviction*," a defect he had also detected in gay writers' plays. In his "meretriciously flashy" work, Zeffirelli dressed Price, "one of the sexiest women on the stage," with "anti-feminist skill," added Kauffmann in odd reasoning. Zeffirelli's overkill was so widely applied—to horses, the entire set, male singers—that to see "anti-feminist skill" made little sense, except in the tradition of condemning gay artists' showiness and misogyny. Kauffmann regretted that "the contemporary fruit of all that effort and expense was a tenor singing on horseback." To him, Barber and Zeffirelli showed what ailed Lincoln Center and American culture.[86]

Whatever Kauffmann's intent, the homintern discourse was more at work than overt hostility to gay artists. Escalating for years, denunciations of gay men's creative sterility and conspiratorial tricks were commonplace by 1966. Real men did not produce sterile products. "We," Bing said on opening night, "have been pregnant for so long."[87] When the child—the opera—was stillborn, it made sense to blame the childless gay men. Rudolf Franz Josef Bing, though faulted for creative conservatism, was too domineering, straight, and powerful to be cast in that role. And, many people agreed, he had successfully sired a new opera house.

Barber's music, on the other hand, seemed slack and unmanly. It was "subtle to the point of being flaccid, passive to the point of boredom," claimed a critic. Flogging a vulgar production and weak music, critics evoked queer decadence—indulgence, sterility, and showiness. Did not Barber's effort "fizzle like a damp firecracker"? If that suggested a limp penis, it seemed attached to someone who had lost sexual heat—Barber's music was "chilly and unimpassioned," claimed *Life*, which found heat only in a house that opened in a "Blaze." Language evoking a sexually spent force suffused comment on Barber's music—"lacking melodic drive and rising only fitfully to the eloquence of Shakespeare's lines," it was said. His "WASPish" and "well-mannered" score suggested that "as a dramatic composer Mr. Barber does not carry even a water-pistol," his music "as uncommunicative as the weakest scores of Strauss's old age." It "seemed too cerebral and cool."[88]

Barber was thereby imagined as a sad, burnt-out queer who had succumbed to Zeffirelli's youthful but empty exuberance, only to be used and abandoned. Assailing Zeffirelli for overwhelming Barber's music, critics suggested that Barber had been too "passive" to resist the Italian's juggernaut. Here were familiar tropes—the trusting American outsmarted by the wily European; the queer elder exhausted by his young companion, who would move on to other triumphs while the older man was left lonely and spent.

Many of the qualities assigned to *Antony* also fell into the category of camp, as Susan Sontag famously defined it in 1964—the "sensibility that, among other things, converts the serious into the frivolous." Indeed, Sontag had dragged Barber into her essay. "Pure Camp is always naive" or "unintentional," she wrote. "One doesn't need to know the artist's private intentions. The work tells all," she maintained. "Compare a typical 19th century opera with Samuel Barber's *Vanessa*, a piece of manufactured, calculated Camp, and the difference is clear." Somehow she knew it was "calculated" without knowing Barber's "private intentions"—but commentators on gay artists usually presumed they could decode intentions from products.[89] Critics did not label *Antony* as camp—perhaps grand opera was too obviously camp to need that label—but they evoked its apparent campiness: its roots in European decadence, its striving for effect, its excessive artifice.

Antony was also vulnerable for its musical idiom. For proponents of high modernism and experimentalism, music by tonalists had reached a dead end, if it was ever alive. Nadine Hubbs summarizes their outlook: "Atonal and dissonant music was perceived as bold and forward-looking, hence masculine, hence straight; tonal and consonant music as gentle and backward-looking, hence feminine, hence gay."[90] That outlook marked criticism of *Antony* and lasted beyond it. Harold Schonberg devoted his final chapter of *Lives of the Great Composers* (1970) to Second Viennese pioneers—Berg, Webern, Schoenberg—who died before composers he consigned to earlier chapters. The message was clear: serialists had triumphed. Tonalists rated scant mention—Britten a half-sentence, Bernstein only as a conductor. Schonberg did not praise postwar serialists' music—it was, he wrote elsewhere, "a hideously misbegotten creature sired by Caliban out of Hecate." But at issue was not who wrote attractive music but instead who advanced music's evolution. U.S. tonalists had been caught in serialism's "backwash," he asserted, and except for Copland they "lacked the individuality to create a lasting body of music," even though Barber, like Copland, "remains very much in the repertory."[91]

Schonberg's book showed no overt homophobia. Explicit on matters once only insinuated, he wrote that Tchaikovsky was "terrified lest his homosexuality become open knowledge" and that he disliked using the "hysteria" in Tchaikovsky's music to discount him as a "weeping machine." [92] He treated most modern tonalists cursorily, not just queer ones. But in arts criticism, homosexuality rarely stood alone. Its relationship to other categories was key. Because most gay composers avoided the course of progress that critics proclaimed for music, Schonberg mostly dismissed them. Among Americans he preferred Charles Ives, that scourge of sissy music.

Beyond musical matters, Barber fell victim to gathering doubts about the vitality of high culture. The Lincoln Center project began with hopes for American preeminence in high culture and the Center's preeminence in American life. By 1966, it was facing waves of criticism for urban bulldozing, showy architecture, bad acoustics, and timid programming. It also endured the continuing triumph of popular culture and the sagging status of national elites as the war in Vietnam ground on. Planned as a beacon to the world and to the masses, Lincoln Center now seemed more a lonely and expensive outpost. When the Met's triumphal opening proved disappointing, blaming *Antony* contained the damage. Barber had embarrassed himself. The Met was off the hook.

Barber's opera also appeared when New York's cultural fortunes were dimming. Ascendant rock, country, and folk music had roots elsewhere, and New York "began to lose ground as a place of cultural innovation" and "became less a site of cultural experimentation than a showplace for work developed elsewhere." America's "political and economic decentralization" dispersed wealth and power beyond the city, just as new agencies like the National Endowment for the Arts dispersed funding widely. Other cities copied Lincoln Center and New York retained primacy as "showplace." Still, the high-water mark of the city's high culture was passing; an ebbing tide caught Barber in its currents. [93]

Finally, Barber's reputation faltered because cultural empire faltered. The Met's opening was a grand imperial event designed to showcase America's cultural supremacy. The aspirations behind it did not vanish. In 1967, composer William Schuman pled the case for Washington's Kennedy Center by arguing that "America is most often pictured as a land of violence, vulgarity, racism, and controversial military actions. The unfortunate result is that the American people are being misjudged the world over." [94] But as his defensiveness showed, confidence about showcasing American culture shrank amid the convulsions of the late 1960s. So also

189

did the urgency. Fewer Americans were convinced that the Cold War had to be won or that its outcome hinged on cultural competition. For many, including an angry President Nixon, the real cultural battle was no longer global but stateside, against the counterculture, feminism, gay culture, black power, and other homegrown challenges. If Barber failed the test of proving American cultural prowess, the test itself was becoming less relevant, and with it the men once summoned to meet it. Awkwardly embraced when empire demanded them, queer artists like Barber quickly seemed like relics of a bygone era of superheated international competition in the arts.

Bing informed Barber, then in Rome, of the opera's demise in a carefully worded letter of 11 November 1966: it would not be offered the next season as originally planned. Bing claimed that "every performance is sold out, and the audiences are quite enthusiastic," although others had noted "painfully apathetic" applause and "the hasty emptying of the hall at the final curtain." Bing made Zeffirelli the villain. The project "is so immensely complicated" and "wildly expensive" because "our friend, Franco, who nobody admires more than I do, has let us down a little bit" by creating something "technically overproduced." He wanted Barber to hear the "reasons from me, rather than to hear distorted or untrue stories from other sources." But Barber only had to read the magazines to know that Bing had been ready from the start to pull the plug. Bing had told *Time*, "Stage a modern work and during the third performance you could put on a blindfold, spray the house with a machine gun and be pretty sure that you would never hit anybody."[95]

Ruin?

Antony's failure fed an old-told tale of Barber's ruin. It also added to doubts about queer artists of Barber's generation, many of them shunted aside after the mid-1960s as the homintern discourse, though diminished in broader culture, persisted among many taste makers. But, at most, the tale of Barber's ruin was only half true. Much else besides *Antony* shaped his final years, and his voice, now less in service to cultural empire, still sounded.

Antony's major figures followed different paths. Damned for his production and libretto, Zeffirelli still emerged unscathed. Schippers enlarged his reputation as conductor (including of Barber's music) but died in 1977, leaving behind gossip about his sexuality. Coyly noting "extramusical considerations" regarding Schippers, one observer reported in

1974 that some people "thought of him as being grand, aloof, a playboy and a social climber," and his work "a big fake"—familiar language about the shallow, devious gay artist. For his part, Schippers insisted that previously "I wasn't leading a secret life . . . I was always a loner until I got married"—certainly news to insiders. Ailey remained a key figure in dance but later faced changing racial politics, health problems, and poverty, dying of AIDS in 1989. Price flourished but deplored Bing's indulgence of Zeffirelli and the racial burden on her at *Antony*'s debut. " 'I really resent someone telling me that opening the new house at Lincoln Center with *Antony and Cleopatra* was a favor,' she sneers," as if " 'I had the plum of the century. That's *not* true, I had the plum of responsibility.' " [96]

Buttressing the view that *Antony*'s failure destroyed Barber was his departure for Italy after opening night—as previously planned, he claimed —and his stay there for several minimally productive years. There were other explanations for his departure: *Antony* had exhausted him, he had long valued his time in Italy, and now he had the financial success to purchase a house there. But it seemed like he had fled America with his tail between his legs.

It was as if his tragic opera became a story of his own doom. "The spectacle [of *Antony]* was almost unanimously panned, and Barber's career was effectively ended," ran one later account. The "controversy" over *Antony* "tragically ended Barber's career," ran another. The opera "was a failure so grand and so public that Barber never fully recovered from the shock." Barber's publisher bluntly commented: "*Antony* was a terrible catastrophe from which he never recovered. . . . He never wrote anything of importance any more." The *New York Times*'s 1981 obituary was headlined, "Samuel Barber, Composer of *Vanessa*," politely ignoring *Antony*. Even Barber's sympathetic biographer crowded "The Last Years, 1967–81," into one chapter, although careful not to see those years as shaped only by "one so-called musical failure." [97]

In his many reflections, Ned Rorem offered conflicting versions of Barber's ruin. The avant-garde in the arts, he argued in 1971, contributed to "murdering our heroes every few years while salvaging, in the guise of influence, the froth of their output. We throw out the baby but keep the bath water," he declared. "Consider the cold dethronings of playwrights Williams and Albee, and of composers Barber and Copland" (he might have added James Baldwin and others). But Rorem was abetting the "dethroning" by reporting it so insistently and often. "The blame fell unjustly on the composer," he wrote a few years later, "who, disgraced in fortune and men's eyes, produced little thereafter." By the time Rorem wrote his memoirs, "little thereafter" became nothing: "When his second huge opera failed," Barber "stopped." Rorem was inconsistent, for he also dated Barber's decline from decades earlier: Barber "grew increasingly sour" after Menotti's success with *The Medium* in 1946; Menotti "became and remained more renowned than his life's companion"; *Medea* (1946) was "maybe [Barber's] best score." Rorem both contested and broadcast the repudiation, practiced also by young gay activists, of Barber and his generation.[98]

That Zeffirelli's career blossomed suggests how complex the construction of Barber's failure was. Had queer-baiting alone been at work, Zeffirelli might have suffered along with Barber, but he bore no burden of carrying American music, and his youth insulated him from the suspicions of creative decline hovering over Barber. If Zeffirelli went over the top, that seemed natural for a young Italian given to flamboyant projects. For Barber to indulge in movie-score surges and faux-Egyptian sound seemed out of step for this older, more reserved man—seen as a sign that he was slipping.

Barber was not so crushed as rumor had it, however. He was confident enough in *Antony* not to reject it and realistic enough to grasp some of its faults. With Menotti's help, he produced in 1975 a shorter, more lyrical version shorn of much that Zeffirelli had contributed, with more revisions later. In revised forms *Antony* was performed several times, notably at Chicago's Lyric Opera in 1991 and in concert version by New York's American Composers Orchestra in 2003—for an American opera to have any staying power for four decades was unusual. A 1983 recording was an improbable Grammy winner.

Divisions among critics changed little, however. The *New Yorker* applauded a suite from the opera performed by Bernstein and the Philharmonic in 1971, and even restored Barber's manhood—he had "escaped the emasculating influence of Nadia Boulanger's school in Paris"—in part by linking his music to Mahler's. Rorem judged the 1975 version as "close to Barber at his most deliciously skilled" even if sometimes "hyperromantic out of Gliere via Elgar and a Hollywood sound track." A 1975 reviewer pointed out that the original had featured an "electric guitar (an operatic first?)" cut from the revised version. In 2003, Anthony Tommasini, assessing music "deemed anachronistic" at its premiere, granted the opera "captivating qualities" cut short by "grand, sweeping passions of conventional opera" or "swamped by fake Egyptian exotica." Still, "Barber's was the real thing" compared to "many derivative Neo-Romantic operas" after it. The *New Yorker* noted in 2003 that this "sensational flop" was "finally becoming better known for its memorable lyricism and dignified dramatics." Some new perspective emerged abroad: Italian critics heard in a version done at Spoleto a vital form of hybridity. Barber's "ability to bring together techniques, languages, and emotions quite dissimilar," as his biographer summarizes Italian responses, "was seen as a strength and, moreover, as a uniquely American asset." Nicolas Slonimsky said much the same, praising music "combining [the] Italianate fervor of bel canto with a flair for intellectually modern melodic configurations, quartal intervallic progressions and acridly euphonious polyharmonies."[99]

Barber maintained his sense of humor—"If I must have a fiasco, it may as well be a monumental one," he quipped in 1971. "As far as I'm concerned, the production had absolutely nothing to do with what I had imagined," he observed, complaining, "I had very little control—practically none," while "management supported every idea of Zeffirelli's." That did not explain why, as his biographer puts it, "Barber—usually so decisive about aesthetic principles—seemed to abdicate his artistic assertiveness in this instance." Still, in 1971, "no brooding, temperamental or electrical qualities hover over him," although his candor persisted: "Most composers bore me, because most composers are boring." He remained unconcerned about his place in music history: "It is said that I have no style at all but that doesn't matter." He noted the resistance he met from Philadelphia's Girard Bank when it was asked to underwrite *The Lovers* (1971), based on work by the "Communist poet" Pablo Neruda, then in Paris serving Salvador Allende's Chilean government. Some "board members raised their eyebrows. Finally, I asked the board whether they still didn't have love affairs in Philadelphia, and learned that they did. Then I said, 'Even Communists have love affairs, you know.' "[100]

Barber's productivity did decline, but for many reasons—aging, deaths of those near him, health problems, alcohol use that led to psychiatric treatment, and trouble with Menotti, which led to the sale of their home, Capricorn, and Menotti moving to Scotland. Those factors did have links to *Antony*'s failure, but variations on them afflicted many artists at his age, and Barber did not single out *Antony* as causing his troubles.

His later years also reflected continuity. Barber was never a prolific composer. His moodiness after *Antony* was a lifelong trait: he titled his first composition, at age seven, *Sadness*, and before *Antony*'s premiere it seemed that his "profound mood is melancholy: he is introspective and often withdrawn." Criticism of *Antony* as old-fashioned carried little sting since he did not pursue fashion: before its premiere he "chuckled" at a claim that he was a "neo-romantic . . . slowly catching up with the twentieth century." "I don't think I've caught up with the twentieth century at all," he said. "You would have to be aleatoric, electronic, and everything else. Even [Pierre] Boulez is out of date."[101]

Decline in his productivity was also exaggerated, or simply assumed. He composed fewer works, but some of his darkest and most creative. He had periods of buoyant creativity and warm contact with others—his sixty-eighth birthday party featured luminaries in the arts and a lobster-bearing Roman chariot labeled "Antony and Cleopatra." He stayed committed to modernist texts—by Robert Graves, Theodore Roethke, James Joyce, and Neruda—despite complaining, "I often get bored looking through modern poetry." "The texts he chose," his biographer notes, reflected "loneliness, rededication, reconciliation, and solitude." As one Roethke poem went:

> When I am undone,
> When I am no one.

Perhaps such moods also influenced nonverbal works like the *Third Essay for Orchestra* (1978), which opens with a long, stark passage for solo percussion. His music continued to evolve, becoming more astringent and featuring "a tendency toward tonal ambiguity—a blurring of tonal centers." *Three Songs* (1972) included a poem by Jerzy Harasymowicz, translated by Czesław Miłosz, which presented "a ludicrous fusion of pianos and cows: 'a herd of black pianos.' " He was not repeating himself.[102]

His music, though not in fashion, still showed his selective engagement with it. Never enamored of cultural nationalism, he was oddly in step with its decline. In the 1970s, he turned to a "Communist poet" for inspiration, grew long hair, composed angry music (as in much of *The Lovers*) when anger ruled the land, and maintained a hybrid style as hybridity was gaining acceptance. In his distanced engagement with fashion, he resembled Menotti, who, Winthrop Sargeant wrote, "stood apart from the academicians," from "the popular musical show," from "the ponderous traditions of opera," and "from Broadway, regarding it as a sink of mediocrity and commercialism" despite his success there. "[Menotti] has worked in Hollywood and for radio and television, but he stands apart from them, too," as he did from modernism, even as Stravinsky was his touchstone.[103] Like Barber, he also established no school of composition, stable of students, or lasting institutional ties except to the Spoleto festival he founded—the usual markers of composers' influence and gravity. Their eclectic engagement with fashion had confounded critics since the 1930s.

Barber remained in the eye of musicians, composers, critics, and programmers, and he attracted high-profile performers—Leontyne Price and Dietrich Fischer-Dieskau, Eugene Ormandy and the Philadelphia Orchestra. But attention diminished. Growing in number for decades, performances of his music by major American orchestras began dipping in the mid-1960s, putting him behind Copland and Britten (the record for regional ensembles may differ).[104] Despite favorable responses to *The Lovers*, his largest-scale work of this period, it was not heard again for two decades.

Still, the claim that *Antony*'s failure ruined him was an exaggeration that served many purposes. It was one thread in the repudiation of his generation of queer composers, a repudiation never just about queerness but rarely free of concern about it. Notions of queer shallowness, sterility, aging, and aesthetic stodginess inflected the dismissal of Barber and other artists.

Barber's work was defined as inauthentic—the worst thing to be in the 1970s, given the importance placed on authenticity in that decade. Suspicion in this regard had followed him from the start, through his association with Toscanini, distance from "Amurhican" music, and lyricism in an age of modernist severity. By the 1970s, creative authenticity was defined in part by transparency—by a close, evident correlation between private self and public product. An ancient tragedy told in Shakespeare's idiom and displayed at the imperial opening of the new Met, *Antony* fell short of that standard. *The Lovers* exhibited more transparency—the chilling last section, "cemetery of kisses," perhaps reflected his pain regarding Menotti. But some critics found a familiar fault. Irving Kolodin felt "that its passion is one step removed from authenticity, that it has been intellectually arrived at through a literary intermediation." Similarly, critic Donald Henahan spotted an "odd emotional distance" in Barber's song cycle *Despite and Still* (1968). In an age of transparency, "emotional distance" did not ring true.[105]

Authenticity had other meanings, including fidelity to cultural traditions, but to some critics Barber was merely true to a European romantic tradition that was itself passé. His verbal texts and musical idioms ranged too widely over time and place to anchor him culturally, and he hardly asked to be regarded as authentically gay—an oxymoron anyway insofar as critics associated queerness with artifice and superficiality. Some figures in the 1970s did announce their queerness—Leonard Bernstein and Ned Rorem among them—but few in either high or popular culture asserted its connections to their creativity. That assertion gained traction only in the 1980s, partly in response to AIDS and to the rebellious and expressive currents in gay life set loose in the 1970s—too late to do Barber any good, except in posthumous reputation.

Authenticity also meant spontaneity—improvisation and immediacy. A "coherent aesthetic of spontaneity," evident in " 'gesture' painting and 'beat' writing" and "bebop jazz," defined much "American art and literature after World War II," Daniel Belgrad argues. It is true that if spontaneity "privileges the unpremeditated act," it was often calculated: authenticity was a virtue imposed on art rather than inhering in it. But Barber seemed to fail this test as well. He was too careful a craftsman, too remote from his audience, too tied to ponderous institutions like the Met, and too reticent in public bearing. If "elegance was the defining virtue" of Barber, as Rorem wrote, it conveyed coolness—an elitist posture at odds with the leveling forces and premium on immediacy coursing through the 1970s.[106]

Some difficult music did gain critical favor, suggesting that authenticity was a slippery standard. Because John Cage treated "music simply as unemotional sound material," he bore no burden of being emotionally revealing. He embraced chance and playfulness, and the effort he put into composing his music was hidden.[107] Serial composers used the tight tone-row system and, like electronic composers, had heavy debts to Europe and to the academy, both often viewed as culturally stodgy. But authenticity was also defined by a willingness to reject middlebrow American culture. In contrast to crowd-pleasing queer tonalists, serial and electronic composers seemed authentic in the 1970s *because* they looked to Europe and disdained the crowd.

Cage too was queer, and a lover to and collaborator with dancer and choreographer Merce Cunningham; yet he suffered few of the insinuations of superficiality and decline that many gay artists faced. The difference points up how queerness intersected other factors. Cage's sexuality had little visibility—to the end of his life he "colluded in the silence" about it "and in a manner that is quite startling given the radicalism he pursued in so many other areas of his life." His radicalism also protected his queerness, earning it a pass not given Barber. His work might seem maddening, but hardly campy or backward, as Barber's music was characterized. Moreover, Cage influenced artists in many fields—a key test of gravity—and his experimentalism freed him from the burden of representing America. If he embodied anything American, it was the freedom to discard tradition. He was outside the standards applied to Barber and thus not charged with failing to meet them.[108]

Serialists and experimentalists also sternly guarded their gates. They issued thundering manifestoes designating the true path of musical progress, and the severity of their music served as emblem of their manly seriousness—no kitsch or camp for them. In contrast, most American tonalists eschewed "theoretical claims for the natural or historical inevitability or the timeless transcendence of their chosen method."[109] That Menotti was indebted to Puccini or Barber's *Antony* to Verdi's *Aida* was the critics' idea, not theirs, reflecting an assumption that queer creativity had to be derivative and that straight men had genuine creative zeal.

If cultural politics set up Barber as failed figure, so did some specifics of his career and music. Earlier an accomplished singer, pianist, and conductor, later in life he was only a composer, with no other roles to sustain his reputation. Copland's critical reputation also fell off—his *Connotations* flopped at the opening of Philharmonic Hall in 1962, and in 1970 Bernstein publicly blamed his use of the twelve-tone method for his declining output. ("How sad for him. How awful for us.") But because Copland had tried nothing as grand as a Met premiere, he had no catastrophic failure on which others could hang a tale of decline, and he sustained a vigorous career with his other hats—mentor, conductor, writer, raconteur, promoter—and his exuberant personality. Barber had little to fall back on. He had, a 1966 profile indicated, an "attitude of cool detachment, so rare and so admirable among composers (and other creative artists), who usually consider everything they put on paper as an immortal message coming from heaven." As symbol of queer aging and decline, a taciturn Barber fit better than an ever-smiling Copland.[110]

Moreover, Barber's music was identified with loss, setting him up for a life-imitates-art role. Its expressiveness was worn on his musical sleeve and in turn heard as overwrought—coded queer through notions of Tchaikovsky's music as weepy and gay men as prone to excess. Bernstein was also criticized for excess—in his music, conducting, personality, and politics—but given his marriage and children, a public identity as queer never stuck firmly to him. The *Adagio* remained immensely popular. "Even as you read these words," Rorem once wrote, "somewhere in the world Samuel Barber's *Adagio for Strings* is being played." But this "national funeral music" evoked yearning and tragedy—sounding in *Elephant Man* (1980) as the film's title character dies, surging as the film *Platoon* (1986) asserts the lost innocence of Americans in Vietnam, swelling in the choral version *Agnus Dei* as Luka on television's *ER* faces savage murderers, humming along during a comically funereal moment in the French film *Amelie* (2001), and even used to parody mourning in *South Park*. Stories of Barber's ruin also reflected his music's association with loss.[111]

Whereas Barber's music was used to underline a suffering America, Copland's best-known music was employed to remember a confident America amid the troubled post-Vietnam reassertion of the nation's martial and moral virtue. Nixon's second inaugural in 1973 featured *A Lincoln Portrait* and selections from *The Tender Land* (Nixon did not choose the program).[112] This was a far cry from the banishment of his music from Eisenhower's 1953 inaugural and from Nixon's private fulminations about queer artists. (I first heard Copland's *Old American Songs* performed by a U.S. military band on the Capitol steps in the middle of the Watergate scandal.) Without protest by Copland, the music of a Jewish leftist queer was taken back into the political mainstream and used in the effort to reconstruct an affirmative America. Bicentennial festivities in 1976 furthered that trend. No tragic tale was applied to Copland for a host of musical, personal, and political reasons.

Like his contemporaries, Barber straddled fault lines that his queerness intersected. In his career and in the claim about his ruin, his sexuality played a role contingent on other factors. Yet even as a contingent factor, queerness was so consistently a factor that it had autonomy. Had a nonqueer team—somehow—produced *Antony*, it might still have been deemed a failure but not one shadowed by an implicit tale of queer sterility and ruin. If Barber's queerness was a sign of other things—of being musical, tonal, cultured, European, old-fashioned, inadequate— it was also a sign that kept appearing. And it was shared with others who fell from grace. Long after Britten's death in 1976, the "assumption" persisted that his "music is dated and retrogressive and therefore not worth the time of day," and a prominent British composer publicly made "a sinister reference" regarding Britten to 'the homosexual, pedophilia thing."[113]

Restoration

Even as composers like Barber and Copland fell from critical grace in the 1970s, their appeal to wider audiences grew. "Ned Rorem has pointed out that as Copland's fame increased, his influence waned," David Denby notes.[114] A similar pattern held for Barber. Their utility as musical emblems of national greatness, affirmation, and mourning fed that appeal, as did other changes.

In the 1980s and 1990s, the label "gay American composer" seemed at last to take hold for Barber, Copland, Thomson, and others. Biographers wrote about their lives and scholars looked for relationships between composers' sexuality and creativity, as did gay composers themselves—Ned Rorem, John Corigliano, Lou Harrison, among others. Celebrants of gay creativity, once past the revolutionary 1970s, claimed older heroes, and moments like the concerts for the twenty-fifth anniversary of the 1969 Stonewall riots also provoked comment. Some interpreted Barber's apparent downfall as illustrating the burden his generation bore—he had been sacrificed to the gods of cold-blooded modernism practiced mainly by straight men.

Designation of Barber and others as gay composers reinforced a surge, barely glimpsed by Barber before he died in 1981, in recording, performance, and appreciation of their work. His 1939 Violin Concerto, once infrequently heard, became a staple of the violinist's repertoire, and post-*Antony* compositions gained attention. Severe modernism's limited appeal was one factor, as was postmodern doubt that music had to follow one path of progress. Once "treated condescendingly by advocates of more advanced and challenging styles," Barber and his kin were now regarded, Alan Kozinn observed, as "right in step with the New Accessibility. Once regarded as a neo-Romantic throwback, Barber can now be seen as a prophet." [115] No longer roadblocks to progress, tonalists were now seen as precursors to postmodern eclecticism, lyricism, and popular appeal. Barber had not seen himself as a prophet, but reimagining him as one helped restore his reputation.

National politics played a less direct role, but it was no coincidence that amid efforts to reassert American might, music by Barber, Copland, and others seemed evocative of mid-century America and its remembered virtue and power. Renewed appreciation of their music reflected nostalgia for a time when composers had cultural cachet, reached large audiences, and made big statements about a nation still coherent enough to warrant them. Other tonalists also benefited—Alan Hovhaness's "melodic music is much-performed and admired, except by those who dismiss it." [116] Too, the celebration of cultural heroes, begun in the Kennedy White House and steeped in national self-congratulation—a new cultural nationalism as older forms faded—returned attention to an older generation. The first classical composers to win Kennedy Center honors were Copland, Bernstein, and Thomson.

The capaciousness of postmodernism—as a broad sensibility more than in the specific field of music—embraced Copland, Barber, and others like Tchaikovsky whose popularity and excess had triggered derision. Critics had bewailed—or like Sontag, uneasily championed—how gay artists prized excess over restraint, abandon over discipline, playfulness over seriousness, artifice over authenticity. Many of the qualities ascribed to queer artists were also associated with postmodernism. Barber, given his modernist's sense of narrative and his faith in music as a universal language, was no postmodernist, and initially postmodernism cast figures like Barber and Menotti aside. But only a blurry line separated modernism from postmodernism, which Barber foreshadowed in his hybrid musical style, disregard for boundaries, rejection of a single vector of progress, and dislike of modernist insularity.

In death he continued to figure in arguments still inflected with suspicion that gay composers lacked gravity. "I've learned a lot from Brahms, whereas I can't say that about Tchaikovsky" and his "orchestral niceties," huffed Milton Babbitt, a senior serial composer, in 2002. "Tchaikovsky has as much to do with real classical music as the Three Tenors have to do with real opera," asserted Robert Einhorn. But as Walter Frisch maintained, "There's a school that concludes, 'If it's popular, how good can it be?' The postmodern view is more inclusive. It's the same problem as those who value Schoenberg and discount Samuel Barber because his work wasn't on the trajectory of modernism. But today you don't have to be ashamed of loving Barber's 'Adagio for Strings.' "[117]

If anything, identification of queer tonalists with America deepened. By 1999, Copland's *Fanfare for a Common Man* (1943) had "become as much an American signature as the faces on Mt. Rushmore" and had been "pressed into service to sell bonds, to raise money for PBS, and to celebrate the building of the Brooklyn Bridge," and his music was also tapped to peddle products in advertisements.[118] Use of Barber's music was more scattered—tragedy and loss do not sell cars or elect politicians —but no less telling. The *Adagio* was conducted by Christoph Eschenbach at the ruins of the World Trade Center, Barber's music sounded in post-9/11 "United We Stand" spots on television, and the *Adagio* was played on CBS's *60 Minutes* during the program's 30 May 2004 display of photographs of Americans who had died in Iraq. The distinction between Copland's music as affirmative and Barber's as memorial dwindled as both assumed their places as musical emblems. Copland's music expressed post-9/11 mourning over the loss of an imagined innocence, while Barber's music offered affirmation of faith and nation. Their music was so woven into national idioms—directly and in imitation by others—that it served multiplying aesthetic, political, and commercial purposes. In death, they were still defining—"composing"—America.[119]

The new attention often left queerness in the gauzy shadows of nostalgia, however—at most as a sidebar to the more essential American category. And notions of queer insufficiency persisted. Alex Ross found in mid-century American composers a "familiar pattern: early promise, early triumph, then a long and lonely winding down"—men who "overreached themselves with Empire State Building–size symphonic utterances."[120] Although Ross did not distinguish queer from straight composers, he echoed earlier intimations that the queer tonalists suffered creative sterility. He played down the length of their composing careers—several decades—and the possibility that their "lonely winding down" was contextual rather than individual. Copland and Barber moved on—it was others who froze them in that "Empire State Building" decade.

The repositioning of composers as queer partook of niche marketing common in the late twentieth century. They were gay American composers in recordings and in commentary for gay audiences, and occasionally in places like the *New York Times*, but otherwise their sexuality stayed on the sidelines. Obituaries for Barber and Menotti (1911–2007) offered few hints of their sexuality and relationship, like treatment of Britten's death in 1976.[121] Some accounts were comically obfuscating: one noted Menotti as Barber's "boyhood friend," although they met late in adolescence, kept a relationship into old age, and were more than "friends." When the Juilliard Opera Center staged *Vanessa*, program notes used old conventions—Barber and Menotti "had enjoyed a close and affectionate friendship since their days as students" and "made a home together for some three decades."[122] Similarly with Copland, the U.S. Army, claiming "America's most prominent composer" as one of its own in releasing Army Field Band recordings of his music, noted his "Jewish heritage" and racial politics but subjected his sexuality to its " 'don't ask, don't tell' policy." The army's "production of American patriotism and nationalism for the new millennium," Nadine Hubbs notes, used Copland as "a national treasure and nationalist figure," though if alive he would have faced "dishonorable discharge from the institution that now brandish[ed]" him.[123] Readers of music criticism and history learned far more about Barber's debts to Brahms or Copland's to Boulanger than about how their sexuality informed their work and reputations. Whether they succeeded because of it, despite it, or apart from it usually remained unaddressed.

It was not easily addressed, of course, any more than other questions about identity—how much does Jewishness explain Copland's work?—but those questions were frequently and comfortably addressed. In contrast, Alex Ross, assessing two Britten operas, insisted, "Sexuality is ultimately beside the point: Britten is most interested in the intricate web of circumstances between innocence and corruption"—as if sexuality had nothing to do with that web. "Ultimately," any specific is "beside the point," yet that claim was rarely made about Britten's Englishness, Wagner's Germanness, and Bernstein's Jewishness. "Like it or not," Ross wrote during the 1994 Stonewall anniversary, "most of the masterpieces of Western tradition have been written according to a code of reticence and transcendence, and they are perhaps best understood according to that same code."[124] That was a surprising retreat to universalism given decades of comment about composers' other identities. "There is this whole notion of high art being edifying," Antony Tommasini usefully noted, "and that maybe we shouldn't stoop to this level. And to talk about a straight person's life is not to stoop to some level, but to talk about a gay person's life is." In his biography of Thomson, Tommasini successfully talked about such a life.[125]

For the most part, the categories of gay, American, and composer still did not fit together in public accounts of Barber and his contemporaries. Of course, identities rarely form a neat package for anyone. Their awkward fit was less a problem for Barber—he had not complained—than a sign of the currents buffeting American culture. Even "American" and "composer" had not been a tidy combination given tastemakers' doubts about Americans' creative worth, but also because "composer" often meant "queer." Many still found questions about queerness uncomfortable. An important survey of American culture was nearly silent. Charged with ignoring his sexuality, Barber's biographer insisted that his "love relations are discussed when they bear on his creativity" and damned "the current emphasis on discussion of sexuality," for it "tends to obscure rather than reveal the individuality of the composer's voice."[126] In the end, bringing together ideas of gay, American, and composer—or artist—was hard because doing so implied admission that gay people had so much shaped—invented—American culture.

Perhaps Barber had not desired that admission. Although greatly formed by his relations with Menotti and other gay men, he saw his creative work as driven by his engagement with texts, by his musical muse, and, especially in Italy, by his surroundings. But he knew more was involved—at some level he had known since writing his mother, "I was not meant to be an athlet[e]. I was meant to be a composer." Having approached Tennessee Williams and James Baldwin, pondered *Moby-Dick* as an opera, set "every day another version of every known perversion" to music, surrounded himself with gay men, joined Menotti in Scotland near the end of his life, and requested music by Menotti at his funeral (Menotti, living with his adopted son and the son's wife and children, made it clear he should be buried beside Barber), he was aware of the complicated sources and objects of his creative muse. "To be a composer" did not erase those things. It merely absorbed and contained them.

5

Aftermath

And then, poof! The notion of a conspiracy of gay artists, so common-place by the mid-1960s, abruptly dissipated, though it hardly disap-peared. So, it seemed, did much else in gay life, as *Esquire* claimed after queers attacked cops in New York's 1969 Stonewall riots. "Pity: just when Middle America finally discovered the homosexual, he died." Gone, or at least irrelevant, was "this thirty-fiveish semi-neuter whom they imag-ine to be the prototypical modern deviate: a curio-shop proprietor with an uncertain mouth, wet basset eyes, a Coppertone tan and a miniature Yorkshire, who . . . mourns Judy . . . and masturbates while watching tele-vised swimming meets." He was superseded by the "guiltless male child of the new morality in a Zapata moustache and an outlaw hat," who had more in common with the "heterosexual hippie" than with the neurotic queens of the past. "Gay kids" discarded Ethel Merman, Judy Garland, and the culture that went with them—" 'theatre,' or 'Broadway'—except of course *Hair*," the show celebrating hippies.[1] Although *Esquire*'s ac-count resembled past treatments in its fixation on men and Manhattan, it captured common beliefs that gay liberation made earlier cultural modes and conflicts passé.

Rupture

Among them, agitation over the homintern. By 1972, one contributor to *Out of the Closets: Voices of Gay Liberation* referred to "the then current theory" of 1967 "about a sort of informal conspiracy in the arts, fashion, and so on that was supposed to be threatening the fabric of American society." Likewise, Peter Fisher's *The Gay Mystique* (1972) suggested that controversy had subsided, asserting that culture rather than innate talent or pathology accounted for "creativity" among gay people: they flocked to the arts because "society decrees that this is where they belong" and because the childless homosexual finds in art "another way to make his mark on the world." For C. A. Tripp, whose book *The Homosexual Matrix* (1975) offered a fresh take on the politics and psychology of homosexuality, "the whole argument" about whether gay people make "any direct contributions to society" had "virtually died out in recent decades." Its demise owed to its "having become a dated cliche" and to "the disappearance of the prize: In an age of counter-culture," with its rejection of high art and high culture, "it is hard to find a Leonardo da Vinci."[2]

Direct challenges to the homintern discourse had emerged. In 1967, Benjamin DeMott offered a wicked summary of prevailing views:

> What is a homosexual artist? A devil and a liar, says the current noisy indictment—a desecrater, a self-server, a character nobody on earth should trust. Sly and sulky, he poisons hope and idealism with the mean flow of his resentment. Sick and exhibitionistic, he jams the media with neuroses, teaching that Women are destroyers and heterosexual domestic life is hell. Worse by far, he is power-mad. Skinnying his way onto established grant committees, prize panels, editorial boards, and other seats of authority, he spurns aspirants not of his clique, thereby creating a tyranny of taste. . . . In sum: The homosexual artist is an enemy of the people, a threat to the quality of American life.

For DeMott, the gay artist was still explicitly male (presumptively, all artists were), "homosexual cliquishness" still ruled some fields, and queers were still outsiders. But not because of pathology, for "like heterosexuality," homosexuality is simply "a complex set of relations between self and society," even as a "tide of suspicion" meets the "intelligent homosexual." DeMott saw real worth in what many queers—Tennessee Williams, Edward Albee, and W. H. Auden among them—produced, even if it was " 'usually thin in political content.' " He attacked claims that they were "incapable of speaking truly to anyone not himself a homosexual," dissected critics like Stanley Kauffmann and Susan Sontag, and deplored the "trick of medical inside-dopesterism" and "chic psychoanalytic chatter" critics often used. To ignore gay artists "is worse than senseless," he concluded. "It is a mockery not only of art and of the suffering that art rises out of and seeks to comprehend: It is a mockery of our famous, preening new liberation as well."[3]

But, as he suggested, queer artists found no secure place in the "new liberation," and his essay was more marker than catalyst of change. The homintern discourse developed gradually out of half-baked assumptions and prejudices rarely challenged, even as the particulars were contested. Claims about queers' flawed creativity and pernicious influence served many purposes, displaying hatred, fear, and admiration. Likewise, diminution of the homintern discourse owed less to formal argument than to shifts beneath the surface. It was not killed off; it simply drifted away from center stage. It persisted in many quarters—in the fate of composer Samuel Barber, in the rants of Richard Nixon, and even in gay liberation. Nor did tolerance suddenly prevail—if anything, queer rebellion elicited intolerance. But shifts in politics and culture made the homintern discourse less urgent to many once involved in or subject to it. It had been sustained by the belief that the nation's fate hinged on a cultural empire whose gay artists helped to define America. In the late 1960s, every assumption—that America's fate hinged on empire, that there was a coherent nation to define, that queers dominated culture—came into question.

Out of the Closets, the most wide-ranging gay tract of the period, revealed a good deal about how that change occurred. Contributors said little about queer creativity. Issued at the peak of gay revolutionary ferment, it devoted more space to such topics as "Cuba: Gay as the Sun" than to "Gay People vs. the Media." The daily mores, rituals, and stereotypes of culture were a concern, but not formal cultural production. Karla Jay, the volume's coeditor, did offer a perceptive essay, "A Gay Critique of Modern Literary Criticism," and John Murphy an informed take on "Queer Books." But earlier issues seemed irrelevant to most contributors, and Aaron Copland, Samuel Barber, Tennessee Williams, and others seemed like spent figures. Lovingly consigned to the past, Williams had expressed gay men's "humanity in the only way allowed to them," teaching that "the source of my humanity lies in the endurance of my victimization." "But now we can and must do more, we must refuse to be victims, losers, queers." Ned Rorem too got short shrift—readers entering his "circle of wits and eccentrics cannot be blamed for feeling confusion, trepidation, and even distaste for the homosexual world." Writers aside, gay creators were barely mentioned except as "decorators and beautifiers [for heterosexuals] ever since Christianity captured the Western World." Many had embodied "the cultural conservatism of the tired old gay trip"—they were "selfish, petty, and vain little men who dedicated their lives to preserving the past and serving our masters, the rich. We called ourselves 'artists,' but greatness in art depends on innovation, not repetition of the old." The dismissal of past "innovation" oddly echoed the antigay discourse, whose victims were mostly brushed aside. After all, if gay people were now "out of the closets," by definition most had earlier been in it and stifled by it. The repudiation of mid-century queer creativity was done in part by a new cohort of activists, unwittingly in league with those who had disparaged that creativity for decades.[4]

A similar "commitment to eradicating the rigid sex role system" of "mainstream society" defined *Lavender Culture* (1978), also edited by Karla Jay and Allen Young. A wider range of the arts got attention, but little went to earlier figures. "Are gays more creative?" Young asked, citing "a common myth." In response, he quoted Williams's comment that homosexuals were more artistic "because they've *had* to develop a greater sensibility because they have been rejected." But Young avoided the question of creativity (it "makes me uncomfortable"). Instead he cited "the danger of co-optation in the mainstream," relating one intellectual's worry that "all of that creative energy would be lost once people come out of the closet and become comfortable with their homosexuality." He rejected "a mere current in the mainstream in which to flow," wanting instead "an entirely new culture," and worried that "gay liberation" might mean "that we are just like everyone else" except in sex. For Young, the issue was not gay creativity's past but its revolutionary potential. So too for Jay, who sought an autonomous women's culture—a "No Man's Land," as her piece was entitled.[5]

How were the issues of queer creativity so abruptly set aside? The ideological rupture of gay liberation played a major role. With the existing culture viewed as patriarchal, sex-phobic, and oppressive, old debates about it seemed irrelevant. "Smash Phallic Imperialism," as a piece in *Out of the Closets* was titled, was the call, and it required immediate action—from protest to alliance with other radical causes—not the slow-moving ways of cultural creativity. Gay rebels were inflamed by hard forms of authority—police and the courts, psychiatrists and mental hospitals, imperialists and their wars. Softer forms of authority—culture—seemed less urgent, except for the "game of roles" and sexist assumptions. That shift from culture to politics meant abandoning an older queer culture, for it seemed "as if most homosexual literature were a game, with elaborate rules, masks, costumes, hiding places." Insofar as liberationists sought to smash the very category of "homosexual," an older creativity born of that category was beside the point. *Out of the Closets* likewise rejected the middle-class concerns that shaped earlier gay investment in the arts.[6]

Queer radicals also had scant leftist tradition of cultural criticism to draw on. The New Left rarely addressed their issues and the old left was despised. ("The Communist Party is probably the most vicious anti-homosexual group on the left today," Allen Young complained.) Insofar as "the left is too prone to accept the old syndrome that violence-proves-masculinity," Dennis Altman wrote in 1971, the left led some gay men "into concealing their homosexual feelings behind a cult of virility not far removed from that of John Wayne." Alliance with Black Power militants was similarly fraught. *Soul on Ice* author Eldridge Cleaver condemned James Baldwin and other "Negro homosexuals" for "acquiescing in this racial death wish," famously declaring that "homosexuality is a sickness just as are baby rape or wanting to become the head of General Motors," although Black Panther leader Huey Newton saw "homosexuals and women as oppressed groups." Feminism offered more, but *Closets* drew largely on its claims about male power in everyday life, not on those about literature and the arts.[7]

Ideological stances in *Out of the Closets* reflected authors' backgrounds. Most were young, with little memory or feel for older voices in these matters. Many were women not about to play second fiddle to gay men — "I will not be your 'nigger' any longer," Del Martin had proclaimed, "and I shall no longer concern myself with your toilet training" — and the homintern discourse had rarely been about women. Their stance was inadvertently justified when John Murphy defined homosexuality as "the actual love of men for men," which excluded women, and for the most part women writers. These rebels sympathized with oppressed groups, not with privileged men in the arts.[8]

Out of the Closets nonetheless reflected the past. Its dismissal of past gay creativity as stale, superficial, and supine echoed the earlier denunciations, and it engaged issues of authenticity that had long bothered Americans. As Martha Shelley complained, adorning herself in "black lace dress, heels, elaborate hairdo and makeup" for a benefit dinner made her feel "like the ultimate in artifice, a woman posing as a drag queen." Attacks on "role playing" stressed the artifice it involved and the need to come "out 'of the closets," which this volume helped establish as the ruling metaphor for the gay past. To come out was to be true to the self and free of artifice, and "in a free society everyone will be gay," or at least liberated from sexism and role playing.[9]

208   The ringing call to come out flung back the accusation that gay people

engaged in deception, as if to say: You don't like our disguises? Well, we don't either, and not yours either. That turnabout animated gay liberation. It was straight men who were deceivers, oppressing others in the name of medical wisdom and religious virtue while themselves remaining sexually sick. The accused were now the accusers, bent on freeing themselves and their oppressors. Gay radicals thereby gained the high ground of authenticity and influence (if rarely admitted by others), since "coming out" became "a general trope in American popular culture. Anyone can emerge from denial, evasion and secrecy to embrace a public identity."[10]

But liberationists seemed unaware that they echoed earlier views of their kind. Viewing coming out as a revolutionary breakthrough, a notion soon romanticized, blocked that awareness. Instead, they agreed about queers' past deficiencies but blamed them on sexist oppression and "phallic imperialism." Their audacity came not in forging a new understanding of queer authenticity but in hurling their tormenters' definition back at them. Gay rebels also worked within familiar imaginative traditions "as heirs of a recurring and peculiarly American injunction to find ourselves," embodying "a modernist moral quest" evident in American literature, Roger Lancaster notes. Their "identity politics" infuriated "cultural traditionalists," but it was "as American as apple pie."[11] Coming out, they seized the enemy's weapon but implicitly conceded that the enemy had been right to wield it.

Beyond *Out of the Closets*, some observers offered a more nuanced sense of the past. Dennis Altman, an Australian scholar in the United States, drew on earlier writers — Baldwin, Genet, Ginsberg, Isherwood — in his *Homosexual Oppression and Liberation* (1971), which astutely observed how gay liberation related to capitalism, black power, the counterculture, and other currents. Noting the claim that Albee's *Virginia Woolf* was " 'really' a play about homosexuals," Altman observed that "the claim suggests that many critics recognize the extent to which gays and straights mirror-image each other." A similar view of mirror imaging came in Tripp's *The Homosexual Matrix*. In such treatments and in fads like androgynous fashion, the sharp homosexual/heterosexual binary faded, while resurgent feminism widened the male-female divide. If "gays and straights mirror-image each other," here was cause to champion queer artists: they spoke to and about all people, not just their own kind. Yet Altman saw "gay culture" as "produced almost exclusively by social ostracism" and agreed with D. J. West "that homosexuals, like most people who are stigmatized, 'strive to avoid all taint of unorthodoxy in opinions and behavior.' " Few artists would be daring until the stigma was

AFTERMATH

gone. That view left little space for past creativity. As a writer claimed in the *Advocate*, "The history of gay fiction, at least in this country, can be divided into two eras., B.L. and A.L.: Before *Loon* and After *Loon*," referring to Richard Amory's *Song of the Loon* (1966).[12]

If gay liberationists neglected how the past shaped the present, so too did their foes. Antigay polemicists—and many earlier ones remained active—had railed against the shallowness, deception, and artifice of gay people. Especially in theater criticism, they had demanded that queers abandon disguise and write honestly about homosexuality, if only to spare others their tiresome games. When gay men and women did what was demanded—if not because it was demanded—some observers responded in horror, while others were more welcoming, grudgingly or not.

Critic John Simon offered one version of that transition. Reviewing Terrence McNally's *And Things Go Bump in the Night* in 1965, he recalled that he had "deplored the crypto-homosexual play in which the pederast appeared disguised as an aging actress, a rebellious Negro or Everyman. Well, now we have an honest-to-goodness homosexual play, and is it ever an abomination," showing how the gay writer "has to wallow in every kind of nastiness, exhibitionism, vulgarity, and destruction. It is not the homosexuality that offends, but all that hysterical ugliness that seems to be its Siamese twin," wrote Simon, whose metaphor suggested that the two were in fact inseparable. In 1968 he recorded his surprise that Matt Crowley's *The Boys in the Band*, "a play about a clutch of homosexuals, ranging from closet to screaming queens, who celebrate an internecine birthday party, would prove one of the very few good shows of the season." But after all, "I have been pleading all along for frankly homosexual drama instead of plays in drag." Simon offered his arch praise of *Boys in the Band* more to vindicate his attacks on Williams and Albee than to embrace the liberated stage character. Others, too, struggled with the shift that critics had demanded. Pauline Kael found director John Schlesinger guilty in *Midnight Cowboy* (1969) of "almost hysterical cleverness" and "his spray of venom" at America "almost overpowering." Kael reprised old attacks on gay artists—a category Schlesinger fit—as being venomous about dominant society. (She did like his 1971 film, *Sunday, Bloody Sunday*.)[13]

Observing the new undisguised homosexual, whether on stage or in the streets, many people expressed the same indignation they had given the old deceiver. Queer truth-in-packaging was as alarming as queer secrecy. Accusations that gay people practiced disguise had rarely addressed what lay beneath the disguise beyond murky pathology. Few had imagined that

210

it was defiance and pride—perhaps experts had convinced themselves that inside every homosexual lay a hidden heterosexual. To be sure, they spotted dishonesty even in the liberated queer, rehashing an old view of those who defied the sickness model: assertions of gay pride were pitiful compensations for the self-loathing that homosexuals felt deep down. But the terms of debate had shifted.

Shifts

Shifts in gender, sexuality, and empire pushed aside the homintern discourse. Resurgent feminism was key. The assault by feminists, and gay liberationists often inspired by them, on misogyny, patriarchy, and male power shifted blame for women's mistreatment away from gay men, now rendered victims of sexism, if still guilty of it as well. That assault challenged a major prop of the homintern discourse—that gay men were hateful to women. Feminism also emboldened lesbians' voices in gay politics, helping to sideline the homintern debate with its focus on men.

Gay liberation was also important for reasons beyond its formal claims. Given the wave of coming out, gay writers and artists were no longer the most visible embodiments of queerness. New ones emerged: Howard Brown, New York City's first health services administrator, whose coming-out in 1973 and book *Familiar Faces, Hidden Lives: The Story of Homosexuality in America Today* (1976) attracted headlines; San Francisco politician Harvey Milk; and thousands marching in protest, asserting visibility and storming groups like the American Psychiatric Association, which dropped homosexuality from its list of mental disorders in 1973. Some of the new faces were in the arts—Rita Mae Brown, an *Out of the Closets* contributor who became a successful novelist; poet and essayist Adrienne Rich; and writers like Edmund White and Larry Kramer. But artists and writers lost their singularity (shared with criminals) in the pantheon of public queerness. Scandalmongers, state-of-America essayists, and inquiring reporters could look elsewhere. The arts no longer served as the primary arena for inquiry into, and abuse about, homosexuality.

This shift was marked in the film *The Boys in the Band* (William Friedkin, 1970), in which gay men gather for a birthday and bare their souls about the plight of the homosexual. It offered arch comments on gay decor and the biting humor often seen as typical of arty gay men. ("It's like the gathering of bitchy ladies in *The Women*," Pauline Kael wrote, referring to George Cukor's 1939 film.) But its core was its characters' everyday lives (and lies), not their place in creativity. They were out-spokenly, if self-mockingly, gay—a far cry from the shadowy figures of *Strangers on the Train*, *Sweet Smell of Success*, and doomsday films, who had endangered the nation, and the lightweight pianists and designers of other movies. That was even more the case with *Midnight Cowboy*, whose queer characters—"homosexual" seems not the right label—cling to the bottom rung of New York life. Although creatures of urban pathology, they were presented sympathetically by Schlesinger rather than scorn-fully. Hollywood still offered dangerous or unpleasant gay characters, as some regarded those in *Boys in the Band*, as well as in *The Killing of Sister George* (1968), about lesbians. "A plethora of plagues is upon us," ob-served the pseudonymous Ronald Forsythe in the *New York Times*. "In books and plays and films we seem to have to commit suicide, murder one another (or be murdered . . .), die 'a la Camille, or at least break off the relationship lest insanity be the result." But the explicitness of many characters' queerness and the ordinariness of their lives diminished the queer artist—or the queer who was "artistic"—as a central figure.[14]

Change flowed also from disruptions at the nexus of cultural empire and queer creativity. The tension between aspirations for cultural empire and dependence on queer creativity had fueled the homintern discourse. That fuel dried up in the late 1960s as the cultural Cold War and the Cold War itself came into question. Against the ugliness of the Vietnam War, it seemed a minor matter whether Lincoln Center or American music com-manded world attention. If the nation's fate no longer hinged on winning the cultural Cold War, it no longer hinged on which black writer or queer composer waged it. America's tarnished image came from its war in Viet-nam, not from its artists. If anything carried American culture abroad, it was not highbrow artists but popular music, commercial culture, and a new counterculture.

Less important, cultural empire also now seemed corrupted—not by a queer presence but by the machinations of the American state. A wave of exposés revealed how much the CIA and other agencies, corporations, and foundations had secretly funded the cultural war against commu-nism. Rather than a noble effort by artists and intellectuals embodying freedom, that war now appeared deeply compromised and politicized. Al-though covert sponsorship had been no secret to many insiders, their ac-quiescence in it only made the enterprise look more corrupt. This take on cultural empire moved old questions about the gay presence in it further to the side.

212   Cultural empire-building still had political and institutional momen-

tum. It figured in the creation of the National Endowment for the Humanities and the National Endowment for the Arts in the mid-1960s and in the completion of Washington's Kennedy Center. And at the Metropolitan Opera House in Lincoln Center, the wealthy and powerful continued to gather. But its gala 1966 opening, troubled even when it occurred, soon looked like the relic of another era. Those deeply invested in the arts—performers, patrons, audiences, and others—cared about these developments, but their place as bearers of American authority shrank. Americans still argued about the content of culture, above all when sex was involved, but the stakes changed once the burden of American culture on the world stage diminished.

Ironically, the United States gained ground in the cultural Cold War just when a sense of its urgency waned. In part because of Eisenhower's initiatives in cultural exchange, Soviet and other communist-regime artists performed in the West, and through their initiative or the forcing hand of Soviet authorities, some defected, often to the United States. Most famous were ballet star Rudolph Nureyev in 1961, cellist Mstislav Rostropovich and his wife, soprano Galina Vishnevskaya, in 1974, and writer Aleksandr Solzhenitsyn, exiled that year. Diverse motives moved the defectors, who did not all embrace American culture and were sometimes greeted as exemplars of a more authentic European culture. But the defections were heralded by U.S. authorities as victories for Western freedom and signs of Soviet cultural rot. American culture had global dominance by the 1970s, and U.S. authorities no longer worried that one misstep would bring the whole thing crashing down. The United States won, if not through creativity then by the sheer dominance of its culture. If anything, danger now lay in resentment abroad and disquiet at home about the American cultural machine. Meanwhile, who occupied the high ground of high culture seemed less important.

As the stakes for American culture began shifting in the late 1960s, so too did debate about authenticity. In the midst of the Vietnam War and other convulsions, America's leaders triggered more concern than America's artists. Lyndon Johnson and Richard Nixon were accused and judged guilty of deceit and dishonesty (of a criminal sort in Nixon's case). There had been nothing like this sustained assault on presidents, which lasted through and beyond Nixon's resignation in 1974. Other battles about authenticity continued—over Black Power, gay liberation, feminism, and much else—but they were often overshadowed by the drama over Vietnam and the presidency. To an extent, Nixon unwittingly moved homosexuals, and many others he hated, off center stage.

As the fortunes of America's cultural empire shifted, the reputations of many gay men who had served it went into eclipse. The two developments were loosely related. Animosity against queer artists may have diminished because they seemed—and in some fields were—less prominent. Many of the major figures—Barber, Copland, Williams—faced aging, health problems, and difficulty in remaining productive and fresh, or at least having others see their work that way. Even James Baldwin, a younger figure, met more critical disapproval. As Barber's case shows, this older generation also endured the stereotype of aging gay men as burnt-out, stale, adrift. It did not help when figures like Williams and Truman Capote made the rounds of television talk shows as rather dazed or sad creatures.

Although younger men like Albee and Stephen Sondheim bridged generations and styles, the homintern discourse waned in part because gay artists were now less prominent, as if that discourse had diminished their stature. In serious music, the 1970s completed the ascendancy of serial and other straight-identified composers like Elliott Carter and Pierre Boulez and younger ones like Philip Glass and John Adams. Bernstein's fame persisted, but more as a conductor and celebrity than as a composer. Gay male film stars of the postwar era were dead (Montgomery Clift) or doing less glamorous work (Rock Hudson, Tab Hunter, Farley Granger, Anthony Perkins), while the new stars (Al Pacino, Dustin Hoffman, Robert Redford) were straight, or at least stalked by few rumors to the contrary. Meanwhile, "the best Hollywood can do," Edmund White observed, "is to mate a lesbian and a gay man, or to sneak a few Sensitives—those Troubled Youths with inclinations toward ballet or suicide— into otherwise dreary features." Nor did rock 'n' roll show a queer face, aside from glam rock and similar offshoots. Dennis Altman deemed it "a little strange, perhaps sad, that gays in the rock world remain closeted while they are coming out in the much more . . . literate worlds of theatre and literature." [15]

If gay men's place in American culture seemed diminished, culture itself seemed less coherent. Whether any social type dominated a niche was less apparent when the niche was in disarray, as many arts were. Several trends—women's increasing voices, the rise of regional themes and artists, a democratization in cultural production, a proliferation of fields—made any accounting of who was on top and who was not difficult. [16] The less coherent the culture, the harder it was to finger one group as controlling it.

Postmodernism also diminished gay men's place in American culture, at least initially. It is true that mid-century modernists—Barber, Bernstein, and Thomson in music, Williams and Albee in drama—anticipated postmodernism, which in turn became associated with feminism, queer theory, and queer intellectuals and artists. But that association developed more in the 1980s and 1990s, with the influence of Michel Foucault, the rise of queer theory, and the cultural production prompted in part by AIDS. As Jonathan Dollimore notes, postmodern fashions may only have reproduced "the consumerist ethic whereby the latest, despite—or rather because of—being little different from the last, renders the latter obsolete."[17] Thus mid-century gay artists were rendered "obsolete" although not so different from their successors. Initial exponents of postmodernism were usually not queer-identified, and their import in many fields was to set aside older figures, many gay.

Similarly, the sexual revolution of the 1960s and 1970s had ambiguous consequences. It was a factor in the more vigorous expression of queer sexuality in theater, film, and other fields, but heterosexuality also gained more vigorous expression, often in explicit or implicit rebuke to a perceived queer tide. As Altman noted, "*Newsweek*'s (approving) review of *Oh! Calcutta!*," a popular 1969 musical, "congratulated it on its 'bracing heterosexuality'—a notice that is reprinted on the theatre's billboards."[18] Many fashions of the time—including most rock 'n' roll and nearly all country music—offered an assertively heterosexual face. By no means did all such writers and artists seek to counter a queer tide, which indeed had its moments in everything from disco music and Armistead Maupin's *Tales of the City* to women's music and revelations about the writer John Cheever. Hence many gay people experienced the 1970s, more than the years before or after, as a time of queer efflorescence. Yet much of it remained blanched of its queer roots in media treatments or dwarfed by a resurgent heterosexuality.

The post-Stonewall political rebellion of the 1970s, with its noise and success, obscured the shakier fortunes of gay people in culture. In standard templates, progress for a group in one arena means progress in others, as indeed happened in the long run—the whole genre of lesbian and gay historical writing, for example, owes much to the 1970s rebellion. But cultural change does not move on the same timetable as political change—otherwise there would have been no gay ascendancy in the arts at mid-century, a time of rampant antiqueer politics. Insofar as another queer moment in American culture did emerge, it came more in the wake of the Stonewall rebellion, not in step with it.

The mid-century generation had been associated with cultural definitions of America—the nostalgia-tinged America of Copland's cowboys and cityscapes, the sophisticated America of Cole Porter, the mourning America of Barber's *Adagio*. Defining America had not always been their intent, but it had been the culturally inscribed result. Among the reasons for their diminished stature by the 1970s was the passing of the America they depicted—indeed, even of the attempt to represent America, which now seemed to many a parochial or chauvinistic act. Even if the attempt was valid, its practicality was in doubt: a coherent, definable America seemed blasted away by divisions over war and foreign policy, presidential misdeeds, and social relations. At best, those who defined America captured its untidiness—America as *The Segmented Society*, as historian Robert Wiebe's 1974 book was entitled—not the commonality remembered by some for mid-century America. Although cultural nationalism had been fading for decades, the convulsions of the Vietnam era made the mid-century American arts seem obsolete. Nationalism was not dead. Its revival in 1976 Bicentennial celebrations, Reagan-era nostalgia, and "America's neo-traditionalist self-celebration" helped restore the luster of men like Copland and Barber.[19] But by then they were voices from a past whose recovery was yearned for, not creators speaking to the present.

The changing fortunes of America's cultural empire hastened the eclipse of the gay artists who had helped sustain it. An empire in disarray had less need for their work, and observers had less need to scrutinize it. With empire shorn of authenticity, so also to a degree were those who once spoke for it. By the same token, discarding them implicitly repudiated the empire they had served. Earlier, they were too valuable to be rejected but too queer to be fully accepted. By the 1970s, neither their value nor their queerness seemed as important.

Persistence

Even as high-profile talk of the homintern diminished, its shards spun off. Struggles over queer contributions continued in many fields, if gaining less attention outside them. Antigay crusaders, now usually on the right wing of politics and culture, condemned the queer presence in entertainment and the arts. Though now less uniformly, experts, in books like *Homosexuality: The Psychology of the Creative Process* (1971), still were doubtful or muddled about queers' fitness for the arts.[20]

Another place these ideas persisted was in the White House. As noted in this book's introduction, in May 1971 the TV sitcom *All in the Family* had led Nixon and John Ehrlichman to bewail the effects of homosexuality and gay artists on past empires and the current American imperium. Nixon privately vented suspicions that others only hinted at in public. Lyndon Johnson had denounced "Nervous Nellies"—code for queers and others of dubious virility—as among those "who will become frustrated and bothered and break ranks under the strain" of waging the Vietnam War. Nixon's vice president, Spiro Agnew, condemned "ideological eunuchs" and others given to "tantrums" who were "insidiously destroying the fabric of American society." "We *are* an effete society if we let it happen here." Johnson and Agnew included queers in the forces undermining America's power and values.[21] They avoided explicit words like "homosexuals," though not because they were afraid of venom. Perhaps the words seemed beneath the dignity of men in power. Perhaps insinuation worked better: they were intent less on identifying real homosexuals than on associating the antiwar movement with queerness.

In any event, Nixon spelled things out in private. He was at it again on 13 September 1971, with H. R. ("Bob") Haldeman, another principal assistant.[22] The subject was the 8 September opening of Washington's Kennedy Center Opera House, an event Nixon refused to attend, instead going to the new Concert Hall the next night. Just as the new Met's debut in 1966 had displayed a gay artist's grand creation, Barber's *Antony and Cleopatra*, so did the unveiling of the Kennedy Center: Leonard Bernstein's *Mass*, a supercharged mix of rock 'n' roll, religious liturgy, and passionate outburst that, like *Antony*, was dubbed by many critics a failure.

Nixon had many reasons to hate this occasion, his hatreds always overdetermined. It honored John F. Kennedy and implicitly the Kennedy family, which Nixon feared and detested, and Jacqueline Kennedy Onassis had commissioned *Mass*. Reviewing press coverage of the opening-night gala, Nixon and Haldeman were agitated by a photo of Joan Kennedy, Senator Ted Kennedy's wife, in an immodest dress "with a slit up to the top of her thighs," Haldeman noted. Nixon was also glad he did not attend because Bernstein and his wife had "put on a damn cocktail party" in 1970—a notorious fundraiser for the Black Panthers mocked by Tom Wolfe in his article "Radical Chic" and regarded later by James McCourt as an effort by "the Uptown Homintern" to appear radical without "doing anything so socially compromising as coming out."[23] Bernstein was also, Haldeman added, "a big buddy of the Berrigans"— the Catholic priests Daniel and Philip Berrigan convicted for their raids on Selective Service offices and now charged with conspiring to kidnap

Nixon's national security adviser, Henry Kissinger. Bernstein had put on a party for the Berrigans in May. "I didn't know that!" Nixon responded to Haldeman.

More likely, he had forgotten that detail, for FBI director Hoover had briefed Haldeman and Attorney General John Mitchell in July about the upcoming Kennedy Center gala and warned that *Mass* had an anti-war message.[24] Bernstein's composition had plenty to offend. Loosely a setting of the Catholic Mass, this "Theater Piece for Singers, Players, and Dancers," as it was subtitled, seemed sacrilegious to many Catholics and others. It was "an attack on all authority," a Bernstein biographer wrote—a loud " 'Fuck You!' " as its conductor, Maurice Peress, recalled.[25] Beyond its words, it was raucous, defiant, and disheveled in musical and theatrical content—an outsized expression of Bernstein's hear-my-pain ego. Its characters' seemingly drug-induced frenzy added another offense to conventional morality.

But what most bewildered Nixon were "nauseating" photos, as Halde-man called them, "of Bernstein kissing everybody he could find" at the premiere festivities. "He's kissing a lot of men on the mouth," Haldeman added, "including the big black guy," Alvin Ailey, who choreographed *Mass* as he had *Antony and Cleopatra*. "Kissing on the mouth?!" Nixon asked in an astonished whisper. "Yeah, right head on!" Haldeman re-plied. "Absolutely sickening," the president commented—"revolting," Haldeman added. The two groped for an ethnic model for such behavior, observing that Jewish, black, and Latin American men often kissed each other. Seen that way, Bernstein's kissing appeared almost understandable to Nixon. "Yeah, but they don't kiss," Haldeman clarified with respect to those groups, "they don't put their lips to the cheek. But the French do." Nixon and Haldeman were disgusted: there was no avoiding that this was *queer* behavior—the kisses of men with passionate loves and friendships, or at least the performance thereof. Ethnicity could not account for it, especially when it crossed the color line. They took comfort that *New York Times* critic Harold Schonberg thought *Mass* "stinks," as Haldeman put it. "Did the Times say Bernstein was vulgar?" Nixon asked. "The New York Times," Haldeman confirmed, Nixon adding an indecipherable reference to Jews. Then they returned to the Attica prison riots, their fear that "radicals" would exploit them, "the homosexual rape of young boys" in prisons, and the Kennedy Center's opening again.

Schonberg condemned *Mass* for its "slick kind of bathos" and "fashionable kitsch." "Cheap and vulgar," its music "as thin as the watery liberalism" of its message, it was the "work of a musician who desperately wants to be with it" but was only good at "lightweight music." "Anyway," Schonberg added in a stinging attack on Bernstein, "the ones who talk loudest about universal love are generally . . . the greatest haters." More came days later, Schonberg calling *Mass* "the greatest melange of styles since the ladies magazine recipe for steak fried in peanut butter and marshmallow sauce."[26] His terms reflected standard attacks on gay artists, although many people hated *Mass* for no visibly antiqueer reasons. *Mass* did find supportive critics and other venues—at the Met a year later and the Vienna State Opera in 1981—and Bernstein was invited by Pope Paul VI to conduct at the Vatican in 1973. He was too needy and ambitious, with other hats to wear when one failed him, to slip away as Barber had after *Antony*, and given his envy of Barber's stature, perhaps eager not to act like him.

The notion that queer artists debased culture was alive and well. It showed in Schonberg's review of *Mass*, which resembled his review of Barber's *Antony*, and in the White House, where there were receptive readers of that review and disgusted viewers of photos. Just as striking was what Nixon did not say. He did not care about what the arts at the Kennedy Center conveyed to the world. He indulged the rituals of cultural empire—obliged as president to attend one performance—but had no investment in their substance. What galvanized him was the war within America, which imperiled American empire, or at least Nixon's rule. It was not a wholly paranoid view: gay rebels and others proclaimed their revolutionary intent. But it was the pinched view of a man who enjoyed having enemies. However defiant *Mass* was, Bernstein was also playing court composer by starring in the Center's opening: he was not going to lead the revolution. But for Nixon, Bernstein's *Mass* and his kisses, like other queer phenomena, showed the rot spread by the "enemies of strong societies," as he had put it months earlier. At least he got the pleasure of having the *Times* as a surprising if momentary ally.

Nixon's responses showed both the continuing salience of older ideas about a gay threat and the repositioning of that threat: cultural empire now mattered less than power within America. Press coverage treated the Bernstein premiere more as a political than a cultural event, not surprisingly given Bernstein's politics and the Kennedy Center's location. Schonberg hoped the Center could be something better, and better supported by the American government, than it was on first view, given that "the American image around the world is one of bloodthirsty imperialism, racism and internal problems." But that rationale for cultural achievement had lost out to the angry politics of the Vietnam War, and

Schonberg was not about to give Bernstein credit for speaking to "blood-thirsty imperialism." It did not help that the Center's architecture was something that Nazi architect and munitions guru "Albert Speer would have approved," Ada Louise Huxtable claimed on the front page of the *Times*, and that "New York no longer has the ugliest opera house in America," according to Clive Barnes.[27]

Like other real or imagined queers, Bernstein aroused Nixon's ire, or at least appeared to. It is hard to determine if that ire was deeply felt or merely grist for the curious male-bonding that he and his staff enjoyed by heaping venom on others. His aides were set-up men, feeding Nixon material from papers and magazines that allowed the lead attraction to carry on his performance. Or perhaps the locker room is a better meta-phor—the put-downs had the strained quality of men trying to prove to each other that the guys in the locker-room were tougher and better than the outsiders.

Homosexuals were only one of many groups that angered Nixon, and perhaps not that frequently, although the voluminous Nixon record has not been systematically searched for all his antigay outbursts. Boundaries between these groups were fluid for Nixon, as he tacked back and forth among homosexuals, Jews, blacks, the French, and Latin Americans. On 13 September he moved from African Americans in Attica prison, to Bernstein's party for the Black Panthers, to his kissing of Ailey, and back to Attica: out-of-control blackness and unchecked homosexuality were loosely but profoundly tied together in his mind. Not that he was a post-modernist attuned to multiple identities. Rather, he perceived so many enemies that they ran together for him. But there was an extra frisson to the rambling by Nixon and his aides about ancient Greeks, San Fran-cisco queers, and kissing artists—a special charge to their disgust, and to their delight in their disgust, at seeing Bernstein kissing Ailey. Not every enemy offered such guilty pleasure. And beyond disgust was a nervous awe—"Kissing on the mouth?!"—a hint that they might not be able to stop the forces displayed in the photographs.

In the raucous 1970s, "homintern," a word Nixon did not use, served antigay agitators poorly—its implication of hidden conspiracy was at odds with the newly un-hidden sight of gay women and men. But many assumptions propelling earlier use of the term remained in force, if any-thing deepened by fury at gay people's new assertiveness. Movements to ban them from public school teaching—California voters narrowly de-feated Proposition 6, offering such a ban, in 1978—and fissures over their presence in many churches measured the fury. Many critics still saw a sinister, if no longer hidden, presence in culture yielding sterile, superficial results.

Something of Nixon's spirit showed in Midge Decter's 1980 *Commentary* piece, "The Boys on the Beach."[28] If Nixon felt mocked by queers brazenly kissing each other, Decter felt mocked by their mere existence. And lesbians "were a living sneer at the straight men." If such men had sex with them, "there would be little triumph, or pleasure, in it for [them]," she observed, not disclosing how she was privy to such moments. Decter updated urbane, often Jewish intellectual commentary on homosexuals and its psychoanalytic style ("for many if not all" gay men, "homosexuality represented a flight from women" and an "escape from the sexual reminder of birth and death"). Once identified as liberal, that tradition by the 1970s was associated with neoconservatives like Decter, Cold Warriors infuriated by détente with the Soviets and by changes at home that weakened America, as they saw it. They included her husband, Norman Podhoretz, and Joseph Epstein, whose 1970 *Harper's* essay had observed, "If I had the power to do so, I would wish homosexuality off the face of this earth" because of the pain it caused queer people "and because, wholly selfishly, I find myself incapable of coming to terms with it." That essay had prompted amply televised protest at *Harper's* offices and debate on TV talk shows. Decter, the essay's editor, now dubbed it "elegant and thoughtful."[29]

She cast her commentary as a reflection on the gay men she had observed on New York's Fire Island in the early 1960s, before she felt squeezed out by them — "being surrounded by homosexuals put our very existence as women on the line," she claimed, reprising the notion of gay men as misogynists. She also reflected on changes since then, including in "gay bars," which she did not claim to have visited. Like many predecessors, she found most gay men to be mama's boys — alcoholic, adolescent in personality, and unhappy, especially now as they succumbed to "drugs, sado-masochism, and suicide" — to "the obliteration of all experience, if not, indeed, of oneself."

In an essay notorious for many reasons, Decter tracked her reactions to the expressive gay culture of the 1970s. She had earlier spotted gay men in a host of creative fields, with their presence sufficient "to define a certain kind of privilege," apparently different from that of intellectuals like herself. She added that "the list could go on" of "businesses and professions" where gay men "have engaged in a good deal of discriminatory practice against others." That charge echoed Jewish male intellectuals' denunciations of affirmative action for women and minorities in the academy.[30] Like the gay men in Arthur Schlesinger's *The Vital Center*, her queers also had the advantage that "they can in a single sweeping glance around a crowded room and with unerring accuracy recognize one another." Among them was "an unaccountably high proportion of extremely talented persons." "Does homosexuality have the effect of releasing talent," Decter asked, "or is it that the talented are more inclined to be homosexual?" But she dropped the matter, for "the question bores. The concrete reality, however, does not," she added ominously.

Decter disliked earlier gay creativity, rehashing old charges: plays by Williams and Albee offered "homosexual relationships as the deeper truth about love in our time. Women have permitted themselves to be rendered breastless, and men to become pocket-book carriers, by homosexual designers." But like many who had condemned indirection and disguise, she liked expressiveness even less. New "homosexual tracts and novels"—she identified no fiction, only Edmund White's *States of Desire: Travels in Gay America* (1980)—were "part of the vast outpouring of confessional literature" of her time. They hovered "somewhere between aggressive exhibitionism and the plaintive appeal for pity." Their authors lacked "the talent and wit that were so characteristic a mark of their predecessors" and featured "an earnestness and callowness and crudity that are the very last qualities one who knew them would have associated with homosexuals." Interpreting "Gay Lib" as seeking "to define homosexuality as nothing more than a casual option," she missed its revolutionary currents, seeing only a neurotic quest for assimilation. As she commented about San Francisco, "where spokesmen for Gay Lib control banks and major businesses," "the freedom to rise, it would seem, is also very much the freedom to sink." She judged gay culture above all by whether it entertained heterosexuals, as if that were its function, deploring how "a strategy of flight, tricky and absorbing, has been transformed into a tactic of frontal assault." In their "'literature'"—Decter used the term only with quotation marks—and lives, homosexuals "have lost their lightness of touch, and with it, whatever lightness of heart it made possible." For Decter, they were no longer fun to be around and their culture no longer fun to observe. Whatever they did was superficial and artificial, but at least once it had been entertaining. Now it was callow, earnest, or patently offensive.

Decter's piece prompted a torrent of responses in *Commentary* and elsewhere, one measure of change from pre-Stonewall days. Many identified a bigotry akin to anti-Semitism, all the more offensive coming from a Jew. "For sheer vim and vigor," Gore Vidal charged, "'The Boys on

the Beach' outdoes its implicit model, *The Protocols of the Elders of Zion.*"
Decter stuck to her guns, suggesting she was a victim of truth telling.
"Homosexuals *do* tend to be more interested than others in aesthetic sur-
faces," she insisted.[31]

Her complaints were not all hers alone. Some were echoed in queer
fiction like Larry Kramer's *Faggots* (1978). Edmund White criticized a
"new macho fascism" among gay men. And just as she decried the loss
of wit and indirection, some gay men mourned the loss they saw of the
pleasures of secrecy, the artifices of camp, and the insights borne of oppression. For them, the 1970s marked a descent James McCourt later
traced in his memoir's subtitle, *Rise and Fall of an American Culture.* If
not for all the same reasons, some gay men too worried that "the freedom
to rise" entailed "also very much the freedom to sink."[32]

But White gave a far more nuanced account of these changes than
Decter. Gay liberation "made the indirection of the past less necessary"
and perhaps "made even art itself less useful, less compelling to the majority of gays." If gay artists once excelled at "delicacy, prettiness, tenderness," and evasiveness, "the current gay taste . . . is moving toward greater
simplicity and explicitness." Registering loss, White also saw gains: "New
York gays" remained "taste-makers for the rest of the country," their
"restlessly evolving style" now "disseminated with alarming rapidity."
He traced change, not declension.[33]

Assimilation?

The homintern discourse rumbled through the rest of the century.
During the 1980s, it showed in AIDS-driven revelations and "culture wars"
over artists like Robert Mapplethorpe. News that actor Rock Hudson was
gay and dying of AIDS unleashed a media frenzy of alarm and admiration about how he had managed to perform heterosexual roles and to disguise—an old complaint about gay men—his sexuality. Politicians like
Senator Jesse Helms voiced outrage that queers like Mapplethorpe had
burrowed into the American arts and been succored by federal monies.
And the deaths of notable figures rekindled notions of gay men's early
creative demise.

But the controversies were no simple replays of the past, their explicitness being one difference. Earlier denunciations had rarely identified
living queer artists, or had done so obliquely, and public rejoinders to
them had been few. The willed coming-out of the post-Stonewall era and
the unwilled coming-out that AIDS often produced meant that names were

named. In his prime, Rock Hudson had endured published innuendo and gossip, but he was never plastered on the cover of magazines as a gay—and AIDS-ravaged—figure. AIDS also exposed figures on the right—lawyer and former Joe McCarthy sidekick Roy Cohn, and scholar Allan Bloom, author of *The Closing of the American Mind* (1987). That exposure, along with the Cold War's ebbing, diluted associations between queerness and radicalism. And alongside queer-baiting and fear-mongering about AIDS came extended comment about gay men's creativity, prompted by the deaths of artists and by a creative explosion among gay artists, often in response to the disease.

Indeed, gay people offered spirited public voices in these matters far different from their muted or indirect role earlier. Women were now prominent among them, in part because both straight and gay women—Karen Finley, Holly Hunter—were fingered as dangerous recipients of federal monies. Queer voices sounded in activism and creatively as well, as in playwright Tony Kushner's commercial and critical success, *Angels in America*, early in the 1990s, reprised in 2003 on television (Mike Nichols, 2001), and in comic Margaret Cho's edgy persona. In addition, a postmodern emphasis on multiple identities muted the singular stress on the sexual identity of entertainers and artists—Cho's identity as Asian American or novelist E. Lynn Harris's as African American seemed as notable in their self-presentation and others' perception of them as their sexuality. Public discourse was often tawdry, smirking, and kiss-obsessed, especially when gay characters or actors kissed others of the same sex—Nixon's antenna for what offended many Americans was accurate. But it was also more unbuttoned and diverse than when gay artists were seen as a hidden conspiracy and their sexuality was treated as singularly defining.

Older notions still appeared in how arts critics spotted artificiality. "Cultural commentators," playwright Mark Ravenhill complained in 1999, "have always welcomed the moments in our history when the Straight Boys arrive to sort everything out," as when they dismissed disco, from "the gay and black community," as "trivial compared with the authentic voice of Punk." Distinctions between straight "authenticity" and queer "artificiality" and " 'deadness' " still "linger in the air," he added—"between the honest simplicity of the heterosexual man and the role-playing artificiality of the gay man." Those distinctions lurked in comments on architect Philip Johnson after he died in 2005. Mark Stevens linked Johnson's pre–World War II fascist sympathies to how he "lived more than ever for the stylish surface," becoming "marvel-

224

ously, provocatively, disturbingly hollow." His famous Glass House was "a stylish stage set" that "seems full of emptiness." Here again was the queer's gift for surface over substance. Still, Ravenhill's phrase, "linger in the air," was apt: invidious distinctions between queer artists and other artists now usually lacked their earlier vigor and bluntness.[34]

In serious music, success by younger straight-identified composers seemed to roll back the Barber-Copland-Bernstein generation. Although the relief some felt was rarely explicit, it was measurable by fierce reaction against scholars' efforts, not always subtle, to find queer themes and people in music's history. The twenty-fifth anniversary of the Stonewall riots was a catalyst for both those efforts and indignant responses. In one dustup, Charles Rosen asserted that claims about Franz Schubert's "cruising for boys" had set loose "consternation among Viennese musicologists and their allies, who saw a takeover of Schubert by the Homintern, and have proceeded to invent an Immortal Beloved for Schubert." Responding, Rita Steblin insisted that "there is no Viennese plot to manufacture a heterosexual Schubert, just a Canadian seeking the truth." But echoes of the homintern discourse were faint, or funny: Rosen was "spoofing" her work, Steblin complained.[35]

Yet the labels "gay" and "American" still rarely coexisted for figures in the arts. One was used, displacing, if also signaling, the other, even in some posthumous treatments of artists. Homophobic venom had diminished, but silence persisted: in 2005, a lengthy *New York Times* piece, "As American as Copland," ignored the composer's sexuality even as it covered most everything else. "American" displaced "queer," but not Copland's urban roots, Jewishness, or other elements of his life.[36] In much media treatment, artists' queerness was either all-consuming—the sole focus—or absent. Placing it in the tapestry of artists' identities was still unusual. In the movie industry, despite much buzz about the homosexuality of actors, producers, and plots, few well-known actors were publicly gay, and, as usual, Englishmen (Ian McKellan, Rupert Everett) were prominent among them. Gay figures gained recognition in major venues like the Kennedy Center Honors, but as Americans, at most implicitly or incidentally as gay.

Silence carried less weight by the century's end, however, for it was swamped by a tide of information within and beyond gay circles about public figures in the arts and other realms. And amid the transnationalism many saw as defining the end-of-century era, "American" lacked the charge and precision it had had in 1945 and 1965, just as "gay" lacked its old weight. Both labels seemed afloat in a multicultural stew of identities.

As a term of abuse or allegation, "homintern" lost resonance with the communist menace as the Cold War ended. Even "homosexual mafia" often appeared as a humorous or belittling reference to the imaginations of bigots, whose own use of the term had narrowed mostly to Hollywood and entertainment, not to the arts generally. In one incident in 2002, Michael S. Ovitz, once treated as Hollywood's most powerful deal maker, blamed his decline on a "gay mafia," referring to, among others, Dream-Works cofounder David Geffen, another deal maker. "I know how hard it is for people to see me as a victim," Ovitz admitted. "But in this case, it's pretty close to the truth."[37] But he was widely ridiculed for his accusation, indicating that such tactics were losing legitimacy. Self-appointed defenders of family and morality denounced queer representations on screen, blaming them on a "homosexual mafia" ("homosexual agenda" was another standard phrase). But their complaints were too routine to have shock value, and queer groups often just defended the product—*Ellen*'s (Ellen DeGeneres) coming-out, cable TV's *Queer as Folk*—rather than refute the charge of queer power, as if that power was now taken for granted.

By century's end, considerable commentary presented gay people as a cultural resource rather than a cultural menace. Even in the 1950s, hand-wringing about that menace had ambivalent strains: it was tricky to denounce gay artists who aided the nation's cultural standing and hard to name straight ones who were better. But ambivalence had then usually simmered beneath the surface rather than gaining explicit voice. In contrast, reported the *Boston Globe*, "college recruiters look for gays," seeking them "because they question the norms," according to Judith Brown, director of the Tufts University Lesbian Gay Bisexual Transgender Center. "They make people question their own assumptions, and that's a key to learning and growing as people.'" Predictably, others saw in such statements the specter of quotas and pressure on applicants to "reorient their sexual preference from AC to DC."[38] But Brown's comments also revealed continuity: for her, queers were outsiders no matter whether they were privileged or poor, Vietnamese or Mormon. The outsider label stuck, though it was now used for new purposes.

Homosexuality gained approval as a spur to *The Rise of the Creative Class* (2002), as Richard Florida's work was titled. To explain why some cities nourished creativity, Florida used a "list of preferred locations for gays." As he told the *Chicago Tribune*: "The 'Eureka!' moment: by and large, the city names were redundant. Places that proved hospitable to progressive young people in alternative living arrangements also were catnip to cool, creative types—and lots of folks, of course, made both lists. . . . He [Florida] mimicked an aging city father's probable reaction to his book: 'You mean having a lot of music in a city *matters*? You mean gay people *matter*?' " Where gays lived, it seemed, creativity—not pathology—thrived.

Yet if that claim was fresh, the murkiness of explanation was familiar. "To some extent, homosexuality represents the last frontier of diversity in our society"—though such frontiers have a way of reappearing. "And thus a place that welcomes the gay community welcomes all kinds of people," Florida explained. "The Gay Index did better than any other individual measure of diversity as a predictor of high-tech industry." Were gay people genuinely creative, or did they just provide good decoration and a welcoming atmosphere for the truly inventive? Was their queerness the essential matter, or their "alternative living arrangements," their youth, their urbanness? Even correlations of homosexuality with creativity and diversity turned out to have "a gaping hole," for "the Creative Economy does little to ameliorate the traditional divide between the white and nonwhite segments of the population. It may even make it worse." Gays were little more than " 'canaries of the Creative Age,' " Florida quoted one researcher—a telling metaphor given notions of gays as decorative. Others did the heavy lifting: Florida assured readers that few " 'engineers and high-tech types' " were gay. It was as if queers were the arts' hosts and hostesses. As one skeptic asked, for writers, "what matters most—a nice neighborhood to write in or a city that's worth writing *about*?" Did not inspiration mean more than Internet cafés and what the *Tribune* called "an effective come-hither look" in a city?[39]

The old glibness lurked in the new praise, as did the idea of queers as decorative in their contributions. They were nice to have around, like a gay cousin, Rupert Everett in a movie, or the guys who spruced up decaying neighborhoods (they were good for real estate too). They provided a certain edge, a dollop of diversity, that enlivened people—presumably straight—around them. In that spirit, a reviewer of *The Substance of Style: How the Rise of Aesthetic Value Is Remaking Commerce, Culture, and Consciousness* (2003) noted "the mainstreaming of gay culture" as among factors that "conspired to make valuing appearances both affordable and necessary. 'Better to look good and be thought gay,' " the book's author was quoted, " 'than to look straight and be thought sloppy, ignorant, ugly or old.' " The bold title of Cathy Crimmins's book, *How the Homosexuals Saved Civilization: The True and Heroic Story of How Gay Men Shaped the Modern World* (2004), promised a look beyond appearances, but sections

227

such as "What Makes a Gay Meal" and "How Gays Invented Recreational Viagra" often kept things light. Queers' association with appearances endured. Once ornamenters of American culture, they were now also ornaments to it.[40]

Both notions emerged on television at the turn of the century. NBC's long-running *Will and Grace* offered the gaily ornamented lives of Karen, Grace, Jack, and Will. With the 2003 "reality" show *Queer Eye for the Straight Guy* (Bravo and NBC), gay men as ornamenters gained explicit expression as a queer team redecorated the dwellings, appearances, relationships, and professional veneers—the lives—of clumsy straight men. In these treatments, queer people—men at least—offered something to American culture, but it literally ran skin-deep, as if they were reprising the role that Midge Decter recalled she had nervously enjoyed in the early 1960s, or were back as heterosexuals' "Court Jesters," a role Allen Young had hoped in 1978 was vanishing. *Queer Eye* "flatters heterosexuals by putting them where they already are, at the center of the action," gay writer John Weir complained.[41] Of course, much depended on how viewers regarded such programs, which might be seen as a playful wink at the idea of gay decorativeness. This was a far cry from Richard Nixon's queers corrupting the core of Western culture. But in placing them on its frothy surface, it reworked another vein of commentary. Homosexuals decorated not only homes, hairdos, and fashions, but, it now seemed, American life.

These developments raised the specter or promise of "assimilation," about which queer people persistently squabbled. They fought over whether gay bookstores and bars were falling to the inroads of giant book chains and trendy new clubs. They argued whether the designation "post-gay" meant a denial of queerness or progress in advancing it. They analyzed each new movie, television show, and entertainment act along the same lines, as they did weightier efforts to end antigay policies in the armed forces and to secure marriage rights for gay people.

Not surprisingly, "assimilation" had different meanings for different people. One involved the incorporation of queer people and themes into the representations, production, and marketing of culture. That meaning embraced developments as varied as advertisements for beer in queer publications, the Chicago Symphony Orchestra's commissioning of John Corigliano's AIDS symphony, *Of Rage and Remembrance*, and the careers of queer actors, especially when playing gay characters. Assimilation as incorporation was content-neutral, reflecting rather than altering gay people, albeit exposing what once had been hidden. They entered an ill-defined mainstream but remained mostly intact in the process.

Another meaning of assimilation was absorption and dilution, or "Co-Optation," as Allen Young had called it. In this meaning, assimilation came at a big cost—a reconstitution of queer people, their behavior, and their culture to fit into a mainstream. Assimilation bleached out the heretical aspects of queer life in order to present queer people as like everyone else in all but one minor way—*Virtually Normal*, as Andrew Sullivan's 1995 book was entitled.[42] Explicitly or not, those who saw assimilation this way often drew on an ethnic-group model whereby Italian Americans, Jewish Americans, and others shed their cultures as they faced coercion during war and the subtler pressures of upward mobility and "fitting in." In this view, the trajectory of John Waters—from creator of filthy 1970s films, to director of *Hairspray* in 1988, to inspiration for its Broadway musical version—showed assimilation through dilution, as did fads like *Queer Eye*.

Building on worries voiced in the 1970s, many observers saw assimilation in the second sense, and as it seemed to quicken, they expressed regret, anger, or foreboding about its effects. In an insightful essay, "In My Father's House Are Many Closets" (drafted in 1989 and published in 2000), Robert Dawidoff captured the "the gay sensibility" of several iconic figures—Walt Whitman, George Santayana, Henry James, Cole Porter, Thornton Wilder, Lorenz Hart ("whose lyrics define what America means by romantic love [and who] was a homosexual")—and placed them in a long-standing, double "closet." Although "the cultural closet" entailed oppression and silence, "the personal closet has often been the ground of a fulfilled and creative if difficult life." Because homosexuals had "to learn American as an alien language," Dawidoff argued, they had special insight into it, and "American gays seem always to have been on the cutting edge of American self-definition." A powerful but one-sided bargain ensued. Gay artists gained voices, even influence. In return, "the culture gets from its closet gays a powerful perception of its most intimate and most important matters," but gets it "for free because the closet keeps the gay from owning his own insight." The artistic result was "subversive of social conventions" but also "curiously conceiving of the conventional whole." Presenting only the closet as a source of creativity, Dawidoff implied that its demise presaged a decline in creativity—at least eventually, since the closet was "still in force."[43]

For the prolific critic Michael Bronski, assimilation meant that queer creations were "Stolen Goods," as his 1991 essay was called—absorbed into a culture that hid their queer origins. "There is no doubt that the gay male sensibility—after it had been assimilated—has been one of the most dynamic transformers of U.S. culture," though rarely given credit. Theft-by-assimilation was common, but with other groups this assimilation "does not totally ignore and lie about their place of origin." Bronski challenged not so much assimilation as the queer-denying terms on which it took place. But, like Dawidoff, he traced innovation to oppression. Due to "religious, social and legal prohibitions" and the "stigma" against them, "homosexual writers and artists created a distinct political, artistic, and social identity." They offered not only criticism of "dominant culture—what Christopher Isherwood has called the 'heterosexual dictatorship'—but an alternative." Demanding that the theft of creativity be admitted, Bronski implied that once it was, the creativity, at least its past version, would dwindle.[44]

What Dawidoff and Bronski hinted at, Daniel Harris spelled out in *The Rise and Fall of Gay Culture* (1997): "Gay sensibility" was in jeopardy. Despite a nod to "armies of gay composers, writers, directors, architects, dancers, choreographers, and curators"—none named—Harris focused on camp, defined as an "aestheticism of maladjustment" created when gay men ransacked celebrity culture to forge a self-mocking but affirming style. That "aestheticism," he argued, was "the source of some of the most valuable contributions that homosexuals have made to American society." An "unconscious act of revenge"—an impulse critics once deplored—"is the secret to our creativity," and without it "the American cultural landscape would be . . . less interesting." But with co-optation by consumer culture, "our distinctive characteristics as a culture begin to dissolve," especially queers' "involvement with the arts and camp" and their "highly mannered style of humor." "Oppression and camp are inextricably linked," Harris warned, "and the waning of one necessitates the death of the other." America always "demands from its minorities nothing less than a voluntary act of subculture suicide," but gay culture was "uniquely jeopardized by assimilation." As the book's dust jacket read, "Gay culture ultimately arose in response to the physical and psychic injuries of homophobia." As a reviewer put it: "In other words, oppression maketh culture, and acceptance taketh it away."[45]

Harris offered the most flawed of the critiques. The "fall of gay culture" loomed, but whose gay culture? Men's, insofar as many critics assumed that men alone were at issue, but even gay men came in many varieties, as did their modes of cultural activity—the bathhouse and the concert hall had overlapping constituencies but produced different cultures; James Baldwin's gay culture had not been Andy Warhol's. Although Harris regretted affluent gay men's surrender to assimilation, he treated them—presumptively white as well—as if they alone constituted gay men, harbored no differences with each other, and had an identity only through their engagement with corporate media and markets.

More important, the claim that marginality accounted for creativity did a disservice to history. Its exponents rarely pondered how historically specific the claim was and how much it owed to antihomosexuality forces eager to present queers as outsiders. There was irony in gay critics' fierce embrace of an outsiderness largely formulated by earlier enemies. But that outsiderness now gained endorsement in many venues. "In a sense, perhaps oppression in part creates genius," wrote a reader of *The Gay and Lesbian Review*, hoping that "integration of sexual minorities" would not destroy "the gay individual's 'sacred outsider' perspective." "After all," a *Wall Street Journal* article suggested, gay editors, "long in the mainstream but not of it," have "*always* had a natural, and quite unaffected, distance from the cultural middle ground."[46] To the contrary: it was not "natural," and it was not always "unaffected."

The assertion of creativity's debt to marginality obscured a great deal. It overlooked how figures like Barber, Copland, and Williams had seen themselves as in the mainstream and indeed had constituted it, rather than merely observing it. It ignored the shifting boundaries between margin and mainstream, terms resistant to precise definition over time. It made the closet a timeless condition rather than a metaphor that at best describes the punitive structures and attitudes at mid-century. Most of all, it robbed queer people of creativity, seen as inhering in their pain more than in their talent. Alarmists treated marginality as the sole source of creativity rather than one of many wellsprings that varied among individuals and over time. "Assimilated"—whatever that meant—queer people would go dull and dumb, as if oppression alone activated their talent. In that reasoning, they should cling to oppression in order to sustain their culture.

A larger obsession with outsiderness reflected and reinforced the queer version. Post-Watergate politicians routinely claimed they were outsiders to Washington, and outsider status was asserted for or by entire groups, whatever their politics (many Christians portrayed themselves as outsiders to a dominant secular culture). To find a place at the center of American life seemed to require first staking out a footing on its margins, as if there were few real insiders left. Outsiderness became a virtue in itself, a mysterious repository of insight into the empty insides of American life, but as such it was drained of meaning. The broad and queer-specific streams of this obsession merged when Jean H. Baker, who wrote the introduction to C. A. Tripp's *The Intimate World of Abraham Lincoln* (2005), asserted that Lincoln's "outsider status would explain his independence and his ability to take anti-Establishment positions like the issuing of the Emancipation Proclamation. As a homosexual, she said, 'he would be on the margins of tradition.' "[47] Elected president twice, Lincoln was still an "outsider" because he was presumably queer. And queers forever lay on "the margins of tradition" even as they did much to make it. The outsider discourse was reaching a silly dead end.

Contention over queer culture also updated a long-running tension in gay life between respectability and rebelliousness. Queer theorist Michael Warner, in *The Trouble with Normal* (1999), rebutted Andrew Sullivan's call for "gays to abandon 'the notion of sexuality as cultural subversion.' " "People who are defined by a variant set of norms commit a kind of social suicide," Warner worried, "when they begin to measure the worth of their relations and their way of life by the yardstick of normalcy." He rejected "the distinction between assimilation and separatism," insisting "that the dominant culture assimilate to queer culture, not the other way around," and pointing to "queer writers of the past" and "critics as different as Pat Califia and Eve Sedgwick."[48]

Warner added gravity to arguments made by Harris and others but overlooked how respectability and rebelliousness entwined each other. Subtler advocates of respectability saw it as a way to change dominant culture by boring within, even as others seemed to imagine only mimicking that culture. Exponents of rebelliousness often occupied the high ground of intellectual respectability, lamenting the masses' false consciousness, as Warner sometimes seemed to do. There was still truth to Dennis Altman's complaint decades earlier that "the desire for acceptance on the left becomes just another form of passing, of seeking to prove revolutionary respectability," and fosters "a tendency for political movements to be puritanical." The views of Harris, Warner, and others were linked to a queer stance on many matters—sex, politics, the academy, theory—that emphasized the shifting, constructed nature of queerness, defined as "identity and ideological nonconformity—not a particular sexual orientation."[49] It was therefore odd that they saw queer marginality as the sole, static source of creativity. But their stance is understandable: gay creativity in modern America had been stunning. If it had arisen from marginality, who would want to lose that?

Of course, many queer Americans did not fear the "fall of gay culture," and many lesbians imagined a different past and future. Despite their nostalgia for an earlier time of lesbian pulp novels, they rarely mourned the end of a golden era. For many, lesbian marginality had been too acute — or was too continuing — to regret its passing, and feminism's surge in the 1970s made that era more their golden age. Only belatedly did lesbian influence gain the recognition that gay men's impact long had had, though often with a similar explanation. "Being an outsider heightens awareness," insisted an expert on lesbians in fashion.[50]

Lesbian critics differed with each other, and some did worry about assimilation. But with less assimilation to claim and a less golden past to recall, their worries had a different charge. Writer Sarah Schulman saw queer artists as "functioning in a parallel world — in fixed and stagnant substructures of companies, bookstores, reading circuits, review pages, and readers' minds." She saw no gain in heightened "visibility," only "an above-board recognizable ghetto in addition to the old secret underground one." Introducing Schulman's essays, Urvashi Vaid, a leader in lesbian-gay politics, wrote that "the Reagan-Bush years were the worst years of our lives." In this view, assimilation was a luxury that affluent white gay men might worry over. In addition, lesbians still found, Schulman wrote, that they "could not believe how sexist gay men were." Despite Ellen DeGeneres, k d lang, Margaret Cho, Susie Bright, and others, the decade after Schulman's *My American History* (1994) left that sense of things intact. When Stacey D'Erasmo saw the new TV series *The L Word*, she admitted that lesbians, who had rarely seen themselves on screen, had a lingering attachment to "the wildness of feeling not only unrepresented but somehow unpresentable." But that was a wistful look back, not indignation over assimilation: she liked *The L Word*.[51]

The tension between valuing queers' marginality and asserting their influence emerged anew with *The Crimson Letter: Harvard, Homosexuality and the Shaping of American Culture* (2003), billed by the *New York Times* as showing "American culture's debt to gay sons of Harvard." Author Douglass Shand-Tucci compiled an imposing list — the *Times* mentioned George Santayana, F. O. Matthiessen, Lincoln Kirstein, Leonard Bernstein, Frank O'Hara, John Ashberry, Philip Johnson. Although not the first look at Harvard homosexuals — Toby Marotta's *Sons of Harvard: Gay Men from the Class of 1967* appeared in 1982 — it was the first to emphasize their collective creativity. But it was odd to deem as marginal men with the good fortune to attend or teach at Harvard, although Martin Duberman insisted, "I was certainly not nurtured at Harvard. I was hounded and belittled." Indeed, in a way Shand-Tucci boasted not of marginality but of power: "The Harvard gay experience is more important in the shaping of American culture, because, in so many ways, Harvard is more important."[52]

That tension also crept into Jess Green's 2003 reflection on artists' response to AIDS. The disease "made its debut among a very cultured group of people," he asserted, a claim influenced by his New York City perspective. Despite citing Sarah Schulman's AIDS activism, Green framed the response as one by gay men, their marginality nourishing creativity. Even nonprofessionals "were knowledgeable amateurs: hiding, encoding and image management were a fundamental part of every homosexual's sentimental education." As he quoted writer Larry Kramer, "We were a bunch of gay people; this is what we know how to do. . . . We know how to pretend. We knew how to make things pretty." Regarding the waning of arts activism and the arrival of shows like *Will and Grace*, Green wistfully added that "when you consciously manipulate imagery to change the mainstream, in effect, you join it."[53]

But only so much marginality can be claimed for those who succeed, however problematic their identity or initial circumstances. For Aaron Copland or Margaret Cho, success undercuts any designation of marginality without erasing it. At the same time, the arts outside of mass entertainment are set apart from the rest of American life—at its margins, if not subordinate to a mainstream. Marginality defines artists whatever their success, muddying matters further: which margins, whose mainstream?

Shand-Tucci and Green also updated the tradition of The List—that accounting of notable queers, especially in the arts. Its endurance indicates a measure of continuity across the mid-century divide created by the homintern discourse. Still circulating in many versions, The List retains its air of defensive pride—we too claim greatness—and its role in tracing history and lineage. If it hints that queers are superior, it usually operates by asserting they have created much, rather than by explaining why they have. Like much else, its endurance suggests that the age of agonized explanation and denial—do they have "special gifts"? do they succeed despite their pathology?—was over, and the deniers had lost. Efforts to explain, deny, or exaggerate gay creativity did not cease. Countering "widely held assumptions" that female dancers will be "surrounded by bitter homosexuals and imperious, poodle-toting prima ballerinas," critic Joan Acocella assured readers that "according to a choreographer I recently spoke to, about half of male ballet dancers are now straight."

234

Christian backers of "reparative" or "conversion" therapy saw artiness as a mark of queerness—much as gay men long had—and viewed both traits as best expunged: a typical patient was a "sensitive, introverted artistic son," one "who doesn't like rough-and-tumble, who is artistic." But these efforts no longer hold center stage. Queer creativity seems more taken for granted, the need to explain it less pressing, its authenticity more accepted.[54]

Accommodation

In the American idiom of the jeremiad, alarms about assimilation equated change with decline, but change usually has murkier consequences—pluses and minuses, for those into scorekeeping, and lateral shifts and complex reorderings that defy numbers. A better word than assimilation for what was happening with gay Americans is accommodation, a term freer of the connotation of selling out. Accommodation suggests a coming-to-terms with change in a social group's fortunes, by both the group and nervous others. It need not involve tolerance of or fondness for a group, though those may ensue for some. Rather, it involves resignation before certain realities and a truce in the face of them. With that term in mind, this historian, as bad at foresight as any historian, throws out three overlapping predictions.

First, modern queer history owed much to America's fears and ambitions on the world stage, and in some fashion that dynamic will continue. The content and valuation of queer creativity will still depend partly on what the nation is and how gay people shape it. A nation struggling to remain the world's hegemon will make demands on creativity different from one whose power recedes or is more effortlessly maintained. Other cultures and nations will also play a role. Transnationalism and globalization are glibly exaggerated, but currents of change do erode boundaries, and as for many groups, the fate of gay people takes shape in transnational networks. Even if the United States resists the expansion of gay rights seen in Canada and much of Europe, isolating it in this realm as in others, it will remain open to influences from abroad.

Second, much gay creativity once went to defining America culturally —often affirmatively, sometimes critically—because the nation sought such definitions and because producing them gave artists a place in cultural life. The arts will bear that burden less insofar as the quest to define a coherent America has subsided and queer influence is more accepted. With that burden eased, queer artists may be freer to be critical observers, and, freed from the masculine terms of mid-century nationalism, lesbians may play a greater role.

A third possibility—the likeliest—is that creativity will simply be a less-charged matter. The discovery of gay people's place in culture—in its tones of shock and dismay, a rather contrived pose to begin with— has played out, and attempts to rekindle the shock have worn thin. A comparison to the place of African Americans in cultural life may be apt. Just as Duke Ellington, James Baldwin, Maya Angelou, Leontyne Price, Toni Morrison, and Henry Louis Gates have been incorporated into American culture even as racial intolerance and difference persist, so have Aaron Copland, Tony Kushner, Alice Walker, and RuPaul. Accommodation does not necessarily yield tolerance or assimilation—it was rash for British writer John Bayley to predict in 2004 that "the day has almost come when nobody will care a farthing any more for who is who sex-wise. . . . Sex will be like the turn-up of the trousers or the length of a skirt." But many people now regard queer creativity as unremarkable, even if few admit the "thriving symbiosis between twentieth-century homosexual subculture and U.S. national culture." Even earlier, some Americans, and many gay ones, were unsurprised that homosexuals flourished in theater and music. Most likely, that outlook will continue to spread.[55]

Despite the assertions that queer creativity sprang from marginality, it has continued even as law, culture, and other forces inched toward accommodation. Look at a badly incomplete list: queer theory (Judith Butler, Michael Warner), poetry (Adrienne Rich, Essex Hemphill, Mark Doty, James Merrill), prose (Edmund White, Andrew Holleran, Paul Monette, Audre Lorde, Armistead Maupin, Jewelle Gomez), music (Stephen Sondheim, Ricky Ian Gordon, John Corigliano, Robert Spano, Jennifer Higdon, Michael Tilson Thomas, Earl Wild—performing into his nineties), drama (Edward Albee, Terrence McNally, Sarah Schulman, Tony Kushner). Although most on that list emerged before the age of accommodation and some are now deceased, many persisted into it and younger ones emerged. Others stayed influential in death—post-9/11 use of their music found Copland and Barber still defining America, or at least used to define it.

Laments over the malign effects of assimilation expressed nostalgia for a golden age of gay cultural prowess. They resembled reflections by some African Americans who warmly recalled the vigor of black communities under segregation. One might as well mourn the passing of other strands of mid-century culture—big band music, flights to the moon,

Elvis Presley, film noir: all parts of an irretrievable past. They have continuing influences, but cannot be sustained as they once were. No artist should try to recreate *Appalachian Spring* or *Cat on a Hot Tin Roof*, nor will men camp it up at the sight of a newfound Judy Garland. That hardly means the end of gay creativity and culture, but forthcoming versions will differ in substance and in the cultural place perceived for them.

The fall of gay culture has not yet happened, but predictions of it continue, and not only from leftists. Andrew Sullivan asserted in 2005 that "gay culture," though perhaps not gay creativity, "is ending." Even "the very concept of gay culture may one day disappear altogether." Sullivan was an older white man, like many giving such predictions. They equated loss of their gay culture with the loss of all gay culture, but there never was the "single gay culture" Sullivan remembered, nor one only "built on oppression" and "primarily about pain and tragedy" — "a gilded cage of exclusion with magnificent ornaments."[56]

Given the historical record, the belief that queer marginality inspired queer creativity was understandable. Jonathan Dollimore, citing the "fierce dialectic of centers and margins" in modern culture, argues that "dissidence may not only be repressed by the dominant (coercively and ideologically), but in a sense actually produced by it, hence consolidating the powers which it ostensibly challenges."[57] His formulation captures how gay artists at the "margins" were often "consolidating the powers" at a nationalist moment. But it is not the only way to read this history. For one thing, it makes "centers" and "margins" more distinct than they were at the time, when gay artists — albeit as American artists — often occupied the centers. For another, it folds together the many different ways that marginality was experienced and perceived — for some, as the loneliness of a queer childhood; for others, as silence and evasion in adulthood; for still others, as benign or even empowering difference.

As the real and imagined historic link between queerness and marginality diminishes, other sources of creativity may surface. A group's cultural distinctiveness may be enhanced by oppression without owing wholly to it. Few people now see American Mormons, Jews, or Catholics as oppressed groups, yet their distinctiveness persists. Queers do not precisely fit the models of religious, racial, and ethnic groups, but they do not depart entirely from them. Those who equate assimilation with cultural death will encounter less assimilation than they fear and more creativity than they imagine. Certainly camp remained vibrant. Not unchanged, of course — less a form of everyday resistance and more a performance mode, as John Epperson's stage character Lypsinka, as Brenda Withers and Mindy Kaling in their play *Matt and Ben* (about actors Ben Afleck and Matt Damon), and as "the sublime Vera Galupe-Borszkh, and her La Gran Scena opera troupe"—but still vital.[58] Creativity, never prompted only by oppression, will persist.

The trend toward accommodation also appears in how comment on queer artists, once dark and heavy, is often now light and humorous. "You got to respect Tchaikovsky for keeping the tragedy in," Susie Day wrote in 2003, spoofing the mythology of gay (male) creativity rooted in pain. "Back then, homosexuals knew about tragedy. How you can only have what you want after death. Now, with the gay liberation, Art is more vapid. They get the sodomy laws repealed, and they forget about the pain of the human condition." The menacing homintern now hangs on often as farce in which queers write the laugh lines, lampooning themselves and fears of them. After Michael Ovitz blasted Hollywood's "gay mafia," screenwriter Paul Rudnick responded in the *New Yorker* with a mock "MEMO TO: All federal agents" about FBI "operatives working under cover as vicious choreographers, neo-con columnists, and chatty House-boys" to unravel "the nation's alleged Gay Mafia." Among their find-ings: "Gay hit men have been known to slaughter a rival simply by enter-ing his apartment, glancing around, and commenting, 'Oh, I love that, you're still doing Mission.'" Rudnick also turned the homintern-in-the-theater routine on its head when he was asked if he foresaw "a day when a straight—non-gay—play can't get on Broadway." "God willing," he re-plied. In coarse humor, *Onion* writer "Lawrence Sharpless" asked, "Who do I have to blow to win the Bancroft Prize in American history?" One committee member, he continued, "or should I just blow the whole lot of them, sucking and slurping phalluses like a Singapore whore?" It was a tasteless parody of old notions of how gay people succeed in the creative arena. Having once won the Bancroft Prize, I just laugh.[59]

Readers of this book's introduction may recall the response once given to the question, "Is there a gay sensibility and does it have an impact on our culture?" Jeff Weinstein answered, "No, there is no such thing as a gay sensibility and yes, it has an enormous impact on our culture."[60] To leave a paradox standing defies the historian's duty to explain, but history is often paradox. Similarly, mid-century gay creativity occurred because of oppression, but also because oppression had limits, and for reasons having little to do with it. An untidy formula, to be sure, but more accu-rate about the past and optimistic about the future than a fond embrace of the sad beauties presumably produced by gay artists facing oppression.

NOTES

Introduction

1. On the origins and meanings of "homintern," see chapter 1.
2. On the Lavender Scare in politics and in Washington, D.C., see David K. Johnson, *The Lavender Scare: The Cold War Persecution of Gays and Lesbians in the Federal Government* (Chicago, 2004), the essential book on this subject.
3. "The Homosexual in America," *Time*, 21 January 1966, 40–41.
4. Composers Recordings, Inc. CD 721 (1996).
5. I draw primarily on Conversation No. 498-5, 13 May 1971, in the Nixon Watergate Tape series, as held by the Nixon Presidential Materials Staff and transcribed for me by David Johnson. Additional comments by Nixon, including those on San Francisco and fashion, I take from "Nixon on Tape Expounds on Welfare and Homosexuality," *Chicago Tribune*, 7 November 1999, by James Warren, a journalist zealous in finding and explaining material from the Nixon tapes. Warren's article first alerted me to this conversation. See also Gene Weingarten, "Richard Nixon: Just What Was He Smoking?" *Washington Post*, 21 March 2002.
6. Nadine Hubbs, *The Queer Composition of America's Sound: Gay Modernists, American Music, and National Identity* (Berkeley, 2004), 4.
7. Vito Russo, *The Celluloid Closet: Homosexuality in the Movies*, rev. ed. (New York, 1987), 326.
8. Edmund White, *States of Desire: Travels in Gay America* (New York, 1981), 238.
9. W. J. Rorabaugh, *Kennedy and the Promise of the Sixties* (New York, 2002), 142.
10. David Caute, *The Dancer Defects: The Struggle for Cultural Supremacy during the Cold War* (New York, 2003); Devon W. Carbado, Dwight A. McBride, and Donald Weise, eds., *Black Like Us: A Century of Lesbian, Gay and Bisexual African American Fiction* (San Francisco, 2002), 27.
11. Anthony Tommasini, *Virgil Thomson: Composer on the Aisle* (New York, 1999); James Campbell, *Talking at the Gates: A Life of James Baldwin* (Berkeley, 2002); Fred Kaplan, *Gore Vidal: A Biography* (New York, 2000). On Barber, see Barbara Heyman, *Samuel Barber: The Composer and His Music* (New York, 1992), essential to my work despite the limitation noted here. On Copland, see Howard Pollack, *Aaron Copland: The Life and Work of an Uncommon Man* (New York, 1999).
12. Tommasini, *Thomson*; Hubbs, *Queer Composition*; George Chauncey, *Gay New York: Gender, Urban Culture, and the Making of the Gay Male World,*

1890–1940 (New York, 1994); Robert Corber, *In the Name of National Security: Hitchcock, Homophobia, and the Political Construction of Gender in Postwar America* (Durham, N.C., 1993); Robert Corber, *Homosexuality in Cold War America: Resistance and the Crisis of Masculinity* (Durham, N.C., 1997); Robert Dawidoff, *Making History Matter* (Philadelphia, 2000), especially his essay, "In My Father's House Are Many Closets," a provocative account of the sources and nature of gay men's place in American culture. Several writings by Brett are cited later in this book.

13. James Baldwin, "The Preservation of Innocence," as quoted in Robert Corber, "James Baldwin," in *The Encyclopedia of Gay, Lesbian, Bisexual, and Transgender History in America*, 3 vols., ed. Marc Stein (New York, 2004), 1:111.

14. Philip Brett and Elizabeth Wood, "Gay and Lesbian Music," *Grove Music Online*, ed. L. Macy, <http.www.grovemusic.com> (25 June 2003).

15. See Geoffrey Wheatcroft, "Finland's Forte," *New York Times Magazine*, 9 January 2000, 40.

16. Quoted in "Dorothy Farnan Dies at 84; Author of 'Auden in Love,' " *New York Times*, 2 November 2003.

17. Robert Alan Goldberg, *Enemies Within: The Culture of Conspiracy in Modern America* (New Haven, 2001), is an excellent study of conspiracy thinking with almost no mention of its antigay versions; quotation, x.

18. Paul Monette, *Becoming a Man: Half a Life Story* (New York, 1992), 176, 206.

19. Alan Helms, *Young Man from the Provinces: A Gay Life before Stonewall* (Boston, 1995), 13.

Chapter One

1. I owe the phrase "face of the Cold War homosexual menace" to Nadine Hubbs, from her remarks on my manuscript.

2. William Barrett, "Innocents Abroad," *Partisan Review*, March 1950, 272–91; Arthur Laurents, *Original Story by Arthur Laurents: A Memoir of Broadway and Hollywood* (New York, 2000), 189; obituary on Phillips, *New York Times*, 14 September 2002, which mentioned the magazine's "landmark essays" but not the piece quoted here nor the review's CIA ties.

3. Jonathan Ned Katz, *Love Stories: Sex between Men before Homosexuality* (Chicago, 2001), 45; John Bayley, "Sex and the City," reviewing Graham Robb, *Strangers: Homosexual Love in the Nineteenth Century* (New York, 2004), *New York Review of Books*, 25 March 2004, 17. See also Caleb Crain, *American Sympathy: Men, Friendship, and Literature in the New Nation* (New Haven, 2001); and James McCourt, *Queer Street: Rise and Fall of an American Culture, 1947–1985* (New York, 2004).

4. Judith R. Walkowitz, "The 'Vision of Salome': Cosmopolitanism and Erotic Dancing in Central London, 1908–1918," *American Historical Review* 108 (April 2003): 337–76. For more on the opera's fate and the quotations about

it I give, see John Dizikes, *Opera in America: A Cultural History* (New Haven, 1993), 315–16.

5. John Loughery, *The Other Side of Silence: Men's Lives and Gay Identities, A Twentieth-Century History* (New York, 1998), 21 (Rainey), 30 ("List"), 60 (Cadmus). On Harrison, see Nadine Hubbs, *The Queer Composition of American Sound: Gay Modernists, American Music, and National Identity* (Berkeley, 2004), 138.

6. Headline reproduced in George Chauncey, *Gay New York: Gender, Urban Culture, and the Making of the Gay Male World, 1890–1940* (New York, 1994), 301; quotation, 309.

7. Rachel Adams, *Sideshow U.S.A.: Freaks and the American Cultural Imagination* (Chicago, 2001), 93 (Adams's emphasis), 64. Locating this use of "freak" in the late 1930s, Adams does not explicitly see the film's freaks as readable as homosexuals.

8. Nugent, quoted in Loughery, *Other Side*, 50. Devon W. Carbado, Dwight A. McBride, and Donald Weise, eds., *Black Like Us: A Century of Lesbian, Gay and Bisexual African American Fiction* (San Francisco, 2002), 30; see generally "1900–1950: Harlem Renaissance," 1–27. See also Chauncey, *Gay New York*, chapter 9.

9. Chauncey, *Gay New York*, 99 ("the effeminate"), 6–7; see also chapter 4; and Loughery, *Other Side*, 58.

10. Chauncey, *Gay New York*, 283, 284; Philip Brett, "Musicality, Essentialism, and the Closet," in *Queering the Pitch: The New Gay and Lesbian Musicology*, ed. Philip Brett, Elizabeth Wood, Gary C. Thomas (New York, 1994), 11, 12, 18; Loughery, *Other Side*, 24.

11. Kaier Curtin, *"We Can Always Call Them Bulgarians": The Emergence of Lesbians and Gay Men on the American Stage* (Boston, 1987), 46 ("a married"), 78 ("I'm"), 72 ("treat"); Chauncey, *Gay New York*, 311 ("farcical"), 312 ("criminalization"), 313 ("depicting").

12. Curtin, *We Can Always Call Them Bulgarians*, 68 ("perverts"), 54 ("province"), 43 ("lesbian"), 44 (Allen), 53 ("one"), 81 ("a calcium"), 100 ("drag"), 47, 58.

13. Ibid., 53, 45.

14. Chauncey, *Gay New York*, 357 (title of chapter 12).

15. Curtin, *We Can Always Call Them Bulgarians*, 12.

16. Hubbs, *Queer Composition*, 90, her words and quoting Wayne Koestenbaum, *The Queen's Throat: Opera, Homosexuality, and the Mystery of Desire* (New York, 1993).

17. Deems Taylor, *Of Men and Music* (New York, 1938), 24–26.

18. Quotations from Leo Treitler, "Gender and Other Dualities of Music History," in *Musicology and Difference: Gender and Sexuality in Music Scholarship*, ed. Ruth A. Solie (Berkeley, 1993), 36, 37. McClary presents a strong case in "Narrative Agendas in 'Absolute' Music: Identity and Difference in

Brahms's Third Symphony" (also in Solie, *Musicology and Difference*), where she uses terms like "tender" and "feminine," but I lean toward Treitler's complicated skepticism about her case.

19. Treitler, "Gender and Other Dualities," 37 (Ives on Wagner and Chopin); Judith Tick, "Charles Ives and Gender Ideology," in Solie, *Musicology and Difference*, 88 ("pansys," etc.), 89n23 ("homophobic," quoting Philip Brett), 95 (Rosenfeld on MacDowell); Howard Pollack, *Aaron Copland: The Life and Work of an Uncommon Man* (New York, 1999), 252; Hubbs, *Queer Composition*, 78 ("Is the Anglo-Saxon").

20. Tick, "Charles Ives," 104, 105, 96, 91. Hubbs, in *Queer Composition*, while agreeing that gender ideology was not a settled scheme for assessing composers, places manliness and queerness more than I do at the center of interwar debates about American music.

21. See Edward Maisel, *Charles T. Griffes: The Life of an American Composer*, rev. ed. (New York, 1984); Donna K. Anderson, *Charles T. Griffes: A Life in Music* (Washington, D.C., 1993). For Griffes within a gay male world, see numerous discussions in Chauncey, *Gay New York*; and Frank Rossiter, *Charles Ives and His America* (New York, 1975), 166 ("did not").

22. Tick, "Charles Ives," 92, 104. Here I use the fine account by Joseph Horowitz but draw out aspects of Toscanini's putative manliness that Horowitz presents only obliquely or offhandedly; see Joseph Horowitz, *Understanding Toscanini: How He Became an American Culture-God and Helped Create a New Audience for Old Music* (Minneapolis, 1987).

23. Anthony Tommasini, *Virgil Thomson: Composer on the Aisle* (New York, 1999), 229. On Copland, see Pollack, *Copland*, 235. On associations between musicality and homosexuality, see especially Hubbs, *Queer Composition*; and Brett, "Musicality, Homosexuality, and the Closet."

24. Pollack, *Copland*, 235.

25. Charles Alexander, *Here the Country Lies: Nationalism and the Arts in Twentieth-Century America* (Bloomington, Ind., 1980), 172 (Copland), 170 (Mason); Terry A. Cooney, *Balancing Acts: American Thought and Culture in the 1930s* (New York, 1995), 207 ("more so"); Barbara Heyman, *Samuel Barber: The Composer and His Music* (New York, 1992), 92 (Downes); Barbara L. Tischler, *An American Music: The Search for an American Musical Identity* (New York, 1986), 147 (Bauer).

26. Virgil Thomson, "On Being American," 1948, reprinted in Virgil Thomson, *A Virgil Thomson Reader* (Boston, 1981), 305; Tischler, *An American Music*, 147 (Copland), 148 (Schuman); Ned Rorem, *Knowing When to Stop: A Memoir* (New York, 1994), 282. For what Copland seemed to evoke, see Pollack, *Copland*, 526–31.

27. Taylor, *Of Men and Music*, 123–24, 126, 197.

28. Cooney, *Balancing Acts*, 211.

29. Horowitz, *Understanding Toscanini*, 253.

30. Hubbs, *Queer Composition*, 32 ("emblematize"), 47 ("renowned," etc.), 20–21 (Downes). Hubbs offers a full reading of the queerness of the opera and the occasion.

31. Tommasini, *Thomson*, 357, 359, 354, 357; see generally chapter 20. The Hanson purges are alleged more in talk and memoir than in documented form; see Hubbs, *Queer Composition*, 127, 225n25.

32. Tommasini, *Thomson*, 360; Loughery, *Other Side*, 106 ("one of the best"); Aaron Copland and Vivian Perlis, *Copland since 1943* (New York, 1989), 63. See also Allen Berube, *Coming Out under Fire: The History of Gay Men and Women in World War Two* (New York, 1990).

33. Erin Redfern, "The Neurosis of Narrative: American Literature and Psychoanalytic Psychiatry during World War II" (Ph.D. diss., Northwestern University, 2003), 56–57, 60, 74.

34. Jack Lait and Lee Mortimer, *U.S.A. Confidential!* (New York, 1952), 279 ("We offer"); Jack Lait and Lee Mortimer, *Washington Confidential* (New York, 1951), 90–91, 98; Michael S. Sherry, *In the Shadow of War: The United States since the 1930s* (New Haven, 1995), 153 (Truman).

35. "Confidential," *One*, July 1953, 8.

36. Brooks Martin, "Skeletons in TV's Closet!" *Confidential*, July 1953, 2–3; "Why They Call Broadway the 'Gay' White Way," *Tip-Off*, April 1956, as "reprinted almost in its entirety" in Martin Bauml Duberman, *About Time: Exploring the Gay Past* (New York, 1986), 187–90.

37. Dr. Arthur Guy Mathews, "Homosexuality Is Stalin's Atom Bomb to Destroy America," with preface by Joshua Mortelling, *Physical Culture* (sometimes cited as *Vitalized Physical Culture*), April 1953, 12–13; *Pageant*, February 1951.

38. *One*, October 1953, 8; "Magazine Goldmine: 'Run an Article on Queers!'" *One*, July 1953, 2, 8.

39. "Homosexuals Form New Organization," *People Today*, 25 August 1954, 3–7; "How Hollywood Handles the Third Sex," *Picture Life*, March 1954, 14–18.

40. "References to such gay-conspiracy theories are, not surprisingly, vastly fewer in the daylight of published prose than in the disavowable discourse of speech acts — which persist on these themes even today," notes Hubbs, in *Queer Composition*, 224–25 (note 23), sketching some of the evidence.

41. *Confidential*, July 1957; John Gill, *Queer Noises: Male and Female Homosexuality in Twentieth-Century Music* (Minneapolis, 1995), 18 (on Britten); Tommasini, *Thomson*, 424; Rorem, *Knowing When to Stop*, 346.

42. Jane De Hart Mathews, "Art and Politics in Cold War America," *American Historical Review* 81 (October 1976): 772–73. Arguably, it was not in the Abstract Expressionists attacked in the late 1940s and early 1950s but in a younger generation with a different style that a large gay male role occurred, with figures like Jasper Johns, Robert Rauschenberg, and Andy Warhol;

see Jonathan Katz, "Opposition, Inc.: The Homosexualization of Postwar American Art" (Ph.D. diss., Northwestern University, 1995).

43. R. G. Waldeck, "Homosexual International," *Human Events*, 16 April 1952, 1.

44. Alfred Towne, "Homosexuality in American Culture: The New Taste in Literature," *American Mercury*, August 1951, 3–27. For the later comment, see Hilton Als, "Unhappy Endings: The Collected Carson McCullers," *New Yorker*, 3 December 2001, 99, on the "exalted status she [McCullers] enjoyed in a milieu dominated by gay editors and writers."

45. Kovacs, quoted in Michael Davidson, *Guys Like Us: Citing Masculinity in Cold War Politics* (Chicago, 2004), 1; "American Mercury," *One*, July 1953, 9; Alfred Towne, "The New Taste in Humor," *American Mercury*, September 1951, 22–27; Waldeck, "Homosexual International." See also Jennifer Terry, *An American Obsession: Science, Medicine, and Homosexuality in Modern Society* (Chicago, 1999), 329, 346.

46. Marya Mannes, "Any Resemblance . . .," *Reporter*, 21 July 1953, 34–35; *One*, October 1953, 9.

47. Robert Duncan, "The Homosexual in Society," *Politics* 1 (August 1944): 209–11, as excerpted with commentary in Jonathan Ned Katz, *Gay/Lesbian Almanac: A New Documentary* (New York, 1983), 591–95.

48. *Strangers on a Train* (Alfred Hitchcock, 1951) ("my mother"). Other quotations: Robert Corber, *In the Name of National Security: Hitchcock, Homophobia, and the Political Construction of Gender in Postwar America* (Durham, N.C., 1993), 70, 72.

49. See Chauncey, *Gay New York*.

50. Lait and Mortimer, *U.S.A. Confidential*, 44–45.

51. See David K. Johnson, *The Lavender Scare: The Cold War Persecution of Gays and Lesbians in the Federal Government* (Chicago, 2004), on the federal government and Washington, D.C.

52. See Hubbs, *Queer Composition*, 8–9.

53. "American Masterpiece" and "'Dear Mother . . . I Was Meant to Be a Composer,'" *Newsweek*, 27 January 1958, 62–63; for more on media coverage of Barber, see chapter 4. See D. A. Miller, *The Novel and the Police* (Berkeley, 1988), 206, 207; for use of Miller's analysis, see also Philip Brett on Benjamin Britten, in "Britten's Dream," in Solie, *Musicology and Difference*, 261, 280.

54. Walter Hixson, *Parting the Curtain: Propaganda, Culture, and the Cold War, 1945–1961* (New York, 1997), 8; congressman quoted in Michael Kammen, "Culture and State in America," *Journal of American History* 83 (December 1996): 801; Mathews, "Art and Politics," 762.

55. Frances Stonor Saunders, *The Cultural Cold War: The CIA and the World of Arts and Letters* (New York, 1999), 220, 74 (Berlin trip).

56. Ibid., 225, 257, 272.

57. Peter G. Davis, *The American Opera Singer: The Lives and Adventures of Amer-*

ica's Great Singers in Opera and Concert from 1825 to the Present (New York, 1997), 448.

58. Saunders, *Cultural Cold War*, 255 (Greenberg), 249 (MacDonald).

59. *New York Times*, 6 November 1955, "The United States Has Secret Sonic Weapon — Jazz." My student Michael Green called this to my attention.

60. Gregory Woods, "The 'Conspiracy' of the 'Homintern,'" *Gay and Lesbian Review* (May–June 2003): 11; Patrick Higgins, ed., *A Queer Reader* (New York, 1993), 287. On Bowra, who "dubbed the gay leftist Oxbridge of his day the Homintern," see Terry Eagleton, *The Gatekeeper: A Memoir* (London, 2001), 146.

61. Pollack, *Copland*, 554 ("heading up"); Hubbs, *Queer Composition*, 224–25 (note 23).

62. Hubbs, *Queer Composition*, 156, quoting Humphrey Burton, *Leonard Bernstein* (Boston, 1994), and on Varèse.

63. Christopher Reed, "Painting, Drawing, and Sculpture: 1890–1969," in *The Encyclopedia of Lesbian, Gay, Bisexual, and Transgender History in America*, 3 vols., ed. Marc Stein (New York, 2004), 3:233.

64. Thomson, "On Being American," 304–6.

65. See Jack Sullivan, *New World Symphonies: How American Culture Changed European Music* (New Haven, 1999).

66. See Hubbs, *Queer Composition*, especially chapter 3.

67. Copland and Perlis, *Copland since 1943*, 51, 52, 53.

68. Michael Denning, *The Cultural Front: The Laboring of American Culture in the Twentieth Century* (New York, 1997), xv. See also, for example, his extensive treatment of Blitzstein.

69. Robert Dawidoff, "In My Father's House," in Robert Dawidoff, *Making History Matter* (Philadelphia, 2000), 92 (on Hart); Redfern, "Neurosis of Narrative," 184–85; Bernard Weinraub, "A Tribute to Isherwood in the Land He Loved," *New York Times*, 7 July 2004, summarizing comments by James J. Berg.

70. On Catholic ascendancy, see Seth Jacobs, *America's Miracle Man in Vietnam: Ngo Din Diem, Religion, Race, and U.S. Intervention in Southeast Asia* (Durham, N.C., 2004), 77–87, which summarizes much recent scholarship.

71. The conversation, if it indeed took place, probably occurred in the 1940s. See Hubbs, *Queer Composition*, 128 and chapter 3 for the issues it raises.

72. Leon Botstein offers a capacious definition of musical modernism that accords with my understanding; see the summary and quotations in Hubbs, *Queer Composition*, 84. Of course, most art, including the severely modernist, is presumably expressive of something, but the term "expressive" captures the more overt or transparent expressiveness of many gay artists.

73. Herbert Muschamp (on Huntington Hartford's Gallery of Modern Art), "The Secret History," *New York Times*, 8 January 2006. Entries in *Encyclo-*

pedia of Lesbian, Gay, Bisexual, and Transgender History in America: William Pencak, "John Cage," 1:185; and Christopher Reed, "Visual Arts: Painting, Drawing, and Sculpture: 1969–Present," 3:237. These and other entries summarize scholarly debate on this matter and cite others' scholarship, especially that of Jonathan Katz.

Chapter Two

1. Edmund Bergler, M.D., *Homosexuality: Disease or Way of Life?* (New York, 1957), title for chapter 8; Havelock Ellis, *Studies in the Psychology of Sex* (1928), quoted in Donald Webster Cory, *The Homosexual in America: A Subjective Approach*, 2nd rev. ed. (New York, 1960), 148.

2. Donald Webster Cory and John P. LeRoy, *The Homosexual and His Society: A View from Within* (New York, 1963), 206–7. Cory elaborates this point in this book and earlier in Cory, *The Homosexual in America*, chapter 14.

3. Quoted characterizations are those of Kenneth Lewes, Ph.D., *The Psychoanalytic Theory of Homosexuality* (New York, 1988), 15, 149.

4. Bergler, quoted in Lewes, *Psychoanalytic Theory*, 114 ("there are"), 136–37 ("will be"); Edmund Bergler, M.D., *One Thousand Homosexuals: Conspiracy of Silence, or Curing and Deglamorizing Homosexuals?* (Paterson, N.J., 1959), 5 ("became the"); Bergler, *Homosexuality: Disease or Way of Life?* 300 ("the *capos*").

5. Lewes, *Psychoanalytic Theory*, 98 (Horney), 196 (Bieber, in 1969); Bergler, *One Thousand Homosexuals*, 163. Dominant views of homosexuality from the 1950s and 1960s still circulate, but their sponsors are now often religious groups; see, for example, Eagles' Wings Ministry, "Can Homosexuals Change?" (copyright 1987–2001), accessed 2001 at <www.ewm.org>, which draws on Bergler and others from this period.

6. Bergler, *Homosexuality: Disease or Way of Life?* 175, 172, 296, 292.

7. Edmund Bergler, M.D., *Fashion and the Unconscious* (New York, 1953), vii–viii; Bergler, *Homosexuality: Disease or Way of Life?* 293, 297 (italicized in original).

8. Gilbert Cant, "The Malady of Sexual Inversion," *New Leader*, 7 January 1957, 25–26; *One* 3 (January 1955): 12.

9. D. J. West, *The Other Man: A Study of the Social, Legal, and Clinical Aspects of Homosexuality* (New York, 1955), 60–66; Edward Hitschmann, M.D., with foreword by Ernest Jones, *Great Men: Psychoanalytic Studies* (New York, 1956), 212; W. David Sievers, *Freud on Broadway: A History of Psychoanalysis and the American Drama* (New York, 1955), 412. On concepts of the homosexual as immature, see Barbara Ehrenreich, *The Hearts of Men: American Dreams and the Flight from Commitment* (New York, 1983), chapter 2.

10. Lewes, *Psychoanalytic Theory*, 203 (Socarides), 150 ("insisted"); Harry Gershman, "Homosexuality and Some Aspects of Creativity," and Irving

Bieber, "Discussant," *American Journal of Psychoanalysis* 24, no. 1 (1964): 29–38; Lawrence J. Hatterer, M.D., *The Artist in Society: Problems and Treatment of the Creative Personality* (New York, 1965), 142, 163–64.

11. Bergler, *Homosexuality: Disease or Way of Life?* 170 (his emphasis); Lewes, *Psychoanalytic Theory*, 149 (quoting contemporaries).

12. Frederic Wertham, *The Seduction of the Innocent* (New York, 1954), 187–93. See also Geoffrey S. Smith, "National Security and Personal Isolation: Sex, Gender, and Disease in the Cold-War United States," *International History Review* 14 (May 1992): 325; Jennifer Terry, *An American Obsession: Science, Medicine, and Homosexuality in Modern Society* (Chicago, 1999), 320; George Chauncey, "The Postwar Sex Crime Panic," in *True Stories from the American Past*, ed. William Graebner (New York, 1993), 160–78; and Alan Helms, *Young Man from the Provinces: A Gay Life before Stonewall* (Boston, 1995), 33. On the TV series, see "Tangents," in *Tangents*, February 1966, 17, drawing on a *Newsweek* account. Gay people's role in mid-century comics is beautifully imagined in Michael Chabon's novel *The Amazing Adventures of Kavalier and Klay* (New York, 2000).

13. Lewes, *Psychoanalytic Theory*, 232, 230, 151, 232.

14. Ibid., 239 ("frequent"), 232 ("remarkable"), 149 (paraphrasing and quoting Kardiner), 189 (paraphrasing Kardiner), 229 (paraphrasing Bieber), 232 ("repeated"); Bergler, *Fashion*, vi; David Riesman and Nathan Glazer, "The Intellectuals and the Discontented Classes (1955)," in *The Radical Right: The New American Right Expanded and Updated*, ed. Daniel Bell (Garden City, N.Y., 1964), 119.

15. Among well-known accounts about therapy, Martin Duberman, *Cures: A Gay Man's Odyssey* (New York, 1992), is detailed, damning, and supplemented by his historian's perspective (quotation, 37). Arthur Laurents, *Original Story by Arthur Laurents: A Memory of Broadway and Hollywood* (New York, 2000), presents a wider range of encounters with therapy. Audre Lorde mentions her therapy in the 1950s briefly and neutrally in *ZAMI: A New Spelling of My Name* (Freedom, Calif., 1982). Paul Monette, *Becoming a Man: Half a Life Story* (New York, 1992), reports extensively and positively on his experience in the 1970s.

16. Laurents, *Original Story*, 51. See also George Chauncey, "Tea and Sympathy," in *Past Imperfect: History According to the Movies*, ed. Mark C. Carnes (New York, 1996), 258–61.

17. See Vito Russo, *The Celluloid Closet: Homosexuality in the Movies*, rev. ed. (New York, 1987), 116.

18. Robert Corber, *Homosexuality in Cold War America: Resistance and the Crisis of Masculinity* (Durham, N.C., 1997), 3. Corber makes a strong case for the subversive messages of writers like Williams but raises doubt that contemporaries grasped the subversiveness he now sees: "Although postwar critics

never specifically addressed the ways in which the writers examined in this study foregrounded the politics of gender and sexual identity in the Cold War era, they were clearly threatened by this aspect of their work" (16).

19. Gore Vidal, *United States: Essays, 1952–1992* (1993), quoted in Charles Kaiser, *The Gay Metropolis: 1940–1996* (New York, 1997), 98–99.

20. Florence Conrad, "A Lesbian Looks at Tennessee Williams," *Ladder*, May 1959, 24.

21. William Phillips, ed., *Art and Psychoanalysis* (New York, 1957), xx–xxi; Dr. Hendric M. Ruitenbeek, compiler and apparent author of the introduction, *Homosexuality and Creative Genius* (New York, 1967), xvi.

22. Charles Jackson, *The Lost Weekend* (New York, 1944). I am indebted for much of my analysis of this novel to Erin Redfern, "The Neurosis of Narrative: American Literature and Psychoanalytic Psychiatry during World War II" (Ph.D. diss., Northwestern University, 2003), especially chapter 2; page 137 offers the "double note" phrase. John Horne Burns, *The Gallery* (New York, 1947), 149.

23. David K. Johnson, *The Lavender Scare: The Cold War Persecution of Gays and Lesbians in the Federal Government* (Chicago, 2004), 8.

24. Robert Lindner, *Must You Conform?* (New York, 1956), 74, 32, 37, 40, 41, 43, 42.

25. P. Schilder, quoted in Lewes, *Psychoanalytic Theory*, 119 ("cultural"); Jennifer Terry, "'Momism' and the Making of Treasonous Homosexuals," in *'Bad' Mothers: The Politics of Blame in Twentieth-Century America*, ed. Molly Ladd-Taylor and Lauri Umansky (New York, 1998), 169 (Terry), 181 (Strecker).

26. On "lesbian invisibility," an earlier treatment is Lillian Faderman, *Odd Girls and Twilight Lovers: A History of Lesbian Life in Twentieth-Century America* (New York, 1991); more recent is Leisa Meyer, "The Myth of Lesbian (In)Visibility: World War II and the Current 'Gays in the Military' Debate," in *Modern American Queer History*, ed. Alida M. Black (Philadelphia, 2001), 271–81.

27. Clara Thompson, M.D., "Changing Concepts in Homosexuality" (1949), reprinted in *The Homosexuals: As Seen by Themselves and Thirty Authorities*, ed. A. M. Kritch (New York, 1954), 255.

28. Lewes, *Psychoanalytic Theory*, 237, 236, 238; Ehrenreich, *Hearts*, 26, 24.

29. Ehrenreich, *Hearts*, 24 (Kardiner), 26 (her emphasis).

30. See K. A. Cuordileone, "'Politics in an Age of Anxiety': Cold War Political Culture and the Crisis in American Masculinity, 1949–1960," *Journal of American History* 87 (September 2000): 530 (Kardiner); see generally 515–45. See also K. A. Cuordileone, *Manhood and American Political Culture in the Cold War* (New York, 2005); and Ehrenreich, *Hearts*.

31. Cuordileone, "Politics in an Age," 532.

32. David I. Freeman, "Literature and Homosexuality," *One*, January 1955, 15.

33. Philip Wylie, *A Generation of Vipers* (New York, 1943), 60, 68, 236, 61, 60, 70, 75. On Wylie, see Truman Frederick Walker, *Philip Wylie* (Boston, 1977).

34. Arthur M. Schlesinger Jr., *The Vital Center: The Politics of Freedom* (Boston, 1949), 151, 127, 36, 40, 81. Here I also draw on Michael S. Sherry, *In the Shadow of War: The United States since the 1930s* (New Haven, 1995), 163–65. Among many analyses of these passages, see Cuordileone, "Politics in an Age."

35. Cuordileone, "Politics in an Age," 521. On Welles, see Robert Dean, *Imperial Brotherhood: Gender and the Making of Cold War Foreign Policy* (Amherst, Mass., 2001), 72; and Benjamin Welles, *Sumner Welles: FDR's Global Strategist: A Biography* (New York, 1997).

36. Dean, *Imperial Brotherhood*, 103, 116. On the phrase "purge of the perverts," see Johnson, *Lavender Scare*, 2, 216n2.

37. On neglect of the Lavender Scare, see Johnson, *Lavender Scare*, 2–5.

38. Dean, *Imperial Brotherhood*, 148, 149, 151.

39. Ibid., 107. On Nicolas Nabokov, see the many references in Frances Stonor Saunders, *The Cultural Cold War: The CIA and the World of Arts and Letters* (New York, 1999).

40. Dean, *Imperial Brotherhood*, 119, 121. See also Frank Costigliola, "'Unceasing Pressure for Penetration': Gender, Pathology, and Emotion in George Kennan's Formation of the Cold War," *Journal of American History* 83 (March 1997): 1309–39.

41. Dean, *Imperial Brotherhood*, 123, 130, 133, 137; David Caute, *The Great Fear: The Anti-Communist Purge under Truman and Eisenhower* (New York, 1978), 12.

42. Dean, *Imperial Brotherhood*, 155, 156–58.

43. Johnson, *Lavender Scare*, 36 ("immoralism"); see also ibid., 69–70, 93; and Riesman and Glazer, "Intellectuals," 119.

44. John Springhall, *Youth, Popular Culture and Moral Panics* (New York, 1998), 7.

45. For this story I rely on Marc Stein, *City of Sisterly and Brotherly Loves: Lesbian and Gay Philadelphia, 1945–72* (Chicago, 2000), chapter 5, for quotations from firsthand sources and Stein's characterizations; on some points I depart from or extend his interpretations.

46. David Russell and Dalvan Mcintire, "In Paths Untrodden: A Study of Walt Whitman," *One*, July 1954, 4–15.

47. The reading of Copland's homosexuality as a target is mine, but I draw on Howard Pollack, *Aaron Copland: The Life and Work of an Uncommon Man* (New York, 1999), 451–60, 520; Antony Tommasini, *Virgil Thomson: Composer on the Aisle* (New York, 1999), 425–27; and Nadine Hubbs, *The Queer Composition of America's Sound: Gay Modernists, American Music, and National Identity* (Berkeley, 2004), 212n60, which paraphrases the Schoenberg broadcast.

48. Anonymous letter to Scott McLeod, 20 April 1953, unfoldered material, Box 12, Lot File 62-d-146, Decimal Files 1953–1960, Bureau of Security and Consular Affairs, Department of State, Record Group 59, National Archives and Records Service, Washington, D.C. I owe this information to David Johnson, who was given by Archives staff, he reports, a "box with 'privacy' material that should have been removed."

49. McCarthy hearings, *Executive Sessions of the Senate Permanent Subcommittee on Investigations of the Committee on Government Operations*, vol. 2, 83rd Cong., 1st sess., 1953, 1267–91, as "Made Public January 2003" (Washington, D.C., 2003) at <www.access.gpo.gov/congress/senate/senate12cp107 .html>. For diary entry, see Aaron Copland and Vivian Perlis, *Copland since 1943* (New York: St. Martin's, 1989), 193. On release of the subcommittee executive hearing records, see "Transcripts Detail Secret Questioning in 50's by McCarthy," *New York Times*, 6 May 2003.

50. Arthur M. Schlesinger Jr., "Whittaker Chambers and His *Witness*" (1952), in Arthur M. Schlesinger Jr., *The Politics of Hope* (Boston, 1963), 183, 186; Arthur M. Schlesinger Jr., "The Highbrow in American Politics" (1953), in Schlesinger, *Politics*, 222–23, 224, 228.

51. Arthur M. Schlesinger Jr., "Look Back in Amazement" (1957), in Schlesinger, *Politics*, 247–53. For Osborne's 1958 denunciation and the welcome of him as a virile playwright, see Mark Ravenhill, "Looking Back Warily at a Heterosexual Classic," *New York Times*, 17 October 1999.

52. Arthur M. Schlesinger Jr., "The Crisis of American Masculinity" (1958), in Schlesinger, *Politics*, 237–46; Cuordileone, "Politics in an Age," 530; Kramer, from *Arts* (1959), as quoted in Gregory Woods, "The 'Conspiracy' of the 'Homintern,'" *Gay and Lesbian Review* (May–June 2003): 12.

53. Edmund Wilson, *The Bit between My Teeth: A Literary Chronicle of 1950–1965* (New York, 1965), 594.

54. Leslie Fiedler, "The Un-Angry Young Men: America's Post-War Generation," *Encounter* 10, no. 1 (1958): 3–12. See also Corber, *Homosexuality in Cold War America*, 1–2, 136.

55. Max Lerner, *America as a Civilization: Life and Thought in the United States Today* (New York, 1957), 546, 683, 877, 934, 935. On Williams and Albee, see Sanford Lakoff, *Max Lerner: Pilgrim in the Promised Land* (Chicago, 1998), 201.

56. Betty Friedan, *The Feminine Mystique* (New York, 1963), 270, 286, 273–75.

57. Barry Werth, *The Scarlet Professor: Newton Arvin, a Literary Life Shattered by Scandal* (New York, 2001), 221; Cory and LeRoy, *The Homosexual and His Society*, x, 193.

58. Terry, *American Obsession*, 166; John D'Emilio, *Sexual Politics, Sexual Communities: The Making of a Homosexual Minority in the United States, 1940–1970* (Chicago, 1983), 140.

59. D'Emilio, *Sexual Politics*, 142, 143. For Becker's linkages among homosexuals, jazz musicians, and drug users, see Howard Becker, *The Outsiders: Studies in the Sociology of Deviance* (New York, 1963); and Howard Becker, "Deviance and Deviates," *Nation*, 20 September 1965, 115–19.

60. Dal Mcintire, "Tangents," *One*, February 1957, 28 ("smutty"). Other quotations and information and most analysis about *The Geisha Boy* are from Naoko Shibusawa, "America's Geisha Ally: Race, Gender, and Maturity in Refiguring the Japanese Enemy, 1945–1964" (Ph.D. diss., Northwestern University, 1998), introduction.

61. Russo, *Celluloid Closet*, 149.

62. Lorde, *ZAMI*, 173,

63. George Chauncey, *Gay New York: Gender, Urban Culture, and the Making of the Gay Male World, 1890–1940* (New York, 1994), 149 (see generally 141–49); Gershman, "Homosexuality and Some Aspects of Creativity," 34 ("distinct," etc.).

64. "Growth of Overt Homosexuality in City Provokes Wide Concern," *New York Times*, 17 December 1963. For background and further commentary, see Kaiser, *Gay Metropolis*, 156–59.

65. Bryan Magee, *One in Twenty: A Study of Homosexuality in Men and Women* (London, 1966), 36, 38–39.

66. Sidney Alexander, in *American Scholar* (Winter 1951–52), as quoted in Paul Carter, *Another Part of the Fifties* (New York, 1983), 158.

67. See the fine account of Hains in John Howard, *Men Like That: A Southern Queer History* (Chicago, 1999); quotation, 222.

68. Quotation from unidentified source, in Sal (presumably Dal) Mcintire, "Tangents" column entitled "Really Putting the Basket Back in Basketball," *One*, May 1962, 17.

69. For programming and other elements of the local scene, I have drawn on scrapbooks, photographs, and program collections of my parents, on family memories, and on Thomas A. Sargent, *The Muncie Symphony Orchestra: 50 Seasons of Music* (Muncie, Ind., 1998). Many of my recollections are confirmed by C. A. Tripp, *The Homosexual Matrix*, 2nd ed. (New York, 1987); Tripp found "large cities that are rigidly conformist" and also "small towns in America—and not all of them are arts colonies—where persons living discreet but undisguised homosexual lives (often in the form of fairly obvious ongoing relationships) make up a sizable portion of the population" (120).

70. James McCourt, *Queer Street: Rise and Fall of an American Culture, 1947–1985* (New York, 2004), 73.

71. On the film and its making, see Sam Kashman, "A Movie Marked Danger," *Vanity Fair*, April 2000, 416–32. On Winchell, see Neal Gabler, *Winchell: Gossip, Power, and the Culture of Celebrity* (New York, 1994), especially 500–503. No commentary I have read offers a queer reading of the film or its char-

acters, though hints appear in Richard Corliss, "That Old Feeling: Sweet Smells," <www.time.com>, 21 March 2002.

72. Laurents, *Original Story*, 224; "2-Hour Broadcast on Homophile Problem," *Ladder*, January 1959, 9.

73. William J. Helmer, "New York's 'Middle-class' Homosexuals," *Harper's*, March 1963, 85–92.

74. Fiedler, "Un-Angry Young Men," 11.

75. Walter Hixson, *Parting the Curtain: Propaganda, Culture, and the Cold War, 1945–1961* (New York, 1997), 159, 156.

76. "I Am a Homosexual Woman," as "Reported by Jane McKinnon," in A. M. Krich, ed., *The Homosexuals: As Seen by Themselves and Thirty Authorities* (New York, 1963), 9.

77. James Barr, *Quatrefoil* (1950; Boston, 1991), 124; Helms, *Young Man*, 52, 56.

78. Barr, *Quatrefoil*, 79, 83, 108, 25, 282, 311.

79. John Loughery, *The Other Side of Silence: Men's Lives and Gay Identities, a Twentieth-Century History* (New York, 1998), 195–97, summarizes the man and his work, as do references in D'Emilio, *Sexual Politics*, which contributes the "scathing" adjective (168).

80. Cory and LeRoy, *The Homosexual and His Society*, 195–97.

81. Cory, *The Homosexual in America*, 164.

82. Ibid., 151, 152, 153, 154; Cory and LeRoy, *The Homosexual and His Society*, 201 ("an intense"); Rorem quoted in Hubbs, *Queer Composition*, 155.

83. Cory and LeRoy, *The Homosexual and His Society*, 206–7.

84. Arthur Kroll, "We Need a Great Literature," *One*, May 1954, 19.

85. Dal Mcintire, "Tangents," *One*, February 1957, 27–28.

86. See Helms, *Young Man*; quotation, 40.

87. Laurents, *Original Story*, 133.

88. Hubbs, *Queer Composition*, 66; Monette, *Becoming a Man*, 272.

89. James Campbell, *Talking at the Gates: A Life of James Baldwin* (Berkeley, 2002), 129, 33, 71.

90. Kaiser, *Gay Metropolis*, 88, 93. Laurents, referring to a review of James McCourt's *Queer Street*, which quotes McCourt as arguing that *West Side Story* was "the supreme encoded queer Broadway musical," wrote to the *New York Times Book Review* ("Letters," 11 January 2004): "I have no idea why [reviewer Maureen N.] McLane feels pretty and even less what is encoded in the play."

91. Laurents, *Original Story*, 349, 358.

92. A. E. Smith, "Coming Out," *One*, June 1962, 6–8.

93. Helms, *Young Man*, 73–78.

94. *Homosexuality and Citizenship in Florida*, A Report of the Florida Legislative Investigation Committee (1964); quotations taken from several portions of this unpaginated report.

95. Schlesinger, Fiedler, and Lindner passages are quoted earlier in this chapter; Hubbs, *Queer Composition*, 142, which adds (211n49) that editors chose this title without consulting Babbitt; Oliver Larkin, *Art and Life in America*, rev. ed. (New York, 1960), 463–70.

96. Albert Ellis, "Homosexuality and Creativity," *Journal of Clinical Psychology* 15, no. 4 (October 1959): 376–79.

97. Meredith Grey, "Homosexuality and Creativity," *Ladder*, February 1959, 7–10; D'Emilio, *Sexual Politics*, 163.

98. Hubbs, *Queer Composition*, 229n54, notes some of the conflicting evidence about the project and what it would have attempted.

99. I owe the quoted phrase to Doug Mitchell, editor at the University of Chicago Press, who suggested it to me in e-mail discussions near the start of this project.

100. Daniel Boorstin, *The Image: A Guide to Pseudo-Events in America* (New York, 1980), 3–4.

101. Williams, quoted in Allen Young, "No Longer the Court Jesters," in *Lavender Culture*, ed. Karla Jay and Allen Young (New York, 1979), 33; Philip Brett and Elizabeth Wood, "Gay and Lesbian Music," *Grove Music Online*, ed. L. Macy (accessed 14 February 2006), <http://www.grovemusic.com>.

102. Dennis Altman, *Homosexual Oppression and Liberation* (New York, 1971), 37; Brett and Wood, "Gay and Lesbian Music."

103. Tripp, *Homosexual Matrix*, 261.

Chapter Three

1. Vito Russo, *The Celluloid Closet: Homosexuality in the Movies*, rev. ed. (New York, 1987), 122; Dennis Altman, *Homosexual Oppression and Liberation* (New York, 1971), 43, 52.

2. John D'Emilio, *Sexual Politics, Sexual Communities: The Making of a Homosexual Minority in the United States, 1940–1970* (Chicago, 1983), 139; Jess Stearn, *The Sixth Man* (Garden City, N.Y., 1961), 18, 47, 259 (titles of chapters 2, 16).

3. Dust jacket as quoted in Edoaurd Marques's review, *One*, July 1961, 22; David I. Freeman, "Literature and Homosexuality," *One*, January 1955, 13 ("many tons"); Stearn, *Sixth Man*, 21, 10; R. E. L. Masters, *The Homosexual Revolution* (1962; New York, 1964), xiv.

4. *One*, October 1953, 8; Jonathan Ned Katz, *Love Stories: Sex between Men before Homosexuality* (Chicago, 2001), 58.

5. Altman, *Homosexual Oppression and Liberation*, 52; Stearn, *Sixth Man*, 17, 28; S. J. Harris, *Saturday Review*, 22 April 1961, 27.

6. Stearn, *Sixth Man*, 23, 76, 96, 95, 93; see generally chapters 6, 7.

7. Undated, unnamed "magazine for executives" of art museums, quoted in "Cross-Currents," *Ladder*, November 1963, 18; Joseph Wood Krutch, "Con-

fessions of a Square," *Saturday Review*, 9 May 1964, quoted in "Cross-Currents," *Ladder*, November 1964, 23.

8. "Homosexuals Proud of Deviancy," *New York Times*, 19 May 1964.

9. Ibid.; *Show Business Illustrated* (April 1962), as quoted in *Ladder*, September 1962, 22; "The Homosexual in America," *Time*, 21 January 1966, 40–41; "Homosexuality in America," *Life*, 26 June 1964, 66.

10. "Homosexuality in America," *Life*, 66.

11. Lee Atwell, "Homosexual Themes in the Cinema," *Tangents*, March 1966, 5, 9; Russo, *Celluloid Closet*, 131, 132. Kael's comment was not repeated in her anthology, Pauline Kael, *5001 Nights at the Movies* (1982; New York, 1991), 814, which judged *Victim* "ingenious, moralistic, and moderately amusing" and "a slick thriller" featuring Bogarde in "a daring role," though she only identifies it as "daring" because Bogarde now "acted his age," not because he was gay, despite one quip of his she quotes—"I was the Loretta Young of England"—which seems very gay indeed.

12. "Magazine Goldmine: 'Run an Article on Queers!'" *One*, July 1953, 2.

13. "The Lesbian in Mass Media," *Ladder*, August 1962, 16–17; "The Fourth Sex—The Lesbian," *Ladder*, January 1964, 4–5.

14. See Lee Atwell, "Homosexual Themes in the Cinema," *Tangents*, March 1966, 5–10, and April 1966, 5–9. See also "A History of Homosexuality in the Movies," *Drum*, October 1967, 13–32.

15. "Magazine Goldmine," *One*, 2; Dal Mcintire, "Tangents," *One*, February 1957, 27–29.

16. Arthur B. Kroll, "We Need a Great Literature," *One*, May 1954, 19–23; Lyn Pederson, "Do Homosexuals Hide behind Great Men?" *One*, May 1957, 4–6; Sal (presumably Dal) Mcintire, "Tangents," *One*, June 1963, 15 ("'one rather'").

17. Anna Frankenheimer, "A Much-Needed Upbraiding of Long-Hair Music," *Fact*, November–December 1964, 11–17.

18. "Tangents," *One*, February 1965, 17; Letters, in *Fact*, January–February 1965, 26–27.

19. *Rockwell Report*, 15 July 1964, quoted in "Tangents," *One*, October 1964, 15.

20. Allen Drury, *Advise and Consent* (Garden City, N.Y., 1959), 288, 290, 294, 295, 433, 447.

21. "Homosexuality in America," *Life*, 66; Ernest Havemann, "Why?" *Life*, 26 June 1964, 76; Lee Edelman, "Tearooms and Sympathy, or, The Epistemology of the Water Closet," in *Lesbian and Gay Studies Reader*, ed. Henry Abelove, Michele Aina Barale, David M. Halperin (New York, 1993), 558. Edelman asked, regarding Havemann's name, "Can this *not* be a pseudonym?" Edelman probably suspected an obvious pun—Havemann as have-a-man. But Havemann (1912–1995), an M.A. in psychology, wrote often for *Life* and other publications and coauthored, with the well-known psycholo-

gist Jerome Kagan, *Psychology: An Introduction* (1976). See "The Havemann Family History Center," <www.havemann.com>, whose list of Havemann writings omits the *Life* piece quoted here.

22. Edelman, "Tearooms," 555.

23. On the Jenkins affair, yet to receive a definitive account, I draw on the provocative essay by Lee Edelman, "Tearooms," and on other sources cited here, including White House phone conversations, heard at <www.c-span.org/lbj/lbjctest.asp> and in excerpts transcribed for me by David Johnson, who also located other documents cited here.

24. *Newsweek*, 2 November 1964, 26.

25. White House tapes: Conversation 5890 with Tommy Corcoran, 15 October 1964; Conversation 5900 with *Denver Post* publisher Palmer Hoyt, 16 October 1964. On FBI suspicions, see Conversation 5888 with Abe Fortas, 15 October 1964.

26. Edelman, "Tearooms," 562 ("Either Way," "behind"). *Newsweek*, 26 October 1964, 31–34, notes the Sioux City placard and other reactions. On advice to LBJ to appear as the "American family," see White House tapes, Conversation 5882 with John Connally, 14 October 1964.

27. White House tapes: LBJ in Conversation 5900 with Hoyt, 16 October 1964; Lady Bird in Conversation 5895 with LBJ, 15 October 1964; Fortas in Conversation 5880, 14 October 1964.

28. Letter from Arthur Luber, 27 October 1964, and Letter from Mrs. James Cronin, 26 October 1964, both in White House Confidential Files, Subject Files, Federal Government, 11-8-1/Jenkins, Box 87, Folder "11/1/64," Lyndon Baines Johnson Library, Austin, Texas.

29. Edelman, "Tearooms," 565.

30. Ibid., 555 (LBJ), 566.

31. Daniel Boorstin, *The Image: A Guide to Pseudo-Events in America* (1961; New York, 1980), 3; the Frisch quotation appears on the title page.

32. Howard Brick, *Age of Contradiction: American Thought and Culture in the 1960s* (1998; Ithaca, N.Y., 2000), 66, 69, 70. In this section I draw on Brick, especially chapter 4, "Authenticity and Artifice." But in contrast to Brick, I see concerns about authenticity as climaxing in the 1960s rather than rooted in it; I ascribe them more to the broad conditions and anxieties of Cold War militarization and social change; and I see homosexuality as more central to them. I also draw on conversations with and preliminary writings by George Chauncey, who will elaborate his views in his forthcoming book, *The Strange Career of the Closet: Gay Culture, Consciousness, and Politics from the Second World War to the Gay Liberation Era*. Also useful is Doug Rossinow, *The Politics of Authenticity: Liberalism, Christianity, and the New Left in America* (New York, 1998). For discussion of how authenticity figured in Barber's career, see chapter 4.

33. Brick, *Age of Contradiction*, 84, 67, quoting Baldwin, *The Fire Next Time* (1963). See also James Campbell, *Talking at the Gates: A Life of James Baldwin* (1991; Berkeley, 2002).

34. Peter Biskind, *Seeing Is Believing: How Hollywood Taught Us to Stop Worrying and Love the Fifties* (1983; New York, 2000), 177.

35. "Tangents," *One*, November 1964, 16. On the poles of rebellion and respectability, see D'Emilio, *Sexual Politics, Sexual Communities*.

36. James Baldwin, *No Name in the Street* (New York, 1972), 53–54. Baldwin here provides summary statement, and sometimes direct restatement, of views on his part that were emerging in the 1960s.

37. Brick, *Age of Contradiction*, 71.

38. Baldwin, *No Name*, 62, 64.

39. Humphrey Burton, *Leonard Bernstein* (New York, 1994), 321; Walter Hixson, *Parting the Curtain: Propaganda, Culture, and the Cold War, 1945–1961* (New York, 1997), 153.

40. Hixson, *Parting the Curtain*, 172–73.

41. Paul Carter, *Another Part of the Fifties* (New York, 1983), 119; Stuart D. Hobbs, *The End of the American Avant Garde* (New York, 1997), 119 ("Cold Warriors"); Burton, *Bernstein*, 307; Barbara Heyman, *Samuel Barber: The Composer and His Music* (New York, 1992), 414, paraphrasing Barber.

42. Harris's comments and *One*'s responses appear in Dal Mcintire, "Tangents," *One*, June 1960, 10–11.

43. For the quotation and information, but not the analysis I offer, see David Caute, *The Dancer Defects: The Struggle for Cultural Supremacy during the Cold War* (New York, 2003), 486–89.

44. Patrick Dennis, "Tennessee Off Broadway," *New Republic*, 27 January 1958, 20; Eric Myers, *Uncle Mame: The Life of Patrick Dennis* (New York, 2000), xii ("the first").

45. *Show Business Illustrated* (April 1962), quoted in *Ladder*, September 1962, 23.

46. Howard Taubman, "Not What It Seems: Homosexual Motif Gets Heterosexual Guise," *New York Times*, 5 November 1961; Howard Taubman, "Modern Primer: Helpful Hints to Tell Appearances vs. Truth," *New York Times*, 18 April 1963.

47. Wilfred Sheed, "Heterosexual Backlash," *Commentary*, 21 May 1965, 289–90, 292.

48. For a brief view of contemporary controversy, see Charles Kaiser, *The Gay Metropolis: 1940–1996* (New York, 1997), 166–67.

49. Philip Roth, "The Play That Dare Not Speak Its Name," *New York Review of Books*, 25 February 1965, 4.

50. See Edward Alwood, *Straight News: Gays, Lesbians, and the News Media* (New York, 1996), 65–69, for a brief, bland treatment of the episode; for a harsher view, see Kaiser, *Gay Metropolis*, 165–66. See also "Tangents," *Tangents*,

March 1966, 21–22. *Tangents* was a new magazine emerging out of disputes at *One*, adopting "Tangents" as title for both the magazine and a section in it.

51. Ned Rorem, *The Later Diaries of Ned Rorem, 1961–1972* (1974; San Francisco, 1983), 167–68.

52. Stanley Kauffmann, "Homosexual Drama and Its Disguises," *New York Times*, 23 January 1966; "On the Acceptability of the Homosexual" (with accompanying letters to the *Times*), *New York Times*, 6 February 1966.

53. "Tangents," *One*, April 1965, 15–16, responding to Roth's piece on Albee.

54. For a brief, shrewd view of Rodgers and Hart individually and together, see David Hajdu, "He Took Manhattan," *New York Review of Books*, 15 August 2002, 40–41, which reviews biographies.

55. "The Homosexual in America," *Time*, 21 January 1966, 40–41; *Time*'s use of Maugham probably derived from Edmund Bergler, *Homosexuality: Disease or Way of Life?* (New York, 1957). Editorial, *Tangents*, March 1966, 2.

56. Kaiser, *Gay Metropolis*, 160–71, gives an extensive account of "The Homosexuals" and reactions to it.

57. Antony James, *America's Homosexual Underground* (New York, 1965); Matt Bradley, *Faggots to Burn!* (Hollywood, Calif., 1962), 103, 12, 13; Tor Erikson, *The Half World of the American Homosexual* (North Hollywood, Calif., 1966), 185. See also Michael Bronski, ed., *Pulp Friction: Uncovering the Golden Age of Gay Male Pulps* (New York, 2003).

58. Leslie Fiedler, *Waiting for the End* (1964), as quoted in Altman, *Homosexual Oppression and Liberation*, 138.

59. Susan Sontag, "Notes on Camp" (1964), in Susan Sontag, *Against Interpretation and Other Essays* (New York, 1966), 275–92.

60. Vivian Gornick, "It's a Queer Hand Stoking the Campfire," *Village Voice*, 7 April 1966, 1ff.

61. Frances Stonor Saunders, *The Cultural Cold War: The CIA and the World of Arts and Letters* (New York, 1999), 382, summarizing and quoting from a *Human Events* article.

62. Gene Marine, "Who's Afraid of Little Annie Fanny?" *Ramparts*, February 1967, 26–30.

63. "Tangents," *One*, October 1964, 14 (Tulane). "Tangents," *Tangents*, March 1966, 1966.

64. John Gerassi, *The Boys of Boise: Furor, Vice, and Folly in an American City* (New York, 1966), 144, 179. On recent controversy, see Thomas C. Mackey's review of the reprint edition, May 2002, published online by H-Urban, which was followed by lively exchanges on the H-Urban site.

65. Gerassi, *Boys*, x, 101.

66. Paraphrase of Battcock's comments by Erika Hastings in her article, "The Homosexual Citizen in the Great Society," *Ladder*, February 1966, 4–6.

67. Review by J. H. (probably Joseph Hansen), *Tangents*, March 1966, 26–27.

Chapter Four

1. Barbara Heyman, *Samuel Barber: The Composer and His Music* (New York, 1992), 8. The following pages draw heavily on Heyman's account.

2. See the sympathetic account in Peter G. Davis, *The American Opera Singer: The Lives and Adventures of America's Great Singers in Opera and Concert from 1825 to the Present* (New York, 1997), 205–8, 211–19.

3. Quoted in Heyman, *Barber*, 7.

4. John Gruen, *Menotti: A Biography* (New York, 1978), 8; Heyman, *Barber*, 69, and on *American Home* feature, 239–41.

5. John Gill, "Burying Benjamin Britten," in John Gill, *Queer Noises: Male and Female Homosexuality in Twentieth-Century Music* (Minneapolis, 1995), 10–25.

6. See generally Barbara L. Tischler, *An American Music: The Search for an American Musical Identity* (New York, 1986), 5 ("nationalists by quotation"). For a more positive view of the American scene in the 1890s, see Joseph Horowitz, "Dvořák and the New World," in Joseph Horowitz, *The Postclassical Predicament: Essays on Music and Society* (Boston, 1995), 67 ("example"). MacDowell is quoted in Joseph Horowitz, "Old Sounds from the New World," *New York Times*, 15 July 2001.

7. Heyman, *Barber*, 53; Anthony Tommasini, *Virgil Thomson: Composer on the Aisle* (New York, 1997), 182 (paraphrase of and quotation from Thomson).

8. Michael Wilcox, *Benjamin Britten's Operas* (Bath, England, 1997), 14.

9. Ned Rorem, *The Later Diaries of Ned Rorem, 1961–1972* (San Francisco, 1983), 391 (23 March 1972 entry); Heyman, *Barber*, 81 ("Amurhican"), 130 ("skyscrapers").

10. Heyman, *Barber*, 173 (Turner), 173–74 (on uses of the *Adagio for Strings*).

11. Nicolas Slonimsky, *Music since 1900*, 5th ed. (New York, 1994), 910; Russell Platt, "Classical Notes: Barber Shop," *New Yorker*, 14 March 2005, 44; Heyman, *Barber*, 144 ("ultra-modern").

12. Kurt List, "The State of American Music," *Partisan Review* 1948 (1): 88–89, 90. In List's view, even John Cage was guilty of "an escapist—also regressive tendency."

13. Heyman, *Barber*, 122 ("Too"), 41 ("businessmen"); Gruen, *Menotti*, 130 ("art," Menotti quoting Barber).

14. Joseph Horowitz, *Understanding Toscanini: How He Became an American Culture-God and Helped Create a New Audience for Old Music* (Minneapolis, 1987), 235, 237; Charles C. Alexander, *Here the Country Lies: Nationalism and the Arts in Twentieth-Century America* (Bloomington, Ind., 1980), 169 (Harris); Heyman, *Barber*, 171 (letter).

15. Heyman, *Barber*, 171–72; Terry A. Cooney, *Balancing Acts: American Thought and Culture in the 1930s* (New York, 1995), 213 ("notion of").

16. Heyman, *Barber*, 188.

17. Horowitz, *Understanding Toscanini*, 255; Heyman, *Barber*, 165 (on Horan, paraphrase and direct quotations).

18. For Barber's wartime service, the Second Symphony, and quotations, see Heyman, *Barber*, 211–31.

19. Heyman, *Barber*, 237, 247, 321; on Barber's music in the Soviet Union as of 1962, see 414.

20. Ibid., 256, on the Cello Concerto.

21. Ibid., 336.

22. Ibid., 403.

23. Aaron Copland and Vivian Perlis, *Copland since 1943* (New York, 1989), 68–69; Oliver W. Larkin, *Art and Life in America*, rev. ed. (New York, 1960), 470; Leonard Meyer, *Music, the Arts, and Ideas: Patterns and Predictions in Twentieth-Century Culture* (Chicago, 1967), viii, 153, 264, and 175 (on Barber). Meyer's essays were written from the mid-1950s to the mid-1960s.

24. Tischler, *American Music*, 122 (Carter); Alexander, *Here the Country*, 264 (Sessions); Horowitz, *Post-Classical Predicament*, 149 (Bernstein); Heyman, *Barber*, 379 (Barber).

25. Heyman, *Barber*, 374, 386, 391, 393; Winthrop Sargeant, "Musical Events," *New Yorker*, 25 January 1958, 109 ("music of such").

26. Heyman, *Barber*, 396; Howard Taubman, "'Vanessa' Again," *New York Times*, 18 January 1959; Richard H. Pells, *Not Like Us: How Europeans Have Loved, Hated, and Transformed American Culture since World War II* (New York, 1997), 180 ("American composers"); Everett Helm, "'Vanessa' in Salzburg," *Saturday Review*, 13 September 1958, 65–66 ("fine," "since").

27. Alex Ross, "Musical Events: Gatsbyesque," *New Yorker*, 10 January 2000, 88, compares *Vanessa*'s place to other American operas; Ethan Mordden, *Opera in the Twentieth Century: Sacred, Profane, Godot* (New York, 1978), 310; James McCourt, *Queer Street: Rise and Fall of an American Culture, 1947–1985* (New York, 2004), 113.

28. Gruen, *Menotti*, 39; see also 69.

29. On Ibel, see Heyman, *Barber*, 412–23; and Gruen, *Menotti*, 130, 53, 48.

30. Nathan Broder, *Samuel Barber* (New York, 1954), 9; "American Masterpiece" and "'Dear Mother . . . I Was Meant to Be a Composer,'" *Newsweek*, 27 January 1958, 62–63; D. A. Miller, *The Novel and the Police* (Berkeley, 1988), 206, 207.

31. Humphrey Burton, *Leonard Bernstein* (New York, 1994), 341 (on Blitzstein); Joan Peyser, *Bernstein: A Biography* (New York, 1987), 357.

32. Heyman, *Barber*, 270 (Thomson); Robert Evett, "Yankee Doodling at the Met," *New Republic*, 27 January 1958, 18.

33. David W. Stowe, "The Politics of Cafe Society," *Journal of American History* 84 (March 1998): 1394.

34. Nadine Hubbs, *The Queer Composition of America's Sound: Gay Modernists,*

American Music, and National Identity (Berkeley, 2004), 141 (notes Thomson's designation of the "complexity boys").

35. McClary, quoted in K. Robert Schwarz, "Classical Music: Composers' Closets Open for All to See," *New York Times*, 19 June 1994; Hubbs, *Queer Composition*, 129; Ned Rorem, *Knowing When to Stop: A Memoir* (New York, 1994), 309; Menotti at a 1952 Juilliard symposium, quoted in Gruen, *Menotti*, 117–18.

36. Irving Kolodin, "Menotti, and Some Other Opera Composers," *Saturday Review*, Summer 1959, 41.

37. Menotti, in Gruen, *Menotti*, 135; Jess Stearn, *The Sixth Man* (Garden City, N.Y., 1961), 20. On others at the festival, see the incomplete list in Heyman, *Barber*, 403.

38. For the text of the opera and a recording featuring some of the original cast, see Vanguard VSD-2083 (record copyright 1968; jacket copyright 1976). Measuring the enduring appeal of *Bridge*, in a long program of American opera selections by Stephen Sondheim, Bernstein, Carlisle Floyd, Aaron Copland, Gian Carlo Menotti, Stephen Paulus, and Kurt Weill, *A Hand of Bridge*, given complete, grabbed the audience as effectively as anything (program titled "American Dreams," Northwestern University, 21 November 1998).

39. Leonard Wallock, ed., *New York: Cultural Capital of the World, 1940–1960* (New York, 1988), 11. For a valuable overview of these shifts in cultural power and related changes, see Eric Hobsbawm, *The Age of Extremes: A History of the World, 1914–1991* (1994; New York, 1996), especially chapter 17.

40. Wallock, *New York*, 11.

41. John Dizikes, *Opera in America: A Cultural History* (New Haven, 1993), 485, 486.

42. Robert A. M. Stern, Thomas Mellins, David Fishman, *New York, 1960: Architecture and Urbanism between the Second World War and the Bicentennial* (New York, 1995), 677.

43. Edgar B. Young, *Lincoln Center: The Building of an Institution* (New York, 1980), 43 ("will almost"); Dizikes, *Opera in America*, 530 ("cultural center"); Alan Rich, *The Lincoln Center Story* (New York, 1984), 17 ("You'd have"). See also Lincoln Center for the Performing Arts, *Lincoln Center for the Performing Arts* (New York, 1964).

44. All from a special Lincoln Center issue of the *New York Times Magazine*, 23 September 1962: advertisements, 6, 9; William Schuman, "The Idea: 'A Creative, Dynamic Force,'" 33; August Heckscher (Kennedy's arts adviser), "The Nation's Culture: New Age for the Arts," 15ff.

45. John D. Rockefeller III, "The Evolution: Birth of a Great Center," *New York Times Magazine*, 23 September 1962, 30; John Rockwell, "New York's Music," in Wallock, *New York*, 213.

46. Stern et al., *New York, 1960*, 677 ("show"), 683 (*New York Times*), 678 ("has been"); Dizikes, *Opera in America*, 528 ("cultural capital," etc.).

47. Young, *Lincoln Center*, 137; Sir Rudolf Bing, *5000 Nights at the Opera* (Garden City, N.Y., 1972), 294; Dizikes, *Opera in America*, 524; William Schuman, "Have We 'Culture'? Yes — and No," *New York Times Magazine*, 22 September 1963, 21.

48. Stern et al., *New York, 1960*, 684 ("the tasks"); David Halberstam, *The Best and the Brightest* (Greenwich, Conn., 1972), 201 (on Taylor); Schuman, "Have We 'Culture'?" 21.

49. Dizikes, *Opera in America*, 532–33.

50. *Public Papers of the Presidents of the United States: Dwight D. Eisenhower* (Washington, D.C., 1958–61), *1959*: 106.

51. Heyman, *Barber*, 429.

52. Ibid., 420, 411, 427.

53. Ibid., 427; Mordden, *Opera in the Twentieth Century*, 298, 304; Coward, quoted in John Ardoin, *The Stages of Menotti* (New York, 1985), 10; Hans W. Heinsheimer, "Birth of an Opera," *Saturday Review*, 17 September 1966, 50.

54. Ned Rorem, *The Paris Diary of Ned Rorem* (New York, 1966), 122; Heinsheimer, "Birth of an Opera," *Saturday Review*, 17 September 1966, 50.

55. Heyman, *Barber*, 377, 430. Barber's hunch on the pitfalls of translating *Streetcar* into opera was echoed forty years later. Reviewing André Previn's opera based on *Streetcar* (1998), critic Bernard Holland noted that "Blanche's long speeches are arias in prose" and "I am not sure that Blanche is a character that opera can ever reach." Bernard Holland, "Pursuing the Soul of 'Streetcar' in Opera," *New York Times*, 21 September 1998.

56. Heyman, *Barber*, 430, which overlooks the mention of Barber's interest in *Moby Dick* noted by Broder, *Samuel Barber*, 45.

57. On scholarly recognition, see Leslie Fiedler, "Come Back to the Raft Ag'in, Huck Honey!" originally published in *Partisan Review*, June 1948, and widely reprinted.

58. Wilcox, *Britten's Operas*, 57 (quoting Donald Mitchell and Walton); Alex Ross, "Musical Events: The Battle of Britten," *New Yorker*, 16 December 1996, 100; Humphrey Carpenter, *Benjamin Britten: A Biography* (New York, 1993), 358 (on *Turn*). On his operas, see especially Wilcox.

59. Herbert Kupferberg, "Barber, the Bard, and the Barge," *Atlantic*, September 1966, 126.

60. Leo Lerman, "The New Met," *Mademoiselle*, May 1966, 180 ("world"); Letter, Barber to Bing, 3 November 1963, Metropolitan Opera Archives, New York City.

61. Lerman, "The New Met," 179, 180.

62. Howard Klein, "The Birth of an Opera," *New York Times Magazine*, 28 August 1966, 32, 107; "The New Met and Its Old Master," *Newsweek*, 19 September 1966, 75 (Bing).

63. Kupferberg, "Barber, the Bard, and the Barge," 126; Heinsheimer, "Birth of an Opera," *Saturday Review*, 17 September 1966, 49.

64. Heyman, *Barber*, 414, 434, 438 (Hoiby).

65. Tommasini, *Thomson*, 475.

66. Rorem, *Paris Diary*, 55; Rorem, *Knowing*, 310–11.

67. Tommasini, *Thomson*, 475; Rorem, *Knowing*, 310; Hubbs, *Queer Composition*, 182n23.

68. Robert Mazzocco, "To Tell You the Truth," *New York Review of Books*, 8 September 1966, 6; Gene Damon, "Reader at Large," *Tangents*, December 1966, 25.

69. For the "ideal of interracialism," see Susan Manning, review of Jennifer Dunning, *Alvin Ailey: A Life in Dance* (1996), *Chicago Tribune Book Review*, 6 October 1966.

70. Alan Rich, "The Met's Season—Last but Not Least," *New York Herald Tribune*, 17 April 1966; "The New Met and Its Old Master," *Newsweek*, 19 September 1966, 78; *Time* cover, 23 September 1966.

71. William Smith, *The Irresponsible Arts* (New York, 1964), 137, 144.

72. "The New Opera House—A Triumph of Technology," *Newsweek*, 19 September 1966, 77.

73. Lerman, "The New Met," 179, 180 ("remindful," etc., "Enormous"); Kupferberg, "Barber, the Bard, and the Barge," 126.

74. Lerman, "The New Met," 180.

75. "Opera: Lord of the Manor" (cover article), *Time*, 23 September 1966, 46; Robert Kotlowitz, "On the Midway at Lincoln Center," *Harper's*, December 1966, 136 ("Lady Bird J"); Shana Alexander, "Culture's Big Super-Event," *Life*, 30 September 1966, 30B; "A Night at the Opera," *Newsweek*, 26 September 1966, 40.

76. "Tony and Cleo," *Newsweek*, 16 September 1966, 98; Shana Alexander, "Culture's," 30B; Maurice Essam, music director of WNCN, review, 16 September 1966, typescript in Metropolitan Opera Archives, New York City; Robert J. Landry, "Tres Chic Chi Bow of $45 Million Metop Faces Very Chilly 'Antony and Cleopatra," *Variety*, 21 September 1966. Many of the reviews and other articles on *Antony* quoted here and below were found in the Clippings File, Metropolitan Opera Archives, New York City.

77. Peter Heyworth, "Miscarriage at the New Met," *London Observer Weekend Review*, 18 September 1966 ("nebulous," etc.); Miles Kastendieck, "'Cleo' in Shining Debut," *New York World Journal Tribune*, 17 September 1966; Winthrop Sergeant, "Musical Events," *New Yorker*, 24 September 1966, 116, 119 ("Barber," etc.); Max de Schauensee, "'Antony and Cleopatra' Bows at New Met Opening," *Philadelphia Bulletin*, 17 September 1966 ("thrills," "choral," "keenly"); Desmond Shawe-Taylor, "Glitter at the New Met," *London Times*, 18 September 1966 ("beautifully"). For an example of how crit-

ics had judged *Vanessa* slow to get going, see Winthrop Sargeant, "Musical Events," *New Yorker*, 25 January 1958, 108.

78. For "Massive Everything," see section heading in "Opera: Lord of the Manor," *Time*, 46; Harold Schonberg, "Onstage, It Was 'Antony and Cleopatra,'" *New York Times*, 17 September 1966; Shana Alexander, "Culture's."

79. As Winthrop Sargeant predicted it would: see "Musical Events," *New Yorker*, 24 September 1966, 114.

80. *Time*, 23 September 1966, 51; Schonberg, "Onstage, It Was 'Antony and Cleopatra,'" *New York Times*, 17 September 1966; Joseph E. Evans, "Dreams Come True," *Wall Street Journal*, 19 September 1966; Roland Gelatt, "Opening Night at the Met," *High Fidelity/Musical America*, November 1966, MA-9 ("snatches"); *Newsweek*, 26 September 1966, 98.

81. See, for example, Sargeant, "Musical Events," 24 September 1966, *New Yorker*, 116.

82. See Melani Mcalister, *Epic Encounters: Culture, Media, and U.S. Interests in the Middle East, 1945–2000* (Berkeley, 2001), chapter 2, for a perceptive treatment of these films.

83. The analysis here is largely mine, but see also Jon Solomon, "The Spectacle of Samuel Barber's *Antony and Cleopatra*," in *Opera and the Golden West: The Past, Present, and Future of Opera in the U.S.A.*, ed. John L. Gaetani and Josef P. Sirefman (Rutherford, N.J., 1994), 244–54.

84. Harriet Johnson, "A Surprise in the Met's Splendor," *New York Post*, 17 September 1966, refers to "the glamorous Negro soprano"; Emily Coleman, "Leontyne Makes a Date with History," *New York Times*, 11 September 1966; "Met's 'Antony & Cleopatra' Glamorous but Complex," *Minneapolis Star*, 17 September 1966 (on Ailey).

85. Alan Rich, "Barber's Opera: Slick & Chic," *New York World Journal Tribune*, 2 October 1966; Heyworth, "Miscarriage"; *Bell Telephone Hour*, "The New Met: Countdown to Curtain," 22 November 1966, copy at the Metropolitan Opera Media and TV Department.

86. Schonberg, "Onstage, It Was 'Antony and Cleopatra,'" *New York Times*, 17 September 1966. The "artifice" quotation got recycled: see David Ewen, ed., *Composers since 1900: A Biographical and Critical Guide* (New York, 1969), 31; and Stanley Kauffmann, "Tenor on Horseback," *New Republic*, 22 October 1966, 23–24.

87. "Opera: Lord of the Manor," *Time*, 46.

88. Kevin Kelly, "Too Few Arias, Too Late," probably *Boston Globe*, n.d. ("subtle"); Douglas Watt column, "Small World," probably *New York Daily News*, 19 September 1966 ("fizzle"); "The Met Opens in the Blaze of Its New Home," *Life*, 20 September 1966, 35 ("chilly," "lacking"); Heyworth, "Miscarriage" ("waspish," etc.); "Singers, Not Score, Praised at Met," *Hartford Times*, 17 September 1966 ("seemed"). All as found in Metropolitan Opera Archives Clippings File, New York City.

89. Susan Sontag, "Notes on Camp" (1964), in Susan Sontag, *Against Interpretation and Other Essays* (New York, 1966), 282.

90. Hubbs, *Queer Composition*, 176.

91. Harold C. Schonberg, *The Lives of the Great Composers* (New York, 1970), 550; "a hideously," as quoted in the obituary on Schoenberg by Allan Kozinn, *New York Times*, 27 July 2003.

92. Schonberg, *Lives*, 353, 354.

93. Wallock, *New York*, 14; Rockwell, "New York's Music," 235. Other essays in this volume also point to the mid-1960s as a moment of cultural crisis, and to a degree of eclipse, for the city.

94. Schuman, press release of speech to Friends of the Kennedy Center, 18 May 1967, in Schuman Speeches Folder, William Schuman Collection, Special Collections of the New York Public Library—Performing Arts, New York City.

95. Letter, Bing to Barber, 11 November 1966, Metropolitan Opera Archives, New York City; *Time*, 23 September 1966, 53. Bing later "admitted that he had overdone things himself in those opening weeks"; see Herbert Kupferberg, "Frank Appraisal by Bing," *New York World Journal Tribune*, 17 April 1967. On applause, see Gelatt, "Opening Night," MA-10.

96. Stephen E. Rubin, *The New Met in Profile* (New York, 1974), 150–51 (Schippers), 66 (Price). Chapter 8 is titled "The Token Black Who Paid Her Dues: Leontyne Price."

97. Entry on Franco Zeffirelli, *glbtg: An Encyclopedia of Gay, Lesbian, Bisexual, Transgender, and Queer Culture* (glbtg inc.: entry copyright 2002), <www .glbtg.com/arts>; *Opera in the Twentieth Century—Part II (1940–1970)*, entry on Samuel Barber: *Antony and Cleopatra*, author/date not indicated, <http: //homepage.mac.com/wincfar/Opera>; Phillip Huscher, program notes, Chicago Symphony Orchestra, 24/25/26/29 October 1991 (all-Barber program), 30 ("a failure so grand"); Heyman, *Barber*, 461 (publisher), 462.

98. Ned Rorem, *Pure Contraption: A Composer's Essays* (New York, 1974), 130; Ned Rorem, *Settling the Score: Essays on Music* (San Diego, 1988), 49 (essay dated 1975); Rorem, *Knowing*, 323, 192 (on Barber and Menotti), 266 ("maybe best"); Gruen, *Menotti*, 68 (Barber). The tensions in Rorem's recollections call into question their reliability regarding a figure in his life as charged as Barber.

99. Winthrop Sargeant, "Musical Events: Hearing Barber Plain," *New Yorker*, 18 December 1971, 116; Rorem, *Settling the Score*, 49, 50; Leighton Kerner, "Amendments and Amends," *Village Voice*, 24 February 1975, on electric guitar; Anthony Tommasini, "Another Chance for a Notorious Work," *New York Times*, 10 April 2003; item in previews of "Classical Music," *New Yorker*, 7 April 2003, 23–24; Heyman, *Barber*, 460; Slonimsky, *Music since 1900*, 775.

264 100. John Gruen, "And Where Has Samuel Barber Been . . . ?" *New York Times*,

3 October 1971; Heyman, *Barber*, 428. Barber "has no identifiable style," Rorem wrote in his diary several months later (Rorem, *Later Diaries*, 391 [23 March 1972 entry]), but he may have uttered the thought earlier, and Barber may have been responding to it in his 1971 comments.

101. Eric Salzman, "Samuel Barber," *HiFi/Stereo Review*, October 1966, 79 (*Sadness*), 78; Kupferberg, "Barber, the Bard, and the Barge," 128.

102. Heyman, *Barber*, 501–2 (birthday), 467 ("I often"), 464 ("The texts"), 465 ("more dissonant," etc.), 490 (*Three Songs*).

103. Sargeant quoted in Ardoin, *Stages of Menotti*, 10–11; on Stravinsky's influence, see 13.

104. Kate Hevner Mueller, *Twenty-seven major American Symphony Orchestras: A History and Analysis of Their Repertoires, Seasons 1842–43 through 1969–70* (Bloomington, Ind., 1973), xxx.

105. Kolodin, "Music to My Ears," *Saturday Review*, 23 October 1971, 14–15; Henahan, quoted in Heyman, *Barber*, 471–72.

106. See Daniel Belgrad, *The Culture of Spontaneity: Improvisation and the Arts in Postwar America* (Chicago, 1998), quotations from 1, 6; and Rorem, *Knowing*, 308.

107. Cage, quoted in Howard Brick, *Age of Contradiction: American Thought and Culture in the 1960s* (1998; Ithaca, N.Y., 2000), 139. Brick, *Age of Contradiction*, chapter 6, has informed this section on authenticity and spontaneity.

108. For quotations about and a brief portrait of Cage, see John Gill, "A Minute's Noise for John Cage," in Gill, *Queer Noises*, 26–35. For Cage's influence in the visual arts, see Kay Larson, "Cage Was Not Only All Ears, He Was All Eyes, Too," *New York Times*, 4 February 2001.

109. Hubbs, *Queer Composition*, 149.

110. Howard Pollack, *Aaron Copland: The Life and Work of an Uncommon Man* (New York, 1999), 516 (Bernstein); Heinsheimer, "Birth of an Opera," *Saturday Review*, 17 September 1966, 50.

111. Rorem, *Settling the Score*, 43. Nadine Hubbs, "Bernstein's Mass Appeal: Homophobia as *Dramatis Persona*, Dirty Laundry as Cultural Knowledge" (unpublished manuscript), offers an acute reading of Bernstein and his public reputation. *ER* episode viewed 2 October 2003; *South Park* episode viewed 27 May 2004.

112. Copland and Perlis, *Copland since 1943*, 189.

113. Wilcox, *Britten's Operas*, 8; Alex Ross, "Musical Events: The Battle of Britten," *New Yorker*, 16 December 1996, 100 ("making a").

114. David Denby, "The Gift to Be Simple," *New Yorker*, 13 December 1999, 109.

115. Alan Kozinn, "Listeners Love Samuel Barber? Well, So What?" *New York Times*, 8 June 1999. Kozinn offers useful general observations as well.

116. Mac Randall, "A Composer Who Took as Many Knocks as Bows," *New York Times*, 20 May 2001.

117. Dirk Olin, "Western Musical World Back on Tchaikovsky the . . ." (title incomplete in original), *New York Times Magazine*, 8 December 2002, 49, 52.
118. Denby, "The Gift to Be Simple," 102.
119. Hubbs, *Queer Composition*, 4, asks: "How did these artists compose a nation?" Hubbs also maintains a familiar distinction: "Barber's work, like Copland's, is decidedly American music, but, unlike Copland's, it is not 'America' music" (3). That is, Barber's music is not taken as offering representations of America. Her distinction may presuppose that Americans like affirmation and nostalgia (what Copland's music is used to evoke) but not loss and mourning (what Barber's music is used to evoke), except when unavoidable: Americans have not seen loss and mourning as essential constituents of the American character. But a turn toward mourning and memorial culture late in the twentieth century, and even more after 9/11, suggests that understandings of that character may be changing, making Barber's work more "America" music. On that possibility, see Michael S. Sherry, "Death, Mourning, and Memorial Culture, 1945–2005," in *Columbia History of Postwar United States*, ed. Mark Carnes (Columbia University Press, forthcoming).
120. Alex Ross, "Musical Events: Native Sons," *New Yorker*, 17 February 1997, 96.
121. At best, Pears was his "life-long friend," while the *Sunday Telegraph* only inferred "a still more private anguish" from "the explicitness of his last opera, *Death in Venice*. See Gill, "Burying Benjamin Britten," in Gill, *Queer Noises*, 20.
122. Solomon, "Spectacle of Samuel Barber's *Antony and Cleopatra*," 252 ("boyhood"); Juilliard School, program notes for *Vanessa*, 11, 13, and 15 December 1991, Performing Arts Files, New York Public Library—Performing Arts.
123. Hubbs, *Queer Composition*, 1–2.
124. Alex Ross, "Musical Events: The Battle of Britten," *New Yorker*, 16 December 1996, 102; Alex Ross, "Critic's Notebook: The Gay Connection in Music and in a Festival," *New York Times*, 27 June 1994.
125. Quoted in K. Robert Schwarz, "Classical Music: Composers' Closets Open for All to See," *New York Times*, 19 June 1994.
126. The survey is Michael Kammen, *American Culture, American Tastes: Social Change and the 20th Century* (New York, 1999); Barbara Heyman, Letter to the Editor, *New York Times*, 10 July 1996.

Chapter Five
1. Tom Burke, "The New Homosexuality," *Esquire*, December 1969, 178ff.
2. John Murphy, "Queer Books," in *Out of the Closets: Voices of Gay Liberation*, ed. Karla Jay and Allen Young (twentieth anniversary ed. with foreword by John D'Emilio, New York, 1992), 87; Peter Fisher, *The Gay Mystique: The Myth and Reality of Male Homosexuality* (New York, 1972), 221, 219; C. A. Tripp, *The Homosexual Matrix*, 2nd ed. (New York, 1987), 259.

3. Benjamin DeMott, "But He's a Homosexual . . . ," in *New American Review* 1 (September 1967): 166–82; and in Benjamin DeMott, *Supergrow: Essays and Reports on Imagination in America* (New York, 1969), 17–34.

4. Jay and Young, *Out of the Closets*, 70–71 (on Williams), 81 (on Rorem), 266–67 ("decorators").

5. Allen Young, "No Longer the Court Jesters," in *Lavender Culture*, ed. Karla Jay and Allen Young (1978; New York, 1979), 23–47; see also Karla Jay, "No Man's Land," in ibid., 48–65.

6. Jay and Young, *Out of the Closets*, 271 ("game"), 89 ("as if").

7. Ibid., 22 (Young); Dennis Altman, *Homosexual Oppression and Liberation* (New York, 1971), 221–22 (Altman), 198–99 (Cleaver), 202 (Newton).

8. Martin, quoted in Altman, *Homosexual Oppression and Liberation*, 209; Murphy, "Queer Books," in Jay and Young, *Out of the Closets*, 86.

9. Jay and Young, *Out of the Closets*, 33 (Shelley), 29.

10. Roger N. Lancaster, *The Trouble with Nature: Sex in Science and Popular Culture* (Berkeley, 2003), 7.

11. Ibid., 7.

12. Altman, *Homosexual Oppression and Liberation*, 33, 142, 170, 151; Carl Driver, in *Advocate*, as quoted in John Francis Hunter, *The Gay Insider/USA* (New York, 1972), 79.

13. John Simon, *Uneasy Stages: A Chronicle of the New York Theater, 1963–1973* (New York, 1975), 81–82, 149; Pauline Kael, *5001 Nights at the Movies* (1982; New York, 1991), 478–79, 728.

14. Kael, *5001 Nights*, 98; Ronald Forsythe (pseudonym), "Why Can't 'We' Live Happily Ever After, Too?" *New York Times*, 23 February 1969.

15. Edmund White, *States of Desire: Travels in Gay America* (New York, 1980), 5; Altman, *Homosexual Oppression and Liberation*, 167.

16. For many of these trends, especially regional changes and country music, see Bruce Schulman, *The Seventies: The Great Shift in American Culture, Society, and Politics* (New York, 2001).

17. Jonathan Dollimore, *Sexual Dissidence: Augustine to Wilde, Freud to Foucault* (New York, 1991), 22.

18. Altman, *Homosexual Oppression and Liberation*, 52.

19. Robert Dawidoff, "In My Father's House Are Many Closets," in Robert Dawidoff, *Making History Matter* (Philadelphia, 2000), 94.

20. Paul Rosenfels, M.D., *Homosexuality: The Psychology of the Creative Process* (Roslyn Heights, N.Y., 1971).

21. Michael S. Sherry, *In the Shadow of War: The United States since the 1930s* (New Haven, 1995), 302.

22. Nixon White House tapes, Conversations 571-1, 13 September 1971, made available to the author on CD by the Nixon Presidential Materials Staff, National Archives and Records Administration, College Park, Md. I was first alerted to these conversations by James Warren, "The Etiquette of Social

Kissing," *Chicago Tribune*, 22 January 2003, whose transcription closely resembles mine.

23. James McCourt, *Queer Street: Rise and Fall of an American Culture, 1947–1985* (New York, 2004), 240.

24. Joan Peyser, *Bernstein: A Biography* (New York, 1987), 414; as Peyser notes, the Hoover memo was published in Jack Anderson, *The Anderson Papers* (New York, 1973).

25. Peyser, *Bernstein*, 415, 414.

26. Harold C. Schonberg, "Bernstein's New Work Reflects His Background on Broadway," *New York Times*, 9 September 1971; Harold C. Schonberg, "On the Risk of Playing It Safe," *New York Times*, 19 September 1971.

27. Harold Schonberg, "The Kennedy Center: What Might Have Been," *New York Times*, 12 September 1971; Ada Louise Huxtable, "Architecture: A Look at the Kennedy Center," *New York Times*, 7 September 1971; Clive Barnes review, *New York Times*, 9 September 1971. See also Nan Robertson, "Ex-Foes and Supporters of Aid to Arts Hear Mass," *New York Times*, 8 September 1971.

28. Midge Decter, "The Boys on the Beach," *Commentary*, August 1980, 35–48. Most of the essay, but with some vicious passages deleted, appears in *Columbia Reader on Lesbians and Gay Men in Media, Society, and Politics*, ed. Larry Gross and James D. Woods (New York, 1999), 601–11.

29. Joseph Epstein, "Homo/Hetero: The Struggle for Sexual Identity," *Harper's*, September 1970, 37–44. Details about the controversy this piece set loose and Decter's role are in Charles Kaiser, *The Gay Metropolis: 1940–1996* (New York, 1997), 225; Edward Alwood, *Straight News: Gays, Lesbians, and the News Media* (New York, 1996), 103–5; and Dudley Clendinen and Adam Nagourney, *Out for Good: The Struggle to Build a Gay Rights Movement in America* (New York, 1999), 66–68. See also David Ehrenstein, "Sexual Snobbery: The Texture of Joseph Epstein," *L.A. Weekly* 24 (30 August–5 September 2002), <www.ehrensteinland.com> (15 August 2003).

30. See Nancy MacLean, *Freedom Is Not Enough: The Opening of the American Workplace* (New York, 2006), chapter 6.

31. Vidal, quoted in Ehrenstein, "Sexual Snobbery"; letters and Decter's response appeared in *Commentary*, December 1980, 6–20.

32. White, *States of Desire*, 47; McCourt, *Queer Street*.

33. White, *States of Desire*, 237–39.

34. Mark Ravenhill, "Looking Back Warily at a Heterosexual Classic," *New York Times*, 17 October 1999; op-ed by Mark Stevens, "Form Follows Fascism," *New York Times*, 31 January 2005.

35. See letter by Steblin and reply by Rosen, *New York Review of Books*, 20 October 1994, <nybooks.com/articles/2116> (10 February 2006).

36. Allan Kozinn, "As American as Copland, Who Forged Our New Sound," *New York Times*, 29 July 2005.

37. "Ovitz Bitterly Bares Soul, and Film Industry Reactions," *New York Times*, 3 July 2002.

38. Patrick Healy, "College Recruiters Look for Gays," *Boston Globe*, 21 May 2002; Lowell Ponte, <FrontPageMagazine.com>, 23 May 2002 (accessed 13 October 2003).

39. Julia Keller, "Hosting the Hip May Be the Best Urban Planning," *Chicago Tribune*, 11 August 2002; the skeptic quoted by the *Tribune* was Northwestern University lecturer Bill Savage. Richard Florida, *The Rise of the Creative Class, and How It's Transforming Work, Leisure, Community and Everyday Life* (New York, 2002), 256, 257, 262–63, 256, 258; p. x gives the book's version of that "Eureka moment"—"the real stunner," as the book calls it.

40. Karen Lehrman, "Does It Come in Chrome"? *New York Times Book Review*, 16 November 2003, 52; Cathy Crimmins, *How the Homosexuals Saved Civilization: The True and Heroic Story of How Gay Men Shaped the Modern World* (New York, 2004).

41. Young, "No Longer the Court Jesters"; John Weir, "Queer Guy with a Slob's Eye," *New York Times*, 10 August 2003.

42. Andrew Sullivan, *Virtually Normal: An Argument about Homosexuality* (New York, 1995).

43. In Robert Dawidoff, *Making History Matter* (Philadelphia, 2000), 84–99.

44. Michael Bronski, "Stolen Goods," in Gross and Woods, *Columbia Reader*, 245–51.

45. Daniel Harris, *The Rise and Fall of Gay Culture* (New York, 1997), 6, 36–38, 34, 5. James Bohling, review of Harris's book, *International Gay and Lesbian Review*, 1998, <cellar.usc.edu:9673/reviews/iglr/review> (30 July 2003).

46. Howard Helvey, letter to the editor, *Gay and Lesbian Review*, January–February 2002, 5; Rex Wockner, "Quotelines," *Windy City Times*, 15 April 2002, quoting "Tunku Varadarajan writing in *The Wall Street Journal*, March 15" (my emphasis).

47. "Finding Homosexual Threads in Lincoln's Legend," *New York Times*, 16 December 2004.

48. Michael Warner, *The Trouble with Normal: Sex, Politics, and the Ethics of Queer Life* (New York, 1999), 52, 59, 74, 75.

49. Altman, *Homosexual Oppression and Liberation*, 220, 221; Devon W. Carbado, Dwight A. McBride, and Donald Weise, eds., *Black Like Us: A Century of Lesbian, Gay and Bisexual African American Fiction* (San Francisco, 2002), xiv.

50. Guy Trebay, "The Subtle Power of Lesbian Style," *New York Times*, 27 June 2004, quoting Valerie Steele, museum director of the Fashion Institute of Technology.

51. Sarah Schulman, *My American History: Lesbian and Gay Life during the Reagan/Bush Years* (New York, 1994), 272, 323, xi (Vaid), xviii; Stacey D'Erasmo, "Lesbians on Television: It's Not Easy Being Seen," *New York Times*, 11 January 2004.

52. "American Culture's Debt to Gay Sons of Harvard," *New York Times*, 29 May 2003.

53. Jess Green, "When Political Art Mattered," *New York Times Magazine*, 7 December 2003.

54. Joan Acocella, "No Bloody Toe Shoes," *New York Review of Books*, 26 February 2004, 7; Mark Benjamin, "The 'Ex-Gay' Agenda," *Gay and Lesbian Review*, November/December 2005, 26–31.

55. John Bayley, "Sex and the City," *New York Review of Books*, 25 March 2004, 18; Nadine Hubbs, *The Queer Composition of America's Sound: Gay Modernists, American Music, and National Identity* (Berkeley, 2004), 17.

56. Andrew Sullivan, "The End of Gay Culture," *New Republic*, 24 October 2005; <www.andrewsullivan.com> (27 November 2004).

57. Dollimore, *Sexual Dissidence*, 26–27.

58. *New York Times*, 14 August 2003 (on Lypsinka) and 12 August 2003 (on *Matt and Ben*); McCourt, *Queer Street*, 112 (on La Gran Scena).

59. Susie Day, "Incident at Swan Lake," *Windy City Times*, 13 August 2003; Paul Rudnick, "The Godfathers," *New Yorker*, 9 September 2002, 164; Rudnick, quoted in "Out & Out," *New York Times*, 1 February 2004; Lawrence Sharpless, "Who Do I Have to Blow to Win the Bancroft Prize in American History?" *Onion* 38, no. 2 (23 January 2002): 1.

60. Vito Russo, *The Celluloid Closet: Homosexuality in the Movies*, rev. ed. (New York, 1987), 326.

INDEX

Abstract Expressionism, 167

Accommodation, 235–38

Acheson, Dean, 67

Acocella, Joan, 234

Adams, John, 214; *Nixon in China*, 6

Adams, Rachel, 241 (n. 7)

Adorno, Theodor, 160–61

Advise and Consent (Otto Preminger, 1962), 70, 106–7, 114–16

Advocate, 210

African Americans: and Thomson/Stein opera, 26; activism of, 113, 138, 190, 208, 213; authenticity of, 123; Dvořák on, 157

African Americans in arts: reaction to, 1; cultural evaluation of, 28, 236; and dependence/revulsion tension, 41; and communities of identity, 86, 91; and Baldwin, 94; cultural moment of, 103; restriction on themes of, 133; Hitler on, 135; and Price, 186, 191

Agee, James, 158

Agnew, Spiro, 217

The Agony and the Ecstasy (film, 1965), 111

AIDS, 196, 215, 223–24, 228, 234

AIDS Quilt Song Book, 3

Ailey, Alvin, 179–80, 181, 186, 191, 218, 220

Albee, Edward: as dominant figure, 44; and Lerner, 78; and homosexual themes, 128; *Who's Afraid of Virginia Woolf*, 130, 139, 209; Kauffmann on, 131; *Tiny Alice*, 131; Marine on, 138; portrayals of women, 139; dethroning of, 191;

DeMott on, 205; Simon on, 210; reputation of, 214; and postmodernism, 215; Decter on, 222; and accommodation, 236

All about Eve (Joseph L. Mankiewicz, 1950), 33, 84–85

Allen, Frederick Lewis, 19

Allen, Maud, 15

Allende, Salvador, 193

All in the Family (television series), 4–5, 6, 216–17

Alsop, Joseph, 70

Altman, Dennis, 102, 105, 107, 208, 209, 214, 232

Amelie (film, 2001), 198

American Composers Orchestra, 192

American culture: shallowness of, 34; men's dominance of, 39; inferiority of, 40–41, 126; definition of, 46–48, 50; movement across high, mid, and popular culture, 48–49; masculine robustness of, 64–65, 87, 123; gays as cultural outsiders, 88–102; and prizing of bigness, 101; maturing of, 101–2; gay magazines addressing, 111; anxieties about, 183; lack of coherence in, 214. *See also* Cultural empire; Gay people's role in American culture; Mass culture; Popular culture

American Home, 156

American Indians, 157

American Mercury, 33

American National Exhibition in Moscow (1959), 125, 126

American Nazi Party, 114

American POWs, 78

American Psychiatric Association, 211

America's Homosexual Underground, 135

Amory, Richard: *Song of the Loon*, 210

Anderson, Robert, 59

Angelou, Maya, 236

Angels in America (Mike Nichols, 2001), 224

Anti-Semitism, 11, 43, 73, 75, 95

Architecture, 49

Ardoin, John, 112

Aristotle, 5

Armed forces, 37, 39, 42, 97, 140

Armstrong, Louis, 41

Arnold, "Hap," 162

Arthur, Jean, 81

Artists: as Cold War weapons, 1; as emblems of nation's freedom, 2, 126; and institutional nature of arts, 86, 98. *See also* Gay artists

Arts criticism: and evolution of artistic forms, 9; and homosexual characters, 19–20, 128, 129–30, 131; and national identity of composers, 21, 24–26; and American cultural inferiority, 40–41; and definition of American music, 46; and authenticity, 125, 134, 195, 224; homosexuals as scapegoats of, 140; and progress, 159, 165, 189; and mass culture, 185

Arvin, Newton, 46, 48, 77, 79, 90, 92

Ashberry, John, 96–97, 233

Assimilation, 228–35, 236, 237

Attica prison, 218, 220

Auden, W. H., 11, 28, 42, 93, 168, 205

Authenticity: language of, 1, 124, 129; gay artists depicted as inauthentic, 1–2, 102, 124–25, 128–34, 138, 141, 191, 224; politics of, 114–25, 138, 255 (n. 32); anxiety about,

121–23, 125; and private and public self, 122, 123, 124, 129, 134, 141, 195; changing definitions of, 135, 136; and Barber, 195–96; and gay liberation, 208–9; and American leaders, 213; of gay creativity, 235

Avant-garde art, 126, 163–64, 191

Babbit, Milton, 98, 200

Bach, Johann Sebastian, 159

Baker, Jean H., 232

Baldwin, James: and multiple identities, 9, 38; homosexuality of, 37; place in cultural life, 44, 49, 236; typecasting of fiction, 47; treatment of homosexual identity, 60; and Left, 77; *Giovanni's Room*, 81, 138; and foreign locales, 82; relationship to Europe, 92; and interaction of identities, 94–95; relationship with academy, 99; on authenticity, 122, 124; on masculinity, 125; and Barber, 175, 177, 203; Cleaver on, 208; and Altman, 209; criticism of, 214; and gay culture, 231

Bankhead, Tallulah, 166

Barber, Samuel: Violin Concerto, 3–4, 199; homosexuality of, 4, 156, 161, 166, 167, 179, 181, 198, 199, 201, 202; biography of, 9, 202; and interwar era, 23; and Menotti, 23, 24, 27, 38, 82, 92, 93, 156, 157, 159–60, 165–69, 179, 193, 194–95, 201, 202–3; manliness of, 24, 156; *Overture to "The School for Scandal,"* 25, 155; as American composer, 26, 46, 48, 157, 158, 159, 164–65, 200–201, 236, 266 (n. 119); and open secret, 38, 166, 169, 173; armed forces sponsors music by, 39, 161–63, 175;

confidence of, 40; as established
figure, 44; and mainstream, 44,
231; *Adagio for Strings*, 45, 46, 48,
158–59, 160, 167, 197, 200, 216;
and Graham, 47; and modernism,
49, 157–58, 159, 163, 194, 200;
and UNESCO, 73; and foreign
locales, 82; and Congress of Soviet
Composers, 126; family background of, 155; and homintern
discourse, 155, 187, 190, 206;
and European influence, 157–58,
162; *Symphony in One Movement*,
158; *Essays for Orchestra*, 158, 161;
Knoxville: Summer of 1915, 158,
163, 165; and international style,
158, 169; Sonata for Piano, 159;
String Quartet, 159; *Agnus Dei*,
159, 198; and patronage, 159–60,
174; and high culture, 159–60,
189; nonpartisanism of, 161; *A
Stopwatch and an Ordnance Map*,
161; Second Symphony ("Flight"),
162, 175; *Capricorn Concerto*, 163;
Melodies passageres, 163; *Nocturne*,
163; Piano Sonata, 163; *Prayers of
Kierkegaard*, 163; Cello Concerto,
163, 165; *Hermit Songs*, 163, 165;
Medea, 163, 167, 192; Pulitzer
Prizes of, 164, 173, 174; *Vanessa*,
164–65, 166, 167, 173, 174, 175,
177, 183, 188, 191, 201; and serial
music, 168; *A Hand of Bridge*,
168–69, 174, 175, 179, 260 (n. 38);
and cultural exchange, 173; opera
commission for Lincoln Center
opening, 173–76; Piano Concerto,
173–74; *Andromache's Farewell*,
174; *Antony and Cleopatra*, 176–
88, 189, 190, 191, 192–94, 195,
197, 198, 217, 219; *Sadness*, 193;
The Lovers, 193, 194, 195; *Third
Essay for Orchestra*, 194; *Three

Songs*, 194; *Despite and Still*, 195;
and authenticity, 195–96; ap-
peal to wider audiences, 198–99;
and postmodernism, 200, 215;
relevancy of, 206; reputation of,
214
Bare, 31, 35
Barkley, Alben, 27
Barnes, Clive, 220
Barr, James: *Quatrefoil*, 89
Barrett, William, 13–14
Batman (television show), 56
Battcock, Gregory, 140
Bauer, Marion, 25
Baxter, Anne, 84
Bayley, John, 15, 236
Beaton, Cecil, 164
Becker, Howard, 80
Beethoven, Ludwig van, 21, 159;
    Ninth Symphony, 21
Belgrad, Daniel, 196
Bellow, Saul, 9
Bell Telephone Hour, 48, 186
Benedict, Ruth, 79–80
Bentley, Gladys, 17
Berg, Alban, 4, 188
Bergler, Edmund: on homosexuality,
    51, 52–55, 56, 79, 134; on fash-
    ion industry, 54, 56, 99; on gay
    creativity, 60, 104; and cultural
    empire, 64; and urban pathology,
    84; Helmer on, 87; and labeling of
    homosexuality, 129
Berle, Milton, 33, 34
Bernstein, Elmer, 85
Bernstein, Leonard: Symphony No. 3,
    "Kadish," 4; and open secret, 38;
    and League of Composers, 43; and
    mainstream, 44; and Copland,
    45, 169–70, 197; *On the Town*, 46,
    47; and Comden, 47; *Candide*, 47,
    173, 175; satire of, 48; masculine
    nature of music, 64; marriage and

family of, 93, 167, 197; *West Side Story*, 95, 167; and cultural exchange, 126; *The Age of Anxiety*, 163; on American music, 164; homosexuality of, 167, 181, 196, 197, 233; and international art, 169–70; Schonberg on, 188; and Barber, 192; and Kennedy Center honors, 199; as Jewish, 202; reputation of, 214; and postmodernism, 215; *Mass*, 217, 218–20; and Berrigans, 218
Berrigan, Daniel, 217–18
Berrigan, Philip, 217–18
The Best Man (film, 1964), 70
Bicentennial festivities, 198, 216
Bieber, Irving, 53, 55, 57
Bing, Rudolf, 170, 171–72, 173, 177, 180, 185–87, 190, 191
Black Panthers, 217, 220
Blitzstein, Marc, 47, 112, 166; *The Cradle Will Rock*, 47
Bloch, Ernest: *Schelomo, Hebraic Rhapsody for Cello and Orchestra*, 4
Bloom, Allan, 224
Bogarde, Dirk, 109, 254 (n. 11)
Bohlen, Charles "Chip," 69, 70–71, 74, 119
Bohn, Jerome, 112
Boise, Idaho, 84, 139–40
Bok, Mary Curtis, 159
Boorstin, Daniel, 101, 121–22
Boston Globe, 226
Botstein, Leon, 245 (n. 72)
Boulanger, Nadia, 43, 157, 192, 201
Boulez, Pierre, 164, 194, 214
Bournet, Edouard: *The Captive*, 19–20
Bowles, Paul, 28
Bowra, Maurice, 42
Boys Clubs, 5

The Boys in the Band (William Friedkin, 1970), 211–12
Brahms, Johannes, 55, 157, 158, 200, 201
Brando, Marlon, 47
Brett, Philip, 9, 18, 22, 102
Brick, Howard, 122, 124, 255 (n. 32)
Bright, Susie, 233
Britten, Benjamin: and modernism, 4; professional circles of, 28; and Walton, 32; *Paul Bunyan*, 45, 176; Wilson on, 77; and Pears, 93, 156–57, 166–67, 176; homosexuality of, 94, 181, 198, 201, 202; assimilation of other composers, 158; *Billy Budd*, 176; *Gloriana*, 176; *Peter Grimes*, 176; *The Turn of the Screw*, 176; *War Requiem*, 176; *Midsummer Night's Dream*, 176, 180; Schonberg on, 188; and American orchestras, 195
Broadway Brevities, 16
Bronski, Michael, 229–30
Brooks, Richard, 59; *The Brick Foxhole*, 47–48
Brown, Howard, 211
Brown, Judith, 226
Brown, Rita Mae, 211
Browning, John, 174
Browning, Tod, 17
Bureau of Security and Consular Affairs, 73
Burns, John Horne: *The Gallery*, 61
Burton, Richard, 185
Busbey, Fred E., 72, 73, 74
Butler, Judith, 236

Cadmus, Paul: *The Fleet's In*, 16
Caesar, Julius, 18
Cage, John, 3, 44, 49–50, 102, 164, 169, 196–97, 258 (n. 12)
Califia, Pat, 232

Call, Hal, 86
Callas, Maria, 167
Camp, 124, 136–39, 188, 196, 197, 230, 237
Cant, Gilbert, 54
Cantor, Eddie, 34
Capote, Truman, 47, 77, 125, 139, 214; *Breakfast at Tiffany's*, 78
Carter, Elliott, 164, 214
Caruso, Enrico, 155
Cassidy, Claudia, 112
Catholic Church, 5, 57–58, 69–72, 88, 218
Cat on a Hot Tin Roof (Richard Brooks, 1958), 59–60
Catton, Bruce, 73
Caute, David, 70
Cavafy, Constantine, 91
CBS, 135
Chakiris, George, 95
Chambers, Whittaker: *Witness*, 75
Chauncey, George, 9, 18, 20, 36, 82, 122
Cheever, John, 215
Chekhov, Anton, 175
Chicago Lyric Opera, 192
Cho, Margaret, 224, 233, 234
Chopin, Frédéric, 22
CIA (Central Intelligence Agency), 39–40, 68, 70, 138, 212
Cinderfella (Frank Tashlin, 1960), 81
Civil rights activism, 114, 122
Cleaver, Eldridge, 208
Cleopatra (Joseph L. Mankiewicz, 1963), 185
Cliburn, Van, 88, 112, 126
Clift, Montgomery, 32, 46, 47, 59, 64, 81, 214
Clinton, Bill, 71
The closet: perceptions of, 8, 17; use of term, 96–97; and outsider model, 102; inventing of, 105–9;

and Barber, 156, 169, 179; and authenticity, 208; and cultural closet, 229. *See also* Coming out
Cohn, Roy, 68, 70, 74, 224
Cold War: and contribution of queer artists, 1; and cultural empire, 8, 38, 39–40, 42, 68, 87–88, 123, 125, 127, 171, 190, 212; homosexual menace of, 13; and masculinity, 29; consensus of, 60; Lerner on, 78; and dominant cultural values, 93; and conservatives, 119; and Tonkin Gulf incidents, 119; and anxiety about authenticity, 122–23; and cultural exchange, 125–27, 171, 173, 213; disruption of, 141; ebbing of, 224
Comden, Betty, 47
Comics, 56
Coming out: *One* magazine on, 96; defining of, 97; and authenticity, 141, 208; as revolutionary break-through, 209; shifts in embodi-ments of queerness, 211; and AIDS, 223–24. *See also* The closet
Comintern, 42–43
Commentary, 129–30, 221, 222
Communism: homosexuals asso-ciated with, 33, 34, 53, 56–57, 67, 118, 123; and cultural empire, 38, 39, 87; support and control of artists, 40; and moralism, 70
Communist International, 33, 42–43
Communist Party, 41, 208
Communities of identity, 86
Composers Recordings, Inc. (CRI): "Gay American Composers," 2–3
Compulsion (film), 107
Confidential magazine, 29–30, 32, 38, 84
Congress for Cultural Freedom, 39
Congress of Soviet Composers, 126

Connelly, Cyril, 42

Conrad, Florence, 60

Conservatives, 68, 119

Conspiracy thinking: and antigay
voices, 11, 243 (n. 40); and gay
presence in politics, 32; and
homintern discourse, 43, 113–
14, 135, 140, 204–5, 220; and
explanations for gay presence in
arts, 52–53, 87, 102, 104; and conspiracy of silence, 53; and urban
pathology, 84; and gays' role in
American culture, 108, 127; and
gay magazines, 110

Conversion therapy, 235

Cooney, Terry, 26

Cooper, James Fenimore, 81

Copland, Aaron: Appalachian Spring,
1, 45, 46; as queer artist vs.
American artist, 2, 7, 47, 199, 201;
Barber compared to, 4, 200–201,
266 (n. 119); biography of, 9, 22;
and interwar era, 23; manliness of,
24; and American music, 24–25,
28, 45–46, 47, 48, 75, 103, 158,
159, 165, 169, 198, 200–201, 216,
225, 236, 266 (n. 119); and Rorem,
25, 32, 191, 198; as leftist, 26, 67,
72–75, 103, 161; lifestyle of, 27;
rumors about, 32; confidence of,
40; and anti-Semitism, 43, 73; as
established figure, 44; and mainstream, 44, 231, 234, 236; Billy
the Kid, 45; Rodeo, 45; and modernism, 45, 49, 157; and Bernstein, 45, 169–70, 197; Fanfare
for the Common Man, 45, 200; and
Graham, 47; masculine nature of
music, 64; Lincoln Portrait, 72, 73,
198; Edmund Wilson on, 77; and
provincial places, 84; and space
for gay artists, 92; as mentor, 93;

197; as Jewish, 94, 103, 161, 202,
225; and Kennedy, 126; and trip
to Russia, 126; criticism of, 163;
film scores of, 167; and Spoleto
festival, 168; The Tender Land,
173, 198; and McCarthy, 175;
Schonberg on, 188; and American orchestras, 195; Connotations,
197; Old American Songs, 198; and
Kennedy Center honors, 199; and
postmodernism, 200; relevancy of,
206; reputation of, 214

Corber, Robert, 9, 60, 247–48 (n. 18)

Corcoran, Tommy, 119

Corey, Wendell, 81

Corigliano, John, 44, 89, 199, 228,
236; Of Rage and Remembrance,
228

Corporations, 40, 97, 98

Cory, Donald Webster: and gay artists as outsiders, 52; Cant on, 54;
and hostile majority, 79; and gay
creativity, 89, 90–91, 98, 99; and
gays as cultural outsiders, 89–
91, 92, 94, 95, 97, 98, 102; and
decoding, 122

Counterculture, 135, 138, 190, 205,
212

Country music, 215

Coward, Noel, 97, 102, 128, 174

Cowell, Henry, 3, 27, 161, 166

Crane, Hart, 46

Crimmins, Cathy, 227–28

Crossfire (film, 1947), 48

Crowley, Matt: The Boys in the Band,
210

Cukor, George, 46, 211

Cullen, Countee, 17

Cult of homosexual superiority, 35

Cultural Center Act (1958), 172

Cultural empire: and homintern
discourse, 1, 14; gay artists as

undermining, 2, 108; America's aspirations to, 8; and Cold War, 8, 38, 39–40, 42, 68, 87–88, 123, 125, 127, 171, 190, 212; and gay artists, 36–43, 103, 127, 161, 173, 206, 212; and communism, 38, 39, 87; and New York City, 169–72; and Barber, 175, 177, 189–90; momentum of, 212–13; changes in, 216; and Nixon, 219

Cunningham, Merce, 49, 196

Curtis, Tony, 85

Curtis Institute of Music, 155, 156

Dalai Lama, 97

Dance, 8, 44, 127, 134, 234

Daughters of Bilitis convention (1962), 110

Davis, Bette, 84–85

Dawidoff, Robert, 9, 229, 230

Day, Susie, 238

Dean, James, 62, 92

Dean, Robert, 69

Deardon, Basil, 109, 254 (n. 11)

Decter, Midge, 221–23, 228

DeGeneres, Ellen, 1, 226, 233

Del Tredici, David, 3

D'Emilio, John, 80, 105–6

DeMille, Cecil B., 182, 184

Democratic Party, 68

DeMott, Benjamin, 205–6

Denby, David, 198

Denning, Michael, 47

Dennis, Patrick, 128, 129; *Auntie Mame*, 128

D'Erasmo, Stacey, 233

Design, 49

Diamond, David, 44, 73

Dinesen, Isak, 175

Dizikes, John, 172

Dollimore, Jonathan, 215, 237

Dondero, George, 32, 42

Doty, Mark, 236

Douglas, Alfred, 15

Douglas, Kirk, 92, 117, 118

Downes, Olin, 25, 26

Dr. Strangelove or: How I Learned to Stop Worrying and Love the Bomb (Stanley Kubrick, 1964), 118

Drury, Allen: *Advise and Consent*, 70, 114–16, 119, 129

Duberman, Martin, 11, 233–34

Dulles, Allen, 39, 69

Dulles, John Foster, 69

Duncan, Robert, 35

Dvořák, Antonin, 21, 157; *From the New World*, 45

Eastman School of Music, 27

Edelman, Lee, 120–21, 254 (n. 21)

Ehrenreich, Barbara, 63–64

Ehrlichman, John, 5, 217

Einhorn, Robert, 200

Einstein, Albert, 48, 159

Eisenhower, Dwight, 40, 69, 72, 75, 126, 173, 198, 213

Elephant Man (film, 1980), 159, 197

Elizabeth II (queen of Great Britain and Northern Ireland), 32, 176

Ellington, Duke, 46, 47, 167, 236

Elliott, George P., 183

Ellis, Albert, 99–100

Ellis, Havelock, 24, 51, 169

Epperson, John, 237

Epstein, Joseph, 221

ER (television series), 198

Erickson, Leif, 59

Erikson, Erik, 123

Eschenbach, Christoph, 200

Esquire, 204

Europe: effect of World War II on cultural resources, 40, 169; American decadence linked with, 68; homosexuality linked with, 82, 92;

superiority of culture, 89, 157,
165, 171, 188; and camp, 136–37;
divisions between America and,
157, 158, 165, 173
Everett, Rupert, 225, 227
Exoticism, 80, 81, 82

Fact, 112, 113
Fadiman, Clifton, 28
Faggots, 136
Fail-Safe (Sidney Lumet, 1964), 116,
118
Fascism, 38, 40, 53, 56–57, 116
Fashion industry: Mannes on, 34–
35; Bergler on, 54, 56, 99; and
McCarthy, 67; Schlesinger on,
76; and urban pathology, 82, 83;
Helmer on, 87; and homosexual
clique, 107; and authenticity, 123,
133; homosexuals in, 124, 134
Faulkner, William, 49
FBI (Federal Bureau of Investiga-
tion), 68, 73, 74, 120
Federal government: and Lavender
Scare, 37, 74, 78; and cultural
empire, 39, 40; antigay hiring and
firing practices, 114; and support
for arts, 223. *See also* CIA; FBI;
U.S. State Department
Feldman, Morton, 169
Feminism, 78, 138, 190, 208, 209,
211, 213, 215, 233
Fiedler, Leslie, 77, 81, 98, 136
Films. *See* Movie industry
Finley, Karen, 224
Fischer-Dieskau, Dietrich, 195
Fisher, Peter: *The Gay Mystique*, 205
Fitzgerald, F. Scott, 49, 60
Florida, 114
Florida, Richard: *The Rise of the
Creative Class*, 226–27
Fonda, Henry, 115, 116
Fonteyn, Margot, 127

Ford, Henry, 182
A Foreign Affair (Billy Wilder, 1948),
81, 82
Forsythe, Ronald, 212
Fortas, Abe, 120
Foucault, Michel, 215
Frankenheimer, Anna, 112–13, 124
Frankenheimer, John, 116–17, 118
Frankfurt School, 160
Franklin, Benjamin, 72
Freak: use of term, 17, 241 (n. 7)
Freaks (Tod Browning, 1932), 17
Freeman, David, 66
Freud, Sigmund, 16, 19–20, 55, 57,
58, 66, 87
Friedan, Betty, 120, 123, 139; *The
Feminine Mystique*, 78–79
Friedkin, William, 211
Frisch, Max, 122
Frisch, Walter, 200
From Here to Eternity (film, 1953), 46,
48, 115
Fulbright, William, 182

Galupe-Borszkh, Vera, 238
Garboursova, Raya, 165
Gardner, Ava, 117
Garland, Judy, 204
Gates, Henry Louis, 236
The Gay and Lesbian Review, 231
Gay artists: depicted as inauthentic, 1–2, 102, 124–25, 128–34,
141, 191, 224; sources of identity,
24, 103–4; and cultural empire,
36–43, 103, 127, 161, 173, 206,
212; and postwar agitation about
discovery, 38; and modernism,
49–50; as pathological outsiders,
52–66; and political affiliations,
69, 70, 74; as cliquish, 77, 107,
108, 112, 124, 205; and urban
pathology, 83, 86; as cultural
outsiders, 88–102; and queer vs.

artistic identity, 93–94; cultural moment of, 103; and the closet, 107; and artificiality in campiness, 124, 136–38; as cultural ambassadors, 127

Gay bars, 16, 20, 61, 83, 92, 107, 221, 228

Gay creativity: relevance of, 3, 8; attitudes toward, 4; as dangerous, 5; and men's dominance of midcentury arts, 10, 17, 63, 103–4, 238; politics linked with, 67–68, 70; deviance linked to, 80; association with foreign locales, 82; Helmer on, 87; and gays as cultural outsiders, 88, 89–92, 97–98, 102, 103, 104; Ellis on, 99–100; stereotypes of, 112; Stainbrook on, 134; Sontag on, 137; and "The List," 140; as derivative, 197; Fisher on, 205; and gay liberation, 206–8; revolutionary potential of, 207; and AIDS, 224; Florida on, 227; and the closet, 229; and marginality, 231, 232, 236, 237; valuation of, 235–36

Gay culture, 190, 209, 221–22, 227, 230–33, 236–37

Gay liberation, 204–11, 213, 222, 223, 238

Gay marriage, 2

Gay people's role in American culture: discovery of, 14, 50, 51; comment on, in 1920s and 1930s, 14–18; and music, 15, 18–19, 20, 44–45, 102; enlargement of, 41, 44, 46, 47, 52; and homintern discourse, 44, 134–35, 138–39, 187, 212; and modernism, 49–50; explanations of, 51–52, 102–4; and urban pathology, 84; and gays as outsiders, 88–102; admission of, 202; diminishing of, 214;

and postmodernism, 214–15; as cultural resource, 226, 228

Gay presence in arts: and homintern, 1; and Lavender Scare, 13; mapping of, in 1920s and 1930s, 15–16, 18; agitation about, 16, 29–30, 34, 35, 36, 141; in World War II era, 28; postwar anxieties about, 36, 37, 42, 50, 51; relative visibility of, 38; and dependence/revulsion tension, 41, 42; and conspiracy thinking, 52–53, 87, 102, 104; and urban pathology, 83; and lack of family responsibilities, 86–87

Gay Renaissance, 136

Gay sensibility, 2–3, 7, 229–30, 238

Gays in the military, 2, 37

Geffen, David, 226

The Geisha Boy (Frank Tashlin, 1958), 81–82

Gender ideology: and music, 22–23, 26, 242 (n. 209)

Gender roles: homosexuality associated with, 18, 36–37

Genet, Jean, 209

Gentlemen's Agreement (Arthur Laurents, 1947), 59

Gerassi, John: *The Boys of Boise*, 139–40

Germany, 40

Gershman, Harry, 55

Gershwin, George, 45, 49, 159, 165, 167; *Porgy and Bess*, 46

Giant (film, 1956), 46

Gide, André, 161; *The Immoralist*, 31, 55

Gielgud, John, 83, 97

Gill, John, 156–57

Gillespie, Dizzy, 41

Ginsberg, Allen, 37, 44, 209; *Howl*, 110

Ginzburg, Ralph, 112, 113

Glass, Philip, 214
Globalization, 235
Goffman, Erving, 80
Gold, Mike, 18
Goldwater, Barry, 113, 117, 119–20
Gomez, Jewelle, 236
Goossens, Eugene, 112
Gordon, Ricky Ian, 236
Gornick, Vivian, 137–38
Grace, Princess of Monaco, 159
Graham, Martha, 46, 47, 163, 174
Granger, Farley, 36, 214
Grant, Cary, 16, 81
Grant Park Orchestra, 3–4
Graves, Robert, 194
Green, Adolph, 47
Green, Jess, 234
Greenberg, Clement, 40, 98
Griffes, Charles Tomlinson, 22–23

Hadley, Henry, 177
Hains, Frank, 83
Haldeman, H. R. ("Bob"), 217, 218
The Half-World of the American Homo-
    sexual, 136
Hall, Radclyffe, 110; The Well of Lone-
    liness, 16
Hamilton, John Wilson, 111
Hammerstein, Oscar: Oklahoma!,
    46–47
Handel, George, 3, 16
Hansberry, Lorraine: A Raisin in the
    Sun, 128
Hanson, Howard, 27
Harasymowicz, Jerzy, 194
Harlem Renaissance, 17
Harper's, 221
Harris, Daniel, 230–31, 232
Harris, E. Lynn, 224
Harris, Roy, 28, 157, 160
Harris, Sydney, 127
Harrison, Lou, 3, 16, 199
Harrison, Susan, 85

Hart, Lorenz, 47, 133, 229
Harvey, Laurence, 116
Hatcher, Tom, 95
Hatterer, Lawrence J.: The Artist in
    Society, 55
Havemann, Ernest, 119, 254–55
    (n. 21)
Hayden, Sterling, 118
Haydn, Joseph, 170
Hearst, William Randolph, 19, 27
Hellman, Lillian, 17, 47; The Chil-
    dren's Hour, 16
Helmer, William J., 87
Helms, Alan, 11–12, 56, 89, 92–93,
    96–97
Helms, Jesse, 223
Helps, Robert, 3
Hemphill, Essex, 236
Henahan, Donald, 195
Henze, Hans Werner, 183
Hepburn, Katherine, 59
Heston, Charlton, 111
Higdon, Jennifer, 236
High Fidelity, 98
Hiss, Alger, 69, 75
Hitchcock, Alfred, 35–36, 59, 84
Hitler, Adolf, 53, 114, 135
Hitschmann, Edward: Great Men, 55
Hoffman, Dustin, 214
Hoffman, Martin, 80
Hoiby, Lee, 3, 178
Holland, Bernard, 261 (n. 55)
Holleran, Andrew, 236
Hollywood. See Movie industry
Homer, Louise, 155, 158, 173
Homer, Sidney, 155
Homintern discourse: and cul-
    tural empire, 1, 14; and depen-
    dence/revulsion tension, 2; on
    gay creative presence, 11; and gay
    presence in politics, 32–33; inven-
    tion of term, 42; and conspiracy
    thinking, 43, 113–14, 135, 140,

204–5, 220; and gay people's role in American culture, 44, 134–35, 138–39, 187, 212; and psychoanalytic discourse, 62; and Frankenheimer, 112–13; and music, 112–13; and authenticity, 123, 125; and pulp publications, 135–36; disruption of, 141; and Barber, 155, 187, 190, 206; challenges to, 205–6, 211, 214; persistence of, 216–23, 225; loss of resonance, 226; continuity created by, 234; as farce, 238

Homosexuality: Nixon on, 4–7, 198, 206, 217, 218, 220, 221, 224, 228; discourse on, 8; and Americanization of globe, 13–14; use of term, 15; as intrusion into culture, 16–17, 29–36, 42; conceptions of, 17–18, 24, 27, 42, 53, 246 (n. 5); pathologizing of, 37, 52–66, 71, 76, 78, 79, 80, 82–87, 88, 91, 99–100, 110, 210–11; and cultural empire, 42; and misogyny, 53, 54, 57, 63, 75, 79, 132, 134, 137–38, 139, 211, 221; stigmatization of, 58; alcoholism conflated with, 61; and master trope of excess, 100–101, 106, 120–21, 197. *See also* The closet; Gay artists; Gay creativity

Homosexuality and Creative Genius, 60

Homosexual mafia, 43, 124, 135, 226, 238

Homosexual matrix, 103

Hooker, Evelyn, 87, 110

Hoover, J. Edgar, 68, 70, 74, 218

Horan, Robert, 161

Horney, Karen, 53

Horowitz, Joseph, 242 (n. 22)

Horowitz, Vladimir, 163

Hovhaness, Alan, 199

Hubbs, Nadine, 7, 20–21, 23, 94,
167–68, 179, 188, 201, 242 (n. 20), 266 (n. 119)

Hudson, Rock, 32, 46, 47, 64, 133, 214, 223–24

Hughes, Langston, 17, 156; "Fantasy in Purple," 156

Human Events, 32

Hume, Paul, 73

Hunter, Holly, 224

Hunter, Tab, 32, 214

Huxtable, Ada Louise, 220

Ibel, Manfred, 166

Illinois, 114

Inge, William, 44, 128, 131

Intellectuals, 66, 67, 70, 75, 79

Isherwood, Christopher, 47, 105, 209, 230

Ives, Burl, 60

Ives, Charles, 22–23, 64, 167, 169, 189

I Was a Male War Bride (film, 1949), 81

Jackson, Charles: *The Lost Weekend*, 47, 61

James, Henry, 41, 229; *The American*, 175

Japan, 40

Jarrell, Randall, 98

Javits, Jacob, 182

Jay, Karla, 206, 207

Jazz, 158, 159, 167, 196

Jenkins, Walter, 119–21

Jews: psychoanalytic discourse on, 57, 65; authenticity of, 123

Jews in arts: reaction to, 1; queerness related to, 4, 32, 34; and Hollywood moguls, 16, 46; and racial liberalism, 34; and communities of identity, 86, 91, 94, 95, 103; as outsiders, 102; cultural moment of, 103; Hitler on, 135

Johns, Jasper, 44, 49–50, 76, 97, 243 (n. 42)

Johnson, Lady Bird, 120, 121, 181–82

Johnson, Lyndon, 113, 114, 119–21, 135, 213, 217

Johnson, Philip, 44, 224–25, 233

Jones, James: *From Here to Eternity*, 48

Joyce, James, 194

Kael, Pauline, 109, 210, 254 (n. 11)

Kaiser, Charles, 95

Kaling, Mindy, 238

Kallman, Chester, 11, 93

Kardiner, Abram, 57, 64, 65

Kastendieck, Miles, 182

Katz, Jonathan, 15

Kauffmann, Stanley, 131–33, 134, 138, 140, 179, 187, 205

Kavy, W. H.: *The Gay Geniuses*, 140–41

Kaye, Danny, 33

Kazan, Elia, 47

Kennan, George, 69

Kennedy, Jacqueline, 97, 217

Kennedy, Joan, 217

Kennedy, John F., 48, 114, 117–19, 121, 126, 159, 171, 199, 217

Kennedy, Robert, 182; *The Enemy Within*, 123

Kennedy, Ted, 182, 217

Kennedy Center, 172, 189, 199, 213, 217–20, 225

Kerr, Deborah, 59, 115

Kerr, John, 59

Khrushchev, Nikita, 119, 123, 126

Kilgallen, Dorothy, 30

The Killing of Sister George (film, 1968), 212

Kinsey, Alfred, 8, 52–53, 64, 100

Kirstein, Lincoln, 44, 233

Kissinger, Henry, 218

The Knack (film, 1965), 111

Koestenbaum, Wayne, 21

Kolodin, Irving, 168, 169, 195

Korean War, 78

Koussevitsky, Serge, 162

Kovacs, Ernie, 34

Kozinn, Alan, 199

Kramer, Hilton, 76

Kramer, Larry, 211, 223, 234

Kroll, Arthur, 91

Krutch, Joseph Wood, 108

Kubrick, Stanley, 118

Kushner, Tony, 1, 236; *Angels in America*, 224

Ladder, 60, 108, 110, 128, 139

Lait, Jack, 36; *Washington Confidential*, 29

Lancaster, Burt, 47, 85, 115, 116, 117

Lancaster, Roger, 209

lang, k d, 233

Language: of authenticity, 1, 124, 129; of medical pathology, 19, 34; of scandal journalism, 32; and war metaphors, 34; postwar changes in, 37; of revelation about secret life, 107; and homintern discourse, 187

Lansbury, Angela, 116

Larkin, Oliver, 163

Las Vegas Sun, 68

Laurents, Arthur, 13, 59, 84, 86, 94, 95, 96, 99, 252 (n. 90)

Lavender Culture, 207

Lavender Scare, 1, 13, 37, 68, 70, 73, 82, 114

League of Composers, 43, 73

Lee, Gypsy Rose, 28

Left and leftism: and Copland, 26, 67, 72–75, 103, 161; homophobic practices of, 41; and Blitzstein, 47; homosexuality associated with, 67; weakness of, 77; and gay liberation, 208

Lehman, Ernest, 85, 95

LeMay, Curtis, 116–17

Leonardo da Vinci, 16, 72, 134, 205

Lerner, Max, 78; *America as a Civilization*, 78

Lesbians and lesbianism: activism of, 8, 10, 110, 208, 211; lesbians in arts, 16–17; as biological treason, 63; invisibility of, 63, 134, 135; Wylie on, 66; and political issues, 68; magazines of, 110; creativity of, 224; marginality of, 233

Levy, Martin David: *Mourning Becomes Electra*, 180

Lewes, Richard, 52, 55–56, 57, 63

Lewis, Jerry, 81–82

Liberace, 32, 37

Liberals: charges of homosexuality against, 68; and containment of homosexuality, 78, 132; patronizing tolerance of, 105; pity of, 109, 116; fissures in, 113; antigay animus of, 114–16; as politically virtuous, 117–18; gays' subversion of, 123; lack of consensus on homosexuality, 140

Life, 108, 109, 118–19, 182, 183, 187

Lincoln, Abraham, 232

Lincoln Center for the Performing Arts, 170–73, 175, 180–82, 185, 187, 189

Lincoln Square Urban Renewal Area project, 170, 172

Lindner, Robert, 65, 80, 98; *Must We Conform?*, 62; *Rebel without a Cause: The Hypnoanalysis of a Criminal Psychopath*, 62

"The List," 16, 18, 83, 88, 91, 97, 140–41, 234

List, Kurt, 159

Literary culture, 33, 35, 44, 47, 77, 89

Locke, Alain, 17

Lodge, Henry Cabot, Jr., 70

Lorde, Audre, 82, 97, 236

Lorenzo's Oil (film, 1992), 159

The Lost Weekend (Billy Wilder, 1945), 47

Loughery, John, 16

Luce, Henry, 45

Lumet, Sidney, 116, 118

Lust for Life (Vincent Minnelli, 1956), 92

The L Word (television show), 233

MacArthur, Arthur, 97

MacArthur, Douglas, 97

MacDonald, Dwight, 40–41

MacDowell, Edward, 22, 26, 157

Mackendrick, Alexander, 85–86

Magee, Bryan, 83

Mahler, Gustav, 170, 192

Mailer, Norman, 136

The Manchurian Candidate (John Frankenheimer, 1962), 116

Mankiewicz, Joseph L., 33, 59, 81, 84–85, 185

Mann, Golo, 28

Mannes, Marya, 34–35

Mapplethorpe, Robert, 223

March, Frederic, 117

Marcos, Ferdinand, 182

Marine, Gene, 138–39

Marotta, Toby: *Sons of Harvard*, 233

Martin, Del, 208

Marx, Karl, 62

Masculinity: and World War II, 29; in American culture, 64–65, 83, 127; and homosexuality, 67; Schlesinger on, 76; Mead on, 80; and arts, 87; science equated with, 88; and gay men's inauthentic claims, 118, 125, 133; in music, 156, 188; and Toscanini, 161; and cultural empire, 172

Mason, Daniel Gregory, 25

Mass culture, 65, 76, 98, 122–23, 185

Masters, R. E. L.: *The Homosexual Revolution*, 106

Mathews, Arthur Guy, 30–31

Mathews, Jane De Hart, 39

Mattachine Society, 31, 90

Matthiessen, F. O., 46, 48, 233

Maugham, Somerset, 2, 53, 134

Maupin, Armistead, 236; *Tales of the City* series, 6, 215

McCarthy, Joe, 67, 68, 70, 73, 74, 75, 175, 224

McCarthyism, 125

McClary, Susan, 21–22, 167, 241–42 (n. 18)

McCourt, James, 165, 217, 223, 252 (n. 90)

McCullers, Carson, 28, 33, 39, 44, 47, 49, 77, 244 (n. 44); *Reflections in a Golden Eye*, 28–29

Mcintire, Dal, 111

McKellan, Ian, 225

McLeod, Scott, 73

McNally, Terrence, 236; *And Things That Go Bump in the Night*, 130, 210

McNamara, Robert, 182

McPhee, Colin, 4; *Tabuh-Tabuhan, Toccata for Orchestra*, 4

Mead, Margaret, 79–80

Medical experts: and explanations of gay artists, 52, 55–56, 57, 58, 61, 83

Melville, Herman, 46; *Moby-Dick*, 175–76, 203

Mencken, H. L., 33

Menotti, Gian Carlo: and Barber, 23, 24, 27, 38, 82, 92, 93, 156, 157, 159–60, 165–69, 179, 193, 194–95, 201, 202–3; *Amahl and the Night Visitors*, 48, 166; and Puccini, 49, 197; and Toscanini, 158; and postmodernism, 160–61, 200;

and Barber's *Vanessa*, 164, 166, 177–78; *The Consul*, 166; operas of, 167, 175; and serial music, 168; and Spoleto festival, 168, 195; *A Hand of Bridge*, 168–69; and New York City, 174; and Barber's *Antony and Cleopatra*, 178; homosexuality of, 181; *The Medium*, 192

Merman, Ethel, 204

Merrick, David, 86, 134

Merrill, James, 3, 44, 99, 236

Metropolitan Opera, 39, 164, 170

Metropolitan Opera House, 173, 180–84, 185, 189, 213

Meyer, Leonard, 163–64

Michelangelo, 16, 18, 50, 72, 88, 111, 134

Midnight Cowboy (John Schlesinger, 1969), 210, 212

Miliukov, Antonina, 4

Milk, Harvey, 211

Miller, Arthur, 46

Miller, D. A., 38, 166

Milner, Martin, 85

Miłosz, Czesław, 194

Mineo, Sal, 62, 91

Minnelli, Vincent, 59, 92

Mitchell, John, 218

Mitropoulos, Dimitri, 164

Modernism: Modernism Lite, 4; shift to postmodernism, 8; ethos of, 9; rebellion against romantic sentimentality, 22; French modernism, 23, 45, 169; and hybridity of style, 26; and cultural empire, 40; and Barber, 49, 157–58, 159, 163, 194, 200; and gay artists, 49–50, 104; and traditional modes, 157, 158, 159, 184; and straight composers, 167; and Lincoln Center, 180

Modern Man, 111

Momism, 66, 116

Monette, Paul, 11, 94, 236

Mordden, Ethan, 165, 174

Morgan, J. P., 15

Morrison, Toni, 236

Mortimer, Lee, 36; *Washington Confidential*, 29

Moses, Robert, 170

Motherwell, Robert, 98

Movie industry: and gay people's role in American culture, 16, 20; and homosexual characters, 17, 35–36, 58–59, 83, 84–85, 92, 105, 106–7, 109, 114, 212; music in, 45, 46; and American idiom, 46; and masculine culture, 64, 107, 118; and urban pathology, 84–86; and image, 94; and institutionalization of arts, 99; and queer resistance, 111; and third sex, 136; and Barber's *Antony and Cleopatra*, 184–85; and gay actors, 225

Muggeridge, Malcolm, 39

Muncie, Indiana, 83–84, 251 (n. 69)

Mundt, Karl, 74

Murphy, John, 206, 208

Murray, Don, 115

Muschamp, Herbert, 49

Music: Finnish ascendancy in, 10; and gay people's role in American culture, 15, 18–19, 20, 44–45, 102; abstractness of, 20–21; Ives on, 22; and gender ideology, 22–23, 26, 242 (n. 209); definition of American music, 24–26, 45–46, 48; place of sexuality in, 27–28; and serial and tonal composers, 49, 77, 93, 98–101, 163–64, 167–68, 188, 189, 196–97, 199, 200, 201, 214; and modernism, 49, 245 (n. 72); and marginality of art, 94; and institutionalization of arts, 98–99; and homintern discourse,

112–13; and cultural exchange, 126–27, 162; homosexual prominence in, 134; and New York City, 170, 171; and Rorem, 178

Musical theater, 46–47

The Music Lovers (Ken Russell, 1971), 4

Nabokov, Nicolas, 68

Nabokov, Vladimir, 68

Nathan, George Jean, 20

National Endowment for the Arts, 189, 213

National Endowment for the Humanities, 213

National security, 58, 61, 79

Nazism, 27, 46, 57

Nelsova, Zara, 165

Neruda, Pablo, 194; *The Lovers*, 193

New Deal, 39

New Leader, 54

New Left, 208

Newman, Paul, 59–60

New Republic, 128, 167

Newsweek, 38, 119, 121, 162, 166, 180, 182, 184, 215

Newton, Huey, 208

New York Academy of Medicine, 108

New York City, 58, 84, 93, 139–40, 169–72, 189

New Yorker, 182, 192–93, 238

New York Philharmonic, 170, 180

New York Review of Books, 131

New York Times: and cultural empire, 39; and urban pathology, 82–83; on homosexuality, 108, 128, 131, 132; and Lincoln Center, 171; and Barber, 177, 183, 191; and Price, 186; and gay American composers, 201; and Bernstein, 218, 219; and Kennedy Center, 220; and Copland, 225; and Shand-Tucci, 233

Nichols, Mike, 130, 224
Nixon, Richard: on homosexuality, 4–7, 198, 206, 217, 218, 220, 221, 224, 228; and kitchen debate, 123, 125–26; and silent majority, 135; and cultural empire, 190; and Copland, 198; and authenticity, 213; and Kennedy Center, 217–20
Norse, Harold, 42
El Norte (film, 1983), 159
Nugent, Richard Bruce, 17
Nureyev, Rudolf, 8, 127, 213

O'Brien, Edmund, 117, 118
Odets, Clifford, 85
Office of War Information, 28
O'Hara, Frank, 44, 233
Oh! Calcutta! (musical, 1969), 215
O'Neill, Eugene, 46
One magazine: on scandal journalism, 30, 31, 35; on Towne, 34; on Whitman, 72; and minority group model, 91; on coming out, 96; and mock shock, 106; and queer resistance, 110–12; and homintern discourse, 113, 139; and cultural exchange, 127; on Roth, 133; Gornick on, 137
Onion, 238
Open secret, 38, 50, 83, 93–94, 166, 169, 173, 178
Opera: demand for American talent in, 40; distinctive American idiom in, 46; growth in, 170; America's debt to Europe in, 173, 185, 188; absence of American tradition in, 174; Anglo-American composers of, 181; effect of *Antony and Cleopatra* on, 183, 186–87
Organized crime, 123, 124
Ormandy, Eugene, 195
Osborne, John, 76; *Look Back in Anger*, 75–76

Oscar Wilde (film, 1960), 109
Out of the Closets, 204–8, 209, 211
Outsiderness: gay artists as outsiders, 51, 52–66, 137; gays as political outsiders, 66–79; gays as social outsiders, 79–88; gays as cultural outsiders, 88–102, 103; continuity in views of gays as, 226; and politics, 231–32; endorsement of, 231–33
Ovitz, Michael S., 226, 238

Pacino, Al, 214
Pageant magazine, 31
Partisan Review, 13–14, 60, 84
Pasternak, Boris: *Doctor Zhivago*, 126
Paul VI (pope), 219
Pears, Peter, 28, 32, 93, 156–57, 166–67, 176
Pearson, Drew, 68
People Today, 31
Peress, Maurice, 218
Perkins, Anthony, 214
Peyser, Joan, 167
Philadelphia Inquirer, 71
Philadelphia Orchestra, 195
Philharmonic Hall, 173, 180, 197
Phillips, William, 14, 240 (n. 2); *Art and Psychoanalysis*, 60
Physical Culture, 30, 31
Picture Life, 31
A Place in the Sun (film, 1951), 46
Plato, 18, 36, 83
Platoon (film, 1986), 159, 197
Podhoretz, Norman, 221
Politicians: on gays as political outsiders, 66–79
Politics, 35
Politics: gays as political outsiders, 66–79; and the closet, 97; gay political activism, 108; of identity, 113–14; of authenticity, 114–25, 138, 255 (n. 32); and gay libera-

tion, 207–8; and outsiderness, 231–32

Pons, Lily, 167

Pop Art, 124

Popular culture, 137, 167, 189, 196, 209, 212

Porter, Cole, 16, 44, 46, 47, 49, 102, 216, 229

Postmodernism: shift from modernism, 8, 199, 200; and Menotti, 160–61; and gay people's role in American culture, 214–15

Post-9/11 mourning, 200–201

Preminger, Otto, 70, 106–7, 114–15

Previn, André, 261 (n. 55)

Price, Leontyne, 41, 165, 167, 176–77, 181–82, 185–87, 191, 195, 236

Production Code, 17, 19, 106

Prohibition, 17, 20

Prokofiev, Sergey, 4, 67, 174

Psychoanalytic discourse: and explanations of gay artists, 35, 51, 52–57, 59, 64, 66; popularization of, 38, 58–59; influence of, 58; contextualizing of gay creativity, 60; and alcoholism and homosexuality, 61; and homintern discourse, 62; and gender norms, 62, 63–64; and causes of homosexuality, 62–63, 66; and belittling of gay artists, 65; class and racial focus of, 65–66

Publishing industry, 33

Puccini, Giacomo, 175, 181, 184

Pulitzer Prize, 164, 166

Pulp publications, 135–36

Queer as Folk (television show), 226

Queer Eye for the Straight Guy (television show), 1, 228, 229

Queer resistance, 109–14, 140

Queer theory, 215, 236

Rachmaninoff, Sergey, 84, 159

Rainey, Ma, 16

Ramparts, 138

Rauschenberg, Robert, 44, 49–50, 76, 168, 243 (n. 42)

Ravel, Maurice: Violin Sonata, 45

Ravenhill, Mark, 224–25

Ray, Johnnie, 30

Ray, Nicholas, 62, 91–92

Reagan-era nostalgia, 216

Rebel without a Cause (Nicholas Ray, 1955), 62, 91–92

Redford, Robert, 214

Red River (film, 1948), 46

Red Scare, 37, 68, 82, 103, 166

Reed, Christopher, 44

Reporter, 34–35

Republican Party, 68, 72–73

Rich, Adrienne, 211, 236

Rich, Alan, 170, 180, 186

Riesman, David, 123

Right, 68, 114, 116–18, 120

Rilke, Rainer Maria, 163

Robbins, Jerome, 95

Robeson, Paul, 126

Rockefeller, John D., III, 170, 171

Rockefeller, Nelson, 170, 182

Rock music, 214, 215

Rockwell, George Lincoln, 114

Rodgers, Richard, 47, 133–34; Oklahoma!, 46–47; The Sound of Music, 133

Roehm, Ernst, 114

Roethke, Theodore, 194

Roosevelt, Franklin, 45, 48, 67, 68, 158

Rope (Alfred Hitchcock, 1948), 59, 84

Rorem, Ned: on mainstream, 3; and Copland, 25, 32, 191, 198; as composer, 44, 90; chronicling of, 92; Paris Diary, 132, 178, 179; and Barber, 158, 168, 175, 178–79,

191–92, 196, 197, 264 (n. 98), 265 (n. 100); and open secret, 178; homosexuality of, 196; and gay creativity, 199; relevancy of, 206

Rosen, Charles, 225

Rosenberg, Harold, 134

Rosenfeld, Paul, 22

Rosenthal, A. M., 83

Ross, Alex, 176, 201, 202

Rossiter, Clinton, 72

Rostropovich, Mstislav, 112, 213

Rota, Nino, 185

Roth, Philip, 131, 133

Rudnick, Paul, 238

RuPaul, 236

Russell, Ken, 4

Russo, Vito, 82, 105; *The Celluloid Closet*, 7

Ryan, James, 71

Sagarin, Edward. *See* Cory, Donald Webster

Salzburg Festival, 164–65

Sanders, George, 84

Santayana, George, 229, 233

Sappho, 110

Sargeant, Winthrop, 194

Saturday Review, 165, 168, 178

Scalero, Rosario, 155–56

Scandal journalism, 29–32, 38, 82, 128

Schippers, Thomas, 166, 179, 181, 186, 190–91

Schlesinger, Arthur, Jr., 75–76, 84, 98; *The Vital Center*, 67, 118, 222

Schlesinger, John, 210, 212

Schoenberg, Arnold, 49, 72, 159, 165, 188, 200

Schonberg, Harold, 112, 183, 184, 186–89, 218–20

Schubert, Franz, 225

Schulman, Sarah, 233, 234, 236

Schuman, William, 25, 171, 172, 189

Schumann, Clara, 55

Schur, Edward, 80

Scott, George C., 118

Scott, Randolph, 16

The Search (Fred Zinnemann, 1948), 81

Sedgwick, Eve, 232

Selby, Hubert: *Last Exit to Brooklyn*, 137

Sellers, Peter, 118

Sessions, Roger, 164

Seven Days in May (John Frankenheimer, 1964), 116–17, 118

Sex criminals, 37, 38, 56

Sexual identity, 21, 76

Sexual object choice: homosexuality associated with, 36, 37

Sexual revolution, 215

Shahn, Ben, 98

Shakespeare, William, 18, 91, 111, 176–77; *Antony and Cleopatra*, 176, 184, 186, 187, 195

Shand-Tucci, Douglass: *The Crimson Letter*, 233–34

Sheed, Wilfred, 129–30, 131

Shelley, Martha, 208

Shostakovich, Dmitri, 67

Show Business Illustrated, 108, 128

Sibelius, Jean, 4, 10, 26, 158

Sievers, W. David: *History of Psychoanalysis and the American Drama*, 55

Simon, John, 210

Sinatra, Frank, 106–7

Sin of Sins, 19

Slonimsky, Nicolas, 159, 193

Smith, William, 180

Socarides, Charles, 55

Social scientists: on gays as social outsiders, 79–81

Socrates, 5, 83

Solzhenitsyn, Aleksandr, 213
Sondheim, Stephen, 95, 214, 236
Sontag, Susan, 136–37, 188, 200,
    205
South Park (television series), 198
Space race, 125–26
Spano, Robert, 236
Spender, Stephen, 98, 161, 164, 175
Stafford, Jean, 33
Stainbrook, Edward, 134
Stalin, Joseph, 29, 30, 42, 72
Stanwyck, Barbara, 138
Stearn, Jess: *The Sixth Man*, 105–6,
    107, 110, 168; *The Grapevine*, 110
Steber, Eleanor, 165
Steblin, Rita, 225
Stein, Gertrude: *Four Saints in Three
    Acts*, 26
Stein, Marc, 71, 72
Stern, Isaac, 84
Stevens, Mark, 224–25
Stevenson, Adlai, 70, 75
Still, William Grant, 43
Stokowski, Leopold, 155–56
Stone, Irving: *The Agony and the
    Ecstasy*, 111
Stonewall riots, 10, 199, 202, 204,
    215, 225
Strangers on a Train (Alfred Hitch-
    cock, 1951), 35–36, 59, 212
Strauss, Richard, 15, 183, 184, 187
Stravinsky, Igor, 11, 67, 84, 165, 194
Strecker, Edward, 63
Suddenly, Last Summer (Joseph L.
    Mankiewicz, 1959), 59, 81, 107
Sullivan, Andrew, 229, 232, 237
Sulzberger, Iphigene, 131
Sunday, Billy, 15
Sunday, Bloody Sunday (John Schle-
    singer, 1971), 210
Sweet Smell of Success (Alexander
    Mackendrick, 1957), 85–86, 212

Taft, Robert, 48, 159
The Taming of the Shrew (Franco
    Zeffirelli, 1967), 185
Tangents, 131, 135, 140–41, 179, 257
    (n. 50)
Tashlin, Frank, 81
Taubman, Howard, 128–29, 130, 131,
    164, 165, 171
Taylor, Deems, 21, 25–26
Taylor, Elizabeth, 59, 60, 130, 185
Taylor, Maxwell, 172
Tchaikovsky, Pyotr: homosexuality
    of, 3, 83, 88, 136, 189; Symphony
    No. 4, 4; marriage of, 4, 21, 60;
    controversies about, 10, 16; and
    gay creativity, 50; emotionality of,
    75; and Barber, 197; and postmod-
    ernism, 200; Day on, 238
Tchaikovsky International Piano
    Competition, 88, 112, 126
Tea and Sympathy (Vincent Minnelli,
    1956), 59, 107
Television industry, 30, 33–34, 38,
    40
The Ten Commandments (Cecil B.
    DeMille, 1956), 184
Thayer, Charles, 68–71, 74
Theater: and gay people's role in
    American culture, 15, 16, 18–20;
    acceptance of homosexuality in,
    31, 109–10; homosexual promi-
    nence in, 44, 54, 82, 83, 86,
    107, 134, 156, 181; and Ameri-
    can idiom, 46; and homosexual
    characters, 128–33, 139, 210
Third sex, 31–32, 136, 139
Thomas, Danny, 34
Thomas, Jess, 182
Thomas, Michael Tilson, 236
Thomson, Virgil: homosexuality of,
    3, 23, 27, 32, 167, 181, 199, 202;
    biography of, 9; on American

music, 25, 44–45; *Four Saints in Three Acts*, 26; on Copland, 43; and modernism, 45, 157; and serial and tonal composers, 49; and spaces for gay artists, 92; and homintern discourse, 112; on German-Austrian musical complex, 157–58; on Barber, 162, 167, 175; as American composer, 165; on "complexity boys," 167; and the closet, 179; and Rorem, 179; and Kennedy Center honors, 199; and postmodernism, 215

Thurmond, Strom, 126

Tibbett, Lawrence, 84

Tick, Judith, 22

Time magazine: on gay artists, 2, 60; on Cliburn, 88; on homosexuality, 108, 109, 134–35, 179; on Lincoln Center opening, 180, 181–82; on Metropolitan Opera House, 184; on Bing, 190

Tip-Off magazine, 30

Tippett, Michael, 157

Toledo Times, 139

Tommasini, Anthony, 9, 192, 202

Tonkin Gulf incidents, 119

Toscanini, Arturo, 23, 64, 89, 156, 158, 160, 161, 181, 195, 242 (n. 22)

Towne, Alfred, 33–34

Transnationalism, 235

Transvestism, 33, 34

Treitler, Leo, 21, 242 (n. 18)

The Trials of Oscar Wilde (film, 1960), 109

Tripp, C. A., 102–3, 205, 209, 232

Truman, Harry, 29, 68

Tufts University Lesbian Gay Bisexual Transgender Center, 226

Tulane Drama Review, 139, 140

Turner, Charles, 158–59, 179

Twain, Mark, 41, 81

UNESCO, 73

Urban pathology, 82–87, 212

U.S.–Soviet Cultural Agreement of 1958, 125

U.S. State Department, 32, 37, 66, 68, 69, 70, 73, 74, 77

Vaid, Urvashi, 233

Vanderbilts, 182

Van Gogh, Vincent, 60

Van Vechten, Carl, 17

Varèse, Edgard, 43

Variety, 182

Verdi, Giuseppe, 181; *Aida*, 155, 185, 197; *Falstaff*, 181

Victim (Basil Deardon, 1961), 109, 254 (n. 11)

Vidal, Gore, 9, 40, 44, 47, 59, 60, 99, 135, 222–23; *The City and the Pillar*, 37, 77; *The Best Man*, 70

Vienna State Opera, 219

Vietnam War, 119, 121, 135, 138, 141, 180, 189, 212–13, 216–17, 219

Village Voice, 137

Vishnevskaya, Galina, 213

Voice of America, 68

Wagner, Richard, 22, 159, 181, 202

Waldeck, R. G., 33, 34

Walker, Alice, 236

Walker, Robert, 35

Wallace, George, 117

Wallace, Mike, 135

Wallock, Leonard, 169

Wall Street Journal, 184, 231

Walsh, David, 27

Walton, William, 32, 176

Warfield, William, 41

Warhol, Andy, 124, 125, 231, 243 (n. 42)

Warner, Michael, 232, 236

Warren, James, 239 (n. 5)

Waters, John: *Hairspray*, 229

Wayne, John, 208

Weaver, Fritz, 116

Weber, Ben, 49

Webern, Anton, 188

Weinstein, Jeff, 7, 238

Weir, John, 228

Welch, Joseph, 68

Welles, Sumner, 67, 119

Welty, Eudora, 9, 33

Wertham, Frederic, 56, 59; *The Seduction of the Innocent*, 56

West, D. J., 54–55, 209

West, Mae, 17, 19; *The Drag*, 19, 20

West Side Story (musical, 1957), 1, 95–96, 167, 181, 252 (n. 90)

West Side Story (Robert Wise, 1961), 95

Whale, James, 17

White, Edmund, 7, 11, 211, 214, 222, 223, 236

The White Sentinel, 111

Whitman, Walt, 3, 10, 15, 18, 46, 71–72, 90, 91, 229

Who's Afraid of Virginia Woolf (Mike Nichols, 1966), 130

Wiebe, Robert, 216

Wild, Earl, 236

Wilde, Oscar, 10, 15–16, 18, 44, 83, 88–89, 91, 97–98, 137; *Salome*, 15

Wilder, Billy, 47, 61, 81

Wilder, Thornton, 18, 44, 48, 164, 168, 175, 229; *Our Town*, 46

Will and Grace (television show), 228, 234

Williams, John: *Music from "Schindler's List,"* 4

Williams, Tennessee: *A Streetcar Named Desire*, 1, 46, 164, 175, 261 (n. 55); as queer artist vs. American artist, 2, 9, 44, 48; and open secret, 38; and cultural empire, 39; *The Glass Menagerie*, 46; fiction by, 47; and modernism, 49; Sievers on, 55; films of plays, 59; *Suddenly, Last Summer*, 59, 60, 79, 128; treatment of homosexuality, 60, 128, 247 (n. 18); Lerner on, 78; relationship to Europe, 92; as Southerner, 94; relationship with academy, 99; and master trope of excess, 100; on gay creativity, 102, 207; *Cat on a Hot Tin Roof*, 128; *Something Unspoken*, 128; as successful playwright, 131; and Barber, 177, 203; Rorem on, 191; production of, 205; relevancy of, 206; Simon on, 210; reputation of, 214; and postmodernism, 215; Decter on, 222; and mainstream, 231

Wilson, Edmund, 76–77

Winchell, Walter, 27, 43, 85

Wise, Robert, 95

Withers, Brenda, 237–38

Wolfe, Tom, 217

Women: place in American society, 13–14; creativity of, 63; gay men conflated with, 63–64; and psychoanalytic discourse, 63–64; Friedan on, 78–79; Southern women as outsiders, 102; and Lincoln Center, 172; increasing voices of, 214. *See also* Lesbians and lesbianism

The Women (George Cukor, 1939), 211

Women's music, 215

Wood, Elizabeth, 9, 102

Wood, Natalie, 92

World Peace Conference (1949), 72

World Trade Center, 200

World War II: and contribution of queer artists, 1; and gender ideology of music, 26; and masculinity, 29; and cultural empire, 38, 39, 40, 169; Wylie on, 66; and dominant cultural values, 93; and

maturing of America, 101; and
Barber, 161–63
Wright, Richard, 94
Wylie, Philip: *A Generation of Vipers*,
66–67
Wynn, Ed, 34

Young, Allen, 207, 208, 228, 229
Young, Edgar, 171

Zeffirelli, Franco, 177, 179, 181–84,
186–88, 190–93
Zinnemann, Fred, 81